Middle Egyptian Grammar

James E. Hoch

SSEA Publication XV

Benben Publications, Mississauga, 1997

Canadian Cataloguing in Publication Data

Hoch, James E. (James Eric), 1954–
Middle Egyptian Grammar

(SSEA Publications ; v. 15)
Co-published by the Society for the Study of Egyptian Antiquities
ISBN 0–920168–12–4

1. Egyptian language—Grammar. I. Society for the Study of Egyptian Antiquities. II. Title. III. Series.

PJ1135.H63 493'.1 C95-932358-9

PREFACE

THE AIMS OF THIS BOOK are two-fold, to serve primarily as an introductory grammar for classroom and self-instruction and only secondarily as a reference grammar for students in their early stages with the Egyptian language. These goals are therefore similar to those of Sir A.H. Gardiner in his monumental *Egyptian Grammar*. Gardiner's grammar was, of course, daunting to beginning students, and while his decision to cite only genuine texts rendered his work more accurate than even his own knowledge of the language, students had a great deal of difficulty in making out the examples, since they were replete with as yet unknown forms and constructions. Although an advanced scientific grammar of Middle Egyptian is a very desirable thing, the need for instructional materials at the elementary level is far more pressing, and this is at all times the main focus of this work. Most of the examples in the early lessons were of necessity "made-up Egyptian." This will, it is hoped, be compensated by presenting the literary constructions at an early stage, in order to permit the reading of extended passages of original texts.

Recent years have seen the appearance of several outlines and handbooks presenting the basics of Middle Egyptian grammar, but the present work seeks to provide a considerably more detailed and more complete accounting of the intricacies and fine nuances of the language as well as a treatment of the basics.

The grammatical approach is for the most part based on the findings of Hans J. Polotsky. Much is owed to many of his works, but the theories and explanations here proposed are not limited to the views of that brilliant scholar. Some new proposals are made, but the main intention was to present the "standard theory." This work also owes a great deal to my first teacher of Egyptian, Ronald J. Williams. And of course, anyone familiar with Gardiner's classic grammar will recognize the enormous debt owed to the work of that great scholar. In particular many examples derive directly from his grammar, and are too numerous for individual acknowledgement.

The terminology used in this book requires a few comments. There was a certain temptation to do away with the old muddle of jargon entirely, and to replace it with a more scientific and descriptive set of terms. In the end, a more conservative approach was taken. Where two terms were roughly equivalent one was generally used as a morphological and the other as a syntactical term. Gardiner's various "virtual" constructions were renamed more descriptively for what they seem to really be. Whenever possible old-fashioned terms were replaced with terms more generally used in the study of ancient Near Eastern languages (e.g. "stative" for the "old perfective" and "bound constructions" for "direct genitive").

The lessons are long and are not intended for coverage in a single hour-long class and should require at least one week per lesson. Later lessons will generally require two weeks per lesson. Instructors may well supplement the exercises with a mid-lesson "drill sheet" that uses simple vocabulary and serves to re-inforce such things as the use of pronouns. Since the vocabulary lists include some vocabulary used in examples cited, it may be useful for students to begin learning the signs and vocabulary before beginning to read the grammatical sections. These vocabulary lists present essential working vocabulary, but also words that contain new phonetic signs—which will enable students to look up other similarly written words encountered at a later time.

This manuscript is a preliminary publication with acknowledged typographical and other deficiencies and is intended to allow the book to be used before its actual publication. Time restrictions prevented the harmonization of Egyptian fonts, leaving an unfortunate mix of hieroglyphic type. The book will be formally published as Volume 15 of the Society for the Study of Egyptian Antiquities Publications. Earlier manuscripts of this book were distributed for use and criticism. Some sections have been significantly revised, and new lessons have been added. The section numbers have, fortunately, not changed. A major shortcoming is the lack of a sign list. (Permission to copy Gardiner's sign list was, however, easily obtained in Toronto.)

At this point I would like to extend a word of gratitude to my students, whose helpful criticism (and keen eyes) have improved almost every page. I would also like to thank Tom Lasinski and especially Mike Dyall-Smith and Wolfgang Schenkel for their careful reading of the earlier drafts and for their many, detailed comments. I have been able to incorporate many of their excellent suggestions in this version, and I intend to address the remaining ones in the next revision. As always, I welcome further criticism. The present version is identical to the one produced in August 1996 apart from a few minor corrections and the pagination.

A Word to the Student

It should be stressed that Egyptian grammar (not to mention the writing system) is not easily learned. For this reason, the grammatical explanations are best read, re-read, and re-read once more. It cannot be overly stressed that repeated *daily* work on the material generally proves far preferable to concentrated efforts on one or two days of the week. Ideally, a regular weekly review of a certain portion of earlier work should be undertaken (e.g. going over old exercises—even from the earliest lessons, since they may be elementary, but they are extremely important).

One of the first tasks facing beginning students is learning the fairly cumbersome script. The signs *must* be learned quickly and thoroughly. Transliteration is a tool used to enable a correct reading of the examples exercises, but it should not be relied upon very heavily. Egyptian is best read in the hieroglyphic script. Learning the signs should not be treated as a burden, but as an aesthetic treat—an enjoyable task. Time-honoured methods include flashcards (preferably ca 3 × 7 cm, punched, and on a ring), but a very enjoyable computer programme, "Scribe of KMT," by Dr. Michael Dyall-Smith is now available on the World Wide Web (ftp://newton.newton.cam.ac.uk/pub/ancient/egypt). Its use is highly recommended.

In general, Middle Egyptian spelling is considerably more standardized than Elizabethan English, for example, but minor variations can be frustrating at first (and there are even mistakes). Students should expect variant writings, and should also be aware that the dictionaries do not provide all the variant writings. Most frustrating of all for beginners is the phenomenon of borrowed determinatives (the use of sense signs properly belonging to another word). Students need to be somewhat flexible, but should not go to extremes.

Translating Egyptian at the early stages is often more like puzzle solving than learning to speak a new language. Nevertheless, Egyptian is a real language—although no longer spoken, and students are encouraged to learn the various sentence patterns as they are presented and to try substituting in other vocabulary items or changing nouns to pronouns for practice. Some mistakes will inevitably be made in such an endeavour, but the familiarity and experience with the language will more than compensate. Egyptian can be learned like any modern language (i.e. largely by internalizing the general rules), but in the early stages, nothing can really replace rote memorization.

There is a great temptation for students in translating to "guess" at the general meaning of a sentence. This is the worst possible approach, since Egyptian writers often said things that surprise us. When looking at a new text (exercises included), rather than looking up the vocabulary first and trying to figure out what is being said, students are by far better served by first analyzing the grammatical relationship of the words (even if they are unknown). When the general relationship of the words is established, then one can plug in the meaning of the vocabulary. This is not a mechanical process, and often the meaning will necessitate a new interpretation. The various factors of language do not occur in isolation, and the process involves a synthesis of various things: syntax (word and phrase relationships), morphology (the particular forms required by a given grammatical construction), and the meaning in the particular context.

In any case, the student should expect to feel the language rather alien, and for the first few years one must constantly ask mechanical questions: "Is there an introductory particle to indicate that this is a new sentence?" "Is there a verb in this sentence?" "What is the subject of the verb?" "Is there a direct object?" "What is the tense?" "Is the voice active or passive?" Often one must hold open two or three possible interpretations. With experience one can eliminate some possibilities, but building experience requires time. A good suggestion is to return to what one thinks is the right answer and then ask if there are any other possibilities. Sometimes one's first inclination is far from the mark, and a good second consideration can lead to better interpretations.

Finally, the examples given in the body of the text are not just for appearance's sake. They are to be examined, studied, questioned, and thoroughly understood. For the most part only grammatical forms and constructions that have already been learned were used, but on a few occasions as-yet unlearned grammatical features could not be avoided. In these cases, explanations were provided in the footnotes. Not all of the vocabulary encountered in the examples and exercises was included in the vocabulary lists within the lessons. This was intentional, and students should look up all new and unknown words—and even known words—for practice in using the glossary and dictionary.

James E. Hoch, Toronto August 25th, 1997

CONTENTS

Abbreviations xvi

LESSON 1 3–16

§1. Egyptian Connections to African and West Asian Languages

§2. The Historical Phases of Egyptian

§3. The Scripts of Egyptian

§4. The Writing System of Egyptian

§5. The Transliteration and Sounds of the Alphabetic Signs

§6. The Direction of Writing

§7. Conventions of Transliteration

§8. The Lack of Articles

§9. The Simple Verbal Sentence: Statements of Fact

§10. The Non-verbal Statement of Fact (with Adverbial Comment)

LESSON 2 17–27

§11. Logographic and Phonetic Writing

§12. Semantic Determinatives

§13. The Use of the Stroke with Logograms

§14. The Egyptian Noun: A Preliminary View

§15. The Egyptian Sentence

§16. Statements of Fact: Main and Subordinate Clauses

§17. The Particle 𓅓𓎡 *mk*

§18. The Egyptian Sentence: Verbal and Non-verbal

LESSON 3 28–44

§19. Declension of Nouns

§20. Adjectives as Modifiers

§21. Adjectives used as Nouns

1) As an ordinary noun

2) The Absolute use of the Fem. Sing. "something that is . . ." "a . . . thing"

§22. Relations Between Nouns

1) The Genitival Relationship:

a) The Bound Construction

b) The Genitival Adjective
   2) Apposition:
§23. The Suffix Pronouns
   1) The Forms:
   2) Use of Suffix Pronouns with Nouns:
   3) Special Forms with Dual Nouns:
   4) Use of Suffix Pronouns with Prepositions:
   5) Use of Suffix Pronouns with Verbs:
   6) Use of Suffix Pronouns in Non-verbal Sentences with Adverbial Comment:
   7) Affinity of Afro-Asiatic Pronouns:
§24. The *M* of Predication
§25. An Introduction to the Suffix Conjugation
§26. Tense in the Egyptian Verb
§27. Derived Stems
§28. Verb Classes
§29. The Circumstantial *Sḏm·f* Form
§30. The Past Tense of the Circumstantial Form (Active Voice): *Sḏm·n·f*
§31. Statements of Fact: *iw sḏm·f / mk sḏm·f & iw sḏm·n·f*
§32. Circumstantial Clauses

LESSON 4   45–57
§33. The Passive Voice
§34. The Passive of the Circumstantial Forms: Present Tense
§35. The Past Tense Passive of the Circumstantial Forms:
   The *sḏm(w)·f* Passive
§36. A Variation on the Statement of Fact: *Noun sḏm·f*
§37. Another Variation on the Statement of Fact: *iw·f sḏm·f*
§38. Circumstantial Clauses that modify Nouns: The Relative Clause with
   Indefinite Antecedent
§39. The Dependent Pronouns
§40. Feminine and Plural Forms of the Particle *mk*
§41. Transpositions in Hieroglyphic Writing
   1) Honorific Transposition:
   2) Graphic Transpositions:
§42. Combination Signs
§43. An Overview of Adjectives
§44. The Predicate Adjective
§45. Exclamatory 𓃀 -*wy* "How …!"
§46. The Impersonal Predicate Adjective + Dative
§47. The Independent Use of the Feminine Singular

§48. The Adjective + Noun: A Bound Construction
§49. The Comparison of Adjectives
§50. The Superlative Notion

LESSON 5 58–72

§51. Word Order in the Verbal Sentence
§52. Abbreviations and Defective Writings
§53. Vocalic (Group) Writing
§54. *Nisba*-adjectives (Relational Adjectives)
§55. The Use of *iry* "Its"/ "Their"
§56. Independent Pronouns
1) Independent pronoun as subject in the sentence with *nominal* predicate
2) Independent pronouns in the sentences with *adjective as* predicate
§57. The Infinitive
1) Preliminary Remarks:
2) The infinitive after prepositions
3) Infinitives and their Logical Direct Objects
4) Infinitives and their Logical Subjects
5) Infinitives and their Logical Indirect Objects
6) Infinitives Serving as Direct Objects of Verbs
7) Infinitives in Captions and Journal Entry Style—The Narrative Infinitive
8) Infinitives as Subjects of Verbs and Predicate Adjectives

LESSON 6 73–86

§58. *Ḥr* + Infinitive: Ongoing Action & Action in Progress
§59. Sentences Expressing On-going / Progressive Action
§60. *M* + Verbs of Motion—Motion in Progress / Immediate Action
§61. Progressive Circumstantial Clauses
§62. The Future Tense Construction: *'Iw·f r sḏm*
§63. Coordinating and Disjunctive Words
§64. Vocative
§65. Cardinal Numbers
§66. Use of the Numerals and Numbers
§67. Ordinal Numbers
§68. Measurements
1) Volume
2) Length
3) Weight
4) Area
§69. Dates & the Royal Titulary
§70. *Sp sn*: "(Read) Twice"

LESSON 7   87–101

§71. The Prospective *Sḏm·f* Verb Form

§72. Prospective *sḏm·f* Forms in Main Clauses: Wishes, Exhortations, etc.

§73. Prospective *sḏm·f* Forms In Other Main Clauses

§74. Prospective *sḏm·f* Forms In Subordinate Clauses of Purpose and Result

§75. Prospective *sḏm·f* Used to Form Noun Clauses
    1) As the Object of Verbs of Speech, Perception, Causation
    2) As the Object of Prepositions
    3) As the Subject of Verbs

§76. The Adjective Verb

§77. The Expressions *Rdi m* & *Rdi r* "To Appoint"

§78. Demonstrative Adjectives and Qualifiers

§79. Noun Phrases as Adverbial Modifiers

§80. Expressions for "Complete" "Entire"

§81. Compound Prepositions

LESSON 8   102–15

§82. The Stative

§83. The Stative Endings

§84. The Stative Form Stem

§85. The Stative as Adverbial Comment ("Pseudo-verbal Construction")

§86. The Stative in Circumstantial Clauses

§87. The Stative as Modifier of Nouns

§88. Past-time Sentences with Verbs of Motion

§89. "To Know"

§90. The Narrative Past Tense Construction: ꜥḥꜥ·n·sḏm·n·f

§91. The Past Tense Passive Voice Construction: ꜥḥꜥ·n sḏm·(w)·f Passive

§92. The Stative in ꜥḥꜥ·n·f šm(w) with Verbs of Motion

§93. The Progressive Past Tense: ꜥḥꜥ·n·f ḥr sḏm

§94. The Stative in ꜥḥꜥ·n·f rdi(w): Quasi-Passives & States

§95. ꜥḥꜥ·n sḏm·n·f with following Parallel Clauses

§96. ꜥḥꜥ·n sḏm·f: A Rare Variation

§97. More About Adverbs

LESSON 9   116–31

§98. The Independent Use of the 1st sing. Stative

§99. The Exclamatory use of the Stative Forms

§100. Existential Sentences: "There is …" "There are …"

§101. Negation
§102. Negation of Non-verbal Sentences with Adverbial Comment
§103. Negation of Existential Sentences ("There is / are no . . ."):
§104. Negation of Nouns: "Without . . ."
§105. Negation of the Infinitive: "Without (doing)"
§106. Negation of the Verbal Clauses & Predicate Adjectives
§107. Past Time: "He did not Hear . . ." / "He was not Heard . . ."
  1) Active Voice *N Sḏm·f* "He did not Hear"
  2) Passive Voice *N Sḏm·tw·f* "He was not heard"
§108. Present Time: "He does not Hear . . ." / "He is not Heard . . ."
  1) Active Voice *N Sḏm·n·f* "He does not Hear," "He cannot Hear"
  2) Passive Voice *N Sḏm·n·tw·f* "He is not Heard"
§109. Future Time: *Nn sḏm·f* "He will not Hear . . ." *Nn sḏm·tw·f* "He will not be heard"
§110. *N sp* + Prospective *sḏm·f* "He never heard . . ." "It was never heard"
§111. *Nty* The relative adjective "That, which, that which, who"
§112. *Nty* + Adverbs / Adverbial Phrases
§113. *Nt(y)t* "that which is . . ."
§114. *Ḥr nt(y)t* "because"
§115. *R nt(y)t* / *Ḥr nt(y)t* "to the effect that" in Letters
§116. *Nt(y)t* "that" after verbs of knowing & seeing

LESSON 10 132–51

§117. The Egyptian Participle
§118. The Basic Uses of the Participle
§119. Adjectival Features of the Participle
§120. Verbal Features of the Participles
§121. Forms of the Participle
  1, a) Imperfect Active Participle
  1, b) Imperfect Passive Participle
  2, a) Perfect Active Participle
  2, b) Perfect Passive Participle
  3, a) Prospective Active Participle
  3, b) Prospective Passive Participle
§122. Translations of the Participle
§123. Extended use of the Passive Participles
§124. Passive Participle + Noun (bound construction) or with Genitival *n(y)* + Noun
§125. *Sḏm·ty·fy*, *Sḏm·ty·sy*, and *Sḏm·ty·sn* Future Active Participles

§126. Possession
 1) "He belongs to X" *N(y) sw X*
 2) "X belongs to him" *Ntf X*
 3) "X belongs to him" *N·f ỉmy X*
§127. *n·f ỉmy* "Of His" / "His Own"
§128. AB Nominal Sentences
§129. Bi-partite Nominal Sentences with *pw*
§130. Bi-partite Nominal Sentences with Other Demonstrative Pronouns
§131. The *Sḏm·in·f* "Then he heard" and Related Constructions

LESSON 11 152–66
§132. The Possessive Article "My," "Your," "His," etc.
§133. Fronting of Nouns with *ỉr* "As for ..."
§134. The "Participial" Statement
§135. Tri-partite Nominal Sentences with *Pw*
§136. *Šmt pw ir(w)·n·f* A Narrative Past Tense Construction
§137. Conditional Sentences
§138. The Second Tense Prospective *Sḏm(w)·f* Forms
§139. Conditional Clauses Without *ỉr*
§140. The Omission of the Subject
§141. The Omission of the Object
§142. The Vocative *Pw*
§143. *Sḏm·f pw*: "This means that he hears" etc. in Explanations
§144. *'Ink pw*: in Explanations
§145. The Imperative (Commands and Instructions)
§146. Polite Requests ("Have X be done ...")

LESSON 12 167–80
§147. The Second Tense Forms
§148. The Explicatory Sentence Construction
§149. The Independent Use of the Second Tense Forms
§150. The Second Tense Forms as Objects of Prepositions
§151. The Second Tense Forms as the Direct Object of Verbs
§152. Reciprocal Sentences (The *Wechselsatz*)
§153. The *ꜥḥꜥ·n sḏm·n·f* Construction
§154. The *Sḏmt·f* Form
§155. The *N Sḏmt·f* Construction " ...before he has/had) heard"
§156. The *Sḏmt·f* Forms as Objects of Prepositions

LESSON 13 181–92

§157. The Relative Verb Forms—An Overview
§158. Perfect Relative Verb Form
§159. Imperfect Relative Verb Form
§160. Prosepective Relative Verb Form
§161. *Sḏm(w)·n·f* Relative Verb Form
§162. Passive Relative Verb Forms
§163. The *Šmt pw ỉr(w)·n·f* Construction
§164. Negation of Wishes and Exhortations
§165. Negatival Complement
§166. Negative Commands
§167. Questions
§168. Questions for Corroboration
§169. Questions for Specification

LESSON 14 193–205

§170. Less Common Classes of Verbal Roots
§171. *'Iri* as an Auxiliary Verb
§172. *Ḫpr* as an Auxiliary Verb
§173. The Auxiliary Verb *Pꜣ(w)* "To Have Done in the Past"
§174. Other Auxiliary Verbs
§175. Negation of Purpose Clauses
§176. Negation of Prospective Forms as Direct Objects of Verbs and Objects of Prepositions
§177. Negation of Conditional Sentences
§178. Negative Infinitives
§179. Negative Participles and Relative Verb Forms
§180. The Negative Verb *Tm* in Other Verb Forms
§181. Rarer Modes of Negation: *Nfr n* & *Nfr pw*
§182. The Ancient Negation *W*
§183. The Negative Relative Adjective *ỉwty*

LESSON 15 206–19

§184. Negations in the Explicatory Sentence
§185. Non-enclitic Sentence Particles
§186. Enclitic Particles
§187. Defective Writing of the Third Plural Suffix Pronoun

LESSON 16 220–34

§188. Second Tense Prospective *Sḏm(w)·f* Forms and Their Uses
§189. Parenthetic Expressions for "So He Said," "So She Will Say," etc.
§190. Verbs Following the Genetival *N(y)* "Such as the King Gives," etc.
§191. The Genetival *N(y)* before Prepositional Phrases
§192. *M*- Preformative Nouns
§193. Abstract Nouns—Idioms with *Bw* and *St*
§194. Colourful Idioms as Nouns
§195. The Reflexive Dative
§196. *'Iw* + Adjective (Stative)
§197. The Offering Formula
§198. The Late Egyptian Set of Pronouns *Tw·ì*, *Tw·k*, etc.
§199. Late Egyptian Writing Conventions
§200. Further Reading

KEY TO SOME OF THE EXERCISES 235–40

EGYPTIAN–ENGLISH VOCABULARY 241–99

GRAMMATICAL & GENERAL INDEX 300–7

VERB CHARTS

Forms of the Mutable and Irregular Verbs
Basic Verbal Constructions I (Active Voice)
Basic Verbal Constructions II (Passive Voice)

SYMBOLS & ABBREVIATIONS

< > Scribal omission

{ } Superfluous signs (including "dittography")

( ) Words supplied for clarity in translation

⌜ ⌝ Text (reading or meaning) uncertain

Ø Zero (ending); Non-existent

* A reconstructed or hypothetical form

** An impossible form or construction

adj.	adjective
adv.	adverb
B.C.E.	before the Common Era
C.E.	Common Era
f., fem.	feminine
infin.	infinitive
m., masc.	masculine
n.	noun
partic.	participle
pl.	plural
PN	personal name
prep.	preposition
sing.	singular
vb	verb

Middle Egyptian Grammar

LESSON 1

§1. Egyptian Connections to African and West Asian Languages

The Egyptian language has usually been taught as a unique language in isolation. But, in fact, it is a member of the large Afro-Asiatic language family. Older works refer to this family as "Hamito-Semitic," but this is not a scientific categorization, since it assumes a false dichotomy between the Semitic languages and the "Hamitic languages." Afro-Asiatic languages were—and still are—spoken by people in central, northern, and eastern Africa, the Arabian Peninsula, the Levant and Mesopotamia.

There are five or six main branches of the Afro-Asiatic family: Berber, Chadic (including Hausa), Cushitic, Egyptian, and Semitic. Each of these branches—apart from Egyptian—has subdivisions into distinct languages. Of the ancient Afro-Asiatic languages, both Egyptian and Akkadian (the Semitic language of Assyria and Babylonia) exhibit a considerable degree of linguistic change, right from the earliest traces in writing. In Egyptian, there are, not surprisingly, many words cognate[1] to counterparts in Hebrew, Arabic, and Akkadian, the best known of the ancient languages. For example, Egyptian  *ḥsb* "to calculate," Hebrew חָשַׁב (*ḥāšab̠*) "to reckon," and Arabic حسب (*ḥasaba*) "to calculate."[2] There are also cognates with many modern African languages, but these have not yet been studied as thoroughly and in any case are more difficult to compare, given the large gap in time.[3] Many of the connections are difficult to recognize because of metathesis (a shift in the order of the consonants) and phonetic changes—some of which are quite drastic. Similarly, there are many affinities in the grammatical features of these languages. The exact grammatical mechanisms may be quite different, but frequently the general approach is similar.

§2. The Historical Phases of Egyptian

Egyptian writing at its incipient stage before 3000 B.C.E. is mostly used to identify individuals and groups by name, as on the Narmer palette, which contains depictions of historical events,

[1] I.e. historically (genetically) related to each other, having descended from a common ancestral language. For example English "cow" is cognate with German *Kuh* and English "father" is cognate with Spanish *padre*. By contrast, English "facade" is a loan-word borrowed from the French *façade*, but is not "cognate" to it.

[2] The cognates will be indicated in the vocabulary lists to show the extent of the relationship with the Semitic languages. Cognates with other Afro-Asiatic languages are not included since almost all of the evidence is from modern languages, and is in any case beyond the scope of an introductory grammar.

[3] A good introduction is J.H. Greenberg, *The Languages of Africa* (Bloomington: 1966), pp. 42–51. Our recently expanding knowledge of Old Nubian, although dating to ca. 1200 C.E., may stimulate scholarship in the relations between Egyptian and other African languages.

symbolic pictograms, and rebus (sound alike) signs for the names. Somewhat later, pictographic signs are used in offering lists to represent such things as a leg of ox, a bundle of onions, and offering loaves. Some of these signs developed directly into hieroglyphic writing; others did not.

The Egyptian language has an extremely long history—spanning some 4,500 years—and can be divided into five main phases, although with some overlaps:

I **Old Egyptian** ca. 3000–2135 B.C.E., Dynasties 1–8

II **Middle Egyptian**, classical ca. 2135–2000 B.C.E., Dynasties 9–12
post-classical, ca. 2000–1300 B.C.E., Dynasties 13–18

III **Late Egyptian** ca. 1550–715 B.C.E., Dynasties 18–24

IV **Demotic** ca. 715 B.C.E.–470 C.E.

V **Coptic** third–sixteenth centuries C.E. (still used as the liturgical language in the rites of the Coptic church, and spoken to a certain extent as a revived language by modern Coptic Christians)

Old Egyptian and classical Middle Egyptian are presumed to be fairly close to the spoken language of their respective eras, and almost certainly reflect the dialect spoken by the royal family or that of the capital city. Old and Middle Egyptian are generally quite similar, apart from a few changes in the verbal system and the use of differing particles. Middle Egyptian continued to serve as the written language into the early New Kingdom (Eighteenth Dynasty) although the spoken dialect had undergone some major structural changes.

Late Egyptian reflects the spoken language of the New Kingdom, but after the Twenty-first Dynasty, monumental inscriptions were written in something approximating Middle Egyptian. The dialects attested in the later periods are all fairly close to Late Egyptian, the major break being between Middle and Late Egyptian.

§3. The Scripts of Egyptian

Over the course of four and a half millennia, Egyptian was written with four distinct scripts:

I **Hieroglyphic** ("holy carving"): The forms closely reflect what they represent; they are often carved in stone; sometimes they are written on papyri, especially for religious texts.

II **Hieratic** ("priestly"): A cursive script for use with pen on papyrus (or on an ostracon—a potsherd or limestone flake—a cheap, common, and very durable writing surface). The cursive forms emerged very early, and there is evidence from the First Dynasty. Only rarely were inscriptions written on stone in this script.

III **Demotic** ("popular"): This is a late (7th century B.C.E. on) cursive script that derives from hieratic, but is much abbreviated. It was used for everyday documents and literary works. Religious texts continued to be written in hieratic and sometimes cursive hieroglyphs.

IV **Coptic** (from Greek *Αἴγυπτος* "Egypt"): The script is Greek, but with additional letters derived from demotic, e.g. ϯ (*ti*), ϣ (*š*), ϥ (*f*), ϩ (*ḫ*), ϧ (*ẖ*), ϩ (*ḥ*), ϫ (*tsh*), ϭ (*gy*).

A comparison of a few signs in the various scripts is presented in Table 1. Of course, as can be easily seen, Coptic is an alphabetic script. The Egyptian script is not directly related to the Semitic and Greek (and Roman) alphabets, but it served as the inspiration. Many hieratic and hieroglyphic signs were used in the ancient Phœnician syllabic script of Byblos (ca. 2000 B.C.E.) that evolved into the western alphabets.[4]

TABLE 1: A COMPARISON OF THE EGYPTIAN SCRIPTS

Sign	Beetle	Ring Stand	Foot	Owl
Value[5]	*ḫpr*	*g*	*b*	*m*
Hieroglyphic	𓆣	𓎼	𓃀	𓅓
Hieratic				
Demotic				
Coptic	ϣⲱⲡⲉ	ϭ	ⲃ	ⲙ

§4. The Writing System of Egyptian

From the earliest phase down to its demise, Egyptian is characterized by two principal features: the use of *logograms* and the *rebus* principle. Logograms are signs that represent words, both concrete and abstract. For instance, the sign ⊙ represents the sun, and could be read variously depending on the meaning: *rʿ* "sun," the god Rēʿ, "(every) day"; *hrw* "day(time)"; *sw* "day x (of the month)" in dates. This is easy enough for simple, concrete words, such as 𓉐 *pr* "house."[6] But how, for example, might one write the preposition "to," the noun "life," or the verb "to become"? The rebus principle was the solution: one used words that sound alike (i.e. have the same root consonants) to stand for these words that could not be easily depicted. Thus, the sign depicting a "mouth" 𓂋 (pronounced *r*) was used for the preposition "to" (*r*). The "sandal strap" ☥ (*ʿnḫ*) was used to write "life" (*ʿnḫ*), and the scarab beetle 𓆣 (*ḫprr*) was used to write "to become" (*ḫpr*). These signs, since they are used for their similar pronunciation and not for their basic meaning, may be termed "phonetic signs." A core group of phonetic signs must be learned by memory, since according to rules of Egyptian orthography, certain combinations of consonants are written *only* with particular phonetic signs.

Very early on in the history of Egyptian writing, certain signs were assigned the values of the Egyptian consonants, thus forming an alphabet of sorts (minus vowels). The Egyptians never

[4]M. Dunand, *Byblia Grammata* (Beirut: 1945), pp. 71–138; G.E. Mendenhall, *The Syllabic Inscriptions from Byblos* (Beirut: 1985); J.E. Hoch, "The Byblos Syllabary: Bridging the Gap Between Egyptian Hieroglyphs and Semitic Alphabets," *Journal of the Society for the Study of Egyptian Antiquities* 20 (1990), pp. 115–24.

[5]The transliteration of the Egyptian signs and their probable phonetic values will be discussed in §5.

[6]The use of the stroke indicates that the sign is to be read as what it represents (and not phonetically, for instance). The stroke will be dealt with in §13.

made exclusive use of the alphabetic signs as an alphabet, and although words were commonly spelled out alphabetically, they were frequently *also* written logographically or were followed by generic sense determinatives (See, §12.). For example, the writing 𓂋𓂝𓇳 (*rꜥ*) with "sun" determinative is "sun"; with the god determinative 𓂋𓂝𓁛 it is the god Rēꜥ.[7] The alphabetic spelling also permitted a clear distinction for words of similar meaning, e.g. 𓉔𓂋𓅱𓇳 (*hrw*) "day(time)."

§5. The Transliteration and Sounds of the Alphabetic Signs

The Egyptian "alphabet" is arranged in a special order devised by modern scholars. The order may seem peculiar, but it must be learned immediately, since the use of the dictionary requires it.

There have been many misconceptions about the phonetic values of some of the signs, and this is unfortunately reflected in the names by which Egyptologists refer to them. The inappropriate names will not be used in this book, but are cited in the footnotes. They should, however, be learned since they are in general use among Egyptologists today.

The alphabetic signs must be thoroughly learned at once. Some signs are distinguished by subtle differences. Note especially that the vulture sign 𓄿 is distinguished from other bird signs by the sharp angle of the upper right-hand portion of its head, and that the owl sign 𓅓 is distinguished by its squarish head in full frontal view (profile view is the norm in Egyptian art and writing). The quail chick 𓅱 is easily distinguished by its immature wings, but in hand written forms of the sign the distinction is chiefly based on its plumpish body shape. The transliterations do not distinguish between variant signs. For instance, both 𓇌 and 𓏭 are transliterated *y*, and both 𓅱 and 𓏲 are transliterated *w*. The signs 𓊃 and 𓋴 were not originally variants, but represented distinct sounds. In Middle Egyptian, however, they are treated as variants. (In works in English on Middle Egyptian they are considered variants, but the German Dictionary,[8] which includes Old Egyptian, treats them as distinct letters.

TABLE 2: THE EGYPTIAN ALPHABETIC SIGNS

Sign	Transliteration	Depiction	Value	Name
𓄿	*ꜣ*	Egyptian vulture	*l*, *r* (?)	Vulture[9]
𓇋	*ỉ*	Reed leaf	ʾ, *y*, *i*	Reed leaf

[7]The early New Kingdom pronunciation of this god's name can be reconstructed from Akkadian cuneiform syllabic transcriptions as *Rīꜥa. The sound of the last consonant does not exist in English and will be dealt with in §5.

[8]A. Erman and H. Grapow, *Wörterbuch der ägyptischen Sprache* (Leipzig: 1927–1963), 7 vols. Beginning students are not expected to consult this work, but it will be useful—absolutely necessary—in later courses.

[9]This sign is commonly called "*Aleph*" (the Hebrew name for the glottal stop). This name should be understood, but avoided.

Sign	Transliteration	Depiction	Value	Name
𓇌	*y*	Two reed leaves	*y*	Double reed leaf
𓏭[10]	*y*	Duality	*y, i*[11]	Oblique strokes
𓂝	ʿ	Arm	ʿ	ʿ*Ayin*
𓅱	*w*	Quail chick	*w, u*	Quail chick
𓏲	*w*	Cursive *w*	*w, u*	(Hieratic) "W"
𓃀	*b*	Foot/Leg	*b*	"B"
𓊪	*p*	Stool	*p*	"P"
𓆑	*f*	Horned viper	*f, pf?*	"F"
𓅓	*m*	Owl	*m*	"M"
𓈖	*n*	Water	*n, l*	"N"
𓂋	*r*	Mouth	*r, l*	"R"
𓉔	*h*	House plan	*h*	"H"
𓎛	*ḥ*	Twisted fibre wick	*ḥ*	Dotted "H"
𓐍	*ḫ*	Placenta?	*ḫ*	Circle "H"
𓄡	*ẖ*	Animal belly and tail	?[12]	Flat "H"
𓊃	*s* (Old Egy. *z*)	Door bolt	*s*	Bolt "S"
𓋴	*s* (Old Egy. *ś*)	Folded cloth	*s*	Tall "S"
𓈙	*š*	Pool	*sh*	*Shin*
𓈎	*q* (*ḳ*)	Hill (cross section)	*q?*	*Qoph*, "Q"
𓎡	*k*	Basket with handle	*k*	"K"
𓎼	*g*	Ring stand for vessels	*g?*	"G"
𓏏	*t*	Loaf of bread	*t*	"T"
𓍿	*ṯ*	Rope for tethering	*tsh*	*Chīma*
𓂧	*d*	Hand	*d?*	"D"
𓆓	*ḏ*	Cobra	*dj?*	*Djandja*

It should be noted that the *exact* phonetic values of the Egyptian consonants are in many cases unknown.

The phonetic values of the following signs, in particular, require some comment. Some of the information in the following paragraphs is rather technical and is intended as supplementary

[10]A variant of "double reed leaf."
[11]This sign is used sporadically to indicate the vowel *i*.
[12]Actual value unknown.

information for those interested in linguistic matters. The recommendations on pronunciation, on the other hand, are admittedly simplistic from the linguistic point of view, but may assist the beginning student in acquiring a passable "accent."

𓄿 *ꜣ* The original phonetic value of this sign is unknown, but by the New Kingdom it was no longer pronounced. In the Old and Middle Kingdom times it was used to transliterate Semitic *l* and *r*. Coptic has *l* and so, presumably, did some Old and Middle Egyptian dialects. Scholars used to think that this was the "glottal stop" (the sound produced in the "Adam's apple" that breaks the vowels in some English speaker's pronunciation of "the ocean" [ðə ˀo:š^{ə}n] and in all English speaker's pronunciation of "Oh, oh!" Whatever the vulture sign is in Middle Egyptian, the glottal stop it is not!

𓇋 *ỉ* has two consonantal values: 1) the "glottal stop" (the sound that breaks the vowels in the English pronunciation of "oh, oh!"). 2) It also has the value of *y*. It also is sometimes used with the vocalic pronunciation of *i*, but this is almost exclusively in foreign names.

The letters 𓇌 *y* and 𓏭 *y* were also used sporadically to indicate the vowel *i*, especially in transcribing foreign names.

𓂝 *ꜥ* is a sound that does not exist in English or European languages. It occurs in Arabic, and in the speech of some speakers of Sephardic Hebrew. It is produced with a restriction in the pharynx and with voicing. It is quite a strong consonant, and in the Afro-Asiatic languages, it is considered one of the "emphatic" series.[13]

𓅱 *w* and 𓏲 *w* can indicate a *u*-vowel, sometimes as a grammatical ending, and regularly in transcribing foreign names.

𓎛 *ḥ* is a pharyngeal aspirate. Pronounce it as a constricted *h*. Cf. Arabic ح. This is the unvoiced counterpart of *ꜥayin*.

𓐍 *ḫ* is an unvoiced velar. Cf. the guttural in Scotch *loch*, German *ach*, Modern Hebrew אַךְ, and Arabic خ.

𓄡 *ẖ* has an unknown value. Perhaps it was a lateral as Welsh *ll*, an unvoiced "hissed l" produced by letting air pass over one or both sides of the tongue.[14] Egyptologists conventionally pronounce it as *ch* in German *ich* (something like a "whispered-h" in "he" in English). In a few cases, *ẖ* sometimes interchanged with *š* and *ḫ*.

[13]The "emphatic" feature is common to the Afro-Asiatic language family, but it is not clear that the sounds were vocalized the same way. In some languages they were glotallized, but in Arabic, for instance, the main feature is pharyngealization.

[14]The Welsh lateral is pronounced by holding the tongue as if to pronounce "lee" and exhaling air (without voicing—and smiling helps). English speakers tend to hear this sound as a type of "lisped s," as in the voice of a famous animated cat's pronunciation of "sl" sounds.

𓈎 *q* was in later times perceived as an "emphatic" consonant by Semitic speakers.

𓎼 *g* is transcribed by both ג *g* and ק *q* in Hebrew, so it may have been both voiced and "emphatic."

𓍿 *ṯ* is conventionally pronounced as English "ch," but it may have been "ts" or had this value as a variant sound. Students familiar with Arabic or Biblical Hebrew should carefully note that Egyptian *ṯ* does **not** represent the interdental that corresponds to English "th" in "thing."

𓂧 *d* is possibly a voiced "emphatic" [ḍ]. In any case it was perceived as an emphatic by Hebrew speakers, who used ט *ṭ* to transcribe it.

𓆓 *ḏ* is conventionally pronouned as "dj," but it may have had the value [ḍẓ][15] or had this as a variant sound. In any case this sound was also perceived as an emphatic by Hebrew speakers, who rendered it with Hebrew צ *ṣ*. Again, students familiar with Arabic or Biblical Hebrew should note that Egyptian *ḏ* is not the voiced interdental (English "th" in "this").

The letters 𓏏 *t* and 𓍿 *ṯ* tended to become variant sounds of each other (allophones) depending on such things as the following vowels,[16] but in earlier Middle Egyptian they are distinct sounds. The same phenomenon occurs also with 𓂧 *d* and 𓆓 *ḏ*. Thus in many Middle Egyptian texts 𓏏 *t* is used in place of original 𓍿 *ṯ*, and 𓂧 *d* in place of original 𓆓 *ḏ*. Other times the reverse is encountered (e.g. 𓆓 *ḏ* for original 𓂧 *d*). These cases are usually "false archaizations."

Most of the variant forms of the alphabetic signs have been given in Table 2. There are, however, a few others from later periods: 𓐝 for *m*, 𓋔 for *n*, and 𓏐 for *t*.

For convenience, Egyptologists have adopted certain conventions in pronouncing Egyptian words.

- Both *ꜣ* and *ꜥ* are pronounced as the vowel *a*.
- *ỉ* is pronounced as the vowel *i*, as *ʾaleph* ("glottal stop") plus *i*, or as *y*.
- *w* is sometimes pronounced as a *w* and sometimes as the vowel *u*. Many scholars are inconsistent in their pronunciation of *w* and *ỉ*.
- Otherwise, we freely insert the vowel *e*, just so we can pronounce the sounds as syllables. This is purely arbitrary and the resulting sounds bear no resemblance to the original spoken Egyptian. There are some conventions generally followed by scholars, but these can be assimilated over time. Students should therefore feel free to just "jump in" and start reading. For

[15] An "emphatic" voiced (?) affricate.

[16] Evidence from later times suggest that *ti* was pronounced [tsi] or [tši], whereas *ta* was pronounced *ta*. Thus the writing *ṯa* would be pronounced [ta]. Cf. J.E. Hoch, *Semitic Words in Egyptian Texts of the New Kingdom and Third Intermediate Period* (Princeton: 1994), p. 429 f.

example, *ỉw ḏd·f n sš nty ḥr w3t* would be pronounced: *yew djedef en sesh enty ḥer wat*. This is a far cry from what Egyptian must have actually sounded like, but this method has served modern scholars well enough.

§6. The Direction of Writing

Egyptian was generally written from right to left. In Middle Egyptian hieratic texts the writing is in columns reading top to bottom and from right to left. Later hieratic was horizontal and always written from right to left. Hieroglyphic inscriptions can be written in any of these ways, and also from left to right; the direction of the signs is normally reversed in such cases. To determine which direction to read, one need only read into (towards) the faces of the birds, animals, and people, as can be seen below. Modern publications of Egyptian texts follow two conventions. Passages that are typeset are usually set left to right for practical reasons. Books that are written by hand follow the direction of the original. With the introduction of computers and new methods of book composition, it will soon be feasible to publish typeset quality books following the original orientation of the texts. In the writing samples, below, the two signs marked "1" are actually inverted, the quail chick should be first in order, but they are transposed for aesthetic reasons (§41, 2).

Left to right, horizontal 

Right to left, horizontal 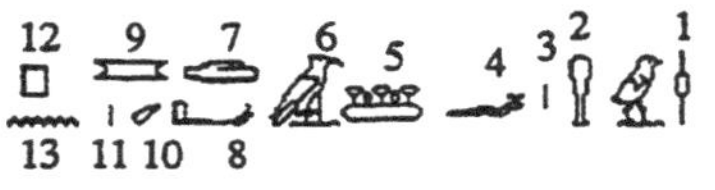

Left to right, vertical 

Right to left, vertical 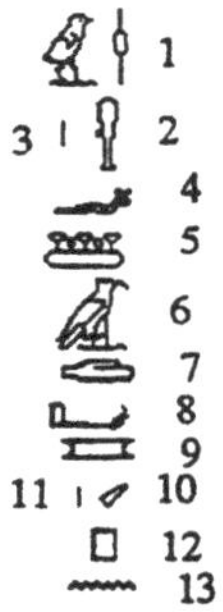

Note that there are no word spaces. There is no punctuation, either. Therefore one must rely upon the grammar to divide sentences, paragraphs, and chapters. The use of semantic determinatives (§12) aids greatly in word division.

With very few exceptions, here assuming left to right orientation, the order in which signs are to be read is as follows: left before right, top before bottom. The exceptions involve transpositions either for aesthetic or honorific reasons, and will be learned later.

Occasionally one encounters retrograde signs (written with the "wrong" orientation). This is particularly the case in left to right inscriptions, since right to left was the normal direction. The sign  *k*, however is supposedly always written retrograde in the hieratic script, and hieratic *k* is conventionally transcribed with the retrograde sign:  .

§7. Conventions of Transliteration

There are two main systems of transliteration, the German and the Anglo-American; the latter is followed in this book.[17] Egyptian contains a number of suffixes, and these are separated by a raised dot. (E.g. *ỉw·ỉ ỉy·kwỉ* "I have arrived," in which *·ỉ* and *·kwỉ* are both suffixes of the first person singular.) The feminine ending *t* is not, however, separated by a raised dot (*sꜣ* "son," *sꜣt* "daughter"). Compound words are connected by a hyphen: e.g. *ỉmy-r* "overseer," *r-pr* "temple," *r-ꜥ-ḫt* "combat." Letters not written but presumed present are placed in parentheses: e.g. *ḥ(n)qt* "beer" and *n(y)t* "of" (fem. sing.). Extraneous letters are placed in curly braces { }, and reconstructed portions in square brackets [ ]. Letters erroneously omitted are placed in angle brackets < >. Words are transliterated only once. This applies in cases where a word is written *both* logographically *and* phonetically—e.g.  is transliterated *ḫpr* and not *ḫ-ḫpr-pr*, or the like. The consonant *r* was not always stable, and sometimes is written with *ỉ* in final position. In these cases, transliterate according to the original writing, e.g.  is *swr*.

§8. The Lack of Articles

Standard Middle Egyptian has neither definite nor indefinite article. The noun  *sš* may be translated "a scribe," "the scribe," or just "scribe." Colloquial Middle Egyptian probably contained articles (see §78), but these are rarely encountered in the texts, except where reflecting the spoken language—in letters, legal statements, and in tomb scene captions as quotations of persons of inferior social status. The articles are sporadically encountered in some literary texts, but these are perhaps later additions.

§9. The Simple Verbal Sentence: Statements of Fact

When the speaker wished to state something, presenting it as a fact (whether true or not, and whether the speaker held it to be true or not[18]), the sentence particle  *ỉw* was employed as an indispensable element. This particle always stands at the beginning of the sentence and in the case of the verbal sentence, it is followed by the main verb of the sentence.

It is extremely important to note that the clause[19] begun with *ỉw* is always the main clause. If

[17] The chief difference is *j* in place of *ỉ* and differences in the use of the dot.

[18] Or simply put, lies and preposterous statements could be presented as statements of fact. Examples of great exaggeration will be encountered in this text.

[19] A "clause" is a major sentence component. Main clauses can stand as complete sentences on their own—even if there are subsequent clauses. Surbordinate (or "dependent") clauses cannot stand on their own, but are dependent on the main clause. E.g. (subordinate clause underlined, main clause not underlined): "Having said that, I should point

there are subsequent clauses, verbal or non-verbal, they are subordinate (or "dependent") clauses.

Word order in Egyptian is very fixed, and like English, the sequence cannot be broken or rearranged without either producing drastic changes to the meaning ("Child bites dog") or else a confused jumble of meaningless words ("yesterday my accident mother a tragic automobile had almost"). Egyptian is, in fact, far more rigid in the word order and clause sequence than English. This will be important to keep in mind when dealing with long, complicated sentences. At this point, however, we are dealing with the sentence at its most basic.

The statement of fact sentence type may be simple, but it forms the basis for many other sentence types, and must be fully understood. The sequence of words must be committed to memory: the particle *ỉw*, verbal predicate, subject, and finally adverbs and adverbial phrases, if there are any. (Adverbs and adverbial phrases relate details about the circumstances: they describe manner, means, cause, motive, quality, state, place-where, time-when, frequency, etc. In Egyptian, adverbs do not really "modify the verb" but usually the entire clause. The uses of the Egyptian adverb differs in many ways from the English adverb, and it should be thought of as a distinct grammatical category.)

1) Particle	2) Verbal pred.	3) Subject	4) Adverbial(s)
ỉw	*ḏd*	*s*	*m pr*
(New Sentence)	"speaks"	"(the) man"	"in (the) house"

"The man speaks in the house."

1) The particle *ỉw* signals the beginning of the main clause of a new sentence. 2) The verbal predicate (relates the point the speaker is making). 3) The subject of the verbal predicate. 4) Additional information—here a prepositional phrase indicating "place-where." It will be learned later that the form of the verb that occurs in slot 2 is called the "circumstantial form." The circumstantial forms of the verb function as adverbs (a large and extremely important grammatical category in Egyptian that will be treated more fully at a later point). The sentence structure is therefore very similar to that of the non-verbal statement of fact to be dealt with in §10, which has an adverbial phrase as its "predicate" (to use the standard terminology).

In traditional terms, the predicate is the *information conveyed about the subject of the sentence*. Examples of predicates in English sentences (the predicate is underlined):

1) The cat is on the chair.

2)She jumped off the cart.

---

out that unlike English, in Egyptian, subordinate clauses never precede the main clause (in this type of sentence)."

3)The movie was long, boring, and full of 1960s clichés.

This construction is very much like the English "Present Tense" ("She speaks French." "They study geometry in Grade 10.") Such statements of fact are timeless statements, generalizations, repeated actions, or they refer to a one-time action. This construction is *not* like the English "progressive tenses" (action in progress: e.g. "I am working on it right now . . ." "Her aunts were playing bridge in the alcove."). Egyptian does, however, have a different construction that corresponds quite well to the English progressive tenses (§§58–61).

The "pidgin English" literal renderings used in the chart above should not be taken as an indication of any supposed primitiveness of the Egyptian language. The grammar is actually very sophisticated, and it is capable of many fine nuances that are impossible to render adequately in English and other modern languages. These overly literal renderings are used here only since no vocabulary has yet been learned. They do, however, conveniently provide an opportunity to warn students not to attempt such renderings when translating Egyptian texts, but rather from the very beginning to deal with Egyptian as a language—on its own terms—and not through the filter of English or another language.

§10. The Non-verbal Statement of Fact (with Adverbial Comment)

The non-verbal statement of fact consists of three main slots: particle, topic, comment. The "topic" is similar to the "subject," but is broader in meaning: it is what the statement is about, and will usually correspond to the subject in English. The "comment" is also a broader term than "predicate": it is what the speaker relates about the topic. The comment will generally correspond to the predicate in English. Since the Egyptian sentences of this type do not normally use a verb "to be," the terms "subject" and "predicate" tend to be misleading (especially when some adverbial verb-forms that fit in slot 3 are learned).

1) Particle	(ø)	2) Topic	3) Comment
 *iw*		 *s*	 *m pr*
(New Sentence)		"(the) man"	"in (the) house"

"The man is in the house." (Or "The man was in the house.")

In this construction, the comment slot is always filled by an "adverb." The comment is sometimes called the "adverbial predicate." (The traditional term for this sentence type is "non-verbal sentence with adverbial predicate.") Here the adverbial comment consists of a prepositional phrase. (All prepositional phrases function as "adverbs" in Egyptian, and any prepositional phrase—within logic—can be plugged into slot 3.) Note that the adverbial comment is not limited to prepositional phrases, and various other types of adverbials that will be learned later also occur in this slot. The meaning and function of the particle *ỉw* will be discussed at a later point. It cannot be translated in English, but it conveniently marks the beginning of a new sentence / main clause.

In English the predicate consists of a verb or a verb and words closely tied to it. In English a form of the verb "to be" is used to form predicates involving prepositional phrases (and other adverbial elements), as in ex. 1, above (§9, 1). The verb "to be" is also used with predicate adjectives, as in ex. 3, above. It is important to note that Egyptian does not use the verb "to be" in either case, so these predicates are called either "adverbial predicates" (§10; the term "adverbial comment" is preferred in the present work) or "predicate adjectives" (§44).

There is basically no way to indicate tense in non-verbal sentences with adverbial comment, and translations must therefore supply past, present, or future forms of the verb "to be," depending upon the context. Problems with tense are rarely encountered.

The terms "adverbial comment" and "adverbial predicate" might sound intimidating, but all that is meant is that the information related about the topic of the sentence is:

- an adverb (e.g. "here," "over there")
- a prepositional phrase (e.g. "on the ground," "in [a state of] joy," "at the feet of ...")
- any other word or phrase in the "adverbial" category.

The distinction between "adverbial comment" and "adverbial modifier" is an important one. Making the distinction is, in fact, less difficult than the terms might suggest. The distinction depends on the function of the phrase in the sentence—is it the main point of the sentence (comment) or is it there for additional information (modifier)? Consider the two sentences that have been presented so far. In the sentence *ỉw ḏd s m pr*, the prepositional phrase *m pr* "in the house" is a modifier—an "adverbial modifier." In other words, "in the house" is not the point that the speaker was making about "the man," but rather it provides additional (or modifying) information—where he speaks. On the other hand, in the Egyptian sentence *ỉw s m pr*, the phrase *m pr* is a comment—the point about "the man" is precisely that he is "in the house."

EXERCISE I

(A) Memorize the alphabetic signs in Table 2.

(B) Learn the following words. Practice writing them in both directions (as with future vocabulary and exercises). Transliterate them. Looking only at your transliteration write the words in hieroglyphs.

 *ỉw*[20] (particle used to begin a statement of fact)

 *ỉm* (adverb) "there"; "therein," therewith," "therefrom" This word is derived from the

[20]Pronounce as "yew."

preposition *m*.

 *bw*[21] (n. m.) "place"

 *pn*[22] (m. sing. demonstrative adj.) "this" (follows the noun, and agrees in gender with it). Sometimes it is better translated "that."

 *pr* "house." (n. m.) "house," "household"; "temple" (of gods); "palace" (of king)

 *m*[23] (prep.) 1) "in," "inside"; 2) "by means of," "with" (instrument);[24] 3) "from," "out of" (with verbs of motion). It is cognate with West Semitic *ba/bi*, e.g. Hebrew בְּ (*bə*) "in," "with" (by means of); Arabic ب (*bi*) "in," "at," "with" (by means of)

 n 1) (prep.) "the dative": (give, say) "to" (someone), (do something) "for" (someone); 2) (going) "to" (a person) Cf. West Semitic *l-*, e.g. Hebrew לְ (*lə*) and Arabic ل (*li*) both "to," "for"

 *r* (prep.) 1) "to," "towards" (a place, or thing); 2) "concerning," "regarding," "with relation to"; 3) "at" (a location) Cf. ? Hebrew אֶל (*ʾel*) and Arabic الى (*ilā*), both "to," "toward"

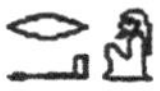 *Rꜥ*[25] Rēꜥ (the solar god)

 *rn* (n. m.) "name"

 *ḥnꜥ*[26] (prep.) "with" (a person), "together with" (things and people)

 *ẖt* (n. fem.—but sometimes masc.) "thing"

 *s*[27] (n. m.) "man" ? cf. Hebrew אִישׁ (*ʾîš*) "man"

 *ky*[28] (n. m.) (precedes the noun) "another"; "another man" (sometimes with a seated man determinative), "another thing"

 *kt* (n. fem.) (precedes the noun) "another"; used as above

 *tn*[29] (fem. sing. demonstrative adj.) "this" (follows the noun, and agrees in gender with it). Sometimes it is better translated "that."

21Pronounce as "bu."
22Pronounce as "pen."
23Pronounce as "em."
24*M* is not used with the sense of "with" a person; another preposition is used.
25The seated god sign is not pronounced—it indicates the general sense. It is, however, an integral part of the writing of this name. The use of such signs will be dealt with in §12.
26Pronounce as "*ḥenaꜥ*."
27Pronounce as "sa." The seated man indicates the general sense.
28Pronounce as "key."
29Pronounce as "ten."

 *ḏd* (vb.) "to say," "speak," "talk," "tell"

(C) 1) Transliterate and translate. 2)For extra practice, write out your translations on a separate piece of paper and translate back into Egyptian (check your own work against the original).

(1)  2)  (3)  (4) 
(5)  (6)  (7) 

(D) Write the following combinations of signs in hieroglyphs. Try to group the signs according to Egyptian conventions.

wbn, *ꜥqꜣ*, *ἰsṯ*, *hr*, *fḫ*, *gḥs* (use tall "s"), *ḫsy* (use bolt "s"), *ḥdb*, *šfꜥ*, *ṯsm* (use bolt "s"), *ḏfꜣw*, *mḫtw*

LESSON 2

§11. Logographic and Phonetic Writing

Although words could be written in a purely logographic manner, without the phonetic spellings there would likely be confusion. Was the intended word "sun," "daylight," "brightness," "time," or "era"? The general practice is to write the words phonetically, but to indicate the general sense of the word with a semantic determinative, which is placed at the end of the word. For instance, the sun sign 𓇳 is used with all the words listed above. Some hieroglyphs are used both logographically and as determinatives. This is the case with the scribe's kit[1] 𓏞 , which has the logographic reading *sš* ("writing," "scribe") but can also serve as the determinative for painting and smoothness. The ear sign 𓂓 has the logographic reading *sḏm* "to hear, listen" but also the phonetic value *ỉd*, and it also occurs as the determinative of words involving hearing and deafness. The various values (and a specification of their types) can be found in the sign list at the end of this book. Normally the writings give enough clues to permit a clear-cut reading.

Phonetic signs can be mono-consonantal (i.e. the alphabetic signs), bi-consonantal (e.g. 𓏞 *sš*), or tri-consonantal (e.g. 𓂓 *sḏm*). A core group of the multi-consonantal signs must be learned thoroughly in the course of the next few lessons.

These signs are essential to read even the simplest text in Egyptian because although the Egyptians *could* have written every sequence of consonants with alphabetic signs, they *did not* do so. For instance, although the sequence *mn* could theoretically have been written 𓅓𓈖, it actually was not written that way within a word, but rather consistently with the group 𓏠𓈖 *mn*. The group here consists of the bi-consonantal sign 𓏠 *mn* with its phonetic complement (the alphabetic sign[s] that complete its writing, in this case *n*). Examples of two divine names that contain the sequence *mn*: 𓇋𓏠𓈖𓀭 *ỉmn*, 𓏠𓈖𓏏𓅱𓀭 *Mnṯw*. Note that this rule of writing only applies *within the word root* and not across word (or root) boundaries. For instance, the sequence *m nhp* "in the early morning" is written 𓅓𓈖𓉔𓊪𓇳, since the *m* is the preposition "in" and stands outside of the word / root boundary of *nhp*. The use of the phonetic complement is regular, and is often a useful way of recognizing one of a group of similar-looking signs. This is particularly useful in reading modern hand-drawn hieroglyphs, since some scholarly handwriting is quite idiosyncratic. For instance the following bird signs 𓅜, 𓅟, 𓅧 can easily be distinguished thanks to their phonetic complements: 𓅜𓐍 *ꜣḫ*, 𓅟𓅓 *gm*, and 𓅧𓈎 *ʿq*. (The bi-consonantal

[1] The kit consists of a palette (with inkwells for black and red ink), water jug, and pen-holder/papyrus smoother, all held together with a cord.

signs will be learned in small groups starting in Lesson 3.)

§12. Semantic Determinatives

Most words have one or more semantic determinatives at their end. Only a few very common words occur without determinatives (as the vocabulary in Lesson 1). Since determinatives are found at the end of the word, they facilitate word division, which is otherwise difficult with no word spaces or other word dividers. Determinatives follow words written in any manner—purely alphabetic, phonetic (using multiconsonantal signs), logographic writings, and any combination of these. Exx. 𓏞𓏛 *sš* plus book-roll determinative is "document, writing," 𓏞𓀀 *sš* with seated man determinative indicates "scribe." Sometimes we do not know the specific meaning or nuance of a given word, but the determinatives can often suggest a general interpretation. The determinatives indicate the sense only and were not pronounced. There is no generally accepted convention among scholars of indicating the determinatives in transliterations. They are simply ignored. For this reason, extended passages cited only in transliteration are often difficult to read. Students should not rely heavily on transliterations, but should become thoroughly familiar with the Egyptian script. (Once learned, it is far easier to read than transliteration, where so much of the important semantic information is lacking.) The following list contains the most important determinatives. Those marked with a bullet (•) should be learned at this time. The others may be learned at a later date with this and the complete sign list to be used as a reference.

COMMON SEMANTIC DETERMINATIVES

• 𓀀 man, person, (also used after a man's name) called "seated man"

• 𓁐 woman, (also used after a woman's name) "seated woman"

• 𓀀𓁐𓏪 people (the three strokes indicate plurality)

𓀔 child, young; sitting

𓀙 old man, old

𓀞 official (there is some confusion between this and the previous sign)

𓀻, 𓀼, 𓀽 revered person, esp. the deceased (after the person's name)

• 𓀭 god, king

• 𓀯 king (with the royal *uraeus* on the brow)

• 𓅆 god, king

• 𓆗 goddess, queen

𓀠 high, rejoice, support

𓀢 praise, homage, supplication

• 𓀜, 𓂡, force, effort, activity. In hieratic (less often hieroglyphic), 𓂡 is used as a substitute.

-  eating, drinking, speaking, thinking, feeling ("man with hand to mouth")[2]

 lift, carry, load

 tired, weak, sitting

 enemy, foreigner

-  enemy, death, evil. Hieratic equivalent: .

 lying down, death, burial

 mummy, statue, likeness, shape

 head, nodding

 hair, mourning, forlorn

 eye, sight, actions of eye

-  actions or conditions of the eye
-  (less fully written: ) nose, smelling, joy, contempt
-  ear, states or activities of the ear (animal's ear)
- tooth, action of teeth, requesting, demanding (elephant tusk)

 offering, presenting

 arm, bending the arm, ceasing, tilting

 enveloping, embracing

-  phallus; less correctly: sexual activity, urination
-  sexual activity, urination; less correctly: phallus
-  leg, foot, action of the feet
-  walking, running ("walking legs"); frequently combined: 

 retreating, backwards motion, backwards (direction), repetition ("backwards walking legs")

-  flesh, meat ("flesh")
-  swellings, wounds, disease, bandaging, odours (depicts a pustule)

 bodily discharges, odours

-  cattle

,  wild, raging, storms ("Seth animal" depicts the animal associated with the god Seth)

-  leather, pelts, mammal, animal (including insects) ("animal"; depicts a hide with tail)

 bone, ivory, harpoons (a stylized fish skeleton)

 bird, insect (i.e. "flying creature")

 bad, evil, nuisance ("bad bird" depicts a sparrow[3])

[2]To be kept distinct from . Note the position of *both* arms.

[3]Perhaps the sparrow is associated with badness because thieving flocks of sparrows would eat freshly planted seeds.

fish

snake, worm

- tree
- plant, flower

vine, fruit

- wood, tree

grain (depicts a sack of grain being emptied)

grain, particles (rarely:)

- sky, above (depicts the upper firmament)
- , night, darkness (depicts the upper firmament with—for unknown reasons—a sceptre or broken and mended oar suspended from it)

star

- fire, heat, cooking (brazier with smoke)

air, wind, breath; sail

- stone (the sign is narrower than the alphabetic sign [š].)
- copper, bronze, metal (depicts a crucible)
- sand, minerals, pellets, particles, spices, metals, etc. (depicts particles)
- water, liquid, actions connected with water
- bodies of water
- irrigated land (irrigation channels seen from above)

land (later often replaces)

- road, travel, position (e.g. after "here," "there," etc.) (depicts a road with shrubs or boundary markers seen from above)
- desert, hilly terrain, foreign country (depicts three hills)
- foreign (country or person) ("throw-stick")
- town, village, Egypt (depicts either a cross-roads, or a circular village with huts)
- house, building, (also: things with interiors—e.g. boxes, chairs; depicts the floor-plan of a simple house)
- door, to open (depicts one of a pair of door leaves, with pivot tangs:)

box, chest; coffin

mat, fibre, basketry

- boat, ship, navigation

to capsize, overturn

- ⛵ sacred bark
- 𓍱 cloth, clothing, linen (a fringed cloth with [folded cloth] below)
- • 𓍼 binding, thread, document (i.e. the string binding a sealed papyrus)
- 𓍢 rope, actions involving ropes and cords
- 𓌪 knife, cutting
- 𓌹, 𓌻 hoe, cultivation, hacking up
- × breaking, dividing, crossing, calculating
- 𓎺 cup
- • 𓏊 (less accurately transcribed ○) vessel, anoint, beverages
- • 𓏐 bread (bread in a pan or bread mold)
- • 𓏏, 𓏒 loaf, bread, offerings
- 𓎱 festival
- • 𓏛 (also vertically 𓏜) book, writing, abstract nouns ("book roll"; depicts a papyrus roll tied and sealed)
- 𓍶 royal name ("cartouche" which encloses the king's main names)
- ı one; the word is the object depicted §13 ("stroke")
- • ııı (also 𓏥, 𓏤, °°°, °°°) plurality ("plural strokes")
- • ↘ substitute for complicated signs that are difficult to draw (mostly used in hieratic)

§13. The Use of the Stroke with Logograms

When logograms are to be read with the meaning of the object they depict, they are regularly followed by a stroke. E.g. 𓇳 r^c "sun," 𓁷 $ḥr$ "face," 𓉐 pr "house." Note, however, that the stroke is also used in some very common words in which it *does not* indicate that the object depicted is meant. These are mostly obvious, and will be learned as separate vocabulary items: 𓅭 $s3$ "son" (not "goose"), 𓁷 $ḥr$ "on" (not "face"), 𓎟 nb "lord, master" (not "basket").

§14. The Egyptian Noun: A Preliminary View

The Egyptian noun has two genders, masculine and feminine. Almost all nouns are consistently of one gender or the other. A very few nouns, however, occur as both masculine and feminine. A number of word roots developed two similar looking forms, one of each gender, and often with slightly different meanings. The masculine is not marked by any special features. The feminine is virtually always marked with the ending 𓏏 t, which is cognate to the feminine ending *-atu* in the Semitic and other Afro-Asiatic languages. (An asterisk (*) placed before a word or part of a word indicates that it is a reconstructed form and therefore not certain. Words that are marked with two asterisks (**) are impossible.)

In Egyptian, unlike the Semitic languages, unmarked feminine words, are almost never encountered. Some place names are not marked with a *t*, but are treated as feminine grammatically, e.g.  *K3š*. Note, however, that not all words that end in *t* are feminine. Some masculine nouns end in *t*, but this is because the final letter of the word root was *t* (the *t* is thus part of the root, and not the feminine ending). E.g.  *ḫt* "tree" and  *ỉt* "father." (The writing of *ỉt* is unusual in that the sign  has the phonetic value *ỉt*.[4])

Just as happened in many of the Semitic languages, the feminine ending *-t* was in the process of being dropped, and probably was no longer pronounced in Middle Egyptian, except when a suffix was attached to the word: e.g.  *dpt* "boat", hypothetically pronounced **dapa*, but with the suffix pronoun *·f*  *dpt·f *dapataf* "his boat." The Middle Egyptian writings are, however, conservative, and all good texts consistently indicate the feminine ending. This ending is also used with feminine adjectives.

There are three categories of number: singular, plural, and dual. The dual is used with things normally occurring in pairs or are perceived as dualities: e.g. feet, ears, sandals, tweezers, the Two Rivals (Horus and Seth), Twin Peaks. At this stage, only singular nouns will be used; the other forms will be introduced and discussed in future lessons.

§15. The Egyptian Sentence

Most scholars classify as **verbal sentences** those which contain a conjugated verb form, i.e. the verb is used *as a verb and is coupled with a subject*. E.g. "The man liked the dog." "The woman could read the mysterious texts." Many sentences that are verbal in English would in fact be nominal sentences in Egyptian and would follow all the rules of nominal sentences. Even the verbal construction used in simple statements of fact is actually a "nominal" sentence since the grammatical function of the predicate is actually adverbial (see below § 29) and not verbal (although few scholars would describe it this way). The verb form used in simple statements of fact is called "the circumstantial form." This form and its several uses will be dealt with later.

Normal word order in the simple statement of fact is as follows:

1) the particle  (*iw*)

2) the verb

3) the subject

4) the direct object

5) adverbial modifiers (prepositional phrases, indirect object), etc.

It cannot be overly stressed that the order in which words occur is the key to understanding Egyptian. In this regard, it is much like English. Unlike Greek, Biblical Hebrew, and many other languages whose distinct forms are written differently, one cannot always rely on the writing of a given word to determine its form (i.e. whether it is a past tense, passive, etc.), but rather, one must deduce which particular form is present from the word order and other elements of its

[4]The reading is based on the Coptic ειοτ (*yot*) "father."

grammatical context and its meaning in context (rather like reading unvocalized Hebrew and Arabic—but without the indication of long vowels!).

One could think of the basic Egyptian sentence as a sequence of slots. So for instance, one can substitute any number of adverbial phrases (and there are several different kinds, including subordinate clauses) into slot 5, i.e. at the end of the sentence. The subject, in slot 3, will be a noun, or a noun derived from a verbal root. The same holds true for the direct object in slot 4. It goes without saying that (virtually) any verb can be put in slot 2. Learning the basic word order thoroughly at this point will save one much grief at a later date.

§16. Statements of Fact: Main and Subordinate Clauses

In statements of fact, the absence of  (*ỉw*) normally indicates that the clause is a subordinate clause. E.g.  *ỉw ḏd s n Rᶜ* "The man speaks to Rēᶜ." But without *ỉw* it is a subordinate (or dependent) clause. ...  ... *ḏd s n Rᶜ* "..., the man speaking to Rēᶜ." In typical Egyptian manner, the exact nature of the connection between the clauses is not explicit. (I.e. one cannot tell whether the relationship is temporal, causal, etc.) Depending on the context, this subordinate clause could therefore be translated:

"..., when the man speaks to Rēᶜ"
"..., while the man speaks to Rēᶜ"
"..., because the man speaks to Rēᶜ"
"..., since the man speaks to Rēᶜ" / "..., for the man speaks to Rē"
"..., whenever the man speaks to Rēᶜ"
"..., although the man speaks to Rēᶜ"
"..., with the man speaking to Rēᶜ"

The function of *ỉw* is identical in non-verbal sentences with adverbial comment.

E.g.  *ỉw s m ky bw*

"The man is in another place."

But, ...  ...*s m ky bw*

"..., the man being in another place." (Or, "..., for the man is in another place," etc.)

An alternate way of looking at the use of the particle *ỉw* is to consider it as a converting particle that converts subordinate clauses (clauses of circumstance, to be precise) to main clauses. This is a non-orthodox concept, but it may be useful to keep in mind. The basic function of the particle, however, would seem to be that of establishing the temporal context between speaker and listener as the here and now—a point of reference.

There are several types of subordinate clauses in Egyptian, but the type that is most frequently encountered is the one presented here. This type of subordinate clause is known as the "circumstantial clause." It is very important to note that circumstantial clauses function as **adverbial modifiers** in the statement of fact construction. Since they are adverbial modifiers, they only occur in "slot 5" at the end of the sentence (§15). In English, similar clauses occur at the beginning as well as the end of the sentence; in Egyptian it is impossible to begin a sentence with a circumstantial clause. Circumstantial clauses will be dealt with in greater detail in §32.

Note that in sentences that are **not** simple statements of fact, the particle *iw* or other particles are not used. These do, however, constitute main (independent) clauses. E.g.  *sḏm sš sḫr m hrw pn* "May the scribe hear of a plan today!" This construction employs the "prospective" verb form (§§71–72) and here is used in a wish. Wishes and other main clause constructions not employing *iw* will be learned at a later stage.

§17. The Particle  *mk*

In addition to the particle  *iw*, the particle  *mk* commonly introduces the main clause of sentences. Either one or the other is used, the two never occurring in the same sentence. *Mk* is quite visual, and corresponds fairly well to French *voilà!* One could also compare Hebrew הִנֵּה (*hinnē*) "behold" and Arabic إِنَّ (*ʾinna*) "truly...." In older books *mk* was conventionally translated "behold," but modern English use requires other translations. In many instances one may translate "there is (so and so) coming down the street" or "here comes the scribe," etc. In declamations, one may also translate "indeed," or the like. Otherwise one may use "look, ..." *Mk* is the form of this particle used when addressing one man (or the reader, in the case of a text). The forms used for a woman and for a group will be presented in §40.

§18. The Egyptian Sentence: Verbal and Non-verbal

There are two main types of sentence in Egyptian verbal and non-verbal, but the distinctions are less pronounced than has been thought in the past. It is also confusing because many sentences that contain verbs are in fact nominal constructions. The Egyptian language tends to use nominal forms of the verb (i.e. forms that, although they convey a verbal idea, function grammatically as nouns) far more than forms that can be called strictly verbal in force. In other words Egyptian verbs are regularly used with a function *equivalent* to that of the verb in modern languages, but the way they function according to the rules and categories of Egyptian grammar is as nouns and adverbs.

The term non-verbal here means simply that there is no verb (including nominal verb forms) in the sentence. This is the sentence structure presented in §10.

VOCABULARY II

Memorize the words given in the vocabulary section of this and subsequent lessons. These words constitute a basic working vocabulary—words that should not have to be looked up in the dictionary. (In later lessons, the vocabulary lists contain words not necessary to commit to memory, but the essential vocabulary will be marked by a bullet.) Note that the forms will be marked as masculine or feminine *only* when there is the possibility of confusion, the final *t* being sufficient indication of the feminine gender.

 *3ḫt* "horizon"

 *Ỉmn* the god Amun

 *ỉtrw* "river," the Nile

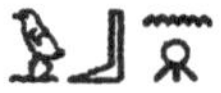 *wbn* "to shine" (said of the sun)

 *pt* "heaven(s), sky"

 *pr* "house"; "household"

 *mw* "water" Cf. Semitic: Arabic ماء (*māʾ*), Hebrew מַיִם (*mayim*), Akkadian *mû* "water."

 *Mnṯw* the god Montu

, var.  *mk* "Look! See!"

 *nỉwt* "city"

,  *nb* "lord, master; owner"

, ,  *rꜥ* "sun"; "day"

 *rwỉ* "to depart, get away" (*r* "from" a place or thing); "to go away"; (transitive) "to leave (a place)"; "to escape (harm, trouble, etc.)"

,  *hrw* "day, daytime"; *m hrw pn* "today"

 *ḥr* "on, upon; on account of, because; concerning, about" (possibly cf. Semitic *ꜥl* "upon")

 *ẖrd* "child"

 *st* "woman" Cf. ? Semitic, *ʾnṯ*: Arabic انثى (*ʾunṯā*) "female"; Hebrew אִשָּׁה (*ʾiššāh*) "woman"

,  *s3* "son"

,  *s3t* "daughter"

 *sḫr* "plan, idea, (piece of) advice"

 *sš* "document, writing"

 *sš* "scribe"

 *sḏm* "to hear, listen"; with the preposition *n* "to": "to listen to (a person)"; "obey (a person)" Cf. Semitic *šmꜥ* "to hear"[5]

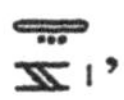, var. , *t3* "land"; "earth"; "ground" Possibly some connection with the Semitic root *tll*,

[5]With metathesis (inversion) of the last two consonants. Note that Egyptian *ḏ* sometimes corresponds to Semitic *ꜥayin*!

e.g. Arabic تل (*tall*) "hill, elevation"; Hebrew תֵּל (*tel*) "mound, hill."

 *dpt* "boat"

EXERCISE II

(A) Review the alphabetic signs and the vocabulary of Lesson 1.

(B) Transliterate and translate:

1) 

2) 

3) 

4) 

5) 

6) 

7) 

8) 

9) 

10) 

(C) ***Parsing***

To parse means to explain the morphology and syntax of a word or phrase. I.e. identify the *form* (in full) and explain how it *functions* in the sentence. One may use abbreviations, but they must be unambiguous. The *art* of parsing is to be as concise *and* as complete as possible. Students unskilled in parsing should err on the side of fullness. (At advanced levels the basics are assumed, and only the salient features need to be mentioned, but at the introductory level students need to demonstrate that they have grasped the basics.) Important note: Rough parsing (mental or written on a rough draft) should be done *before* attempting a translation. Polished parsing can then be written out after the translation.

For verbs 1) identify the verb form and type of subject (noun or pronoun: e.g. "circumstantial verb form with 3rd. masc. sing. suffix pronoun as subject" (suffix pronouns to be learned later); 2) comment on its use: e.g. "in main clause of a verbal statement of fact," "in circumstantial clause." These factors will become more important when more forms and constructions are learned.

For nouns 1) identify the form and suffixes: e.g. "fem. pl. noun + 1st common pl. suffix pronoun" 2) comment on its use: e.g. "subject," "direct object," "indirect object," "object of preposition," etc.

For phrases 1) identify the type of phrase (e.g. "prepositional phrase"); 2) specify its members (e.g. "prep. *m* + fem. sing. noun"); 3) explain its function: e.g. "adverbial modifier" or "adverbial comment"; and other factors, if of interest: e.g. "indicates means" (or manner, instrument, time, place at, place to, etc.).

Parse the words and phrases from the following sentences of part B:

(D) Write in hieroglyphs and transliterate:

N.B. Words in parentheses are aids to translation, either adding a word that is required in Egyptian (with quotation marks) or supplying a word not in the Egyptian, but required by English (no quotation marks).

1) The child obeys the woman.

2) The man is in the boat (when) Rēᶜ shines in the horizon.

3) This city listens (when) the lord speaks.

4) Look, the boat is on the ground.

5) The sun shines in the daytime.

6) Another scribe hears this plan.

7) The house is in the city.

8) This woman listens to the scribe.

9) See, a child is in the house with the woman.

10) The horizon is in another land.

LESSON 3

§19. Declension of Nouns

Nouns are differentiated by gender and number, but do not exhibit case. The forms are as follows:

TABLE 3: THE DECLENSION OF THE NOUN

	Masculine	Feminine
Singular	ø	-*t*
Dual	-*wy*	-*ty*
Plural	-*w*	-*(w)t*

The grammatical endings, when written out, are placed before the determinatives. The masculine singular has no special ending. The *w* of the various endings are frequently omitted in the writing; in such cases, one supplies it in parentheses in transliterations. The *w* is almost never written in the feminine plural forms. There are various ways to write the forms, and since the writings are clearly distinguished, the endings are often totally dispensed with as redundant. Since some of these are normal (not defective) writings, the endings are not placed in parentheses. A few nouns exhibit slight anomalies in the writings of their plurals. These will be pointed out in the vocabulary lists.

An old method of indicating the plural was to write the logogram (or word) three times: *s3w* "sons," *rnw* "names." Sometimes only the determinative is written three times, e.g. *sšw* "scribes." Such writings are generally archaic in Middle Egyptian. For the dual, however, the logograms or determinatives (or both!) are regularly written twice, e.g. *ʿnḫwy* "ears," *T3wy* "The Two Lands" (Egypt). The dual endings -*wy* and -*ty* are often written out, and may serve as the sole indication of duality, e.g. *ʿwy* "arms." The oblique strokes \\ (*y*) are also known as the "dual strokes" since they were originally the determinative of duality. By association with the dual forms, the sign acquired the phonetic value *y*. Sometimes the dual strokes are not oblique, but perpendicular.

In standard Middle Egyptian, the plurals are regularly indicated by the use of the plural strokes or, much more rarely, plural dots (ııı, ⁝ , etc.), which are a type of determinative placed below or beside the semantic determinative. Since plurality is obvious, the endings are usually left off:

 *wʿb(w)* "priests,"  *dp(w)t* "boats." Note that the plural strokes may be employed with singular nouns that are *semantically* plural. This is regularly the case with feminine singular collective nouns, e.g.  *mnmnt* "cattle." However, these words are usually treated grammatically as singular.

Some nouns, especially abstract nouns with the ending *-w*, are written as if they were plurals by false analogy with the plural endings, e.g.  *ẖrdw* "childhood."

§20. Adjectives as Modifiers

The Egyptian adjective, when used as a modifier, follows the noun that it modifies in accordance with the general rule that modifiers take second position. The adjective so used agrees in gender and number with the noun that it modifies. The adjective is declined exactly like the noun, but the dual forms are not common. Examples:  *dpt nfrt* "a good boat,"  *dp(w)t nfr(w)t* "good boats,"  *sꜣ nfr* "a good son,"  *pr(w) nfrw* "fine houses."

§21. Adjectives used as Nouns

1) As an ordinary noun The adjective can stand on its own as a noun, as regularly in French, and occasionally in English ("the rich," "the wicked," etc., but these are usually generic in English, as opposed to Egyptian usage: "the rich [man]," "a wicked [child]"). If the gender of the noun or individual is specified, the corresponding form is used. When used with persons, an appropriate human determinative is frequently used (and likewise the divine determinative with deities). Exx.  *nḏs* "a poor (man),"  *nfrt* "a beauty" or "a fine piece" (referring to a chair),"  *ʿꜣt* "the Great One" (referring to a goddess).

2) The Absolute use of the Fem. Sing. "something that is..." "a...thing" Particularly important to note is the special use of the fem. sing. adjective on its own with the meaning "something that is" of a certain quality. The use corresponds roughly with the use of the neuter in Latin, but the term "neuter" should be avoided. E.g.  *nfrt* "a good thing,"  *ʿꜣt* "something great." Some of these are listed in the dictionaries as separate entries, but many are listed only as the masc. adjective. The plural forms are also used when pluralities are involved.

§22. Relations Between Nouns

1) The Genitival Relationship: The genitival relationship is most generally termed a relationship of possession, but as in all languages, the sense of "possession" is fairly broad. In English we express the genitive in two ways:

1) by the use of the genitive case: -'s (apostrophe "s"); possessive pronouns—"the boat's interior," "my mother";
2) by use of the preposition "of"—"the bottom of the ocean."

In Egyptian there were also two different ways of expressing this relationship, the choice depending mainly upon the closeness of the relationship, the closer relation being expressed as a compound noun phrase, the looser relation using an adjectival modifying phrase. Other factors also determined the choice, and there seems to have been overlap in use.

a) The Bound Construction (Also known as the "direct genitive.") This construction consists of simply placing one noun in front of the thing possessed (or otherwise connected). For instance, 𓎟𓏤𓉐𓏤 *nb pr* "the owner (lord) of a house." The bound construction is very frequently used to form compound words, e.g. 𓉐𓌉𓉐 *pr-ḥḏ* "treasury" (literally "the house [𓉐] of silver [𓌉 *ḥḏ*])." (The second house sign at the end of the word is the determinative.) Although not important for modern readers, the bound construction affected word accent, as we know from Coptic. The first word had reduced vowels and lost its word accent. The technical term for this reduced form is *status constructus*.

In the case of such compound words, modern scholars conventionally link the words with a hyphen, but grammatically there is no distinction in the original Egyptian. Another way of looking at the bound construction is to see the unit as a noun followed by its modifier. (An important fact is that in Egyptian, the modifier always *follows* the word it modifies.[1]) Thus, in the case of 𓎟𓏤𓉐𓏤 *nb pr*, we have: "the owner"—what kind of owner?—"of a house." A very similar construction occurs also in English noun phrases, e.g. "chair leg," which means "leg of a chair." The only real difference here is that the modifier ("chair") precedes the noun it modifies ("leg") in conformity with the normal English word order (modifier preceding the noun it modifies). The use of the bound construction is quite restricted in Egyptian in comparison to the Semitic languages. It occurs mostly in titles ("overseer of construction"), epithets ("Lord of the Heavens"), and set phrases (*pr nsw* "palace," lit. "house of the king").

b) The Genitival Adjective (Also known as the "indirect genitive.") In Egyptian there exists a category of adjective that derives from prepositions and nouns indicating various relationships called *nisba* adjectives (after the Arabic grammatical term) and will be further discussed in §54. The *nisba* adjective derived from the preposition 𓈖 *n* "to" means very literally "belonging to," but in actual use, it is equivalent to English "of," and should almost always be translated "of." Being an adjective, it follows the noun it modifies and agrees in gender and number with it. The forms are as follows:

[1]The astute reader will now ask, "But what about *ky* and *kt*, learned in Lesson 1?" The answer is simple. *Ky* and *kt* are *not* modifiers, but nouns meaning "another one." Thus to translate literally, *kt s3t* means "another one—of the category daughter," or in plain English, "another daughter." So the rule of following modifier is actually in full force, even with *ky* and *kt*.

TABLE 4: THE GENITIVAL ADJECTIVE *N(Y)*: "OF"

	Masculine	Feminine
Singular	*n(y)*	*n(y)t*
Plural	, *n(y)w*	*n(yw)t*
Dual (Very rare[2])	*n(y)wy*	*n(y)ty*

Particular care must be taken with the masc. sing. *n(y)* since it is indistinguishable in appearance from the preposition *n* "to, for" (the dative). In reading the phrase (noun X) *n* (noun Y), one must ask the question: Is it "the X *to/for* the Y", or is it "the X *of* the Y"? The context will generally permit an exact determination.

Exx.

 *pr n(y) sš* "the house of the scribe"
(or, of course, "the scribe's house")

 *dpt n(y)t wꜥb* "the boat of the *wꜥb*-priest"

 *ḫrd(w) n(y)w ỉmy-r[3] pr* "the children of the steward"

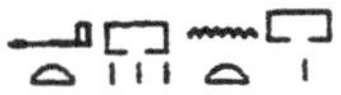 *ꜥ(w)t n(yw)t pr* "the rooms of the house."

The masc. plural *n(y)w* tends to be replaced by *n(y)*. This also occurs with the feminine forms, but less often. The dual forms were also replaced by *n(y)*.

2) Apposition: As in English and other languages, nouns and noun phrases can be used to modify other nouns. As expected, the qualifying word or phrase is placed directly *after* the word (or name) it modifies without any intervening words or particles. More than one phrase may follow.

Exx.

ỉt·f, wꜥb n(y) pr Ptḥ
"... his father, a *wꜥb*-priest of the Temple of Ptah, ..."

Ỉmn, nṯr ꜥ3, nḥm nḏs
"... Amun, the great god, the saviour of the poor, ..."

[2]The dual forms need not be memorized, but are included for future reference.
[3]The word *ỉmy-r* "overseer" is always written as an abbreviation.

§23. The Suffix Pronouns

1) The Forms: Of the three sets of pronouns, the suffix pronouns are by far the most widely used, since they are attached to nouns (and nominal forms) to express the genitival notion and additionally they are attached to verb forms to express the subject. The basic function is genitival (even with verbs) and corresponds more or less to the English possessive pronouns "my," "his," "their," etc. Of course, when used as the subject of verbs, they must be translated by English nominative pronouns: "I," "he," "they," etc. The pronouns are attached directly to the word—after the determinative—and absolutely nothing can separate them from the word to which they are affixed. These pronouns must be thoroughly memorized. Most of the pronouns distinguish gender, but the first person forms are of *common gender* (i.e. there is only a single form). It is unclear whether the 2nd and 3rd person plural forms were differentiated by different vowels in the spoken language, but they are listed as common gender, since they are not distinguished in the writings. The gender is that of the "possessor" (as in English "his mother"/"her brother") and not the gender of that which is "possessed" (as in French *sa mère, son frère*). The forms are as follows:

TABLE 5: THE SUFFIX PRONOUNS

	Gender:	Common	Masculine	Feminine	
Singular	1st Person	, , *-i*			"My"
	2nd Person		*-k*	, *-ṯ, -t*	"Your"
	3rd Person		*-f*	*-s*	"His"/"Her"
Plural	1st Person	*-n*			"Our"
	2nd Person	, *-ṯn, -tn*			"Your"
	3rd Person	*-sn*			"Their"

There are variant (later) writings of the 2nd fem. sing. and the 2nd plural forms that use *t* in place of *ṯ*. The plural strokes are only rarely omitted in the plural forms. For the 2nd fem. sing. suffix, occasionally the seated woman *(·t)* was used, especially in letters.

When the speaker is a king, the 1st sing. suffix pronoun may be written , *(·i)*, and when a god, *(·i)* is used. The 1st sing. suffix was regularly left off in Old Egyptian. In older Middle Kingdom texts this is sometimes the case. In later instances, the lack of indication of the suffix may be due to carelessness. The use of for the 1st sing. suffix is found mostly in earlier texts, and is not particularly common. A few texts indicate this suffix with the single stroke .

When the 1st comm. sing. suffix is attached to a noun ending with the seated man determinative, this sign is frequently written only once, thus doing double duty for the determinative and suffix pronoun: e.g.  could be read either *s3* "son" or *s3·i* "my son," depending on the context.

2) Use of Suffix Pronouns with Nouns: In transliteration, the suffix is separated by a raised dot. Exx.:  *pr·i* "my house,"  *s3t·f* "his daughter,"  *s3(w)·s* "her sons." The suffixed noun may be followed by an adjective that agrees in gender and number with the noun.  *ẖrd·sn nfr* "their good child."

The Egyptian suffix pronoun is often ambiguous, and different translations are sometimes required. For instance,  *snḏw·i* should be translated "the fear of me" (i.e. fear of the king) and not "my fear" (which suggests that the king was afraid). Or,  *sḫ3w·i* should be translated "the memory of me"—and *not* "my memory." In uncertain cases, one must ask if the person referred to by the pronoun was the doer or else the recipient (beneficiary) of the implied action, and if the doer, one translates "my...." In cases where others are doing the implied action, one can translate "of me," etc. Very frequently the particular nouns in question involve "loving," "fearing," "esteeming," etc.

3) Special Forms with Dual Nouns: When the 3rd masc. sing. suffix is attached to a dual noun, it occurs as  *·fy*. The 3rd fem. sing. suffix after duals is  *·sy*. The 2nd masc. sing. suffix after duals is  *·ky*:  *irty·fy* "his eyes,"  *ꜥwy·sy* "her arms,"  *spt(y)·ky* "your lips." Sometimes the writing is abbreviated by leaving off the oblique strokes after the suffix. The *y* should be indicated in the transliteration in parentheses.

4) Use of Suffix Pronouns with Prepositions:  *n·i* "to me/for me," 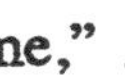 *ḥr·s* "upon it,"  *r·sn* "towards them." With the preposition *ḥr*, the *r* is generally written under the face sign when followed by a suffix. The preposition *m* "in" requires a reed leaf when suffixes are attached:  *m pr* "in the house," but  *im·f* "in it."

5) Use of Suffix Pronouns with Verbs: The function is that of the subject. The suffix is attached directly to the verb. Only verbal suffixes (to be learned later) can intercede between the verb and the pronoun. Exx. (With noun subject)  *iw sḏm sš* "The scribe listens." (With pronominal subject)  *iw sḏm·f* "He listens."

6) Use of Suffix Pronouns in Non-verbal Sentences with Adverbial Comment: When the subject of a sentence with adverbial comment is a pronoun, the suffix pronoun is attached to the particle  *iw*. Exx.: with noun subject:  *iw s3t·i m pr* "My daughter is in the house." With pronominal subject:  *iw·s m pr* "She is in the house." The suffix pronoun is *not*, however, used in conjunction with the particle  *mk* "look." (With , a different set of pronouns is used [§39]).

Since the suffix pronouns cannot stand on their own, but must be attached to something, the use of  *iw* is necessary *even in circumstantial clauses, which are subordinate*. (With noun subjects, however, the absence of  *i͗w* indicates that the clause is subordinate.) With a pronominal suffix as subject, the clause could be either a subordinate clause, or it could be a new main clause. One must judge by context. E.g.  *i͗w·f m dpt* "He is in the boat." *Or* "…, when/because/while/since/although he is in the boat"—or the convenient (unspecific) "…, he being in the boat."

7) Affinity of Afro-Asiatic Pronouns: The Egyptian suffix pronouns correspond very closely to those of the Semitic languages. This is true of the other sets of pronouns, as well. With the suffix pronouns, only the 3rd masc. sing. is anomalous. The functions of §23:1–4 are identical to those in the Semitic languages, but the other two uses are unique to Egyptian. Note the following correspondences:

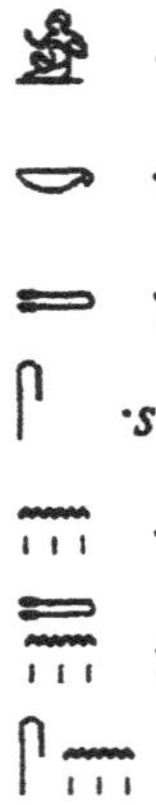

·*i͗* = Semitic -*ī* / -*iya*

·*k* = Semitic -*ka*

·*ṯ* = Semitic -*ki* (In Egyptian *ki has shifted to *chi* (*tši*) or something like it.)

·*s* = Semitic -*hu/hi* and Akkadian -*šu* and -*ša*

·*n* = Semitic -*na*, -*nu*

·*ṯn* = Semitic -*kina*

·*sn* = Semitic -*hen, hem, hum*, Akkadian -*šunu*, -*šina*

§24. The *M* of Predication

To say someone (or something) is something or serves in a certain capacity, one uses the preposition  *m* to form an adverbial comment. It literally means "in (the position/capacity of)." The sentence (or subordinate clause) follows all the rules of the sentence with adverbial comment (§§10; 16; 23, 6). E.g.  *i͗w sꜣ·i͗ m sš* "My son is a scribe." But,  *Ỉmn m ḥmw·i͗* "…, since Amun is my steering-oar (i.e. guide)." Sometimes one can translate it with "as" (i.e. "in the capacity of"). (For instance the previous phrase could have been translated: "…, with Amun as my steering-oar.")

The use of the *m* of predication is very common. What follows *m* is usually a secondary feature or an acquired (or temporary) feature. In other words, it serves to identify people and things by *function* rather than by *essence*. The *m* of predication cannot be employed when the connection between the two members is inherent or intrinsic. (I.e. one would not say to one's own son **i͗w·k m sꜣ·i͗*, but this might be said metaphorically of a person other than one's own son: i.e. "You are [like] a son to me." When the connection is intrinsic, a completely different construction is employed (§§56, 1; 129; 135).

§25. An Introduction to the Suffix Conjugation

The term "suffix conjugation" designates the five basic conjugated verb forms used as part of a subject and verb unit, whether the subject is a noun or a pronoun. The designation of the model forms as "*sḏm·f*," "*sḏm·n·f*," etc. also refers to verbs with noun subjects, and the respective verb forms are identical whether the subject is a noun or suffixed pronoun. The 3rd masc. sing. suffix pronoun *·f* is used for mere convenience in the names of these verb forms.

The student of Egyptian grammar must accept the fact that the standard terminology of the verbal system is worse than inadequate—it is outright misleading. Scholars have generally not been consistent in their use of terms, and above all have failed to avoid confusion between form and function (morphology and syntax). The names of the verb forms should be taken as arbitrary *labels* alone, and not as indications of the way the forms are used, or of what they mean.[4] The names of some forms have no inherent or logical meaning, e.g. "second tense" (§147) and are unique to Egyptological jargon. The terminology used in this book strictly separates form from function, and although the terms here employed are not always in common use, they should be understood by all scholars in the field. Some new terminology has been introduced, but only when it was felt to be necessary.

§26. Tense in the Egyptian Verb

The tenses of the Egyptian verb forms are *relative to their context*, rather than absolute tenses as is usually the case in the Indo-european languages.[5] The use of a form with relative present meaning expresses concomitant action, whether in the past, present, or future. A relative past in a past context serves as a pluperfect (the past within the past: "they had heard"). A past verb form in a future context indicates priority of action.[6]

§27. Derived Stems

Egyptian did not have the complex system of derived conjugations found in the Semitic and other Afro-Asiatic languages, the only derived conjugation in standard use being the *s*- causative stem (formed with the prefix *s*-).[7] Possible vestiges of other earlier stems may be preserved in verbs with *n*- prefix (§170), but they are probably fossilized in only a few roots and are treated as separate vocabulary items, as are also those used in the *s*- causative. I.e. roots that are used in the *s*- causative stem are listed under the letter *s* in all dictionaries and glossaries. (E.g.  *smn*

[4]E.g. the "circumstantial *sḏm·f*" form is in no way limited to its use in circumstantial clauses.

[5]Most Egyptian constructions, however, are entirely unambiguous with regard to tense, but the forms employed in them, in and of themselves, do not express absolute tense. Means of expressing the future tense and progressive aspect ("is doing"), are also found in Egyptian, but they utilize the so-called pseudo-verbal constructions (§§58-61).

[6]English uses the present perfect in like situations: "She will realize its importance when she has seen it herself."

[7]This stem is related to the Hebrew *hiphʿil*, Arabic *ʾafʿala*, and the Akkadian Š-stem. N.B. "Stem" here refers specifically to the derived conjugations, which have a different meaning from the basic conjugation, and are distinguished by prefixes, infixes, doubling of consonants, etc. "Root" refers to the combination of consonants (also called radicals) that comprise any given word.

"to make firm, to establish" is listed separately from the basic root  *mn* "to be firm.")

§28. Verb Classes

Several CLASSES of verbal roots are distinguished in Egyptian based on the number and nature of the radicals (root letters) comprising the root. Like the Semitic and other Afro-Asiatic languages, there is a preference for roots with three consonants. The main classes are the following:

- **Bi-consonantal roots:**  *ḏd* "to speak,"  *rḫ* "to learn,"  *ḫm* "to not know"
- **Tri-consonantal roots:** ("strong verbs"):  *sḏm* "to hear,"  *wbn* "to shine,"  *h3b* "to send"
- **Third weak roots:** (also called *tertiae infirmae* or *3. inf.*):  *ḏ3i* "to cross,"  *h3i* "to go down,"  *iri* "to do"
- **Second geminating roots:** (also called *secundae geminatae* or *2. gem.*):  *m33* "to see,"  *qbb* "to be cool"
- **Fourth weak roots:** (also called *4 infirmae* or *4. inf.*):  *ḥmsi* "to sit down"

The bi-consonantal roots simply have two consonants. Tri-consonantal roots have three strong consonants; these are known as "strong verbs." Third and fourth weak roots have one of the "weak" consonants, either *i/y* or *w*, as the final root letter.[8] This letter is almost never written in the Egyptian, but transliterations should always indicate the final weak radical. (This class of verbal root can be determined in the vocabulary list and in the dictionary by the presence of final *i* or *w*.) Some of the four conjugated verb forms of the third weak roots exhibit "gemination" (reduplication of the second root letter, e.g. *irr·f* from the root *iri*) and others do not, so presence or absence of gemination is a significant factor in identifying the particular form. In the second geminating roots the second and third radicals are identical. The second geminating roots also have gemination in some, but not all forms. (In this case "gemination" is actually a graphic phenomenon rather than "reduplication": when the second and third radicals are separated by a vowel they are written twice, but when they fall together, they are only written once. I.e. **qabābaf* is written *qbb·f*, but **qabbaf* is written *qb·f*.)

Each class exhibits a few characteristics peculiar to itself, and the student should therefore learn the class of each new verb encountered. Because of the non-indication of vowels, none of the four *sḏm·f* forms of the "strong verbs" can be determined from their writings. Verbs of the third weak and second geminating classes do, however, exhibit some graphically distinct forms, and are therefore known as "mutable verbs." (See the verb chart "Mutable and Irregular Verbs," Appendix 1) There may possibly have been a number of "irregular" verbs in Egyptian, but if so,

[8]The consonant  *3* is not a weak consonant by this definition.

the irregularities must have been mostly in the vowels, of which there is no trace in the writing. Only five or six verbs show minor anomalies, and then only in one or two forms. Egyptian verb forms, contrary to their reputation, are quite simple and regular in comparison with those of the Semitic and Indo-european languages. The chart of the "Mutable and Irregular Verbs" contained in the appendix is quite complete. The peculiarities of the various classes and those of the irregular verbs should be committed to memory as each new verb form is studied. *In particular, the forms of the third weak and second geminating classes must be thoroughly memorized.*[9] The verb chart of mutable and irregular verbs should be of use in learning the forms.

The chief difficulty with the study of Egyptian verb forms is that different forms tend to be written alike in spite of different pronunciations. Also, the Egyptians, not feeling the need to indicate every detail, regularly left off the endings, or other markers that we would consider indispensable. Although a knowledge of both morphology and syntax is necessary for a correct analysis of an Egyptian phrase, one must very often deduce the morphology from the syntax and the meaning in context.[10] A thorough grasp of Egyptian syntax is therefore essential. Close attention to word order and grammatical context is key to understanding Egyptian syntax.

§29. The Circumstantial *Sḏm·f* Form

The term "circumstantial *sḏm·f*," often employed by Egyptologists, is misleading, for although circumstantial forms do indeed occur in clauses of circumstance, they are also the usual form employed in the main clauses of simple statements of fact.[11] Although somewhat surprising to speakers of Indo-european and Semitic languages, the circumstantial forms are "adverbial"[12] in nature. The circumstantial forms cannot stand on their own, and always modify or depend on something (even if it is only the particle  *ỉw*).

The grammatical category of "adverb" is a large and important one in Egyptian. (Most of the predicates in Egyptian sentences are adverbial.) Phrases beginning with circumstantial forms occur in virtually any place that an adverb or adverbial phrase does.

The circumstantial *sḏm·f* forms are the following for the various verbal classes:

Bi-consonantal Both root letters:  *ḏd·f*

[9]E.g. **Circumstantial Form:** 3rd weak no gemination; 2nd geminating with gemination. **Second Tense Form (§147):** 3rd weak with gemination; 2nd geminating with gemination, etc.

[10]Unlike Akkadian, Latin, or Greek, where the morphology plays a greater role in analyzing the syntax. In this regard, Egyptian is much like English, where word order, contextual meaning, and syntax are also crucial to identifying the form in question. (E.g. "living" is both the gerund [verbal noun] and the participle [verbal adjective]. Gerund (noun): "Living in the city is becoming ever more expensive." *versus* Participle (adjective): "I saw a living specimen of the rare coelacanth in a Japanese aquarium."

[11]N.B. the Egyptian "old indicative" forms are quite restricted in use, and apart from the archaic affirmative use, only occur after the negation *n*. See §106 ff.

[12]The category of adverb is almost certainly broader than that of Indo-european languages. "Adverbs" in Egyptian seem to qualify nominal elements (including the particle *ỉw*) more often than genuine verbal ones. They do, however, often correspond to adverbial elements in Indo-european languages.

Tri-consonantal All three consonants:  *wbn·k*

3rd & 4th Weak Without gemination:  *mrỉ·s*,  *ḥmsỉ·ỉ*

2nd Geminating With gemination:  *mȝȝ·ṯn*

§30. The Past Tense of the Circumstantial Form (Active Voice): *Sḏm·n·f*

The past tense (of the active voice[13]) is formed by the insertion of the verbal suffix *n*, which precedes the subject, whether a noun or a suffix pronoun: *sḏm·n·f* or *sḏm·n* + noun subject.[14] If the context is in the past, a circumstantial *sḏm·f* form refers also to past events, normally in a circumstantial clause. Similar, to the circumstantial *sḏm·f*, the circumstantial *sḏm·n·f* form expresses a past relative to its context. In the case of *ỉw* + circumstantial form (simple statement of fact), the function of the particles *ỉw* and *mk* is to establish the context as here and now, and they cannot really be translated in English. The particle *ỉw* is quite weak, but *mk* is fairly vivid.[15] The construction *ỉw sḏm·n·f* means: "with respect to (us) here and now, he heard." Thus, although the verb form on its own expresses only relative time, most constructions are unambiguous in their time reference: *ỉw sḏm·f* conveying present time, and *ỉw sḏm·n·f* past time.

There are three *sḏm·n·f* forms (of which the circumstantial *sḏm·n·f* is one). Unfortunately, they are all written identically, unlike the present tense *sḏm·f* forms, which have clearly differentiated forms (as we know from the mutable verbs). **There is never gemination with either 3rd / 4th weak or 2nd geminating roots in the *sḏm·n·f* forms.** Presumably the forms were somehow distinguished in pronunciation, but we do not know how. The existence of various different *sḏm·n·f* forms—including the circumstantial *sḏm·n·f*—is assumed from their different uses and based on analogy with the present tense constructions.[16]

Examples of the "Circumstantial *sḏm·n·f*:

Bi-consonantal.  *ỉw ḏd·n·sn* "They said."

3rd weak No gemination:  *ỉw mrỉ·n sš* "The scribe loved."

[13]The past tense of the passive voice ("was heard") employed a different form, the *sḏm(w)·f* passive (§35), but it belongs very much in the "circumstantial family."

[14]N.B. Some scholars do not admit the existence of distinct *sḏm·n·f* circumstantial forms, maintaining that one or two varieties of *sḏm·n·f* merely function in a variety of ways. Although the forms cannot be differentiated morphologically, they occur in constructions in which only the circumstantial *sḏm·f* is otherwise used. We presume, for instance, that a circumstantial *sḏm·n·f* occurs in the construction *ỉw sḏm·n·f* by analogy to the circumstantial *sḏm·f* occurring in the *ỉw sḏm·f* construction. In spite of the fact that there is no distinction in writing, and even if the pronunciation were identical, we would be justified in identifying them as distinct forms based on grammatical meaning. Cf. English grammar, which distinguishes three distinct forms all written identically: **1)** "Writing quickly she rushed through the exam." (participle = adjective). **2)** "Writing too quickly can result in illegibility." (gerund = verbal noun). **3)** "Ancient writing was discovered on the wall." (common noun).

[15]Cf. French *voilà*, Hebrew הִנֵּה. The translation "Behold!" is to be avoided, if possible. "Look, " or "see, " are somewhat better. Sometimes one can translate along the lines of "Here she comes now!" or "There he is, sitting in the corner."

[16]There are additional clues provided by the differing ways that they are negated and other such factors.

2nd gem. -No gemination:  *ỉw m3·n·ṯ* "You (fem. sing.) saw."

The *sḏm·n·f* form used in the *ỉw sḏm·n·f* construction is presumed to be the "circumstantial *sḏm·n·f*," and it should be so identified when parsing. With *sḏm·n·f* forms of 3rd weak roots, scholars generally do not indicate the final weak letter. The practice of transliterating it at this stage is, however, helpful in distinguishing the verb classes.

§31. Statements of Fact: *ỉw sḏm·f* / *mk sḏm·f* / Noun + *sḏm·f*, etc.

The typical construction consists of introductory particle (or other word) + circumstantial *sḏm·f* (or circumstantial *sḏm·n·f*) form. Introductory particles include *ỉw* and *mk*. Other words may, however, be used to start the sentence. These include the topic of the sentence and a few particles (e.g. *ḫr m-ḫt* "Now later, ..."). The basic constructions are:

-  *ỉw sḏm·f* "He hears."
-  *mk sḏm·f* "See, he hears."
- Noun (the topic) +  *sḏm·f*. The suffix pronoun (subject) agrees in number and gender with the topic since the subject is the same person or thing as the topic (as in French "ma sœur, elle bavarde trop").[17] This construction is not particularly common. E.g.  *ỉt·ỉ sḏm·f* "My father hears."

Exx.

 *ỉw mdw·k n·ỉ*

"You speak to me." (Shipwrecked Sailor, 70.)

 *ỉw ḫrp·n·ỉ k3(w)t ꜥš3(w)t*

"I directed many construction projects." (Urk. IV 1494, 8.)

Verbs of motion (i.e. involving movement in space: go, come, sail, run, travel, return, arrive, etc.) never occur in the *ỉw sḏm·n·f* past tense construction. Instead, the stative is used (§§82, 88).

Although the present tense construction *ỉw sḏm·f* must have been very common in speech, it is less well attested in the texts than one might think. The past tense, however, is common in recorded speech and autobiographies. Literary texts generally employ other constructions for narrative passages (cf. §§90 ff.; 136), but the *ỉw sḏm·n·f* construction is also used. The past tense construction *ỉw sḏm·n·f* may be translated "He heard" or "he has heard."

The charts listing the basic verbal constructions (Appendix 2) should be consulted as each new construction is learned. They contain almost all the main constructions (except the common literary past tense constructions). The charts should provide a convenient reference once the other constructions are introduced, and should help for review of previously learned material.

17 It is difficult to translate the nuance in standard written English, which unlike the colloquial does not allow "My father, he hears." An almost identical construction is, however, common in French.

§32. Circumstantial Clauses

The circumstantial *sḏm·f* and *sḏm·n·f* forms are used in subordinate clauses of circumstance, ***without*** introductory particles. These clauses convey information about current circumstances (with *sḏm·f*) or circumstances prior in time (with *sḏm·n·f*). They may indicate reason or motive ("because," "since," "for"), a concession or exception ("but," "although..."), and very often a temporal relationship ("when," "as," "while," "whenever"). Typically, the Egyptian writer did not specify the exact nature of the relation, leaving it up to the reader to make the proper connections.[18] The circumstantial clause, which is "adverbial" in nature, occurs later on in the sentence and *always* follows the main clause. (Just as word order is quite rigid in Egyptian, so too is the order of clauses. One may, however, find it convenient to use a different clause order in the translations.) Circumstantial clauses are very widely used in Egyptian, and often they occur in a fairly long series of clauses.

Ex.:

ḏd·in[19] *Nmty-nḫt pn, m33·f ꜥ3w n(y) sḫty pn ...*

Then this Nemty-nakhte, seeing the donkeys of this peasant, said "(...)." (Peas. R 41–2.)

One might also translate "Then this Nemty-nakhte said when he saw the donkeys of the peasant: ..." Or "because he saw," etc. Here the English past tense is used in the translation—because the context is in past time—but the Egyptian uses the present circumstantial form. By using the English participle ("seeing"), one can often avoid determining the specific connection, and retain some of the ambiguity of the original.[20] The following example uses the *sḏm·n·f* form to indicate prior action in a past context:

h3t pw ir(w)·n[21] *sḫty pn r Kmt, 3tp·n·f ꜥ3w·f m i33w, rdmwt, ḥsmn, ḥm3t*

And so this peasant went down to Egypt, having loaded his donkeys with reeds and rushes, natron and salt ... (Peas. R 7–11)

The peasant first loaded his donkeys, and then went down to Egypt. Here one might also translate "after having loaded," "when he had loaded," etc.

[18]There actually were words and phrases that could specify the exact relationship, such as *ḥr* "on account of," *n* "because," or *ḫft* "when," but they were not frequently used. One would be wrong to consider this ambiguity a "primitive" feature of the Egyptian language, for several modern languages, such as Japanese, regularly employ rather ambiguous circumstantial clauses in preference to precise conjunctions (or equivalents). In fact, the less precise circumstantial clause is more a feature of scholarly or literary English than colloquial idiom.

[19]This is a literary past tense form (§131) indicating action in sequence.

[20]If the subject differs from that of the main clause, one can sometimes translate "the official seeing," but this construction can be awkward or confusing. In these instances one may need to supply a conjunction in the English translation.

[21]This is a literary past tense construction: *sḏm pw ir(w)·n·f* literally "hearing is what he did" (§136).

Note that with a non-verbal circumstantial clause with adverbial comments, when the topic is a pronoun, the particle *ỉw* is required as a prop for the suffix pronoun, which cannot stand on its own.

ỉw wpỉ·n·f r·f r·ỉ, ỉw·ỉ ḥr ẖt·ỉ m-bꜣḥ·f

He opened his mouth to me as I was on my belly in front of him. (Shipwrecked, 67)

VOCABULARY III

ꜣṯp, later *ꜣtp* "to load" *m* "with"

, , *ỉmy-r*[22] "overseer," "superintendent," *ỉmy-r pr* "steward"

, *ỉrỉ* "to do"; "make"; "carry out (a project, activity, etc.)"

ỉt "father" (the *f* is not pronounced!). Note that this writing can also stand for *ỉt·ỉ* "my father."

ꜥ (dual *ꜥwy*) "arm," "hand"

ꜥꜣ "great, large, grand"

ꜥꜣ "donkey" Possibly onomatopoeic cf. Coptic ⲉⲓⲱ (*ỉꜥō?) "donkey" from original *ꜥīꜥā

wỉꜣ sacred bark

wꜥb the "*wꜥb*-priest"

wpỉ "to open"

bꜣk "servant"; *bꜣkt* "female servant"

bỉn "bad"

mꜣꜣ "to see," "to look at," "to regard" with prep. *m* "as" Perhaps cf. Sem. *ʾmr* cf. Akkadian *amāru* "to see"; Ugaritic *ảmr* "saw"

mwt "mother" Prob. cf. Sem. *ʾimm*, *ʾumm*, *ʾēm* "mother"

See under *ỉmy-r*

nb (adj.) "all," "every," "any," "all kinds of"; *ḫt nbt* "everything"; *ḫt nbt nfrt* "all sorts of fine things"; *s nb* "everyone"; *ḥr nb* "everyone"; , *rꜥ nb* (The variant is not to be misread as **hrw nb*!) "every day"

[22]The word is always written as an abbreviation. Note that some scholars transliterate *mr* or *ỉmy-rꜣ*. These are not considered standard in the Anglo-American practice.

Note that although *nb* is an adjective (and therefore follows the noun it modififes), it cannot be used as a predicate adjective, nor as a noun.

nb (noun) "lord," "master," "possessor," "owner"; "the Lord" (meaning the king), which is also written ; *Nb T3wy* "Lord of the Two Lands" (an epithet of the king)

nbt "lady"; "possessor"; *Nbt t3* "Lady of the Land" (queen)

nfr "good, fine, fair, nice," "kind"; "happy"

nfrt (adjective as an abstract noun §21, 1) "a good thing; good" (also in plural)

nḏs "small, little"

nḏs "poor man," "commoner"

rḫ "to learn, find out," "to learn of (something)"; in past tense "to know" (i.e. having learned something is to know it)

r "mouth"; "statement," "words"; "opening," "entrance"

ršwt "joy," "a state of joy"

rd "foot"; abbreviated: *rdwy*, prob. cf. Sem. *rgl* "foot, leg"

h3i "to go down," "descend" This word must be clearly distinguished from *h3b* "to send."

h3b "to send (a person on an errand, etc.)"; *h3b . . . r* "send to (a place)"; *h3b . . . n* "to send (word) to (a person)"; *ḥ3b ḥr* "to send (word) about (a matter)" This is not a "verb of motion." Cf. ?? Sem. *špr* "to send" cf. Ar. سفر (*safara*) 2nd stem (*faᶜᶜala*) "to send away"; Akkadian *šapāru* "to send" (*h* vs. *š*; *b* vs. *p* and metathesis)

k3t "construction project"

t3wy "the Two Lands" (refers to Egypt—Upper and Lower)

ṯ3ty "the vizier" (The highest official in Egypt)

ḏ3i "to ferry (someone) across"; "to cross (sky, river, etc.)" *Ḏ3i* is not a "verb of motion."

EXERCISE III

(A) Learn the bi-consonantal signs: with *3* as the second consonant (which is usually written out—"the phonetic complement").

ᶜ3 *w3* , , *b3*

b3   p3[23]   m3
ḥ3   ḫ3   h3
s3   s3   š3
k3   t3   t3
ḏ3

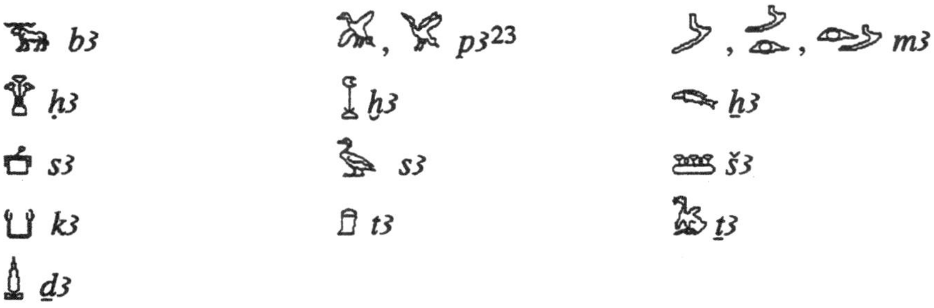

(B) Transliterate and translate:

1) [hieroglyphs]

2) [hieroglyphs]

3) [hieroglyphs]

4) [hieroglyphs]

5) [hieroglyphs]

6) [hieroglyphs]

7) [hieroglyphs]

8) [hieroglyphs]

9) [hieroglyphs]

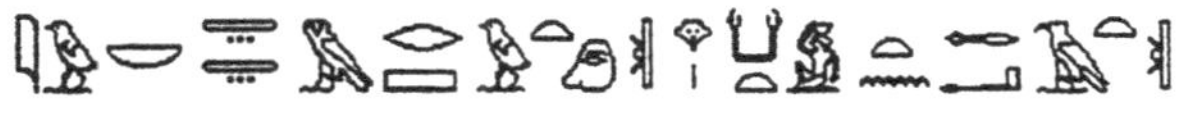

(C) Parse the words and phrases from the following sentences of part B:

1) [hieroglyphs]. 2) The verb. 3) [hieroglyphs]. 4) [hieroglyphs]. 5) [hieroglyphs] 6) [hieroglyphs]
7) [hieroglyphs] 8) [hieroglyphs] 9) The verb; [hieroglyphs].

(D) Write in hieroglyphs and transliterate:

1) His fine boat is in the river.

2) The steward sees the daughter of the vizier in it.[24] (in the boat)

3) The daughter spoke to her father when she saw the female servant upon his donkey.

4) This scribe's hands are in the water, but his feet are on the ground.

5) The Lady of the Heavens[25] sees the horizon every day as she is in her sacred bark.

[23] The writing with both wings to the back is from hieratic, and that with one on each side of the body is hieroglyphic. These should be kept distinct.
[24] Cf. §23, 4.
[25] Use the bound construction.

6) We cross over when the scribe sends (word).

7) Your servant is in (a state of) joy on account of your words.

8) You are a father to[26] this town.

9) He crosses over to this city, his daughter being with him.

10) The Lady of the Land is a mother to everyone.

[26]The "dative."

LESSON 4

§33. The Passive Voice

The Egyptian verb expresses both the active voice ("He eats lots of olives.") and passive voice ("Great quantities of olives are eaten in this region."). The passive forms of the suffix conjugation are mostly very distinct from their active counterparts. There are two ways of forming the passive (depending on particular verb form), but the most common uses the verbal affix (in-fix) *tw*. The affix *tw* derives from the word *tw* meaning "one" (French *on*, German *man*), which continues in this use, although is far less common than the true passive suffix *·tw*. In Eighteenth Dynasty texts written in Middle Egyptian, the word *tw* "One" is used euphemistically to refer to the king.

§34. The Passive of the Circumstantial Forms: Present Tense

The present tense circumstantial form uses the affix *tw* attached immediately after the active circumstantial *sḏm·f* form, normally after the determinative: *sḏm·tw·f*, 3rd weak *iri·t(w)·f*, 2nd gem. *m33·tw·f*, etc. Of course, noun subjects may occur in the place of the suffix pronoun. The agent may be specified by the particle *in* "by."

Ex.

iw sḏm·tw r·f "His words are heard."

iw m33·tw·f in s nb
"He is seen by everyone."

Sometimes *tw* is abbreviated to just *t*; this is especially the case when placed before the determinative: *iw d3i·t(w)·s* "She is ferried across."

§35. The Past Tense Passive of the Circumstantial Forms: The *sḏm(w)·f* Passive

The past tense circumstantial passive forms are not formed with *·tw*. Instead, a completely different verb form is used. This form is called the "*sḏm(w)·f* passive," but it is an integral part of the "family" of circumstantial forms. Its grammatical function is *adverbial* as with all the other circumstantial forms. Like its present tense counterpart, the *sḏm(w)·f* passive forms are used in all the constructions employing circumstantial forms or wherever an adverbial word or phrase can be employed:

1) in statements of fact (beginning with *ỉw* or *mk*),

2) in subordinate clauses of circumstance following a main clause,

3) in other constructions yet to be learned.

It must be stressed that the "*sḏm(w)·f* passive" is a *past* tense form, even though it does not use the usual past tense marker *n*, and that it is a *passive* form, even though it does not employ the regular passive marker *tw*. It is not at all a rare form, although it has the (undeserved) reputation of being quite obscure. The *w* ending is sometimes written when the subject is a noun, but it is almost never written when a suffix pronoun occurs as subject. The 3rd weak roots sometimes have a final *y* instead of *w* (*ỉ*+*w* > *y*): *ỉw mry·ỉ* "I was loved."

The *sḏm(w)·f* passive forms by root class are as follows:

Bi-consonantal roots: both consonants

Strong roots: all consonants

3rd weak roots: no gemination *ỉr(w)*, *mrw*

2nd gem. roots: no gemination *mꜣ(w)*

Irregular: "to give," both with and without *r* *rd(w)*, *d(w)*

Exx. *ỉw mꜣ(w)·f ỉn ḥr nb*

"He was seen by everyone."

ỉw rdw n·ỉ ḥmw ḥm(w)t

"I was given male and female servants." (Or "Male and female slaves were given to me.")

ỉw dꜣỉ·n·ỉ, rd(w) n·ỉ dpt

"I crossed (the river), having been given a boat." Or "a boat having been given to me" or "when a boat was given to me," etc.

Since the *w* of the *sḏm(w)·f* passive is regularly left off, the forms tend to look like active circumstantial *sḏm·f* forms (with relative present time reference). The student should, as a rule of thumb, take such a form as active at first, but then try to analyse it as a *sḏm(w)·f* passive, especially if the meaning is odd, such as **"The bread gives to the hungry man." Another clue to the presence of the *sḏm(w)* passive forms is their occurrence in a past-time context or in a construction that requires a past tense form (as with the literary past tense construction *ꜥḥꜥ·n sḏm·n·f* §90, ff.). Since the passive forms are not as common as those of the active voice, they should be learned all the more diligently, because they are less likely to be drilled into the memory through the exercises and reading passages.

Note that in the last two examples above, the dative unit *n·ỉ* "to me" has moved up closer to the verb, and thus precedes the noun subject. This forward movement is a regular feature and it will be dealt with later (§51).

The family of circumstantial forms

	Active	Passive
Present	*sḏm·f*	*sḏm·tw·f*
Past	*sḏm·n·f*	*sḏm(w)·f*

§36. A Variation on the Statement of Fact: *Noun sḏm·f*

Instead of starting with *ỉw* or *mk*, one can simply place the noun that would be the subject of the sentence at the head of the sentence, and then conjugate the verb with the appropriate suffix pronoun. Ex.  *ṯ3ty Ỉmn-ḥtp*[1] *s3 Mnṯw-nḫt*,[2] *ḏd·f*: ... "The vizier Amen-ḥotpe son of Montu-nakhte says: ..." In general use, this construction is not very common, but it is probably used in mortuary inscriptions to introduce the speech of the tomb owner, where it is the norm. The construction also occurs in literary texts, including verse.

§37. Another Variation on the Statement of Fact: *ỉw·f sḏm·f*

This construction places a noun—usually corresponding to the subject—before the verb, directly after *ỉw*. Suffix pronouns may occur after *ỉw* if the person or thing has been mentioned previously (*ỉw·f sḏm·f*). Some scholars have maintained that this construction was used to express repetitive action, maxims (gnomic statements), aphorisms, sayings, and the like. Not all examples, however, fit this description. This construction probably involved a ***subtle*** shift of focus onto the word placed after *ỉw* by means of the linguistic phenomenon sometimes called "fronting" (i.e. putting it at the head of the sentence)—other scholars refer to this as "topicalization," i.e. making this word the "topic" of the sentence (with the following suffix pronoun serving as the actual "grammatical subject").[3] In English it is translated exactly as if it were the normal statement of fact. (In French and other languages that permit fronting, one could, however, imitate the Egyptian word order rather successfully.)

Ex.

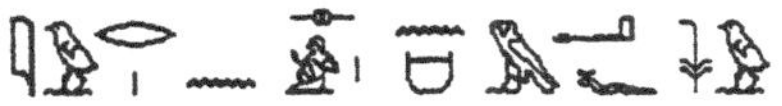 *ỉw r n(y) s nḥm·f sw.*

"A man's speech saves him." (Ship. Sail. 15.)

Perhaps the sense is something along the lines of: "A man's speech—that's what saves him."

[1]The names are inverted for honorific purposes, see §41, 1.

[2]The various words from the root *nḫt* "to be strong" are usually spelled out in full; the "man with stick" is, however, a very common abbreviation in names.

[3]Other similar constructions also occur (§§133, 134), but the shift in focus there is much more pronounced.

§38. Circumstantial Clauses that modify Nouns: The Relative Clause with Indefinite Antecedent

A "circumstantial" clause may modify a noun as a relative clause ("who . . . ," "which . . . ," or "that . . ." clause). This construction is almost always employed when the antecedent (the word referred to) is not defined (i.e. in English it would be preceded by the indefinite article "a" / "an").[4] The concept of definite / indefinite seems to have existed even though Egyptian did not yet have the corresponding articles.[5] Other factors that render a word definite include the use of the suffix pronoun ("her father" i.e., the speaker is referring to a specific individual), specification by name "Nofret's father" (whether using the direct or indirect genitive), and the use of demonstrative adjectives ("this house").

Ex.

 . . .

iw rḫ·n·i nḏs ḥmsi·f m Ḏd-Snfrw.

"I have learned of a commoner who lives in Djed-Snofru . . ."

When the verb is in the passive voice and involves prior action, the *sḏm(w)·f* passive is used, as in ordinary circumstantial clauses of this sort.

Ex.

iw gmi·n·i sḫty ꜥwꜣ(w) ḥnw·f

"I have found a peasant whose property has been stolen."

In the last example the relative clause was translated as a possessive "whose," the sense being not only clear from context (the property was stolen, not the peasant), but also required by the use of the suffix pronoun attached to *ḥnw* "property" (the subject of the *sḏmw·f* passive form *ꜥwꜣ[w]*). The circumstantial clause means literally: "(a peasant) his goods having been stolen."

It is particularly important to note that the circumstantial clause, like all modifiers in Egyptian, always *follows* the noun that it modifies. At this stage, students should ask whether a circumstantial clause seems to modify the entire preceding main clause, or whether it modifies only the noun immediately in front of it (if there is one). In the former case, it is a normal circumstantial clause. If it modifies the noun, it is a relative clause "who/which/that. . . ." Usually one interpretation will be considerably better than the other. Since the ordinary circumstantial clause is by far the more common, special attention must be paid to this particular use as a relative clause. This type of relative clause is not rare, but ordinary circumstantial clauses are extremely common.

[4]A different construction involving the relative adjective *nty* "that which" (§111, ff.) is used when the antecedent is defined.

[5]But cf. §§66, 78 for early examples (at least in colloquial speech).

§39. The Dependent Pronouns

The basic use of the dependent pronouns is as the direct object of verbs (i.e. they correspond to the English accusative [direct object] pronoun series "me, him, her, them," etc.). They are also the type of pronoun that is used with *mk*, e.g. *mk wỉ* "look (at) me" or "here I am." (Cf. French *Me voilà!*) Unlike the suffix pronouns, they are treated as separate words. This set of pronouns must be thoroughly learned. A review of the suffix pronouns (§23) should also be undertaken, if these are not yet firmly committed to memory. Special stress may be placed on learning the 2nd person, especially feminine forms, since these are less common and therefore will not become as familiar. The forms are as follows:

TABLE 6: THE DEPENDENT PRONOUNS

	Gender:	Common	Masculine	Feminine	
Singular	1st Person	*wỉ*			"Me"
	2nd Person		*ṯw*	*ṯn*	"You"
	3rd Person		*sw*	*sy*	"Him"/"Her" "It"
Plural	1st Person	*n*			"Us"
	2nd Person	*ṯn*			"You"
	3rd Person	*sn*			"Them"
Alternate	3rd Person	*st*			"Them" / "It"

The 2nd person forms also have later variants with *t* instead of *ṯ*: *tw*, *tn*, *tn*. The 3rd fem. sing. *s(y)* is also written defectively without the oblique strokes. It is distinguished from the 3rd fem. sing. suffix pronoun by the grammatical requirements of the context. There pronoun *st* is commonly used for the 3rd plural "them" and for (often unspecified) "it."

The dependent pronouns when used as the direct object of a verb tend to get as close to the verb as they can, and they precede the subject when it is a noun.

Exx.

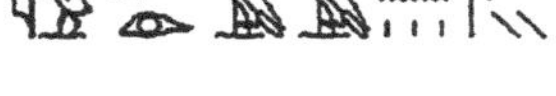 *ỉw m33·ṯn sy* "You (pl.) see her."

 *ỉw m3·n sw s3t·f*

"His daughter saw him."

As the direct object, they can also be used reflexively with the meaning "himself, herself, myself," etc. As mentioned above, these pronouns can be introduced by *mk*: *mk sw ḥr w3t*. "There he is on the road." *mk sy* "Here she is."

§40. Feminine and Plural Forms of the Particle *mk*

The particle *mk* actually contains the 2nd masc. sing. suffix pronoun (·*k*) and is used when addressing a single male individual (and in written documents and literature). When addressing a female, the particle takes the appropriate 2nd person suffix: *mṯ*. Similarly, when addressing a group of people, the particle takes the 2nd. common plural suffix ending: *mṯn*. The fem. sing. and the plural equivalents of *mk* have later variants with *t* instead of *ṯ*: *mt* and *mtn*. Note also the common hieratic writings of *mk* (etc.): , , both read *mk* (i.e. with no ʿ).

§41. Transpositions in Hieroglyphic Writing

1) Honorific Transposition: The bound constructions (§22, 1*a*) were sometimes written in reverse order to place the second element in first place out of deference or respect. This is regularly the case with compounds involving the word *nṯr* "god" and *nsw* (not **swtn*!) "king." In titles, the latter is often abbreviated: *nsw*. The transposition is not, however, indicated in the transliterations. Exx. *pr-nsw* "palace" (lit. "house of the king"); *ḥm-nṯr* "*ḥm-nṯr*-priest" ("servant of the god"); *wḏ-nsw* "royal decree" ("decree of the king"); *S3 Rʿ* "the Son of Rēʿ" (part of the royal titulary); *mry Mnṯw* "beloved of Montu," etc.

A special type of honorific transposition was used in identifying one's father in the Twelfth Dynasty and earlier. Although the bound construction is used, the father's name is placed first. As with the cases above, they are simply read in reverse order: *Mry s3 ꞽIntf* "Mery son of Intef" (and not Intef son of Mery!). After the Twelfth Dynasty, this form of honorific transposition was dispensed with, and the names were written in the order that they were to be read. The other forms of honorific transposition were, however, retained in full force.

2) Graphic Transpositions: Sometimes signs were written in reverse order for aesthetic reasons in order to avoid unsightly gaps, etc. So, for instance, occasionally one finds for *wt* and for *q3*. Narrow vertical signs tend to precede the birds that should follow them: e.g. for *wḏ* "decree," *3ḫt* "field." In particular, note the word , which is read *ḫft* (not **ḫtf*!) "according to"; "corresponding to"; "when."

§42. Combination Signs

Some signs can be combined with others either to produce a new sign or to write the two in a more compact manner. Of the former category are in *ii* "to come," *in(i)* "to bring," *is* "Go!" and *šm* "to go," in which the "walking legs" are an integral part of the sign. Signs optionally joined for aesthetic reasons include *wʿ*, *m3*, *33*, *mm*, *šmʿ(w)* "Upper Egypt." The sign is read *m* (originally *mi*), but its variant writings and can be read as *m* and less often *m*ꜥ. The sequence *m*ꜥ is usually written , but this can also be read as *m*, especially in writings of *mk* "see!" (§40). The words in which such combination signs occur will be learned later; those presented here are intended only to provide examples of the phenomenon.

§43. An Overview of Adjectives

Adjectives can be used in three ways:

1) **As a Qualifier:** modifying a noun, *sẖr nfr* "a good plan"

2) **As a Predicate:** forming a sentence, *nfr sẖr* "The plan is good."

3) **As a Noun:** *nfr* "a good one"; *nfrt* "something good"

As has been seen previously, adjectives as qualifiers follow the noun they modify and agree with it in gender and number: *ẖt nbt nfrt*[6] "all sorts of fine things," *dpt·ỉ tn nfrt* "this fine boat of mine," *sẖr pn bỉn* "this bad plan." (Note that the adjectives *pn*, *tn*, and *nb* are used before other adjectives.)

The words *ky* and *kt* "other," "another" do not follow the noun because they are not adjectives, but nouns meaning "(an)other one." The noun that follows is standing in apposition (§22, 2) and specifies what category the "other" thing/person belongs to.

§44. The Predicate Adjective

The adjective, as in English and other languages, not only serves as a modifier of nouns ("the big boat"), but can serve as the predicate of a sentence ("The boat is big."). The adjective, when serving as predicate, occurs only in sentence initial position, i.e. as the first word of the sentence. It occurs almost always *without* introductory particle. It can be preceded by *mk*, but never by *ỉw*.

The predicate adjective is invariable with regard to gender and number and does not agree with the subject. If the subject is a pronoun, the dependent series is used. The idea of tense is not present in sentences employing the predicate adjective, but there is little problem translating them, since the time reference can be established by context. Egyptian does not permit the compounding of predicate adjectives in sentences comparable to the English sentence: "The boat was big and beautiful."

Exx.

ꜥꜣ *dpt tn*. "This boat is large."

ꜥꜣ *sy* "It is large."

[6] Possibly one should transliterate this as a plural: *ẖ(w)t nb(w)t nfr(w)t*, but this common phrase is almost always transliterated as if it were singular.

 *nfr pr n(y) ṯꜣty* "The vizier's house was nice."

 *nfr sw* "It was nice."

§45. Exclamatory  *-wy* "How...!"

The dual form of the adjective (ending in  *-wy*, written after the determinative) is used as a predicate adjective with an exclamatory force: "How ...!" This is known as the "exclamatory *-wy*." Originally it meant "doubly bad," "twice good," and so on, but the original meaning was not retained, and these exclamations should not be translated as duals.

Exx.

 *nfrwy sy* "How good she is!"

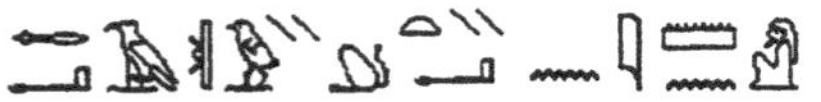 *ꜥꜣwy pḥty n(y) Ỉmn!*

"How great is the might of Amun!"

§46. The Impersonal Predicate Adjective + Dative

The predicate adjective—without a subject—can be followed by a dative, mostly with the meaning "Things are [adjective] for a person." Sometimes English would prefer a verb and adverb "It goes well for." "Things will turn out fine for," etc. The term "impersonal" means that the "subject" is non-specific, i.e. "things in general," "circumstances," etc. In English one must use a "dummy" subject like "it" or "things," but in Egyptian, one could simply omit the subject altogether.

Exx.

 *bỉnwy n·ỉ*

"How bad it is for me!" / "How bad things are for me!"

 *ꜥšꜣ n·f m mnmnt·f*

"He became rich in cattle." (Literally, "It was plentiful for him in his cattle.").

 *nfrwy n pr nsw*

"How good it is for the palace."

 *nfr n·k ꜥꜣ ḥnꜥ·ỉ*

"It will go well for you here with me."

§47. The Independent Use of the Feminine Singular

As noted in §§21; 43, adjectives can be used as ordinary nouns. Of particular importance is the use of the fem. sing. form of the adjective to mean "something that is ...," "what is ...," or "a ... thing." Exx.  *nfrt* "a good thing," "good" (as a noun);  *bint*," "what is bad";  *ꜥ3t* "something great."

§48. The Adjective + Noun: A Bound Construction

With reference to people and gods, Egyptian frequently uses an adjective followed by a noun to modify a preceding noun, the whole phrase constituting a bound construction (§22, 1*a*). A very similar construction is found in English, but it sounds archaic or convoluted:  *nfr ḥr* "fair of face" etc. Sometimes one can translate along the lines of "with fair face" or "whose face is fair," or the like. A particularly favourite expression was 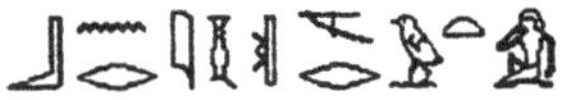 *bnr*[7] *mrwt* "sweet with regard to love," or "whose love is sweet," or "lovable." Certain combinations are idiomatic only in Egyptian and are best translated by a single term. Some expressions are flattering, others not. Exx.  *q3 s3* "high of back" = "arrogant," "presumptuous" (and as a noun denoting such a person); 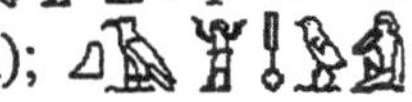 *q3 ḫrw* "high of voice" = "noisy" ("loud-mouth");  *3w ib* "long-hearted" = "joyous," "happy";  *3w ḏrt* "long-handed" = "generous" (i.e. always extending the hand to help others). When adjectives are used as modifiers, they agree in gender and number with the antecedent. E.g. 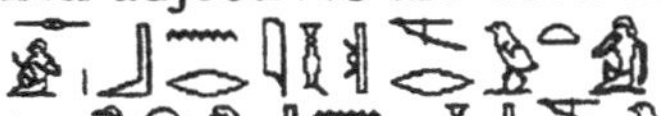 *s bnr mrwt* "a lovable man," but the fem. sing. adjective is required in 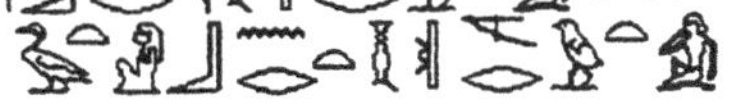 *s3t bnrt mrwt* "a lovable daughter."

§49. The Comparison of Adjectives

As with the ancient Semitic languages, there are no comparative or superlative forms of adjectives (e.g. corresponding to *bigger*, *biggest*). The concept, of course, was very much a part of the language. In fact, Egyptian writers were quite given to hyperbole; often things were not just "good," they were "the best in the entire land," and "so fine that nothing like them had ever been seen (or done) since the era of the primeval gods," and so on. The comparative notion is conveyed by use of the preposition *r* "with respect to," "compared to." This use is known as the "*r* of comparison."

Ex.

 *ꜥ3 s3·i r s3 n(y) sš pn.*

"My son is bigger than the son of this scribe." (Literally, "My son is big by comparison to the son of this scribe.)

The use of the preposition *r* can occur with adjectives used as modifiers or with the predicate adjective. The use of *r* "more than" is fairly broad and can even be used with some verbs when the idea involved is "doing more/better/farther than," etc.

Exx

 *nfr st r ḫt nb(t)* "It was finer than anything."

[7] In words with a final *r* there is a tendency to shift to *i*. The older form with *r* is used in transliteration.

mk ḥnqt bnrt r dpt n(y)t bỉt

"Here is a beer (that is) sweeter than the taste of honey."

ỉw mrỉ·n·f ṯsm r s3t·f

"He loved the dog more than his daughter."

§50. The Superlative Notion

There were no special adjectival forms. Rather, the concept of the superlative ("biggest," "tallest," etc.) was expressed by a genitive construction (either bound or with genitival *n[y]*) in which the second element is the plural form of the first element: *wr wrw* or *wr n(y) wrw* "great (one) of the great ones" or "greatest," *ꜥ3 ꜥ3w* "grand (one) of the grand ones" or "the most grand." The idea is identical to that of "king of kings" (first among kings) familiar from literal translations of Biblical Hebrew. Additionally, the phrase *r ḫt nb(t)* "more than anything" often conveys the superlative notion.

Ex.

(He said):

ỉmy-r pr wr, nb·ỉ, wr n(y) wrw ...

(He said): "High steward, my lord, greatest of the great ..." (Peas. B 53)

VOCABULARY IV

ỉb "heart," "mind" Cf. Semitic *lb*, *lbb* "heart, mind"

ỉn (preposition) "by, through" (expresses agent or means in passive constructions)

ỉqr adj. "excellent, dependable, reliable, worthy" Cf. Hebrew יָקָר (*yāqar*) "precious, highly esteemed"; Arabic وقور (*waqūr*) "dignified, venerable"

ꜥš3 adj. "many, numerous"; (of people) "rich" *m* "in/with (things)" (The plural strokes are a semantic determinative.) Cf. (?) Semitic *ǵṯr* Hebrew עשׁר (*ꜥšr*) "to be rich"

w3t "road," "path," "side"

wꜥb adj. "pure"; verb "to purify (oneself)," "to bathe"; also with dependent pronoun "to bathe oneself"

wr (adjective) "great"; abbreviated, and as noun "great one," "ruler (of a foreign land)"; in titles "chief," etc.; *ỉmy-r pr wr* "high steward" Cf. (?) the Semitic roots *rbb*, *rbᵓ* "great."

bỉt "honey"

bnr "sweet, pleasant" (of taste; of a person's disposition)

pr-nsw "palace" (lit. "house of the king")

pḥty (n. masc.) "might, power" (of god, king), "strength"

mꜣꜥ "true, just, fair, right, correct"; "innocent" (as legal term)

mỉ (preposition) "like"

mrỉ "to love," "like"

mrwt noun "love"

nḥm "to rescue," "save"; "to take away," "to take out"; "to withdraw" Cf. Arabic حمل (*ḥml*) "to bear, carry, take"; stem VIII (*iftaʿala* stem) "to carry off, take away"

nṯr "god"; *ḥm-nṯr* the *ḥm-nṯr*-priest; pl. *ḥmw-nṯr* "*ḥm-nṯr*-priests"

rdỉ, (irregular verb) (hieratic variant *rdỉ* not *rꜥ*!) "to give"; "to put, place"; *rdỉ ꜥ n* "to give a hand to (a person)," "to help (a person)" Possibly a remote connection to Semitic *ntn*, *ndn*, *ytn* "to give, put, place."

Rdỉ is a third weak class verb, but it has a particular feature: some forms have initial *r* and some do not: check the mutable verb chart (Appendix 1) as each new verb form is learned. The circumstantial *sḏm·f* form is usually *dỉ·f*; but examples with initial *r* are also found. The circumstantial *sḏm·n·f* form is with initial *r*: *rdỉ·n·f*.

ḥm "slave," "servant"; fem. *ḥmt* "slave," "servant woman"

Ḥm·f "His Majesty" (said of the king); *Ḥm·ỉ* "My Majesty" (said by the king)

ḥmsỉ (4th weak) "to sit"; with *m* "to live (in/at a place), dwell"

ḥnqt "beer" Cf. (?) the Semitic root **ḥmḏ* "to be sour, fermented."

ḫm "to not know (something/somebody)"; "to be ignorant (of something)"

ḫrw "voice, sound"; , abbrev. , *mꜣꜥ ḫrw* (said of deceased) "justified," "vindicated" (I.e. in the trial court of the hereafter, the deceased has been declared innocent, and is admitted to the hereafter.)

sḫꜣ "to remember"

š "pool," "pond," "lake"

qꜣ "tall, high"; "exalted"; "loud" (cf. English "at the top of one's voice")

gmỉ "to find" Cf. (?) the Semitic root(s) **mḏʾ / mṯʾ / mǵy* "to find; come; come upon," e.g. Hebrew מָצָא (*māṣāʾ*) "to find," Ugaritic *mǵy* "to come upon."

t "bread"

dpt "taste"; "experience"

ḏw "misfortune," "evil"; and adjective "bad," "wicked"; "sad"

EXERCISE IV

(A) Learn the bi-consonantal sign groups: with *ỉ* as the second consonant:

mỉ *mỉ* (also written) *tỉ*

With ᶜ as the second consonant:

*w*ᶜ *ḫ*ᶜ

With *w* as the second consonant:

3w *ỉw* *mw*

nw *nw* *rw*

ḥw *sw* *šw*

ḏw

The sign has the bi-consonantal value *šw*, but since this feather is the emblem of the goddess Maᶜat, it occurs as a "phonetic determinative" in the writing of words from the root *m3*ᶜ.

With *b* as the second consonant:

3b (but also *mr*) *nb*

With *p* as the second consonant:

wp

(B) Transliterate and translate:[8]

1) 

2) 

3)  (The context is past time.)

4) 

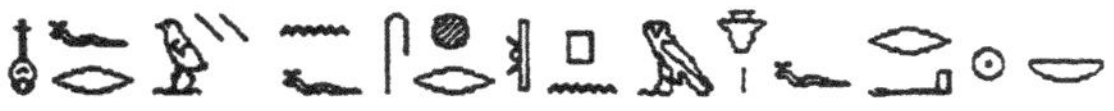

5) 

[8]Some of the texts contain more than one sentence. The particles and predicate adjectives should help indicate the sentence breaks.

6) 

7) 

8) 

9) 

10) 

(C) Parse the words and phrases from the following sentences of Part (B):

1) The verb. 2) . 3) . 4) . 5) . 6) .
7) . 8) The verbs; . 9) . 10) .

(D) Write in hieroglyphs and transliterate:

1) How fine is this house of yours! Here it is in my sight (lit. "face") like heaven!
2) A man remembers a bad thing, (although) he does not know the good therein (Lesson 1 vocabulary).
3) (See,) you are with me as a servant woman.
4) She is meaner ("bad") than her daughter.
5) (Behold,) misfortune is on every side (lit. "road").
6) We were found on the road by a servant of our Good Lord who had been sent from (*m*) the palace.
7) Everyone is in joy when they hear it.[9]
8) Here is a woman who lives in this city.
9) How excellent is this plan of yours, to my mind ("upon my heart"),[10] my lord!
10) My father likes bread more than (§49) honey.

[9]Egyptian often uses a plural suffix in reference to a collective noun (i.e. a noun that is singular in form, but plural in meaning). This also occurs in English: e.g. "The whole class was talking about their history project."

[10]Or "in my opinion" or more freely, "How excellent this plan of yours seems to me."

LESSON 5

§51. Word Order in the Verbal Sentence

The basic word order in verbal sentences is, as has been seen, that displayed in paradigm I. This sentence pattern (i.e. its word order) should be learned now, if it has not already been learned. In Egyptian the order of words is crucial in understanding "who did what to/for whom."

I. Basic Order: Subject, Direct Object, Indirect Object (when all nouns)

1	2	3	4	5

ỉw	*ḏd*	*ḥm-nṯr*	*r pn*	*n sš*
particle	verb	subject	direct object	indirect object

"The priest says this (magical) spell for the scribe."

When slots 3–5 are all nouns, this pattern is invariable. When, however, some of these slots are filled by pronouns, the general rule is that the pronouns (including the dative *n·f*, *n·ṯn*, etc.) take precedence over nouns and they jump as far as possible to the beginning of the sentence.[1] Nothing can intervene between the verb and its suffix pronoun (as subject) except for verbal infixes, such as the passive marker *·tw*, and the past tense marker *·n*.

II. Direct Object is a Pronoun (Dependent Pronoun moves forward)

1	2	3	4	5

ỉw	*ḏd*	*sw*	*ḥm-nṯr*	*n sš*
particle	verb	direct object	subject	indirect object

"The priest says it for the scribe."

[1]Cf. modern languages, such as French: *J'ai vu le spectacle*. *Je l'ai vu*. The shifts are less complicated in Egyptian than in French.

III. Indirect Object is a Pronoun (Dative phrase moves forward)

1	2	3	4	5
ỉw	*ḏd*	*n·f*	*ḥm-nṯr*	*r pn*
particle	verb	indirect object	subject	direct object

"The priest says the (magical) spell for him."

IV. Subject and Both Objects are Pronouns (Indirect before direct object)

1	2	3	4	5
ỉw	*ḏd*	*·f*	*n·f*	*sw*
particle	verb	subject	indirect object	direct object

"He says it for him."

Note that the suffix pronoun of the dative phrase takes precedence over the dependent pronoun, and the whole dative unit (*n* + suffix pronoun) jumps ahead of the dependent pronoun. The only source for confusion lies in sentences of type III, where *n·f* (the dative) might be at first mistaken for the past-tense marker and suffix pronoun subject. Such a reading must be ruled out since there are too many nouns after it, including a likely candidate for the subject. Only rarely is the sentence truly ambiguous, and in such cases, the context virtually always permits a certain interpretation.

§52. Abbreviations and Defective Writings

The Egyptian writing system is generally compact and abbreviated and defective writings are very common. By defective is meant only that the writing is not as full as it could have been, not that it is an erroneous writing. If two identical alphabetic signs come together, they are sometimes only written once (e.g. *m* in place of *mm*). This also happens with the seated man determinative and the 1st sing. suffix pronoun, where it can do double duty for both: e.g. *s3* "son" or *s3·ỉ* "my son"; *ỉt* "father" or *ỉt·ỉ* "my father," and even *ỉt·f* (the viper sign, which was not pronounced in *ỉt*, is thus doing double duty here for the suffix *·f*).

Common expressions, especially honorific interjections, are usually abbreviated. The most common are *ᶜnḫ(w), (w)ḏ3(w), s(nbw)* "may he live long, prosper, and enjoy good health!," which is said after reference to the royal family and the palace. We conventionally abbreviate this as "l.p.h." (for "life, prosperity, health"). The epithet *m3ᶜ ḫrw*, "justified" or "vindicated" said of the deceased, is regularly abbreviated to: . The word *nsw* "king" is commonly abbreviated to : , e.g. *sš nsw* "royal scribe" (note the honorific transposition §41, 1), and in the royal title *nsw bỉty* "King of Upper and Lower Egypt."

Based on evidence from Coptic (where the missing letters were spelled out with Greek letters), some words were always written defectively. The most common are 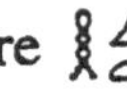 *ḥnqt* "beer,"  *rmṯ* "person," and the fem. sing. collective noun  *rmṯt* "people."

On the other hand, sometimes superfluous signs were added. Often this is by confusion with another similar looking word. For instance a *t* and stroke are frequently found with words employing the town determinative—the scribe was reminded of the word  *nỉwt* and wrote it:  *Ḫnw* "the Residence," i.e. royal city. These superfluous signs are generally ignored in the transliterations.

§53. Vocalic Writing

Towards the end of the Old Kingdom a system of indicating the significant vowels (*i/e* and *u/o*) was devised, primarily to write the names of foreign towns, people, and so on. In this system, the reed leaf  *ỉ* was used to indicate *i* and *e*, and the quail chick  *w* was used to indicate *u* or *o*. The vowel *a* was not indicated, except in one or two possible cases,  ⸢ꜣa⸣. Most of the signs were alphabetic, but some bi- and tri-consonantal signs were also used. Bi-consonantal signs ending in *ꜣ* represent the given consonant + *l* or *r*. This writing system continued to be used in the Middle Kingdom with very few modifications.[2]

During the Hyksos period, however, an attempt was made to also indicate the vowel *a*. It was at this time that bi-consonantal signs ending in *ꜣ* were beginning to be pronounced without the consonant *ꜣ* (originally close to *l* or *r*). These signs were *mostly* assigned the value of the given consonant plus *a*, but sometimes they could represent syllables with other vowels. The vocalic writing system was probably at a transitional phase in the Hyksos period and both systems were in use. Some of the older conventions can be found as late as Thutmose III in the Eighteenth Dynasty. After that period the newer conventions are in place. Since in the newer system sign groups (rather than alphabetic signs) are the rule, the script is known as "group writing."

In the New Kingdom group writing was much used (and abused) by all scribes, and since it was the product of a long evolutionary process it is not always consistent and reliable. For this reason its vocalic nature had been long denied by prominent scholars. There now seems little doubt that group writing was an attempt to indicate vowels, but that in actual practice, scribes tended to be rather careless. New Kingdom group writing is encountered in later manuscripts of good Middle Egyptian texts. Exx.  *ꜣA-bi-na* (a man's name), 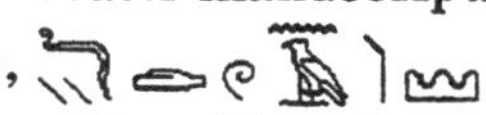 *Ḏi-du-na* Ṣidon. By convention, the *ꜣ* may be disregarded in the transliterations. Late Egyptian group writing is a very cumbersome system, and students of Middle Egyptian are not expected to have any control over it.

[2]For a discussion of the development of vocalic scripts from the Old Kingdom on, see James E. Hoch, *Semitic Words in Egyptian Texts of the New Kingdom and Third Intermediate Period* (Princeton: Princeton University Press, 1994), pp. 487–504.

§54. *Nisba*-adjectives (Relational Adjectives)

There exists within the Afro-Asiatic languages a category of adjective that is derived from nouns and prepositions. The term *nisba* "relative" is taken from Arabic grammar. In the Semitic languages, it is largely used for the "gentilic," indicating a person's origins (place or cultural group). These adjectives are quite analogous to English derived adjectives ending in -er, -ern -(i)an: "upper" (from the preposition "up"), "southern" (from the noun "South"), "African," etc. In Egyptian, *nisba* adjectives are very widely used, and they can also be derived from prepositions to create adjectives denoting relationships, e.g. "which is above," "who is below," "pertaining to," and "belonging to" (the last has already been learned as the genitival adjective *n(y)* "of" [§22, 1*b*]—deriving from the preposition *n* "to").

The forms are identical to those learned for the genitival adjective, and are indicated in table 7. Note that masc. *nisba* forms may be derived from feminine nouns, e.g. *bỉty* "King of Lower Egypt" (literally "he of the bee") from the feminine word *bỉt* "honey bee."

TABLE 7: THE *NISBA* ADJECTIVE ENDINGS

	Masculine	Feminine
Singular	-*(y)*	-*(y)t*
Plural	-*(y)w*	-*(yw)t*

In nouns ending with *t* (either as a root letter or as the feminine ending), the masc. plural -*tyw* is usually written with the sign *tỉw*. (This sign is distinguished from *3* by means of its rounded head in contrast to the angular head of *3*.)

Sometimes the *nisba* adjective is written as if it were a dual, probably because the forms were pronounced similarly. Thus we have *nṯr nỉwty* "the local god" (literally "the god who is of the city") and *3ḫty* "who is from the Horizon." The use in these two expressions is virtually identical to the so-called "gentilic" of the Semitic languages. This use, to indicate an individual's origins, is also attested with Egyptian place and geographical names: from *ḫ3st* "foreign land" derives *ḫ3stỉw* "foreigners" (used as a masc. pl. noun).

The word *ỉmy-r* "overseer," "superintendent" is a bound construction whose first member is the *nisba* adjective derived from the preposition *m* "in" and means "(he) who is in the mouth." There is a commonly used playful (but not humorous) variant writing with the tongue sign . This sign is normally read *ns* "tongue," but as a title it is transliterated *ỉmy-r* (It is based on the pun: "that which is in the mouth" being, literally of course, the tongue!).

Some of the forms derived from prepositions are written differently than the preposition itself. The two most important examples are (, ,) *ỉmy* "which is in" (from the preposition *m)* and *ỉry* "thereto," "connected to," "associated with" (and hence the word *iry* "companion," i.e. "[one] who is associated with"), which is derived from the preposition *r* "to." Both of these *nisba* adjectives form a number of compound words (bound constructions) with a following noun: E.g. *im(yw)t-pr* "transfer of title to an estate" (literally "the things that are in the house"), *imy-ib* "favourite" ("who is in the heart"), *iry-ꜥꜣ* "door-keeper" ("he who is at the door"), etc. Such compound words are treated as vocabulary items in the dictionaries and will be learned as separate items in the vocabulary.

There are many compound prepositions[3] in Egyptian, e.g. *m-ḥꜣt* "before." As *nisba* adjectives, it is the first element that requires the proper ending:[4] *imyw-ḥꜣt* "who were before," or as a noun "those who were before," i.e. "ancestors" or "predecessors." Note that the plural strokes may be written after the second element, since the whole was thought of as a unit.

Words indicating relation to the cardinal points are derived from nouns. E.g. *imnty* "western" derives from *imnt* "the West," (which in turn derives from *imn* "right hand," which is cognate with Arabic يمن [*yaman*] "right-hand side"; "south" and Hebrew יָמִין [*yamin*] "right hand"; "south."[5]) The names of the other cardinal points (and their related adjectives) are treated similarly.

§55. The Use of *iry* "Its" / "Their"

The *nisba* adjective *iry*, var. *ir(y)* is used invariably (without regard to gender and number) *after* nouns as a periphrastic ("round about") way of expressing "its" or "their." The suffix pronouns are not used, but the appropriate pronoun may be used in translations. (This is a more idiomatic way to translate than the traditional "thereto," "thereof.") The expression sometimes expresses the notion of "proper" or "belonging to." There is a variant *irw*. E.g. *m st iry* "in their (proper) place(s)" (meaning something like "in good order"); *mitt iry* "it's likeness" ("the likeness thereof"), "something like it"; *hp irw* "the law (applicable) to it" (said of a crime).

§56. Independent Pronouns

The pronouns of this category have the force of the nominative case, that is, as the subject of a sentence. The use of the independent pronouns is, however, very restricted, and as we have seen, the suffix pronoun is used as the subject in verbal and as the topic in non-verbal sentences. The independent pronouns are *never* used as the subject of a verb. These pronouns also are fairly emphatic when used (cf. Latin *ego*, etc.). The plural forms are not very common. The 1st sing. is directly related to the Semitic pronoun e.g. Hebrew אָנֹכִי (*ʾānōḵî*), Akkadian *anāku* "I." The 1st

[3]Equivalent to compound prepositions in English, e.g. "in front of," "on top of," "at the bottom of," etc.

[4]In a manner not unlike the English plurals "passers by," "mothers-in-law," etc.

[5]The use is practically identical, only the West Semitic speakers' geographic orientation was facing East (hence South, to the right-hand side) and the Egyptians' orientation was facing South (thus the right hand-side is West).

plural is likely directly related as well. The other forms are probably ultimately related, but from within the Egyptian system; they seem to be built on a stem *(ỉ)nt* followed by the corresponding suffix pronouns. There are three basic constructions employing the independent pronouns, of which two are dealt with in this lesson.

TABLE 8: THE INDEPENDENT PRONOUNS

Gender:		Common	Masculine	Feminine	
Singular	1st Pers.	*ỉnk*			"I"
	2nd Pers.		*ntk*	*ntṯ*	"You"
	3rd Pers.		*ntf*	*nts*	"He/She"
Plural	1st Pers.	*ỉnn*			"We"
	2nd Pers.	*ntṯn*			"You"
	3rd Pers.	*ntsn*			"They"

The variant writings of the first common singular pronoun are: , .

1) Independent pronoun as topic in the sentence with *nominal* comment

The construction is called the "AB nominal sentence" since noun element A is simply juxtaposed to noun element B with no connecting words. In this case element A is the independent pronoun and constitutes the topic. Element B is a noun or noun phrase that constitutes the comment. E.g. *ntk s* "You are a man." *ntf ỉt·s* "He is her father." *ntsn nbw pt* "They are the lords of Heaven." Note that in contrast to the *m* of predication (§24), here the link is essential or inherent. The idea is that of *identification* and not description. This construction is *never* introduced by the particle *ỉw*, but *mk* (and its various forms) may occasionally occur.

The independent pronouns cannot be used in non-verbal sentences with adverbial comment. One may say *ỉw·k m pr* "You are in the house." Or, one may say *mk ṯw m pr* "There you are—in the house." But a similar construction with the independent pronouns is impossible.

2) Independent pronouns in the sentences with *adjective* as comment

This use is actually a sub-set of the previous AB nominal sentence construction. Here, however element B consists of an adjective rather than a simple noun. It is very likely that the adjective was used as a noun (i.e. "one who is good," etc.). The use is almost exclusively with the 1st sing. Ex. *ỉnk nfr* "I am one who was good." *ỉnk ỉqr* "I am one who is worthy."

§57. The Infinitive

1) Preliminary Remarks: The Egyptian infinitive is a nominal form derived from verbal roots. It functions fully as a noun (denoting verbal action), and occurs in any place that one might use a noun: with suffixes, as the direct object of verbs, after prepositions, etc. The infinitive may serve as the subject of a sentence with a conjugated verb or even as the subject of a predicate adjective. In meaning, the infinitive is often closest to the English gerund (also a verbal noun): "my going," "much shouting," "swimming after eating," etc. English idiom sometimes prefers the use of the English infinitive "to go," as in "I decided to go at the last minute." Sometimes, it may be more convenient to translate with other derived verbal nouns: e.g. "the arrival," "our descent," etc.

The Egyptian infinitive has no tense and no voice (i.e. it is neither active nor passive, and therefore can be translated either way—of course the active sense is by far the more common). Infinitives are by definition non-conjugated forms (they do not form a unit with a subject). In fact, that is often precisely why one used the infinitive rather than one of the conjugated nominal verb forms (to be learned later). Before examining the uses of the infinitive, the specific features of the infinitive by verb class are detailed. The most notable feature is the occurrence of an ending *t* in some roots (most notably the 3rd weak class). This *t* corresponds to that found in certain forms of the West Semitic infinitive especially in the final weak verbs: e.g. the root *ʿly* whose infinitive construct in Hebrew is עֲלוֹת (*ʿălōt*) "going up."

Bi-consonantal: both consonants— *ḏd* "speaking"

***S*-causative forms of bi-consonantal roots:** take *t* ending— *smnt* "establishing" (derived from *mn* "to endure")

Strong verbs: all consonants— *sḫ3* "remembering"

3rd weak: no gemination, but almost always with *t* ending— *irt* "doing," *h3t* "descending."

There are a few apparently 3rd weak verbs that do not have the *t* ending: e.g. *ḥḥy* "to search (for)";[6] *ḥsy* "singing."[7] In such cases, the *y* is usually written: . This may indicate that in some verbs, *y* was treated as a strong consonant. Verbs of this class whose infinitives do not have *t* will be noted in the vocabulary. The dictionaries do not indicate such infinitives.

2nd gem.: gemination is present— *qbb* "being cool"

4th weak:[8] Most verbs of this class take *t*— *ḥmst* "sitting; dwelling" (dictionary form *ḥmsi*), but some verbs have an infinitive without *t* (these are usually written with *y*) *ḫrty* "travelling overland"

[6] P. Westcar, 7, 7. Five more examples could be cited here from a range of texts.
[7] P. Westcar, 12, 1.
[8] This is a small class of verbs with *i* or *y* as the fourth radical, e.g. *ḥmsi*.

Mutable & Irregular Verbs:

Šm: with *t*  *šmt* "going"; *šm* is not, however, a 3rd weak root.

'Ii, iw: both roots  *iit* and  *iwt* "coming"

'Ini:  *init* "bringing"

Rdi: usually with *r*  ,  , and hieratic  *rdit* "giving," "placing," "causing"

M33: various forms— *m33*,  *m3n*,  *m3* "seeing," the first is by far the most common. The writing with *n* may have arisen for phonetic reasons (*3* pronounced as *l*?[9]), and it might therefore not be a variant *form*, but only a variant *writing*.

2) The Infinitive as Object of Prepositions The infinitives occur after any number of prepositions, usually with very predictable meanings. These phrases (including subsequent words), since they are prepositional phrases function as adverbs, and occur in almost all places where adverbs do. Some of the more notable specific uses are as follows:

***R* + infinitive:** expresses purpose— *r irt* "in order to do"  *r h3t* "in order to go down," etc. This is a very common use. Much less commonly, the *r* has the force of the comparative/superlative (§§49–50):  ... *mnmnt* ʿ*š3t r ip* "... and cattle too numerous to count." (Note that in the translation, however, the comparative/superlative affects the *adjective*. The Egyptian is literally: "cattle numerous with respect to counting.")

***Ḫft* + infinitive:** expresses temporal relationship—"when." E.g.  *ḫft iit* "when (someone) got there" or "upon arrival,"  *ḫft m33* "when seen" (note here that the infinitive is translated as if it were a passive—it is neutral with respect to voice, but the English requires a passive). The subject may have to be supplied in the translation, but is not needed in the Egyptian.

***M-ḫt* + infinitive:** expresses prior action—"after (doing)" or "after having (done)." E.g. 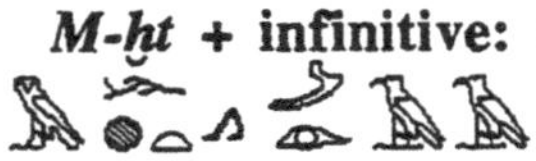 *m-ḫt m33* "after seeing."

***Ḥr* + infinitive:** expresses action in progress—equivalent to English progressive tenses "am doing," "was doing," "will be doing" (or "will continue to do").  *ḥr irt* "is doing,"  *ḥr sḏm* "was listening." This use will be dealt with at length in the next lesson. Although rare by comparison with the progressive use, *ḥr* can be used with the infinitive in its other senses, e.g. *ḥr wnm·f* "on account of its eating (a person's barley)."

***M* + infinitive of *verb of motion*:** Mostly the equivalent of *ḥr* + infinitive: 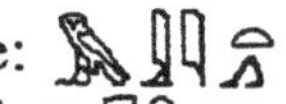 *m iit* "is coming" (Lesson 6). Less commonly, *m* has a temporal meaning "at": 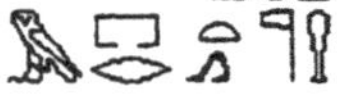 *m prt ḥm-nṯr* "at the coming forth of the *ḥm-nṯr* priest."

***M* With verbs other than verbs of motion**, various meanings are encountered, e.g.  *m irt·s* "in doing it," "by doing it" (means).  *m ḏd* "quote" (literally, "in saying" this is used to introduce direct discourse—reported speech—and is used exactly like Hebrew לֵאמֹר [*lēmōr*] "saying"). The infinitive is also used in such expressions as  *m wḥm* "again" (literally

[9]Egyptians regularly transcribed Semitic *l* with Egyptian *n* in later times.

"in repeating"), e.g.  *ˁnḫ m wḥm* "living again." Specific idioms are mostly noted in the dictionaries and will be presented in the vocabulary lists as separate items.

3) Infinitives and their Logical Direct Objects Infinitives can be followed by what would have been the direct object if it were a conjugated verb "logical direct object." Note than unlike the true direct object, which uses the "accusative" dependent pronouns, the relationship here is usually genitival, since the suffix pronouns are almost always used (the dependent pronouns are used, however, when the dative or other words must intervene between the infinitive and the pronoun).[10]

Exx.

m-ḫt irt·s

after making it (literally "after the making of it")

r m33 ḥr n(y) Nb·i

in order to see the face of my Lord

r m33·f

in order to see it

m-ḫt gmt·f in ṯ3ty

after the vizier's finding him[11] (literally "after the finding of him by the vizier")

4) Infinitives and their Logical Subjects Since infinitives are specifically forms that do not conjugate (unite with a subject), the need to indicate the logical subject (i.e. what the subject would be if this were a conjugated verb) seldom arises. But just as one can say "thanks to my knowing the manager,[12] we got front row seats," so too can one express the logical subject in Egyptian.

With *intransitive* verbs (verbs that do not take a direct object, e.g. verbs of motion like "going," "coming," "arising," etc.), the logical subject is expressed either with the suffix pronoun attached to the infinitive or the bound formation with a noun following the infinitive. Examples are not uncommon.

[10]It should not be surprising that both types of relationships should be found, since the infinitive is verbal in meaning and functions as a noun. The nominal relationship is dominant here.

[11]The translation is admittedly awkward, but it retains some of the flavour of the original. A polished translation for publication might render it more naturally and note the deviation from the original.

[12]The logical subject of the knowing is the speaker.

Exx.

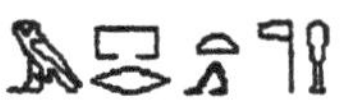

m prt ḥm-nṯr
at the going out of the *ḥm-nṯr* priest

m prt·s m hrw r mȝȝ pr·s
at her going out into the daylight in order to see her house (said of the deceased's *bȝ* leaving the tomb to visit what she wishes)

With *transitive* verbs (verbs that can take a direct object) the logical subject may be specified, but *only* when the direct object is *also* specified. In this case the logical subject is either a suffix pronoun attached to the infinitive or a noun in a bound formation following the infinitive. The direct object follows, and if this is a pronoun, the dependent pronouns are used. Such phrases are not particularly common.

Exx.

ḫft gmt ỉt·(f) sw
when his father found him (literally "at the time of his father's finding him")

ḫft gmt·f sw
when he found him (literally, "at the time of his finding him")

5) Infinitives and their Logical Indirect Objects When the logical direct object is not expressed, the indirect object is expressed by the dative *n* + noun (or *n* + suffix pronoun), which simply follows the infinitive *ỉrt n·f* "(the) making for him."

If the direct object is expressed and is a suffix pronoun, then the dative group follows, as expected: *ỉrt·f n·f* "making it for him" (or more literally, "the making of it for him").

When the logical direct object is expressed by *st* "it," "them," the dative *follows st*: *ỉrt st n·f*. (This would appear to contradict the rules of §51, but there, the *verbal predicate/subject/objects* relations were involved, and here, the rules governing *noun phrases* are involved. Since *ỉrt* and *st* form a bound construction ["the making of them"], they cannot be broken up by intervening words or phrases, and the dative phrase *must* follow.)

6) Infinitives Serving as Direct Objects of Verbs As a nominal form, the infinitive can also serve as the direct object of certain verbs. In particular the verbs have to do with commanding, perceiving, saying, wishing, thinking, and causing.

Exx.

wḏ[13] *Ḥm·f šꜣd mr pn m-ḫt gmỉt·f sw ḏbꜣ(w)*[14] *m ỉnrw*
His Majesty commanded the dredging of this canal after his finding it blocked up with stones. (Thutmose III, Canal Inscription)

ỉw mꜣ·n·f prt wḫt
He saw the emergence of the darkness.

The use of *rdỉ* "to put, place" (in any verb form) + infinitive to express the meaning "grant (to someone) to do something" is not very common. It does not appear to be a causative construction (§75, 1), and typically occurs parallel to the "granting" of favours to the king.

Ex.

Šw, dỉ·f n·k ỉrt ḥḥw m ḥbw-sd ʿšꜣw m ʿnḫ, wꜣs, ḏt
Shu grants to you the making of millions of jubilees, often, and in health and dominion for ever. (Urk. IV 570, 12)

When the verb *rḫ* takes an infinitive as a direct object it almost always means "to know how to" or "to be able to." One should remember that the meaning of *rḫ* in the present is "to learn (of)," but in the past tense (and the stative [§§82, ff.; 89]) it means "to know."

Ex.

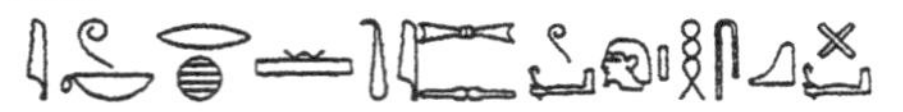

ỉw·k rḫ·tỉ[15] *ṯs tp ḥsq(w)*[16]
You know how to attach a severed head. (West. 8, 13)

7) Infinitives in Captions and Journal Entry Style—The Narrative Infinitive Just as in English, Egyptian captions and journal entries are often terse and abbreviated phrases that do not comprise grammatically complete statements. Instead of using a conjugated verb, the infinitive without introductory particle is used. If the actor is specified, it can follow the infinitive directly in a bound construction "the returning of so-and-so." If, however, other words intervene, it is introduced by the agent particle *ỉn* "by."

Exx.

ỉỉt sꜣ nsw m Tꜣ Nṯr
The return of the prince from God's Land.

[13] *Wḏ* is the narrative infinitive, §57, 7.
[14] *Ḏbꜣ(w)* is the stative (§82) "blocked up."
[15] *Rḫ·tỉ* is the 2nd masc. sing. stative (§§82, 89).
[16] *Ḥsq(w)* is the 3rd masc. sing. stative (§82).

ỉỉt m ḥtp ỉn s3 nsw
The return in safety by the prince ...

These can also be used in commemorative inscriptions and historical narratives (in the latter presumably to imitate or include journal entries made on military campaigns). In such cases these are better translated as full sentences:

wḏ3 Ḥm·f ḥr wrryt·f n(y)t ḏꜥmw
Then His Majesty proceeded upon his chariot of electrum. (Literally: "The proceeding of His Majesty ....")

Such caption / journal entry type statements can be distinguished from ordinary sentences in several ways (often by a process of elimination): 1) the absence of the particle *ỉw*; 2) the final weak verbs (and *šm*) have final *t*; 3) the context is past, and there is no past-tense marker (*·n*)—and it is not a *sḏmw·f* passive. This use of the infinitive is known as the "narrative infinitive." The narrative infinitive occurs in literary verse, as well as historical prose, narratives.

8) Infinitives as Subjects of Verbs and Predicate Adjectives As a noun, the infinitive can occur as the subject of a verb or as the subject of a predicate adjective.

Ex.

3ẖ sḏm n s3
Listening is useful for a son. (Ptaḥḥ. 534)

VOCABULARY V

3w "long," "extended"; with *3w ỉb* "happy," with *3w ḏrt* "generous"

3wt "length"; *3wt ỉb* "happiness," "joy"

3ẖ "good, "useful," "beneficial"

ỉỉ and *ỉw* (anomalous verb; infinitives: *ỉỉt* and *ỉwt*) "to come," "arrive"; "return." These two related roots are not exactly interchangeable, and usually a particular form prefers one root over the other. (Check the mutable verb chart [Appendix 1] for the various forms that have already been learned, and also for each new form learned in future lessons.)

ỉry, var. *ỉr(y)* *ỉrw* (*nisba* of *r*) "thereto," "thereof," "belonging to it"; "its," "their": see §55.

ꜥnẖ "to live" (exist); not in the sense "to live (in a place)"

Note the expression *ꜥnẖ(w), (w)ḏ3(w), s(nbw)* "may he live long, prosper, and be healthy!" or "l.p.h." The verb forms used in this expression have not been learned yet, but will be presented in Lessons 8–9 §§82, 99. Treat this just as an expression for now.

, *wḏ* "to command," "order," "decree"; (noun) "command," "decree" Cf. Arabic وصى (*wṣy*); Hebrew (with metathesis) צִוָּה (*ṣāwā*) "to order, command, decree"

wḏꜣ adj. "sound," "in good condition," "prosperous"

wḏꜣ "to go, set out, proceed" (cf. Semitic **wḏy*, e.g. Hebrew יָצָא (*yaṣā*) "to set out, go forth")

prỉ 1) "to go / come out" *m* "from," *ḥr* "through" (a door); 2) "to ascend, go up" *r* "to"

m-ḫt[17] (compound preposition) "after," "following," "behind"

m ḏd "saying" (*ḏd* is an infinitive) used to introduce direct discourse (a word for word quotation); it can be left out of translations if colon and quotation marks are used.

Also occurring with the same function is the phrase *r ḏd* "saying"

mꜣw "new"

mꜣwt "something that is new," "a new thing" (§21, 2); *m mꜣwt* "again," "anew," "afresh" (literally "as a new thing")

mỉtt "likeness"

nỉwty (*nisba*) "local," "of the city"

r-pr "temple"

rmṯ "person"; pl. *rmṯw* "people"; *rmṯt* (fem. sing. collective) "people"

There is some confusion between the use of the masc. pl. and the fem. sing. collective.

ḥry (*nisba*) "upper"; "(one) who/which is above/over"; *ḥry-pr* "chief of household staff"

ḥtp "to be satisfied" *m* "with"; "be at peace," "go to rest," "set" (of sun); transitive: "to satisfy," "make content"

ḥtp noun "peace," "contentment"; *m ḥtp* "safely" (when travelling)

ḫꜣst "country," "foreign land"

ḫꜣstyw "foreigners"

ḫft "in accordance to"; "corresponding to"; "in front of"; "opposite"; *ḫft* + infinitive:

[17]The *t* is a root letter and not the feminine ending.

"when." Following verbs of speech: "to" (a person of high rank or royalty), i.e. one does not speak *to* the king, but merely *in his or her presence*. Note the writing! This is a case of graphic transposition (i.e. the *t* is placed in a convenient space for aesthetic reasons).

ḫfty "enemy" (a *nisba* "[one] who is opposed"), pl. *ḫftyw*

h̲r (preposition) "under," and from the idea of being "under a burden": "bearing," "carrying," "holding," "having"; "(being) in" (a state or condition)

h̲rt "belongings," "property," "possessions"

ḫs or *ḫs(y)* "cowardly"; "vile" (of enemy)

st "place"; "seat," "throne"; *m st ỉry* "in good order" (literally: "in their [proper] places"). Cf. ? Arabic است (*ʾist*) "buttocks"; Hebrew שֵׁת (*šēt*) "buttocks," שָׁת (*šāt*) "foundation"

snb adj. "healthy"; "safe"; vb. "to be healthy" (cf. Semitic *šlm* "to be whole, in good condition, safe"—here Egy. *n* corresponds to *l* and with interchange of *m* and *b*).

qd "to build"

K3š (place name, feminine in gender) Kush

ḏrt "hand"

EXERCISE V

(A) Learn the bi-consonantal sign groups with *m* as the second consonant:

ỉm	*nm*	*ḥm*
km	*gm*[18]	*tm*

With *n* as the second consonant:

ỉn[19]	*wn*	*wn* (rare)
mn	*nn*[20]	*ḥn*
h̲n	*h̲n*	*sn*
šn		

With *r* as the second consonant:

[18]The distinguishing feature of this sign is that the bird is looking down at the ground, having spotted something (food?), cf. *gmi* "to find."

[19]Note the long straight dorsal fin of the *int* fish.

[20]This sign is distinguished from the *sw* sign. *Nn* has only one pair of off-shoots, and *sw* has two.

 *ir*  *wr*[21]  *pr*

 *mr*  *mr*[22]  *ḥr*

 *ḫr*[23]  *ḏr*

(B) Transliterate and translate:

1) 

2) 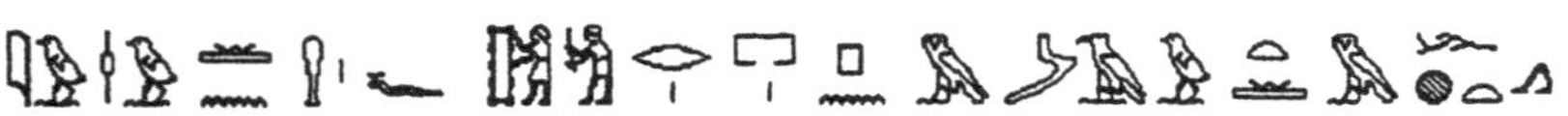

3) 

4) 

5) 

6) 

7) 

8) 

9) 

10)  (Cf. §§ 47, 38)

(C) Parse the words and phrases of (B):

1) . 2) . 3) . 4) 
. 5)  in the phrase . 6) .
7) . 8) The second 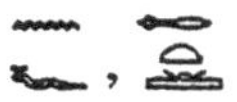. 9) . 10) .

(D) Rewrite in hieroglyphs the following sentences from section (B) according to the directions:

3) Replace the nouns and noun phrases with pronouns. 6) Replace the nouns with pronouns (first clause only). 8) Replace the pronouns with nouns or noun phrases of your choice in the phrase .

[21]This is the swallow sign. It is distinguished from the "bad bird" determinative ( a sparrow) by means of the swallow tail, which flares slightly and has sharp points, compared to the sparrow's narrow, rounded tail.

[22]This sign also has the value *ꜣb*.

[23]This sign must be distinguished from  *g*.

LESSON 6

§58. *Ḥr* + Infinitive: Ongoing Action & Action in Progress

The infinitive following the preposition *ḥr* has a special function—to express ongoing action and action in progress. In general it corresponds to the English progressive tenses "is doing"/"was doing" and French *en train de faire*. E.g. *ḥr ỉrt* "while doing," *ḥr mꜣꜣ·f* "while looking at him."

Note that since the infinitive is involved, the logical direct object is in a genitival relation with the infinitive [§57, 3], and if a pronoun, the suffix pronoun series is used. In addition, the pronoun *st* "it"; "them" also occurs as a logical direct object.

The construction consists of a prepositional phrase, and is therefore adverbial. It can form the adverbial comment in sentences of the "non-verbal type." Such sentences are said to involve the "pseudo-verbal" construction (a regrettable, but well entrenched, term).

Like other Egyptian adverbs and adverbial phrases, this construction may be used to modify nouns, especially the direct object of *gmỉ* "to find" and *mꜣꜣ* "to see."

Ex.

wḏꜣ pw ỉrỉ·n·f (§136) *ḥnꜥ·f r mryt ḥr rdỉt n·f ꜥ·f*

He proceeded with him to the river-bank, giving him his hand. (West. 8, 2)

gmỉ·n·f (§147) *sw ḥr prỉt m sbꜣ n(y) pr·f*

He found him just[1] as he was going out the door of his house. (Peas. 1, 34–35)

The construction is conveniently translated by means of the English participle (a verbal adjective). The preposition *ḥnꜥ* "together with" can be used to link two of these phrases, and here has the meaning "and." (Egyptian generally does not attempt to express the notion "and." See §63.)

§59. Sentences Expressing On-going / Progressive Action

Since *ḥr* / *m* + infinitive are adverbial, they can serve as the adverbial comment in a non-verbal sentence (§10). Just as one can say *iw·f m pr* "he is in the house" (*m pr*:

[1] This is not a statement of fact, but an "explicatory sentence" (§148), which highlights the circumstances: "How he found him was as he was going out . . ."

prepositional phrase = adverbial comment), one can also say  *ỉw·f ḥr ꜣtp ꜥꜣ·f* "he is loading his donkey" (*ḥr ꜣtp*: prepositional phrase = adverbial comment). This sentence construction is quite frequent. Like other sentences with adverbial comment, the verb "to be" does not occur, and therefore there is no tense distinction. One must rely on the context to establish the time frame. Thus, if the context is past time, one would translate "he was loading." The rules concerning the presence and absence of *ỉw* apply here.

Ongoing action does not need to take place at the moment the speaker was talking (or writing). The *ỉw·f ḥr sḏm* construction can also refer to action that takes (or took / will take) place over a period of time, and may include the present time. It can also refer to regularly repeated action. This use is close to the English present perfect constructions: "I have been living in Rome for years." "She has been swimming since she was four years old."

Ex.

ỉw·f ḥr wnm t 500, rmn n(y) ⸢ỉḥ⸣ m ỉwf·(f), ḥnꜥ swr ḥnqt ds 100 r-mn-m hrw pn.

He has been eating 500 (loaves of) bread, a side of beef as (his) meat, and has been drinking 100 jugs of beer down to this day.[2] (West. 7, 2–4)

If  *mk* is used in place of *ỉw*, the dependent series of pronouns must be used (as with other sentences with adverbial comment, §39).

Exx.

ỉw ỉt·ṯn ḥr wnm t

Your father is eating bread.

 *mk sw ḥr wnm·f*

Look, he is eating it. *Or*, Look at him eating it.

 *mk sw m ỉỉt*

There he is coming. / Look, he is arriving.

§60. *M* + Verbs of Motion—Motion in Progress / Immediate Action

Verbs of motion (except *šm* "to go") and certain intransitive verbs (e.g. *ḫpr* "to become, come into existence") can be used in a similar construction. The preposition used is often  *m* rather than  *ḥr*, but both are used. Besides conveying the notion of "motion in progress" the construction *m* + infinitive can mean "going to (move)," "to be about to (move)," or "be on the point of moving" (or even "will be [moving]," and cf. French *futur proche* "*Je vais faire ...*").

[2]This refers to a certain magician's incredible daily rations.

Exx.

ỉw mꜣ·n·f sy m ỉỉt
He saw her coming.

ỉw gmḥ·n·f sw m hꜣt r mryt
He spotted him going down to the shore.

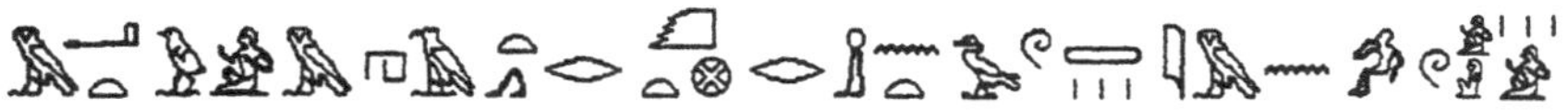

mt (§40) *wỉ m hꜣt r Kmt r ỉnt ꜥqw ỉm n ẖrdw·ỉ*
Look, I'll be going down to Egypt to bring back some provisions from there for my children. (Peas. R 2 f.)

§61. Progressive Circumstantial Clauses

With noun subjects, the absence of *ỉw* indicates subordination—a circumstantial clause (§16). These can be used in the normal fashion to modify the entire preceding clause, or they can be used as nominal modifiers: the relative clause with indefinite antecedent (§38).

Exx.

(I heard a thunderous sound. I thought it was a wave of the ocean,)

ḫtw ḥr gmgm, tꜣ ḥr mnmn
but the trees were breaking, and the ground was shaking. (Sh.S. 59 f.)

ḥfꜣw pw[3] *ỉw·f m ỉỉt*
It was a serpent that was coming. (Sh.S. 60)

In the second example, the clause *ỉw·f m ỉỉt* modifies only the noun *ḥfꜣw* "serpent" as a relative clause: i.e. "what kind of serpent?" "one that was coming." When modifying the entire main clause (whether past or present tense), these circumstantial clauses typically refer to on-going activity that was (or is) taking place when a certain action took (or takes) place.

Ex.

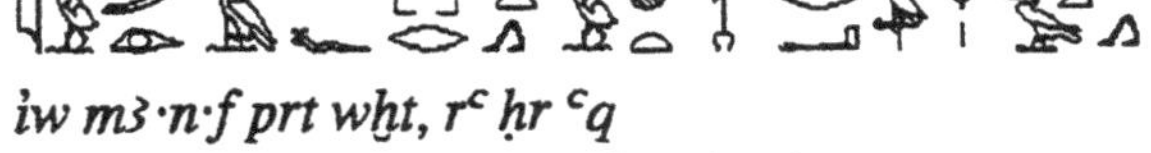

ỉw mꜣ·n·f prt wḫt, rꜥ ḥr ꜥq
He saw the emergence (§57; 57, 6) of the darkness as the sun was setting.

[3]The construction *X pw* expresses the idea "it is/was x" (§129).

§62. The Future Tense Construction: *ʾIw·f r sḏm*

This sentence pattern is exactly like the structure of the progressive constructions *ỉw·f ḥr sḏm* and *ỉw·f m ỉỉt*. All the rules of the non-verbal sentence with adverbial comment are expectedly in force. The preposition used is *r* "to, towards" with the sense of futurity. (The notion involved is very similar to English "I am going to do" and French "je vais faire," which also involve the idea of "motion to.") In this role, the preposition *r* is referred to as "the *r* of futurity." The passive was formed by means of the pronoun *tw*: *ỉw tw r sḏm* "one will hear."

There were a number of ways of introducing the future tense, but the particle *ỉw* is by far the most common. The particle *mk* is used, and as expected the dependent pronoun series is used for the topic.

Also attested, but less common are: NOUN *r sḏm* and the quasi passive *tw r sḏm* "one will hear," which may be a Late Egyptian construction. In neither case is any introductory particle used. The pronoun *tw* is here not used as the passive suffix (as it almost always is), but rather it is used as an independent word "one." Structurally, the construction is identical to NOUN *r sḏm*.

As with the progressive constructions (and otherwise with infintives), when the logical direct object is a pronoun, it is of the *suffix pronoun* series: *ỉw·s r m33·f* "She will see him." In addition to the suffix pronouns, the dependent pronoun *st* "it"; "them" may occur as the direct object.

Exx.

ỉw dpt r ỉỉt m ḫnw

A ship will come from home. (Sh.S. 119–20)

mk wỉ r nḥm ꜥ3·k, sḫty, ḥr wnm·f[4] *šmꜥ·ỉ*

Look, I will take your donkey, peasant, on account of its eating my Upper Egyptian barley. (Peasant B1, 11)

ỉb n(y) Ḥm·k r qbb n[5] *m33 ḫnn·sn*[6]

Your Majesty's mind will be refreshed at seeing how they row.[7] (West. 5, 15.)

ỉw tw r šnt st r pr-ḥḏ

[4]The infinitive. Here the preposition *ḥr* has the meaning "for," "because," "on account of" and is *not* the progressive *ḥr* + infinitive (§58).

[5]The negative arms are here used as a variant writing of the preposition *n*. *M33* is the infinitive.

[6]This is a second tense form (§147) and means "how they row." It is a nominal unit and serves as the logical direct object of the infinitive *m33* "seeing."

[7]The context is that of a rowing exhibition performed by women as a royal entertainment.

One will investigate it at the treasury. (Urk. IV 694)

tw r šsp ḫꜥw nw ꜥḥꜣ

One will take up weapons of war. (P. Petersburg 1116B, 39)

§63. Coordinating and Disjunctive Words

Egyptian does not require the use of a co-ordinating word equivalent to English "and." E.g. *t ḥnqt* "bread and beer," *s ḥmt·f* "a man and his wife." Although such a sequence would appear to be identical to the bound construction, this can be ruled out on the basis of the meaning: "bread of the beer" and "man of his wife" do not make good sense.

Similarly, there is no common word for "or." Again one must rely upon the meaning in context.

Occasionally the preposition *ḥr* "on top of" is used with something like the meaning "and": *ḏꜥ ḥr ḥwyt* "wind storms in addition to rain." Sometimes *ḥnꜥ* "together with" may be used: *rmṯw ḥnꜥ mnmnt* "people along with the cattle." In progressive sentences, one can use *ḥnꜥ* to join infinitives *iw·f ḥr wnm t… ḥnꜥ swr ḥnqt* "He has been eating bread … and drinking beer."

§64. Vocative

There is no vocative case in Egyptian to indicate direct address to an individual (or individuals). One may start a sentence with such an address, end with it, or insert it at some convenient place in the middle. In funerary inscriptions, the text often begins with the vocative particle *i* "O (you)." Personal names were probably often thrown into the sentence as vocatives, but this use is not common in written texts.

Exx. 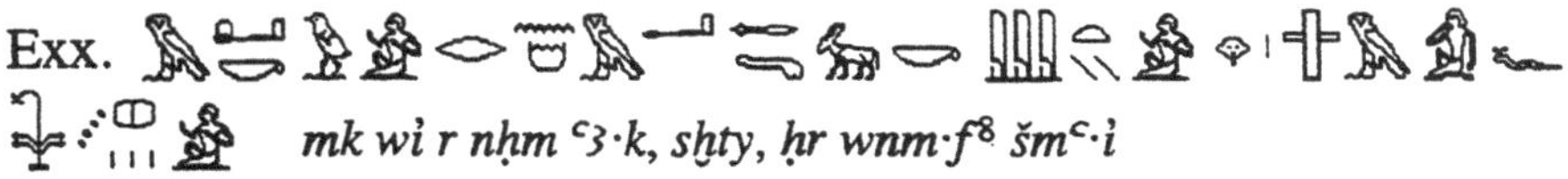

mk wi r nḥm ꜥꜣ·k, sḫty, ḥr wnm·f[8] *šmꜥ·i*

Look, I will take your donkey, peasant, on account of its eating my Upper Egyptian barley. (Peasant B1, 11)

i ꜥnḫw tpyw tꜣ (§54)

O you living beings who are upon the earth …

§65. Cardinal Numbers

The Egyptian cardinal numbers are as shown below. The actual names of the numbers need not

[8] The infinitive.

be committed to memory, since in practice Egyptologists do not attempt to reconstruct the Egyptian numerical system, and instead the numbers of the translation language are used. The numerals are indicated by various signs representing various powers of ten. Ones are indicated by a stroke (𓏺), tens by a hoop (𓎆), and so on. The signs are written as many times as required: 𓎈𓏻 32, 𓎉𓐀 47, etc. Many of the Egyptian numbers are directly related to their Semitic counterparts (*ḫmnw* : **ṯmn* "8," but the relations are considerably obscured by unexpected phonetic correspondences (e.g. Egyptian *ḫ* for Semitic *ṯ*). The corresponding Semitic numbers are listed in parentheses in the following chart.

1	𓏺	*wꜥ(w)*	(**wḥd*)	**6**	𓏿	*srsw / sỉsw*	(**šdṯ*)
2	𓏻	*sn(wy)*	(**ṯny*)	**7**	𓐀	*sfḫ(w)*	(**šbꜥ*)
3	𓏼	*ḫmt(w)*		**8**	𓐁	*ḫmn(w)*	(**ṯmn*)
4	𓏽	*fdw*		**9**	𓐂	*psḏ(w)*	(**tšꜥ*)
5	𓏾	*dỉw*		**10**	𓎆	*mḏ(w)*	

The number one is frequently written out: e.g. 𓌡𓂝𓏤 *wꜥ*, 𓌡𓂝𓏏 *wꜥt*. The number two is also fairly often written out; it is a dual form: 𓌢𓈖𓅱𓏭 *snwy*. Other numbers are only very rarely spelled out. The numbers had feminine forms to agree with feminine nouns, but these are not indicated in the writing, apart from the number one when it is spelled out.

The other units are as shown below. Note in particular the sign for 100 𓍢 which resembles the *w* sign derived from hieratic 𓏲 . The 100 sign descends farther and is less round than *w*.

The names for the units 100–1,000,000 need to be learned, but the others can be dealt with in the translation language.

20	𓎇	[?]	90	𓎎	*psḏyw*
30	𓎈	*mꜥbꜣ*	100	𓍢	*št*
40	𓎉	*ḥm*	1000	𓆼	*ḫꜣ*
50	𓎊	*dỉyw*	10,000	𓂭	*ḏbꜥ*
60	𓎋	*sr(syw)*	100,000	𓆐	*ḥfn*
70	𓎌	*sfḫ(yw)*	1,000,000	𓁨	*ḥḥ*
80	𓎍	*ḫmn(yw)*			

Numerals are written in combinations beginning with the highest unit in descending order. For example, the number 236,258 would be written: . The numerals are not transliterated; instead the Arabic numerals are used. The sign  *ḥḥ* falls into disuse with the meaning "one million," but continues to occur as a word meaning "a great number."

§66. Use of the Numerals and Numbers

The numerals are written after the noun, which is usually written in the singular. E.g.  *pr 4*, "four houses";  *dpt 12* "twelve boats." This use is probably derived from inventory style, in which things were itemized and followed by a number indicating quantity. This practice is particularly evident when the demonstrative adjective (§78) is used with enumerated nouns—the singular demonstrative is used: 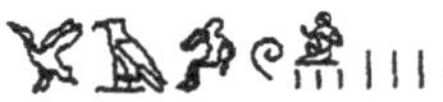 *p3 ẖrdw 3* "these 3 children." *P3* is the masculine singular form "this" (§78). The demonstrative agrees in gender with the noun that is enumerated, but only the singular is used: 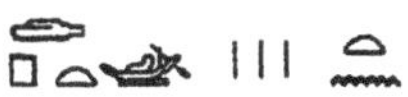 *dpt 3 tn* "these three boats."

With the numbers 100 and 1000, the demonstratives were used differently. In this case, the demonstrative must agree in gender with the number: feminine for 100 (*št*) and masculine for 1000 (*ḫ3*). As with other numbers, however, only the singular is used. Exx.  *t3*[9] *t 100* "these 100 loaves (of bread),"  *p3 t ḫ3* "these 1000 loaves (of bread)."

It seems likely from later evidence that in actual spoken Egyptian (apart from Egyptian as it was read from written documents), the number was generally said first and was followed by the plural noun. (This would presumably be the bound construction [§22, 1*a*] meaning, "four of houses.") This was not, however, the case with number two, which even in Coptic follows the noun.

When the number one is written out, it usually follows the noun and agrees in gender. In addition to "one" it can mean "unique," "sole," "only," etc. E.g.  *w3t·f wꜥt* "one side of it," 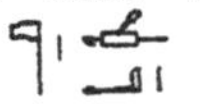 *nṯr wꜥ* "the unique god." Sometimes it precedes the noun and is linked by the genitival adjective *n(y)*: 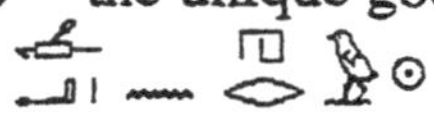 *wꜥ n(y) hrw* "one day." This later became the indefinite article "a," "an," and some early examples can be found in Middle Egyptian.

"One of a group" can be expressed by the preposition *m*: 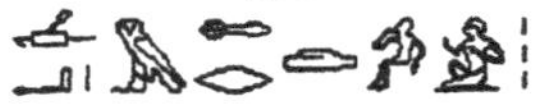 *wꜥ m ẖrdw* "one of the children,"  *wꜥ im·ṯn* "one of you." This use is known as the **partitive**.

The number one can be used as a noun in its own right, e.g. in the expression 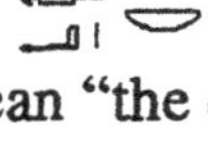 *wꜥ nb* "every one." The expressions 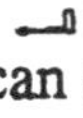 ... 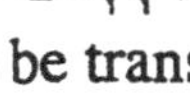 *wꜥ*... *ky* and 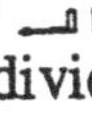 ... 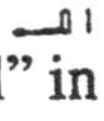 *wꜥ*... *wꜥ* mean "the one ... the other." The word 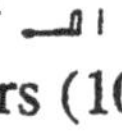 *wꜥ* can also be translated as "individual" in some contexts.

The higher numbers (1000 and above) are usually written before the noun and either the *m* of predication or the genitival adjective *n(y)* connects the number to the noun. E.g.

[9] *T3* is the fem. sing. demonstrative pronoun "this" (§78).

ḫ3 m t ḥnqt "a thousand (loaves) of bread and (jugs) of beer" (a standard line in the funerary offering formula), *ḥḥ n(y) sp* "a million times."

The Egyptians had a very cumbersome system of fractions, and it should be examined by students only at a more advanced level.[10] A few fractions are, however, fairly common: *gs* ½, and much less often *r 4* (hieratic equivalent × *ḥsb*) ¼, and *rwy* ⅔. (Apart from ⅔, all Egyptian fractions have only 1 as the numerator. One had to add a series of fractions with differing denominators until the right total was achieved.)

§67. Ordinal Numbers

For "first" the *nisba* adjective *tpy* (var. ,) derived from the preposition "on top of" *tp* is used (i.e. "to head the list"). As expected with the *nisba* adjectives, it follows the noun *m sp tpy* "on the first occasion," *ḥmt·f tp(y)t* "his first wife." It can also mean "chief" or "head" (i.e. "number one") *ḥm-nṯr tpy* "chief *ḥm-nṯr*-priest."

The ordinal numbers "second" to "ninth" are formed with the suffix *-nw* attached to the cardinal number: *sn-nw* "second," but other numbers are usually written with the numerals *2-nw* "second," *3-nw*, "third," etc. for the masculine. The suffix *nwt* is the feminine form. In earlier Middle Kingdom texts, the ordinal number is placed before the noun, and agrees with it in gender: *5-nw sp* "the fifth time," *m 2-nwt·f st* "in his second position." In later texts, the ordinal numbers are treated like adjectives and follow the noun: *rnpt 3-nwt* "the third year," *sb3 4-nw* "the fourth door."

Ordinals from "tenth" and higher were formed by use of the word *mḥ* and its feminine form *mḥt* "filling up," "completing" (these are grammatically participles—verbal adjectives [§117 ff.]). The cardinal number is placed at the end of the construction: *wnwt mḥt 12 n(y)t hrw* "the 12th hour of the day."

§68. Measurements

There were a great many measures some precise and standardized, but others were not at all accurate (e.g. *ds* "jug"). Only the more important units of measure are here indicated. Some measurements were actually standardized, but the standards occasionally were changed. And we know from actual texts that the standards were sometimes (often?) subverted or at least differed regionally. (One gentleman farmer instructed his agents to use his personal measure in order to collect *everything* owing to him.)

1) **Volume.** The basic grain measure was the *ḥq3t* (ca. 4.54 litres) written variously: , , , , , . A larger unit was the (var.) *ḫ3r* "sack," which held 20 *ḥq3t* (ca. 90.8 litres). A measure for liquids (beer, milk, honey, etc.) was the *hnw* "*hin*" (ca. 0.5 litre). (This word is probably the origin of Biblical Hebrew הִין (*hīn*) a much larger liquid

[10] A fairly complete outline of the fraction system can be found in Gardiner, *EG* §265 ff.

measure.) Rather common for beer is 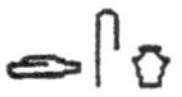 *ds* "jug," of unknown size (if it was even partially standardized is unknown). All of these measurements are placed directly after the item, e.g. 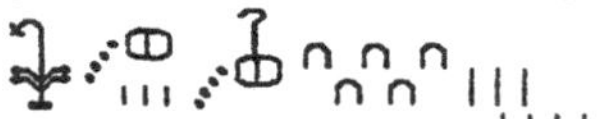 *šmᶜ ḥq3t 53*, "53 *heqats* of Upper Egyptian barley,"  *ḥnqt hnw 47* "47 *hins* of beer."

2) Length. The cubit  *mḥ* was a common measure of length (ca. 52.3 cm). It was subdivided into smaller units, but these are normally encountered only in technical and mathematical texts. There were several units for measuring long distances (e.g.  *ḫt* 100 cubits), but these can be treated as vocabulary items to be looked up in the dictionaries if encountered. E.g.  *š n(y) mḥ 150* "a pool of 150 cubits." The phrases  *m 3w·f* "in its length" and  *m wsḫ·f* "in its width" may follow measures of length. The suffix pronoun of course agrees with the gender and number of the object(s) measured, and one may translate the phrases as "in length" and "in width."

3) Weight. From the Eighteenth Dynasty on, metals (gold, silver, copper) were measured by the *deben* 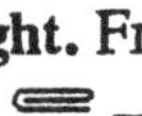 *(dbn)* of ca. 91 grams. The *deben* was subdivided into 10 *qidet*: 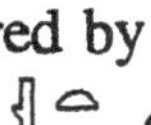 *qdt.* E.g. 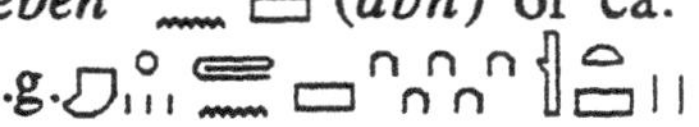 *ḥmt, dbn 50, qdt 2* "copper, 50 *deben*, 2 *qidet*."

4) Area. The main unit of land measurement was the Egyptian *aroura* (by its Greek name):  *st3t* measuring 100 cubits squared (2735 sq. meters or a little more than ⅔ acre). E.g. 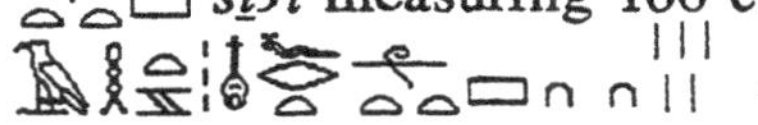 *3ḥwt nfr(w)t st3t 25* "25 *arouras* of good arable land."

§69. Dates & the Royal Titulary

The Egyptian year was divided into twelve months (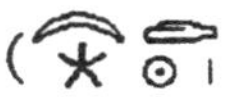 *3bd)* and three seasons:  *3ḫt* "inundation," 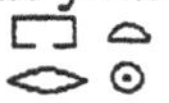 *prt* "winter," and  *šmw* "summer." Each season had four months of thirty days, for a total of 360 days, but the year was "filled out" to 365 days with the inclusion of the five "epagomenal" (added) days. Dates begin with the signs for "regnal year":  *ḥ3t-sp* (the normal word for "year" is 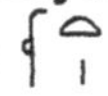 *rnpt*). This is followed by a numeral, then the following sequence: *3bd X 3ḫt/prt/šmw, sw Y* "month X of inundation/winter/summer, day Y." The word for "day" in dating sequences is ,  *sw* and it probably means "date" as opposed to just "day," although it is to be translated "day." E.g.  *ḥ3t-sp 1, 3bd 2 3ḫt, sw 8* "Regnal year 1, second month of inundation, day 8." The numbers of the day of the month are regularly written *horizontally* in hieratic texts, as in the example above. The number before the season is very likely the ordinal even though it is not particularly indicated. In hieratic texts  *3bd 1* occurs without variation, but in hieroglyphic inscriptions, we usually find the writing 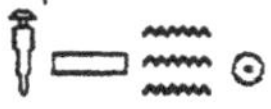 *tpy šmw* "the first (month) of summer" (without the word *3bd*).

The last (thirtieth) day of the month was called  *ᶜrqy*. It does not occur in conjunction with  *sw*. It can be translated "last day (of the month)."

Dates were given by the regnal year of the current king, and therefore the royal titulary is a major and integral part. After the date, the titulary formula follows, with the royal name enclosed in a cartouche: *ḥr Ḥm n(y) nsw-bity Mn-ḫpr-Rʿ* "under the Majesty of the King of Upper and Lower Egypt Men-kheper-Rēʿ." This is the minimal formula, and even this would be followed by the laudatory or honorary interjection: "given life!"

The full titulary consists of five names, and these are listed in a specific order, and particular epithets are associated with the different names. The full titulary—established and proclaimed immediately upon accession to the throne—consists of 1) *Ḥr*: Horus name, 2) *Nbty* Nebty ("Two-Ladies"[11]) name, 3) *Ḥr nbw*: Golden Horus name, 4) *nsw-bity* ("King of Upper and Lower Egypt") + Prenomen in a cartouche (the prenomen almost always contains the name of Rēʿ), 5) *sꜣ Rʿ* "the Son of Rēʿ" + Nomen in a cartouche (the name borne before taking the throne), 6) laudatory epithets, e.g. *di ʿnḫ ḏd wꜣs mi Rʿ ḏt* "given life, stability, and dominion like Rēʿ, forever." The order of these elements was very strictly followed. The only variation is with the laudatory epithets, and even here, only three or four set phrases were used. Since the full titulary is very long, abbreviated formulas are the norm, the prenomen being the most crucial to the identification of the particular king. It often occurs alone or with just the nomen. Within a dynasty it was common to use the same one or two nomen over many generations. (We distinguish like-named kings by such designations as Amenḥotpe I, Ramses IX, etc., but the Egyptians relied mainly on the nomen and the associated prenomen.) The other names are not placed in a cartouche, and are customarily translated—they are usually highflown and difficult to translate. They frequently employ the adjective + noun bound construction (§48). The full titulary of Thutmose II:

Ḥm n(y) Ḥr: Kꜣ-nḫt, wsr pḥty (§48), *Nbty: Nsyt-nṯr, Ḥr nbw: Sḫm-ḫprw, nsw-bity ʿꜣ-ḫpr-n-Rʿ, sꜣ Rʿ Ḏḥwty-ms, nfr ḫʿw* (§48), *ḥr st Ḥr* (§22, 1*a*) *n(y)t ʿnḫw*

The Majesty of Horus: Mighty Bull of powerful might, The Two-Ladies: Kingship of the God, Golden Horus: Powerful of Forms, King of Upper and Lower Egypt ʿA-kheper-en-Rēʿ, the Son of Rēʿ Djeḥuty-mose whose appearance in glory is grand, upon the Horus throne of the living. (Urk. IV, 137)

The royal titularies are quite complicated, not to mention the fact that kings sometimes changed their names, or used minor variants, or added certain epithets inside the cartouche, etc. A convenient source book in English that is approachable by beginning students is not yet available. All the kings' names are, however, contained in German translation in a lexicon of Egyptian kings.[12]

[11]The "two ladies" in question are the goddesses Nekhbet and Edjo.
[12]Thomas Schneider, *Lexikon der Pharaonen* (Zurich: Artemis, 1994).

§70. *Sp sn:* "(Read) Twice"

The sign sequence *sp sn* "two times," "twice" indicates to the reader that one or more sign or even a complete utterance is to be repeated. Frequently it is used to repeat a word for intensification: *nfr sp sn* = *nfr, nfr* "very good." Only in magical spells does *sp sn* indicate that a whole sentence or phrase is to be repeated. (And there, it may even be *sp 4* i.e. to be read four times, etc.)

VOCABULARY VI

3ḥt "field" (specifically agricultural land)

, abbrev. *Ỉmn-nḫt* Amen-nakhte (a name)

ỉnỉ (anomalous 3rd weak; infinitive *ỉnt*) "to bring"; "get," "acquire," and many other idioms. (This is not a "verb of motion."). Note that the *sḏm·n·f* forms are written *ỉn·(n)·f* and *ỉn·n·f*.

ꜥḥ3 "to fight"; "to wage war"

ꜥq "to go in" with *m* (a place); with *r* "to a person"; *ḥr* "by (a door)"; of sun "to set"

wnwt "hour"; and general "time"; "moment"

wnm "to eat," "consume"

, *m-b3ḥ* "before," "in the presence of" (used of an audience with the king, or when ushered in before the gods)

mryt "shore," "bank"; "quay"

Mryt Merit (a name)

mḥ "to fill" with *m* "with"; , *mḥ, mḥt* + cardinal number = ordinal number (§67)

mḥ "seize," "grasp"; "take (into detention)" (for a crime)

mḥ "cubit" (52.3 cm)

mdw 3rd weak verb (infinitive *mdt*): "to speak," *mdw n* "speak to (a person)"; *mdw ḥnꜥ* "have words with (a person)," "dispute," "contend (with a person)"; noun: "speech"

mdt "speech," "word," "words"; "thing," "matter"; *ḥr mdt n(y)t* (a person) "on (account of) the word of (a person)"

nbw "gold" (depicts a gold collar or necklace)

nhy n(y) "a little (of something)," "some," "a few"

nṯrt "goddess"

ḥbs "garment"; pl. "clothing," "clothes"

, *ḥmt* "wife," "woman" Cf. ? Semitic **ḥmt* "husband's mother"

ḫꜥw "weapons"; "equipment, tools"; *ḫꜥw n(y)w ꜥḥꜣ*, *ḫꜥw ꜥḥꜣ* "weapons of war"

ḫpr "to come into existence"; "to become," "to happen," "to take place"; "to change," "turn" *m* "into"; "to come / arrive" (of time), and other meanings / idioms to be looked up in the dictionary (Cf. ? Semitic **ḫlf* "to pass on"; derived stems "to change"

ḫr (preposition) "with," "by," "near," (a god or king)"; "under" (a king's reign)"; (speak) "to" (a king)

ḫt, (noun masc.) "tree," "wood," "lumber"; "mast" (of ship) pl. *ḫtw*

, *swr* "to drink" (? an *s*-causative cognate to Semitic **rwy* "to drink one's fill")

sbꜣ "door"

sp "time," "occasion"; "deed"; "misdeed," "fault"

sp sn "twice" This indicates to the reader that some signs need to be repeated. (See §70.)

, *smꜣ* "to kill," "slay"

sḫt "fields," "meadow," "country" (in contrast to the town)

sḫty (*nisba* from *sḫt*) "peasant"

sḫpr (*s*-causative) "to create," "bring into existence," "cause to be," "bring about"

stꞽ "to shoot"

šmꜥ "Upper Egyptian barley"

šnꞽ "to investigate," "enquire into" (a matter); "to curse"; "to conjure," "exorcise" (an illness)

šsp "to take," "accept," "receive"

qd "reputation," "character," "nature"; "extent," *mꞽ qd·f* "in its entirety"

km "to complete"; *m km* (infinitive) *n(y) ꜣt* "in the completion of an instant"

grḥ "night" *m grḥ* "at night," "in the night," *grḥ mꞽ hrw* "both night and day"

tp noun "head"; preposition "on"

(var.) *tpy* (*nisba*) "which is on"; "principal," "chief"; , "first" *ḏbᶜ* "finger"; "10,000" (cf. Semitic *ˀṣbᶜ "finger")

EXERCISE VI

(A) Learn the bi-consonantal sign groups: with *ḥ* as the second consonant:

bḥ[13] *pḥ* *mḥ*

nḥ

With *ḫ* as the second consonant:

3ḫ

With *s* as the second consonant:

ỉs *ms* *ns*[14]

ḥs *šs*[15] , [16] *gs*

With *q* as the second consonant: *ᶜq*

With *k* as the second consonant: *sk*

(B) Transliterate and translate the following sentences.

1)
2)
3)
4)
5)

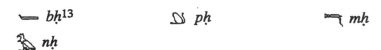

[13]This sign also has the value *ḥw*.

[14]This sign is also used to write the word *ỉmy-r* "overseer," "superintendent."

[15]To be distinguished from *šn*.

[16]The longer sign also has the alphabetic value *m*; the shorter sign is always *gs*.

[17] is the subject.

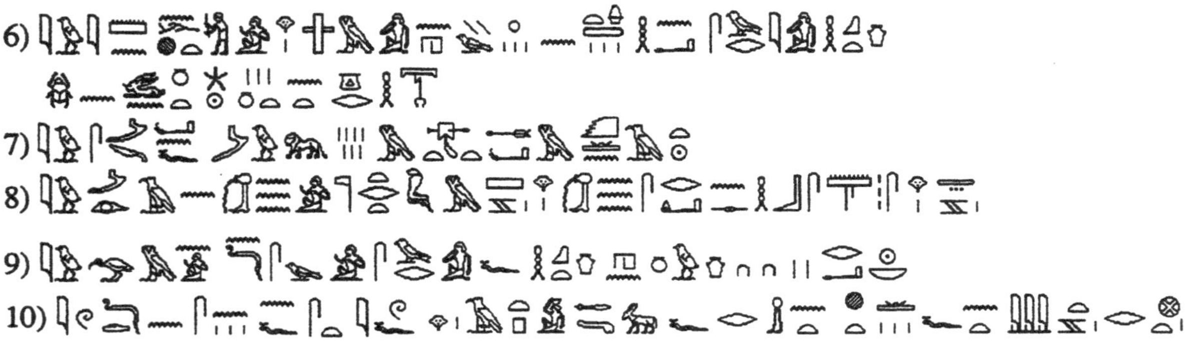

(C) Parse the words from the following sentences of (B).

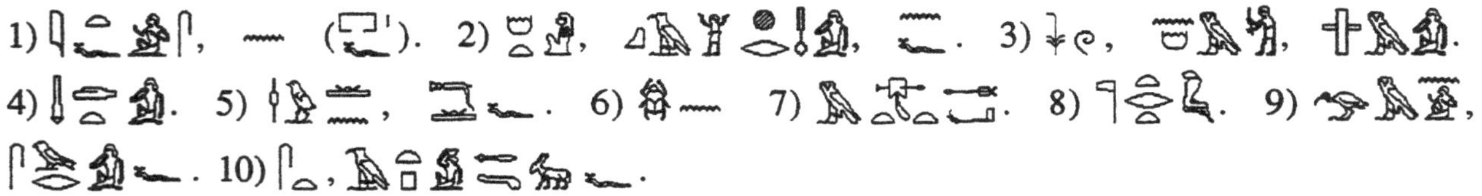

(D) Translate the following sentences into Egyptian.

1) He ferried me (across) in a boat of[18] 14 cubits after[19] I had given him[20] 2 *qidets* of gold.
2) The scribe is going to town to drink beer with his associates while his wife is in the house making bread.
3) Good is a daughter who listens to her father. She is finer than gold.
4) Amen-nakhte was writing while his wife was talking with his friends.
5) Your (fem. sing.) father was in the city when his donkey was taken away by the steward.
6) I am a scribe with excellent fingers (§48). (Literally: "excellent of fingers," i.e. "manually highly skilled")
7) Behold, you are looking (at) a mother whose children have been seized (§38) on the word of[21] a man of wicked character (§48).
8) I saw Meryt as I was going down to the shore.
9) We will enter the temple in order to place[22] the gold before the majesty of the great god.
10) Look, I will give you 25 sacks of new Upper Egyptian barley (§68, 1), because you rescued my son when he was in the river.

[18]Use the genitival adjective.
[19]Or "when." The Egyptian does not use a word for "after," "when," "since," etc.
[20]This is the dative in English.
[21]Use the genitival adjective.
[22]Use a a form of the verb *rdi*.

LESSON 7

§71. The Prospective *Sḏm·f* Verb Form

The prospective *sḏm·f* is nominal in nature and it occurs in almost any place that one might use a noun. It can even be used to form nominal clauses that serve as the subject of a conjugated verb! The prospective refers vaguely to the future, and its modal values are that of the optative (also known as precative) and subjunctive. In other words, the prospective form basically expresses what the speaker considers "desirable / possible / liable / ought" to happen. The prospective is also used to express purpose "that one might do...."[1] The notion of tense is, as usual, relative to the context, and can be used in past time contexts in subordinate clauses of purpose (§74) or as nominal phrases (§§75, 1–2).

The prospective forms are often used in clauses similar to the English "that clause" (which is also a nominal construction) occurring after verbs of saying, thinking, causing, perceiving, etc. As, for example, "I think that you should return early." The nominal phrase "that you should return early" is the direct object of "think." The Egyptian use is very similar, except that there is no special word "that" required, since the prospective form *itself* conveys the meaning of English "that," French, *que*, German *daß*, etc.

(Some confusion may arise *in English*, since there are several distinct uses of "that." In English, the "*that*" that corresponds to the Egyptian prospective forms *is not the relative pronoun*: I.e. it is *not* used to say such things as "the tomb *that* I built," but only in such noun phrases as "His Majesty granted *that* I might build my tomb [in such and such a place, etc.]." As in Egyptian, these phrases are nominal and can serve as the direct object of verbs—in this case answering the question: "What did His Majesty grant...?")

Strong verbs (e.g. bi- and tri-consonantal roots) do not distinguish the prospective from other *sḏm·f* forms. The prospective *sḏm·f* forms from the mutable and irregular classes are as follows:

3rd Weak: no gemination, sometimes with *y* ending— *iri·k*, *iry·i*

2nd Gem.: no gemination— *qb·f*

ii/iw "to come": only the root *iw*, and with *t*— *iwt·s*

ini "to bring": with *t*— *int·k*

rdi "to give": without *r*— , *di·f*

m33 "to see": *m3* and *m3n*— *m3·ṯ*, *m3n·sn*

[1]This use is similar in meaning to *r* + infinitive "in order to...," but the clauses with the prospective forms were used when the subject was required, and the *r* + infinitive when there was no need to indicate the subject.

In particular note the forms of the anomalous verbs *ỉỉ/ỉw*, *ỉnỉ*, and *mꜣꜣ*. The verbs *ỉỉ/ỉw* and *ỉnỉ* take a final *t* on the base stem in standard Middle Egyptian. In later Middle Egyptian, and in later copies of texts originally written in standard Middle Egyptian, the *t* has been dropped. Make note that the *n* that sometimes occurs in the prospective form of the verb *mꜣꜣ* looks like a *sḏm·n·f* past tense form. One must depend on the meaning and on the syntax. (I.e. does it occur where one expects a prospective and not a *sḏm·n·f* form?) The writing with *n* possibly stems from phonetic factors, and it may be only a variant in *writing*, but not in actual *form*.

A general rule is that with the prospective forms, there is no gemination in verbal classes where it does occur. The 3rd weak class verbs often have an ending in 𓏭 *y* in their prospective forms. Certain verbs occasionally have a 𓅱 *w* ending.

The prospectives form their passive voice by means of the suffix 𓏏𓅱 *tw*: *sḫꜣ·tw·t* "that you (f. sing.) be remembered." The basic stem of the verb forms of the mutable and irregular verbs are identical to those of the active voice with regard to the presence or absence of gemination. However, the passive of the verb *ỉnỉ* "to bring" is *ỉn·tw*. The other verb taking *t* in the prospective, *ỉw* "to come," is an intransitive verb of motion and therefore cannot be used in the passive.

Although the verb "to be" is not required in simple statements of fact (non-verbal sentences with adverbial comment), the somewhat irregular verb *wnn* "to be" is required in order to express the various notions conveyed by the prospective forms. Prospective forms of *wnn* are used in all of the constructions in the following sections (§§72–77). Like other second geminating verbs, the prospective form of *wnn* does not exhibit gemination: *wn·f* "may he be."

§72. Prospective *sḏm·f* Forms in Main Clauses: Wishes, Exhortations, etc.

The normal construction is simply bare initial[2] prospective *sḏm·f* or prospective *sḏm* + Noun Subject "May he hear." When the speaker is referring to himself, an English translation as "let me do" (rather than "may I do") is usually preferable.

Exx.

wḏꜥ wỉ Ḏḥwty. ḫsf Ḫnsw ḥr·ỉ. sḏm Rꜥ mdw·ỉ

May Thoth judge me. May Khonsu fend for me. May Rēꜥ listen to my speech. (*Lebensm.* 23 ff.)

sbỉ·f tw m ꜥḥꜥw nfr n ỉtw·k ỉmyw ẖrt-nṯr (§54)

May he send you—in a good span of time—to your ancestors who are in the necropolis. (West. 7, 22 f.)

[2]I.e. no introductory particles are used.

sḏd·ỉ bꜣw·k n ỉty, dỉ·ỉ sšꜣ·f m ꜥꜣ·k

Let me recount your might to the Sovereign. Let me acquaint him (literally "cause that he become familiar" §75, 1) with your greatness. (Sh. S. 139)

Strictly speaking, these clauses are not main clauses in origin, but nominal "that" clauses serving as the direct object of the implied "I wish" or "I hope." However, in practice—if not origin—these clauses are always main clauses. Cf. the French: "Qu'il soit..." "May it / he be..." which uses a "that" clause in exactly the same way.

Non-verbal sentences with adverbial comments can be transformed into wishes, but require the use of the prospective form of the verb *wnn* "to be."

Ex. 

wn·k m pr·k ḥnꜥ ḥmt·k ẖrdw·k.

May you be in your home (once again) with your wife and children.

Passive wishes beginning with *sḏm·tw·f* are not very common, but do occur. In early texts and in religious texts the *sḏm(w)·f* passive is used in wishes. (This was likely a special prospective *sḏm(w)·f* passive that was distinct from the circumstantial past-time *sḏm(w)·f* passive [§35], but the evidence is not yet certain.) Note that passive *requests* (e.g. "Let a goose be brought to me.") do not take the form of wishes, but rather use a special imperative construction (§146).

Ex. 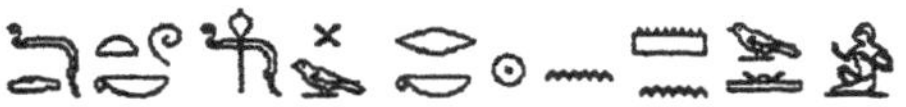

ḏd·tw·k ḥḏ[3] *rk n(y) mn*

May you be called: "The one who ended the time of pain." (Merikare 142)

Wishes, exhortations, and requests are found in recorded speech, e.g. in letters, prayers, etc. and as quotations within narratives.

§73. Prospective *sḏm·f* Forms In Other Main Clauses

The prospective *sḏm·f* forms are also used in sentences with the meaning "(one) is to (do)," "(one) is supposed to (do)," "(one) ought to (do)," or "(one) must (do)." These are never introduced by the particle *ỉw*. Polite requests may be introduced by the particle *ḥꜣ* or *ḥwy*, the latter often being followed by *ꜣ* "please." The particle *ỉḫ* + prospective form is also used in requests, particularly in requests made by a superior to a person of lower social status. Otherwise no introductory particle is used.

Exx.

[4]

msỉ·s m ꜣbd 1 prt, sw 15.

She is supposed to give birth on the first month of Winter, day 15. (West. 9, 15)

[3] *Ḥḏ*: a masc. sing. perfect (active) participle = "the one who ended" (§§ 117 ff.; 121, 2a.

[4] Note that the numbers for the day are written horizontally (§69).

ḏs·k ỉrf Ḥr-dd·f, sꜣ·ỉ, ỉnt{w}·k[5] *n·ỉ sw.*

Now, you, yourself, Hardedef, my son, are to bring him to me. (West. 7, 8)

ḥwy ꜣ wḏꜣ Ḥm·k r š n(y) pr-ʿꜣ, ʿnḫ(w), (w)ḏꜣ(w), s(nbw),
ʿpr(w)[6] *n·k bꜣw m nfr(w)t nb(w)t n(yw)t ḫnw ʿḥ·k*

Would your Majesty please go forth to the lake of the Palace, l.p.h., when a galley has been equipped for you with all the beautiful women of the inside of your palace. (West. 5, 1 ff.)

ỉḫ ỉn·t(w) n·n m sš sḏm·n st

(They)[7] are to be brought to us in writing so that (§74) we might hear them. (Peas. B, 80)

§74. Prospective *sḏm·f* Forms In Subordinate Clauses of Purpose and Result

The prospective *sḏm·f* forms are used without introductory particles or prepositions in subordinate clauses of purpose, and can be translated as "in order that one might do . . . ," or "(so) that one might / could / would do. . . ." The use is similar to *r* + infinitive (§57, 2), but the prospective forms were generally used when the subject was specified.

Ex. 

ỉw wpỉ·n·ỉ r·ỉ wšb·ỉ n·f

"I opened my mouth that I might reply to him."

The verb  *wnn* "to be" can be used in this construction in clauses with an adverbial comment.

Ex. 

ỉw pḥ·n·f pr·f wn·f ḥnʿ snw·f

He reached his home in order that he could be with his brothers.

The chief difficulty in distinguishing this construction from the circumstantial clause is that only in a few verbs is a distinctly written form used (i.e. 2nd geminating class verbs). When the correct prospective form—distinct from that of the circumstantial *sḏm·f*—occurs, then there is little problem, but otherwise one must rely on the meaning in context. Generally this is less difficult than might be thought. One must, however, ask the question: was the speaker or writer

[5]The scribe has written the prospective form of *ỉnỉ* as if it were the passive, but the intention was to indicate the *t* ending of the prospective in this verb.

[6]Most translators have taken this as an imperative "Equip for yourself . . . !" However, given the polite, deferential tone, the *sḏm(w)·f* passive (§35) in a circumstantial clause seems preferable.

[7]The subject has been left out since it was obvious. This is not common with subjects, but direct objects are not infrequently left out when the context was clear. (See §141.)

relating the circumstances contemporary to a certain action or specifying the motive for the action? E.g. the choice between "he went to town so that he might sell his leather goods" and "he went to town when he sold his leather goods" is not difficult in context.

Also, certain constructions favour the use of purpose clauses. For instance, they are particularly to be found in "explicatory sentences" which allowed the speaker to draw attention to such things as *why* actions were undertaken. (See §148.)

Closely related to purpose clauses—from the point of view of Egyptian grammar—are result clauses. They are, however, quite rare by comparison with purpose clauses. Result clauses do not relate intention on the part of the doer of the action, but rather the action resulting from a prior action or pre-existing situation. The use of the prospective in Egyptian implies a connection of the actions or situations. In English such clauses can be expressed through the conjunction "so" followed by the indicative: "The bridge has been completed, so we can cross over without making the detour." In other situations, English can use "then": "Be good to your chum, then he will treat you fairly." (This is different from the temporal or sequential use of "then": "I had dinner, then I had a cup of coffee.")

Ex.

ir[8] *qn·{n}k*[9] *dȝr ib·k, mḥ·k qni·k m ẖrdw·k, sn·k ḥmt·k, mȝ·k pr·k*

If you are brave, control your thoughts (literally "heart"), then you will fill your embrace with your children, then you will kiss your wife, and then you will see your house. (Sh. S. 133 ff.)

§75 Prospective *sḏm·f* Used to Form Noun Clauses

1) as the Object of Verbs of Speech, Perception, Causation The prospective forms were used in clauses that serve as direct objects to verbs of speech and perception. These correspond to the "that" clause of English: e.g. "He said that he would fight with me."[10]

Particularly to be noted is the extremely common use of the prospective after the verb "to give" (*rdi*), which has a **causative** meaning: "make (someone) do," "have (someone) do," or "let (someone) do." It corresponds to French *faire faire*, and German *tun lassen*. The *s*-causative stem (§27) is used only with certain verbs in Egyptian, and although existing *s*-causative forms remained in use, the function was being replaced by the use of *rdi* plus prospective.

Exx. 

di·i sḏm·k mitt iry

[8]The particle *ir* "if" introduces conditional sentences (§137 ff.).

[9]Verb forms ending in *n* are occasionally written as if the were *sḏm·n·f* forms. Here the superfluous *n* is indicated in braces.

[10]The underlined "that" clause here serves as the direct object of "said."

"Let me tell you something like it." (May I cause <u>that you hear the likeness thereof</u>.)[11]

ꜥḥꜥ·n[12] *rdi·n·f ini·tw n·f ḫt-ꜥꜣ*

"He had a *ḫt-ꜥꜣ*-bird brought to him." (He caused <u>that a *ḫt-ꜥꜣ*-bird be brought to him</u>.) (West. 8, 23 ff.)

2) Prospective Forms as the Object of Prepositions As a nominal form used in "that" clauses, a prospective form can also occur as the object of a preposition. Fairly common is the compound preposition *n mrwt* + prospective form "in order that" (lit. "for the love of"), and the preposition *r* "to," usually with the meaning "until," but also with the meaning "in order that" (purpose) or "so that ..." (result; purpose).[13] Purpose clauses without introductory prepositions (§74) are, however, much more common.

Less expected, but quite well attested is the use of the prospective after the compound prepositions "after," "when" and "after." The tense/mood normally associated with the prospective would seem to be lacking, but the selection of this form logically arises from its nominal nature.

The phrase *ḫr m-ḫt* + prospective *sḏm·f* "Now after he heard" can stand at the head of a sentence and introduces main clauses, including the narrative past-tense construction *ꜥḥꜥ·n sḏm·n·f* (§90). This counters the rule of adverbial modifiers occurring in sentence final position, but it is perhaps better to consider this a case of fronting a noun phrase.

Exx.

sḫm·k m mw r ḥtp ib·k

May you have access to water so that your heart might be satisfied. (Paheri, 5.)

iw rdi·n·f wi m imy-r kꜣwt n mrwt qd·i n·f mnw wr(w)

He appointed me as chief of construction in order that I might build great monuments for him. (§77)

(But the storm arose) 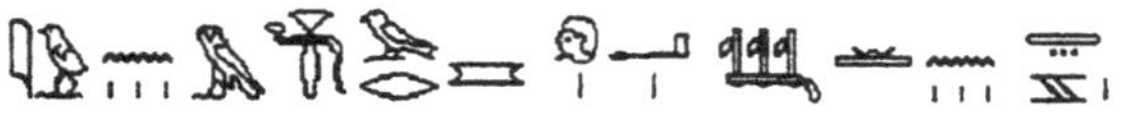

..., *iw·n m wꜣḏ wr, tp-ꜥ sꜣḥ·n tꜣ*

... while we were at sea, before we could reach land. (Sh. S. 32 ff.)

[11]The first verb form (*di·i*) is a prospective in a wish. *Sḏm·k*, also a prospective form, heads a clause serving as the direct object of *di·i*.

[12]The construction *ꜥḥꜥ·n sḏm·n·f* is a common literary past tense. See §90 ff.

[13]In English the distinction between result and purpose clauses is determined by verbal mood. "So that" + indicative mood indicates *result*; "(so) that + modal auxiliaries ("might," "would," "could") indicates *purpose*.

mꜣ[14] *wỉ r-sꜣ sꜣḥ·ỉ tꜣ, r sꜣ mꜣ·ỉ dpt·n·ỉ*[15]
See me—after I had reached land and after I had seen what I had experienced! (Sh. S. 179 ff.)

ḥr m-ḫt spr·f r Ḏdỉ, ꜥḥꜥ·n wꜣḥ(w) pꜣ qniw
Now after he reached Djedi, the palanquin was set down. (West. 7, 13–14)

3) Prospective Forms as the Subject of Verbs

The prospective forms could even be used to start "that" clauses that could serve as the subject of a sentence. In the following example, the noun phrase *swꜥb·k pꜣ r-pr n(y) ꜣbḏw* serves as the subject of a *sḏm(w)·f* passive verb.

mk wḏ(w)[16] *swꜥb·k pꜣ r-pr n(y) ꜣbḏw*
"See it has been commanded that you purify the temple of Abydos." (*Lesest.* 76, 6–7)

§76 The Adjective Verb

The term "adjective verb" is used of adjectival roots that are used as verbal forms. In other words, the root is primarily used as an adjective, but the same root is also conjugated as a verb. The adjective verb only occurs in some verb forms. Fairly common is the use of the prospective adjective verb in various uses: wishes "may you be happy of heart"; in the causative construction after *rdỉ* "caused that Her Majesty be great"; in purpose clauses "in order that it be splendid."

Other verb forms of the adjective verb include the imperative (commands, §145) "be happy" and the stative (§82) "the eyes have become dim." The negative equivalent of the predicate adjective uses a verbal conjugation (§106). Adjectival roots were not, however, used in the circumstantial *sḏm·f* and related forms in statements of fact—for this the predicate adjective construction was used.

§77. The Expressions *Rdỉ m* & *Rdỉ r* "To Appoint"

The verb *rdỉ* has as one of its many meanings "to appoint" when used in conjunction with the *m* of predication or the *r* of futurity. The literal meaning is something along the lines of "to place in (the capacity of)" and "to place to serve (in the future) as." With *m* one can translate "appointed

[14]*Mꜣ* is the imperative (§145).
[15]*Dpt·n·ỉ* is the fem. sing. *sḏm(w)·n·f* relative form (§§157, 161) "what I had experienced."
[16]*Wḏ(w)* is the *sḏm(w)·f* passive. The "subject" of this passive form is the whole nominal clause beginning with *swꜥb·k* "that you purify the temple...." English requires an impersonal construction with "it" as a dummy subject. The Egyptian is literally: "that you purify the temple has been commanded."

as" and with *r* one can render "appointed to be" or "appointed to serve as."[17]

Ex. 
mk rdỉ·n tw Ḥm·f m ỉmy-r pr wr
See, His Majesty has appointed you as the chief steward.

ỉw rdỉ(w)·f r sš nsw
He was appointed (to serve) as a royal scribe.

§78. Demonstrative Adjectives and Qualifiers

In addition to the common  *pn* and  *tn* "this" (occasionally "that"), there were several other demonstrative adjectives in use. The plural demonstrative of the *pn*, *tn* series is 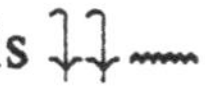 *nn n(y)* "these." *Nn n(y)* precedes the noun that it modifies. *Nn* is actually a pronoun ("this," "these"). In Middle Egyptian it is followed by the genitival adjective *n(y)*, but in later times *n(y)* was dropped. *Nn* is invariable in gender. E.g.  *nn n(y) rnp(w)t* "these years." Note that when another adjective is used in conjunction with *tn* and *pn*, this adjective follows the demonstrative adjective. The pronoun *nn* can be used on its own meaning "this":  *ỉw ḏd·n·f n·ỉ nn* "He told me this."

There was also a series of demonstratives expressing "that (over there)," "those," etc.: masc.  *pf* (var.  *pf3*,  *pfy)* and fem.  *tf* (var.  *tf3*). E.g.  *hrw pf* "that day,"  *ḫ3st tf* "that foreign land." The plural form (corresponding to *nn n(y)* "these") is  *nf n(y)* "those." E.g.  *nf n(y) ḫftỉw* "those" enemies. The *pf*, *tf*, *nf n(y)* series was often used to distance the speaker from what was being mentioned. I.e. "that (despicable) fiend" or "that (awesome) day." For this reason, the *pn*, *tn*, and *nn n(y)* series was sometimes used in cases where English would prefer "that" rather than "this." *Pf* and *tf* precede other adjectives, as with *pn* and *tn*.

The series  (var. , hieratic: ) *p3*,  *t3*,  *n3 n(y)* (later just  *n3*) also means "this," but already in the spoken language it was coming to represent the definite article "the." In literary texts it usually is a demonstrative, but in everyday documents (e.g. legal documents), they are regularly the definite article. All three of the series are placed *before* the noun: e.g.  *p3 pr* "this/the house";  *t3 ḥwt-nṯr* "this/the temple"; 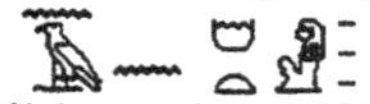 *n3 n(y) ḥm(w)t* "these/the women." Rarely  *n3* is used on its own meaning "these (ones)" and even with a non-plural meaning "this (one)."

A much rarer set of demonstrative pronouns is also encountered in religious, magical, and other such texts: masc.  *pwy* and fem.  *twy* "this." These are used as adjectives following the noun that they modify. Also encountered in these texts are the archaic demonstratives 

[17]The use of *r* corresponds exactly to that of its Hebrew cognate לְ (*lᵊ*) "to" in the expression לְ שִׂים (*śīm lᵊ-*) + office "to appoint as."

pw,  *tw*, and  *nw* "this, these," which also follow the noun.

number:	Singular		Plural
gender:	masculine	feminine	common
"This"	 (noun) *pn*	 (noun) *tn*	 *nn n(y)* (noun)

number:	Singular		Plural
gender:	masculine	feminine	common
"That"	 (noun) *pf*	 (noun) *tf*	 *nf n(y)* (noun)

number:	Singular		Plural
gender:	masculine	feminine	common
"This"/"The"	 *p3* (noun)	 *t3* (noun)	 *n3 n(y)* (noun)

§79. Noun Phrases as Adverbial Modifiers

Nouns and noun phrases may be used as adverbial modifiers (but not as adverbial comment/predicates in non-verbal sentences [§10]). Some are quite obvious, e.g.  (var. ) *rꜥ nb* "every day." In these cases a preposition is not required in the Egyptian, although a preposition may be required in translation.

Ex. 

bin·wy n s nb hrw pf n(y) snd

How bad (it will be) for every man on that day of fear!

§80. Expressions for "Complete" "Entire"

Certain adverbial phrases had rather idiomatic uses. Very frequent is the use of  *r ḏr·f* "to its limits / borders" (from the word  *ḏrw* "limit, border) in the phrase  *m t3 pn r ḏr·f* "in this land in its entirety," or "in this entire land." It is also used in other contexts, e.g.  *iw sꜥnḫ·n·i niwt·i r ḏr·s* "I kept my city in its entirety alive (during the drought)." The suffix pronoun attached to *ḏr* agrees in gender and number with the antecedent.

The phrase  *mi qd·f* also can be translated "in its entirety" or "entire." E.g.  *ḥwt·f tn mi qd·s* "that entire estate of his."

Another similar expression is  *r 3w·f* "to its length," but figuratively "in its entirety." Sometimes it is used without suffix pronoun:  *r 3w* "to the (maximum) length" = "in their entirety." E.g. 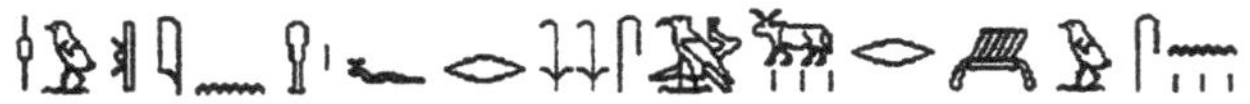 *wḏ·in*[18] *Ḥm·f r nn sm3w r 3w·sn* "Then His Majesty proclaimed concerning these wild bulls in their entirety..." (*Rb.* 66, 5–6)  *msw·sn r 3w* "their offspring in their entirety" (*Rb.* 59, 11).

§81. Compound Prepositions

Egyptian compound prepositions are by and large bound constructions consisting of preposition + noun, e.g.  *ḥr-tp* "on top of." Students should become familiar with the compound prepositions introduced in this section. Others can be learned as they arise. These compounds are almost all listed in the dictionary, and they are often listed under the second element (e.g.  *m-ḫt* "after," "following," "behind";  *m-b3ḥ* "in the presence of," etc.), but also under the first element (e.g. 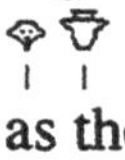 *ḥr-ib* "in the middle of,  *ḥr-tp*, etc.). A number of these use parts of the human body as the second element:

 *ḫft ḥr* "before the face of," "in front of"

 *m-ᶜ* "in the hand," "in the possession of," "by the hand of," "with" (a person), "because of," "from the hand of" (i.e. a letter)

,  *m-b3ḥ* "before," "in the presence of" (important people and gods)

Other important compounds include:

 *m-m* "among" (people)

 *m-ḥ3t* "in front of," "before" (temporally and spatially)

 *m-ḥr* "before (a person)," "in (one's) sight"

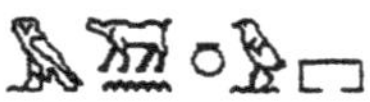 *m-ẖnw* "inside" (literally "in the interior")

 *m-s3* "after," "in the back of"

 *r-s3* + infinitive "after" (doing something), and with nouns "behind, after"

 *m-q3b*[19] "in the midst of" (people, places, things)

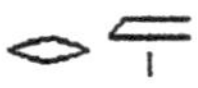 *r-gs* "beside," "at the side of," "next to"

Nisba adjectives can be formed from compound prepositions. The *nisba* adjective endings are placed on the preposition (the first element) and the second element remains unchanged. Only the *nisba* adjective is declined by gender and number (cf. English "passers by").

From  *m-ḥ3t* "before" is  *imy-ḥ3t* (pl. *imyw-ḥ3t*) "former," "previous," "which was before."

[18]This is the literary *sḏm·in·f* "Then he heard..." (§131).

[19]The phrase is cognate to the Semitic *b-qrb*, cf. esp. Hebrew בְּקֶרֶב (*bᵊqereḇ*) "in the midst of." In both language families the expression involves *qrb* "inner parts," "intestines."

From  *m-ḫt* "after" is  *imy-ḫt* "one who will come after," pl. *imyw-ḫt* "those of later times," "future generations."

From  *ḥr-tp* "upon" is  *ḥry-tp* "who / which is upon," "chief," and as a noun, "headman," "master."

Such *nisba* adjectives function as ordinary adjectives, and thus follow the nouns they modify, or stand alone as nouns in their own right (§21). Although in one or two cases *nisba* adjectives can serve as predicate adjectives (§44), this is not the case with those derived from compound prepositions. The meanings of the derived *nisba* adjectives are sometimes not quite what one expects, and these must be learned as separate vocabulary items. E.g. 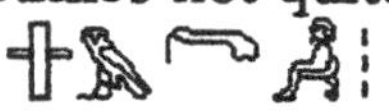 *imyw-bꜣḥ*, which in addition to meaning "(those) who are in the presence (of a god)," also means "ancestors."

VOCABULARY VII

 *iꜣbty* (a *nisba* adjective) "eastern"

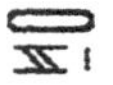 *iw* "island" Cf. Hebrew אִי (*ʾî*) "island"; "coast"

 *ifd* "to flee"

 *iry-pꜥt* "hereditary nobleman" (This is an abbreviated writing. *Iry* is the *nisba* adjective of *r* = "one belonging to" and the *pꜥt* was the social stratum of the nobility usually translated "the patricians.")

 *irf* "then," "now" (a particle, often left untranslated)

 *ꜥ* "condition," "state" (e.g. of a person's health)

 *ꜥntiw* "myrrh"

 *wꜣḏ-wr* "the sea" (lit. "the great green one") for  *wꜣḏ* "green," "fresh," cf. Semitic *wrq* "green," "foliage" e.g. Hebrew יֶרֶק (*yereq*) "green"; Arabic ورق (*wariq*) "green," "verdant"; cf. also Egyptian  *iꜣqt* "vegetables," "greens"

 *wnn* (irregular 2nd gem. verb) "to be"

 *wr* (adjective) "great"; as noun  "great one"; "ruler (of a foreign land)"

 *pḥ* "to reach" (a place, person as direct object) not a verb of motion

 *m* (preposition) with verbs of motion, e.g. come "from," go "out of," etc., but also enter "into" (the meaning depends very much upon the verb used—most major uses are noted in the dictionaries)

 *mšꜥ* "soldiers, troops, army"; "crew, gang";  "military expedition" ,  *mt* "to die," "to perish" (ships); noun masc. "death" (Cf. Semitic *mwt* "to die.")

nsw (not *swtn*!) "king" Note: this word derives from a *nisba* compound: *n(y)-swt* "He who belongs to the *swt*-reed." (The *swt*-reed was a symbol of Upper Egypt.)

nsw-bỉty "King of Upper and Lower Egypt"

ḥ3ty-ꜥ "count" (a regional governor, mayor)

ḥwỉ "to beat," "strike"; "tread" (on a road); verbal adjective: *ḥwy* "well-trodden," "beaten" (path)[20]

ḥwt "estate," "large building"; *ḥwt-nṯr* "temple"

ḥkn verbal adjective: "(he who is) praised"

ḥḏ "silver"

ḫ3ꜥ "to throw down," "cast aside," "abandon (property)"

ḫntw "outside"

ẖnw "interior"; "home"; "royal city," "the Residence"

ẖr(y) qnỉ "porter" ("he who is under the baggage")

ẖrt-nṯr "necropolis"

s3 "back," *m-s3* "behind," "at the back of," *r-s3* "behind, after" (+ infinitive or prospective *sḏm·f*— "after hearing" or "after he heard/has heard/had heard")

, *s3ḥ* "arrive," "reach"; with *t3* as direct object: "to land" (from a ship), "to reach land"

sꜥq (*s*-causative of a bi-consonental verb—see §57, 1) "to cause / make to enter," "to send in"

sbỉ "to send (a person)" (but *not* letters); "to lead," "accompany" (someone) *n* "to (a person)," *r* "to (a place)"

sn "brother," *snt* "sister"

snb "recovery" (from illness)

snḏ verb "to fear"; noun "fear"

ṯ3w "wind"; "breath," *ṯ3w ꜥnḫ* "the breath of life / life-giving breath"

dỉ ꜥnḫ, ḏd, w3s "given life, stability, and dominion" (an exclamation used after the mention of the king's nomen, see §69; the verb form of *dỉ* will be presented in §121, 2b)

dp "to taste"; "to experience"

ḏs· "~self" requires suffixes: *ḏs·f* "himself," *ḏs·s* "herself," *ḏs·k* "yourself," etc. (The words formed with *ḏs·* are emphatic and are not used for the simple

[20]The water determinative is "borrowed" from a related word meaning "to surge up."

reflexive. I.e. the sense is like French *moi-même* "me–myself" and not "myself" as in "I saw myself in the mirror.")

Welcoming Death: This is a poem (ca. 1990–1850 B.C.E.) about a man for whom life has been painful. A couple of minor corrections have been made and one line has been omitted. Consult the dictionary for the new words. A few forms that have not yet been learned are indicated in footnotes—follow the supplied translations; these forms and their uses will be learned in due course.

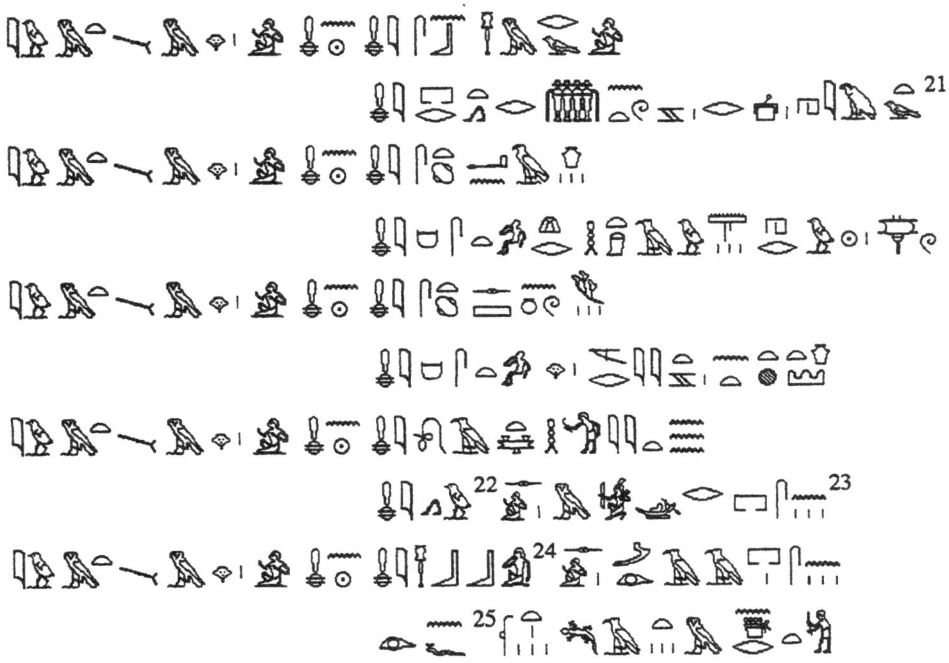

EXERCISE VII

(A) Memorize the bi-consonantal signs:

With *t* as the second consonant:

mt *mt/mwt* *ḫt* *st*

[21] The last word in this line is to be read *ỉḥmt* (graphic transposition).

[22] *Ỉw* is a "second tense" form (§§147, 150) and is translated "how [the subject] returns" (or "the way [the subject] returns").

[23] Egyptian is less consistent with the agreement of number and person: "their house" is used because it is the house of the man's family, as well.

[24] This is the second tense form of *ꜣbỉ*: "how [the subject] desires / longs."

[25] *Ỉrỉ* also has the meaning "to spend (time)."

With *d* as the second consonant:

 *šd*[26]  *qd*  *dd*

With *ḏ* as the second consonant:

 *ꜥḏ* *wḏ*  *nḏ*  *ḥḏ*

(B) Transliterate and translate. Consult the dictionary for a few new words and expressions.

1) 

2) 

3) 

4) 

5)  [29]

6) 

7) 

8) 

9) 

10) 

[26]To be distinguished from  *mḥ* primarily by the two prongs at the left end.

[27]The Golden Horus name is placed *before* the Golen Horus sign, in this text. The name is to be read *Ḥrw-mꜣꜥ*. (This is not a case of transposition.)

[28]Read the foreign land signs as *smwt* "deserts" in this title.

[29]The town boundaries had become confused during a period of upheaval. In Egyptian the idea of distinguishing one thing "from" another is expressed with the preposition *r* "to." Egyptian tends to be elliptical in making comparisons, e.g. Egyptian gets by with "their hearts were braver than lions," whereas English requires a second genitive "than (the hearts of) lions," or "than those of lions." (In other words, in Egyptian one *can* compare "apples and oranges!") Here translate "its boundary from (that of) another town." The repetition of *niwt* … *niwt* conveys the idea of "one" and "another."

(C) Parse from *(B)*:

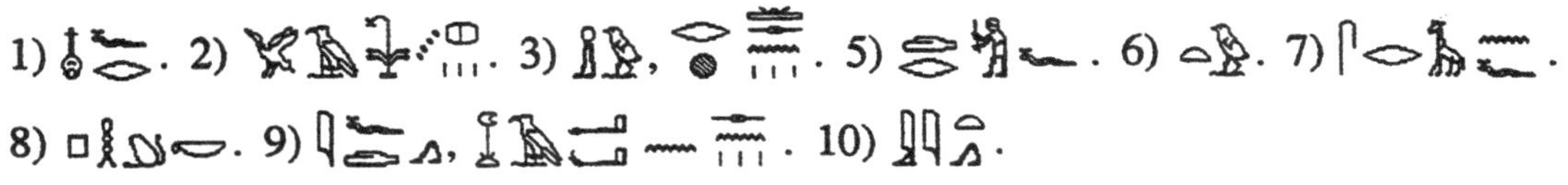

(D) Translate into Egyptian:

1) May you return in safety, having carried out ("done") all the commands of the vizier.
2) You are to write ("send") to me in order to let me know (literally "to cause that I learn") your condition (and) the condition of your brother.
3) May that vile enemy flee after finding them(selves)[30] in the presence our Lord.
4) His majesty commanded that this expedition be undertaken (literally "be done") in order to place fear in the hearts of those foreigners.
5) His might is greater (*ꜥꜣ*) than (that of) any former king in this entire land. (§§44, 49)

[30] This is simply the direct object in Egyptian. Do not use *ḏs·* "(one)self." The Egyptian *ḏs·* is quite emphatic, and does not serve as a "reflexive" pronoun.

LESSON 8

§82. The Stative

The Egyptian stative verb forms (also known as the "old perfective" and in old books also called the "pseudo-participle") do not form part of the suffix conjugation. The stative is, however, related in form to the West Semitic "perfect" and is especially close to the Akkadian stative in both form and function. The stative focuses on the result of an action (a state) and not on the action itself. With verbs of motion the idea is that a person "has arrived," or "has gone out," etc. With other intransitive verbs, the actor is associated with the result of the action: for instance the stative form of the verb *ꜥḥꜥ* "to stand up" conveys the sense that the person "is standing" (i.e. having stood up, the actor is now standing). It often indicates a condition: "fallen into ruins."

With transitive verbs, apart from *rḫ* "to learn" (§89), the stative indicates that the person or thing has undergone the action, and is translated as a passive in English (although in Egyptian it was not considered a "passive" form): "clogged up," "having been removed," "is open," "has been equipped with," etc.

Many adjectives can be used as verbs (mostly as the prospective *sḏm·f*, imperatives (§145), and the stative forms). When "adjective verbs" are used in the stative, they indicate the state or condition of something "was hungry," "awake," "is glorious." One can often translate "has become . . . ," and this is the best translation, when it is possible.

Note that the stative forms are *adverbial* in their grammatical function. In particular they often occur in the same sentence types as those involving *ḥr* + infinitive. E.g. *ỉw·f ḥr prt* "He is going out." *ỉw·f pr(w)* "He has gone out." The two constructions are known collectively as the "pseudo-verbal construction," an unfortunate, but widely used, term. Being adverbial, however, they also occur wherever one expects the grammatical category of "adverbial."

§83. The Stative Endings

Unlike the suffix conjugation, where the subject of the verb—when a pronoun—is indicated by the use of the suffix pronouns, the stative involves different endings depending on the person, gender, and number. These endings do not serve as the subject of the stative forms, and in fact it is best not to think of a subject–predicate relationship, but rather an "antecedent–modifier" relationship. The endings are as follows:

TABLE 9: THE STATIVE ENDINGS

		Common Gender	Masculine	Feminine
Singular	1st Pers.	~*kwi*		
	2nd Pers.	~*ti* , *t(i)*		
	3rd Pers.		~*w* , Ø	~*ti* , *t(i)*

		Common Gender	Masculine	Feminine
Plural	1st Pers.	~*wyn*		
	2nd Pers.	~*tiwny*		
	3rd Pers.	~*w* , Ø		

The writing of the 1st sing. ending is occasionally written in variant forms: , , , , and . The endings are normally written after the determinatives, but the 2nd pers. and 3rd fem. sing. forms may be written with *t* placed before the determinative. The *w* of the 3rd pers. masc. (sing. and common pl.)—when it occurs—is also written before the determinative. More frequent is zero-ending. Quite rarely the 3rd. masc. forms (sing. and pl.) have a *y* ending.

§84. The Stative Form Stem

The stative forms normally do not exhibit gemination in any of the mutable roots. There are a few examples of stative forms with geminated stems, but these are mostly late, and in medical and mathematical texts. The normal forms by verb class are as follows:

3rd Weak: no gemination— *h3i·kwi*, sometimes with *y* in place of ·*w*: *h3·y*

2nd Gem.: no gemination— *qb·(w)*

***ii* / *iw*:** both roots are used, *ii·t(i)*, *iw·(w)*

***ini*:** *ini·ti*

***wnn*:** no gemination— *wn(w)*

***m33*:** no gemination— *m3(w)*

***rdi*:** mostly with *r*: *rdi·k(w)i*, but also without *r*: *di·t(i)*

§85. Stative as Adverbial Comment ("Pseudo-verbal Construction")

Since the stative functions grammatically as an adverb, it can serve as the comment in non-verbal sentences with adverbial comment that are usually—but not always—introduced by *iw* or *mk*. Sentences beginning with a noun (and not introduced by *ỉw* or *mk*) that are followed by the stative are well attested. Grammatically, the construction is identical to: *mk sw m pr* "look, he is in the house" / *ỉw·f ḥr wnm* "he is eating," but the comment consists of the stative form and word(s) associated with it (i.e. it is not part of a prepositional phrase). The stative forms do not indicate tense (except that the action is over and resulted in a particular state or condition). Note the word order carefully. The structure is essentially presentation of the topic *followed* by the adverbial comment (here, the stative). It is incorrect from the point of view of Egyptian grammar to call the sentence topic, whether a noun or pronoun the "subject" of the stative form. It is rather the antecedent, with which the stative form must agree in gender and number.

Note that adjectives can be used as statives in this construction. They can be translated as "has become weak," "have gone deaf," etc.

Exx.

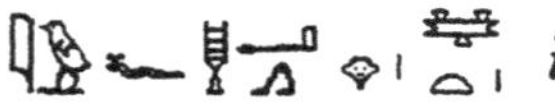 *ỉw·f ꜥḥꜥ(w) ḥr wꜣt*

He was standing on the road. (Having gotten up he was therefore "standing.")

mk ms[1] *sy šm·tỉ r ḏd: ỉw·ỉ r šmt wṯs·ỉ*

But look, she went off saying: "I will go so I can make an accusation." (West. 12, 22 ff.)

tnỉ ḫpr(w), ỉꜣw hꜣw ... ỉrty nḏsw ꜥnḫwy ỉmrw (main clause without *ỉw*)

Old age has arrived; the senior years have descended.... The eyes have become feeble and the ears have gone deaf. (Ptaḥ-ḥ. 1, 4 ff.)

ỉw·s mḥ·tỉ ḥr ḥtp(w)t ḏfꜣw

It (a tomb) is full of offerings and provisions. (*Lesest.* 87, 5)

§86. The Stative in Circumstantial Clauses

As expected, the particles *ỉw* and *mk* are not used. And as always with the stative forms, there must be an antecedent (a noun or pronoun). The antecedent may be part of the preceding clause, or, if a noun, it may stand at the head of the circumstantial clause (without *ỉw*, of course). Note that with verbs of motion, the sense regularly corresponds to a simple past tense in English (i.e. the stative sense is impossible to render in English): e.g. *...~ỉ, šm·kwỉ r Ḫnw* "... me, when I went to the royal city" and not necessarily "when I had gone to the royal city."

Circumstantial clauses with the stative are somewhat vague with regard to time and sequence of events, as opposed to the circumstantial *sḏm·f* and *sḏm·n·f* forms, which provide precise

[1]*Ms* is an enclitic particle that is usually translated as "surely," "indeed," but whose meaning is not exactly certain. Gardiner, *EG* §251 maintained that it expressed surprise that some thought or statement had been overlooked by the person addressed.

information concerning the time and sequence of events. Thus, the action expressed by the stative may be subsequent to that of the main verb and *not* prior to it.

Ex.

ỉw pḥ·n·f wỉ ꜥḥꜥ·kwỉ ḥr wꜣt

He reached me as I was standing on the road.

In this case the antecedent is the dependent pronoun *wỉ* "me," with which the stative form agrees in person and number. If the antecedent is not mentioned in the preceding clause, it must be supplied at the head of the circumstantial clause before the stative form.

Ex.

ỉw grt·k[2] *mt·(tỉ), rn·k ꜥnḫ(w)*

Now, you are dead, but your name is alive. (*Lebensm.* 36–37)

The circumstantial clause begins with *rn·k* "your name," which is the antecedent of the stative form *ꜥnḫ(w)* "lives" or "is alive." (In the actual context—a debate between two living entities—one might better translate: "Now you might be dead (i.e. at some point in the future), but your name will live on." The idea of mood ["might be"] and tense ["will live"] are not conveyed by the stative forms, but the context suggests these notions.)

In meaning, circumstantial clauses employing the stative of transitive verbs (those that take a direct object) are fairly close to those employing the *sḏm(w)·f* passive, and the translations may end up almost identical. These two types of circumstantial clause are, however, easily distinguished by word order. The stative requires an antecedent (either within the main clause, or, as fairly common, supplied in the circumstantial clause itself). The *sḏm(w)·f* passive, on the other hand, requires a subject that follows it. The word order is therefore as follows:

With Stative

NOUN/PRONOUN + VERBAL FORM (Look for stative endings)

With Sḏm(w)·f *Passive*

VERBAL FORM + NOUN (If a suffix pronoun follows, it cannot be stative.)

[2]The particle *grt* often means "moreover," "also." Here the 2nd. masc. sing. suffix pronoun is attached to it, but this is not at all common.

The following example illustrates the Egyptian inclination to multiply circumstantial clauses! Circumstantial clauses of all types may be freely intermixed, as will be seen in this example.

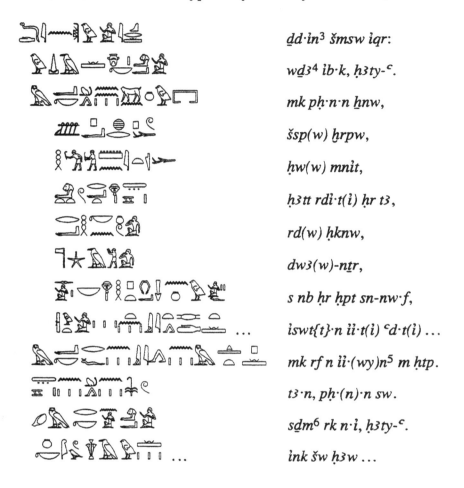

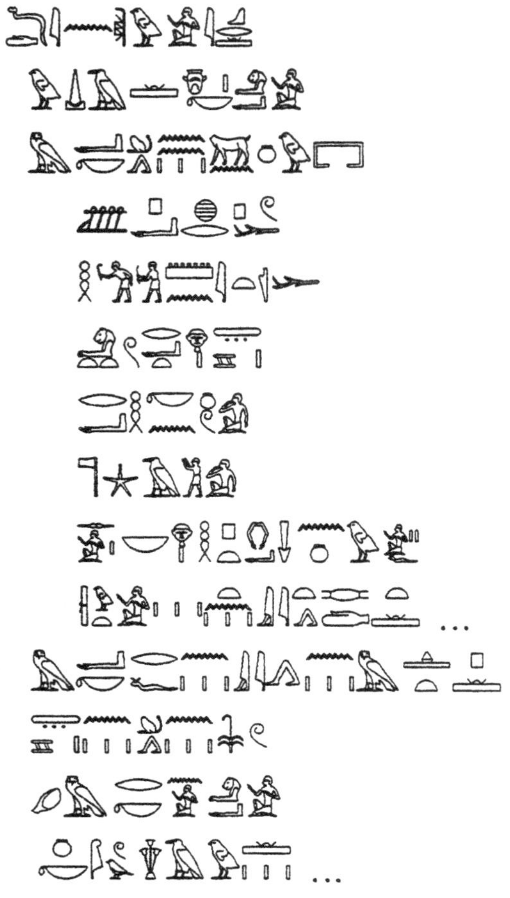

ḏd·ỉn[3] *šmsw ỉqr:*
wḏꜣ[4] *ỉb·k, ḥꜣty-ꜥ.*
mk pḥ·n·n ẖnw,
šsp(w) ḫrpw,
ḥw(w) mnỉt,
ḥꜣtt rdỉ·t(ỉ) ḥr tꜣ,
rd(w) ḥknw,
dwꜣ(w)-nṯr,
s nb ḥr ḥpt sn-nw·f,
ỉswt{t}·n ỉỉ·t(ỉ) ꜥḏ·t(ỉ) ...
mk rf n ỉỉ·(wy)n[5] *m ḥtp.*
tꜣ·n, pḥ·(n)·n sw.
sḏm[6] *rk n·ỉ, ḥꜣty-ꜥ.*
ỉnk šw ḥꜣw ...

Then the trusty retainer said: Cheer up, governor. See, we have reached home, the mallet having been taken up, and the mooring post having been driven in, the bow-warp having been placed on land, praise having been given, and thanks having been given, while every man was embracing his mate, our crew having arrived safely ... Now look, we have returned in safety. Our land—we have reached it! Now listen to me, governor. I am one who is free of exaggeration ... (Shipwrecked Sailor 1–13—*To be continued in the reading passage.*)

§87. The Stative as Modifier of Nouns

Just as circumstantial clauses can modify nouns (e.g. relative clause with undefined antecedent

[3] This is a narrative *sḏm·ỉn·f* form (§131) that indicates sequence.
[4] This is the imperative (command) form (§145) of the adjective-verb. Literally "Be cheerful of heart."
[5] If this is not a stative defectively written, then the sentence must be an explicatory sentence (§148), in which the speaker would be focusing on the notion of safety.
[6] An imperative form.

§38), so too can stative forms (and phrases or clauses involving stative forms) be used to modify nouns. E.g. *šmꜥw ḥḏ(w)* "damaged Upper Egyptian barley" (i.e. "U.E. barley that has become damaged"); *ḥr wrryt·f bꜣk·tỉ m nbw* "upon his chariot worked with gold" (or "wrought with gold"—i.e. gold-plated), *dpt mḥ·t(ỉ) m mw* "a boat full of water" (i.e. "a boat that has become full of water"). This use is quite commonplace in Egyptian. Note that the modified antecedent can also be a pronoun: *m-ḫt gmt·f ḏbꜣ(w) m ỉnrw* "after it was found blocked up with stones" or "after finding it blocked up with stones."

Also very common is the use of the stative to describe the direct object of verbs meaning "to find," "to see," and "to cause." For example, *gm·n·ỉ st wp(w)* "I found them open." (The explicatory sentence §148, literally "how I found them was open.")

§88. Past-time Sentences with Verbs of Motion

It was stated in §31 that the construction *ỉw sḏm·n·f* (*ỉw / mk* + circumstantial *sḏm·n·f*) was not used with verbs of motion. The corresponding construction uses the stative in the "pseudo-verbal" construction: *ỉw·f pr(w)* "He went out"; *mk sy šm·tỉ* "See, she has gone." Note that these sentences can be translated by either the English simple past tense "went out" or the perfect "has come," depending on the context. Egyptian literary narrative texts generally use a different (but related) construction (§92).

Exx.

mk wi ỉỉ·kwi

See, I have come! (West. 8, 12)

mt Sꜣ-nht ỉw(w) m ꜥꜣm

Here is Sinuhe having come as an Asiatic! (Sinuhe B264–65)

§89. "To Know"

The verb *rḫ* means "to learn," "to find out." To express the idea "to know," Egyptians used mostly the stative (but also the past tense) of *rḫ* (i.e. "being in the state of having learned" = "to know"). Fairly common is the use of the infinitive as the direct object of *rḫ*, and the meaning is regularly "to know how (to do something)."

Exx.

ỉw·ỉ rḫ·kwỉ ṯn, rḫ·kwỉ rnw·ṯn

I know you, and I know your names. (BD 125)

dỉ·k m3·n sy. mk n rḫ·wyn smsy[7]

You should let us see her. You see, we know how to deliver (a woman in childbirth). (West. 10, 5)

§90. The Narrative Past Tense Construction:

ꜥḥꜥ·n sḏm·n·f

A very common past tense construction in narrative texts of all types is the basic construction *ꜥḥꜥ·n sḏm·n·f*. The verb *ꜥḥꜥ* (without the walking legs determinative) probably derives from the verb meaning "to stand up, arise," and the original sense may have been something like: "and so it arose..." In practice, it was simply used as an auxiliary verb. The construction is never preceded by the particles *iw* or *mk*. The particular verb form of *ꜥḥꜥ·n* will be dealt with in §153. The verb form occurring after *ꜥḥꜥ·n* is the circumstantial *sḏm·n·f*. This can be ascertained since a variety of circumstantial clauses occur in this position. Intransitive verbs of motion use a variation of this construction (§92). Only very rarely is the subject placed after *ꜥḥꜥ·n*, a pronominal subject is then placed on the following circumstantial *sḏm·n·f*.

It is important to take note of the fact that the elements following *ꜥḥꜥ·n* are always adverbial. They can therefore consist of such things as circumstantial verb forms, progressive *ḥr* + infinitive, and stative constructions. Not all adverbials, however, can follow *ꜥḥꜥ·n*: only phrases containing some form of a verb are permissible. For example, non-verbal clauses with adverbial comment (e.g. topic + *m pr*) cannot occur here.

Exx.

ꜥḥꜥ·n sḏm·n·ỉ ḫrw qri
I heard the sound of thunder. (Sh.S. 55, ff.)

ꜥḥꜥ·n rdỉ·n sr wḏt m ḥr·ỉ m ḏd mk wḏ(w)[8] *swꜥb·k pȝ r-pr n(y) 3bḏw*
The official brought the order to my attention[9] saying: "See it has been commanded that you purify the temple of Abydos." (*Lesest.* 76, 6–7)

ꜥḥꜥ·n Rdḏdt wꜥb·n·s m wꜥb n(y) hrw 14
Redjedet purified (herself) with a purification of 14 days. (West. 11, 18 f.)

---

[7] Infinitives of many *s*-causatives derived from 3rd weak roots do not have *t* (§170).

[8] *Wḏ(w)* is the *sḏm(w)·f* passive. The "subject" of this passive form is the whole nominal clause beginning with *swꜥb·k* "that you purify the temple...." English requires an impersonal construction with "it" as a dummy subject. The Egyptian is literally: "that you purify the temple has been commanded."

[9] Note the vivid expression *rdỉ m ḥr* "to put in (one's) face," which means "command," "call someone's attention to."

§91. The Past Tense Passive Voice Construction:
ꜥḥꜥ·n sḏm(w)·f Passive

The passive counterpart of the *ꜥḥꜥ·n sḏm·n·f* construction uses the *sḏm(w)·f* passive (§35). There is nothing particularly remarkable about the construction, other than the fact that the subject is virtually always a noun and not a suffix pronoun. There are cases of an impersonal use with omitted subject, e.g. "(It) was done according to . . .".

Exx.

ꜥḥꜥ·n mꜣ(w) nꜣ n(y) kꜣwt

These construction projects were inspected. (*Lesest.* 76, 15)

ꜥḥꜥ·n rdỉ(w) ꜥḥꜥ n·f qꜣqꜣ 2 ḥnꜥ ỉst·sn

Two ships and their crews were provided to him. (Lit. it was caused that two ships . . . attend to him.) (West. 8, 4)

ꜥḥꜥ·n ỉr(w) mỉ wḏt[10] *nbt Ḥm·f*

It was done in accordance with all that His Majesty had commanded. (Impersonal construction) (West. 5, 13)

§92. The Stative in *ꜥḥꜥ·n·f šm(w)* with Verbs of Motion

This is the construction used with intransitive verbs of motion. Since the stative forms must have an antecedent (whether a noun or a pronoun), *ꜥḥꜥ·n* always takes a subject in this construction. The stative form, of course, agrees with the subject of *ꜥḥꜥ·n* in person and number (and gender if applicable).

In some texts the 1st sing. suffix pronoun is frequently omitted after *ꜥḥꜥ·n*. This is probably an abbreviated writing—i.e. *ꜥḥꜥ·n·(i)* or *ꜥḥꜥ·n·<i>*[11]—rather than being a distinct construction.

Note that verbs of motion in this construction must generally be translated as simple past tense forms in English (cf. §86), since English does not have a true stative.

Exx.

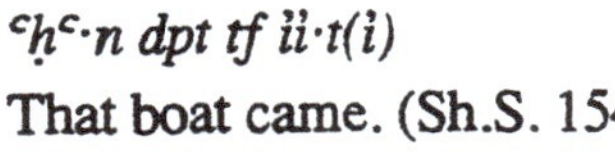

ꜥḥꜥ·n dpt tf ỉỉ·t(i)

That boat came. (Sh.S. 154 f.)

[10]This is a fem. relative form (§158) used as a noun with *Ḥm·f* as subject: "what His Majesty had commanded." These forms will be dealt with at a later time.

[11]The "angle" brackets are for mistakes of omission.

ꜥḥꜥ·n·i šm·kw(i) ḥnꜥ·f
I went with him. (*Lesest.* 76, 6)

§93. The Progressive Past Tense: ꜥḥꜥ·n·f ḥr sḏm

This variation on the pattern is not terribly common, but it is quite straightforward. Its structure is grammatically identical to that presented in §92, only here the adverbial phrase consists of a prepositional phrase rather than the stative.

Ex.

ꜥḥꜥ·n·i ḥr i̓ꜣš n mšꜥ
I was calling out to the crew. (Sh. S. 170)

§94. The Stative in ꜥḥꜥ·n·f rd̩i(w): Quasi-Passives & States

This construction could be used with transitive verbs to form a quasi-passive. With intransitive verbs, the notion conveyed is of a state or the result of the action. Here again, the 1st. sing. suffix is sometimes not written after ꜥḥꜥ·n, although it was presumably supplied by the reader.

Exx.

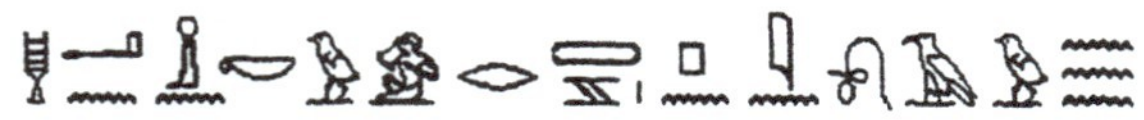

ꜥḥꜥ·n·(i) i̓ni·kwi r i̓w pn in wꜣw
I was brought to this island by a wave. (Sh.S. 109 f.)

ꜥḥꜥ·n·s gr·ti
She became motionless (not rowing). (West. 5, 17)

§95. ꜥḥꜥ·n sḏm·n·f with following Parallel Clauses

Frequently, one or more *parallel* circumstantial clauses (often employing the sḏm·n·f) follow the initial clause. These are not to be understood as *subordinate* clauses (which would indicate that the action took place prior to that of the initial clause). The sequence of events in the following sentence illustrates how this parallel construction works.

ꜥḥꜥ·n·i šm·kwi,

rdi·n·(i) wi ḥr ḫt qꜣ,

si̓ꜣ·n·i ntiw[12] m-ḫnw·s.

---

[12]For *ntiw* "those who (were)," see §§111–12.

I went,
and I got myself up a tall tree,
and I recognized those who were in it (a ship).[13] (Sh.S. 155 ff.)

§96 *ꜥḥꜥ·n sḏm·f:* A Rare Variation

The construction *ꜥḥꜥ·n sḏm·f* is used in past narratives, but it is rare. In one instance, there are two parallel *sḏm·f* clauses that follow, indicating that this form was not simply a textual error. The use of the relative present *sḏm·f* may have been as a "vivid" past.

Ex.

ꜥḥꜥ·n rdỉ·f wỉ m r·f
He put me in his mouth.... (Sh.S. 75)

§97 More About Adverbs

Although the grammatical category called adverbial is extremely large in Egyptian (and important as predicate in all types of sentences), there are almost no "adverbs" proper, apart from a few adverbs of time and place[14] (but these are probably mostly nouns, anyway). By "adverb" proper is here meant any word similar in function to English "quickly," "greatly," "nicely." There is no real void, however, since Egyptian uses either a circumstantial clause ("..., hurrying as they went") or a prepositional phrase ("in haste"). In addition, adjectives could be used in this capacity, as in German and informal English.

Exx.

ꜥḥꜥ·n dwꜣ-nṯr·n·f n·ỉ ꜥꜣ r ẖt nbt
He thanked me most greatly. ("He praised god for me greatly, more than anything.") (*Lesest.* 76, 13)

Sometimes a *w* ending is encountered, and these may be true adverbs. This is especially the case with prepositions that have no suffixes. These may be derived adverbs—they have some resemblance to *nisba* derivatives, but the exact relation is not certain. The *w* ending is usually not written. It is possible that *ỉm* "therewith" is to be also transliterated as *ỉm(w)*, but this is less certain. The similarity to *ỉry*, *ỉr(w)* "thereto" (§55) is, however, quite apparent.

Ex.

wn·ỉn (§131) *sẖty pn ḥr rmyt ꜥꜣw wrt*
Then this peasant was crying very greatly. (Peas. B1 24 ff).

[13]A sentence with the following meaning is impossible: "I went, after I had gotten myself up in a tall tree, having previously recognized those in it." Clearly the sailor saw a ship in the distance, climbed a tree to see it better, and then recognized his former shipmates.

[14]E.g. "tomorrow," "here," "over there," etc.

nn[15] *wỉ ḥnꜥ(w)*
I was not with (them). (Sh. S. 130)

The feminine singular noun *wrt* "greatness" can be used to modify adjectives—both qualifiers and predicate adjectives. This was probably a type of bound construction (§48), but can be conveniently translated by "very" in English.

Exx.

ỉsṯ[16] *štꜣ wrt wꜣt . . . r ḫt nb*
Now, the road . . . was very difficult—beyond anything. (*Lesest.* 77, 7)

sbḥ ꜥꜣ wrt . . . a very great cry. (Sinuhe 265–66)

VOCABULARY VIII

ỉḥ "ox," "cow" (generic)

ỉsft "injustice," "falsehood," "chaos"

Ỉty "Sovereign" (a title of the king)

ꜥꜣm "Asiatic" (i.e. the people living to the north and east of Egyptian borders)

ꜥḥꜥ "to stand up"; *ꜥḥꜥ r* "to rise up against"; in stative "to be standing"

wḥmyt exact meaning unknown, perhaps "howling"

wsḫ "width" Cf. ? Semitic *wsꜥ*, e.g. Arabic (*wsꜥ* "to be wide")

bỉꜣw "mining-region"

pds "box," "chest"

fꜣỉ "to raise," "lift up"; idiomatic use with *ṯꜣw* "wind" perhaps as direct object "to sail \ run before the wind" or else as subject "to pick up," "rise up"

m-ꜥ compound preposition "in / by the hand (possession, charge) of," "through" (agency); "because of"; with *ḫpr* "happen to / with" (a person)

mꜣꜥt "justice," "truth," "order"

mꜥkꜣ "brave"

msḥ "crocodile" Cf. Arabic تمساح (*timsāḥ*) "crocodile"

[15]*Nn* (§102) is used to negate non-verbal sentences with adverbial coment. Here *ḥnꜥ(w)* is the adverbial predicate.

[16]*Ỉsṯ* is a sentence particle (like *mk*). Cf. §185.

nwyt "wave"

rf a particle (cannot be at the beginning of a sentence) "then," "now," cf. *ỉrf*

, *ḫrw* "enemy"

sʿnḫ (*s*-causative): "to feed," "provide food for"; "to keep alive"

sm3-t3 "to unite the land," "to be buried"; noun "interment"

sqdỉ (*s*-causative of 3rd weak verb, apparently without *t* in the infinitive): "to sail," "to sail on" (can be transitive); (more generally) "to travel" (even on land)

sqdw "sailor"

stpw "the choicest" "the pick"

sḏd (*s*-causative of *ḏd*) "to relate," "recount," "converse"

šmʿw "musician"

šms "to follow," "accompany"; *šms wḏ3* "a funeral procession"

šmsw (noun) "retainer," "attendant"

Kmt "Egypt" ("the Black Land")

tw indefinite pronoun: "one" (Can begin a future tense sentence without introductory particle.)

dw3-nṯr compound verb: "to praise god"; *dw3-nṯr n* + (person) = "to thank" (a person) (literally, "to praise god for a person")

EXERCISE VIII

(A) Reading Passage:

[17]The phrase *mitt ỉry* is treated grammatically as a masculine. The following word, *ḫpr(w)*, might be a stative form, but it is more likely a participle (§117 ff.; §121, 2,a) "that happened" (the use tends to overlap somewhat).

[18]Cf. §41, 2.

[19]In this sentence we have a pair of parallel prospective *sḏm·f* forms used with the meaning "whether they ... or whether they." The use is very similar to the French subjunctive *soit* ... *soit* "whether it be ... or it be...." A literal rendering in English might be accomplished with the modal auxiliary "should": "Should they ... or should they...." And just like the French subjunctive or English "should" clauses, these prospective clauses lead into a main sentence construction, which follows. The construction will be dealt with later in its extended context: the "conditional" mood (§§138–39).

(B) Transliterate and Translate. Additional vocabulary to be found in the dictionary.

1) 

2) 

3) 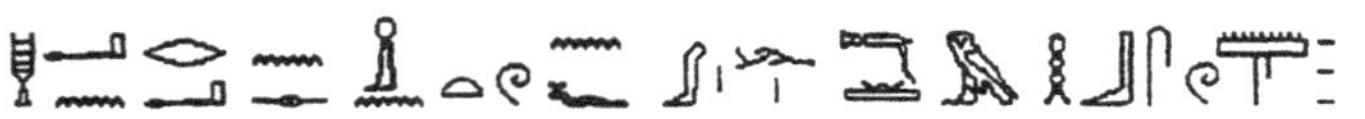

4) Said by the king to an elderly courtier:

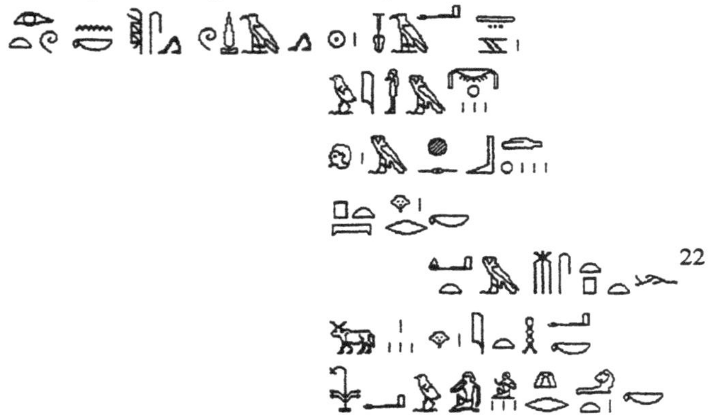

5)  (From a letter that almost certainly exaggerates the current circumstances in the writer's vicinity.)

[20]*Mt* is an abbreviated writing. The *t* is doing double duty for the root letter and for the appropriate verbal suffix. The word order (and meaning) should indicate which form is required!

[21]The suffix *·f* refers to a commoner who was having an affair with a magician's wife.

[22]A depiction of the night sky was painted on the ceiling of the shrine. The deceased thus was thought to be able to look up at it.

[23]The "negative arms" *n* is used for the preposition *n*.

[24]This is an "impersonal" construction (§91). The expression *šꜣꜥ* + *m* + infinitive means "to begin to...."

6) 

7) 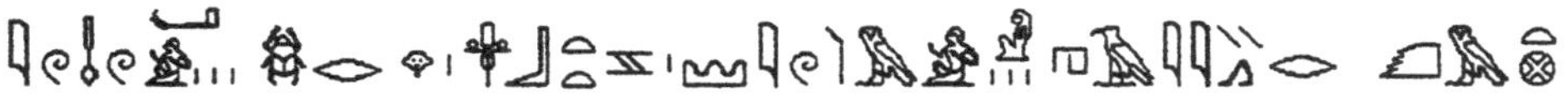

8) 

(C) Parse from section *(B)*:

1) 

4) 

7) 

[25] The word order *seems* peculiar, but the genitival construction was probably split up for a good reason—perhaps involving the function of  in the sentence.

[26] *W3t* here means "course."

LESSON 9

§98. The Independent Use of the 1st sing. Stative

There is a fairly rare independent use of the 1st person sing. stative in main clauses. The construction does not require an antecedent and does not use the introductory particle *ỉw*. It does not occur except with the 1st person singular.

Ex.

rd·kwỉ r pr s3 nsw, špssw ỉm·f (§38), *sqbbwy ỉm·f*
I was put in a prince's house with splendid things in it, and with a cool hall in it. (Sinuhe B 285 ff.)

sd·kwỉ m p3qt, gs·kwỉ m tpt, sḏr·kwỉ ḥr ḥnkyt
I was clothed in fine linen; I was anointed with fine oil; and I was laid down upon a bed. (Sinuhe 289 ff.)

§99. The Exclamatory use of the Stative Forms

The 2nd and 3rd person stative forms could be used alone as exclamations, and may occur at the beginning, middle, or end of an utterance. The use is restricted to a few phrases, some of which, were much used, especially in the royal titulary. The most common is the phrase *ʿnḫ(w), (w)ḏ3(w), s(nbw)* "may he live, prosper, and be healthy," which has already been encountered as an exclamation occurring in conjunction with the mention of members of the royal family, the palace, etc. Similar is the phrase *ʿnḫw ḏt* "may he live forever" and the feminine counterpart *ʿnḫ·tỉ ḏt* "may she live forever," which often occur after the king's nomen or prenomen (§69).

Such exclamations were not limited to royalty, however, and in the speech of commoners we find the phrases *ḥs·tỉ* "may it please you"; *snb·t(ỉ)* "may you be healthy" (meaning "have a safe journey!"); *ỉỉ·tỉ* "welcome!"; *s33·tỉ*[1] + *ḥr* "beware!" "take care not to (do)"

Ex.

snb·t(ỉ) sp sn, nḏs, r pr·k

[1] The gemination is unusual (but known) in stative forms of final weak verbs.

Safe journey, safe journey, little man, to your home. (Sh. S. 158 f.)

§100. Existential Sentences: "There is..." "There are..."

To express the idea, "there is / are ..." (French *il y a* ..., German *es gibt* ...), the verb *wnn* is used in a verbal sentence beginning with the particle *ỉw*. Note that although *wnn* is basically a 2nd geminating verb, its circumstantial form does not exhibit gemination (see, Verb Chart, Appendix 1): *ỉw wn*. The sentence type was no doubt common in everyday speech, but examples in the literature are not all that abundant. In place of *ỉw*, one also finds the particle *ỉsṯ* / *ỉst* "now," but perhaps also meaning "too," ("and then there is ...")

Ex.

ỉw wn nḏs Ḏdỉ rn·f, ḥmsỉ·f m Ḏd-snfrw, m3ᶜ-ḫrw

There is a commoner by the name of Djedi who lives in Djed-Snofru (a town), justified. (West. 6, 26–7, 1)

ỉst wn ḥmt·f, Mrt rn·s

And then there was his wife whose name was Merit. (Peas. R2)

There are also cases of non-verbal sentences that do not use the verb *wnn*. These use only the particle *ỉw* followed by the noun or noun phrase. One also finds *ỉm* "there" as the adverbial comment, with additional modifiers, if necessary. (Literally, "X is there ...")

Ex.

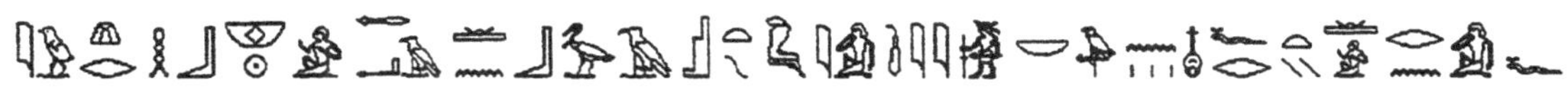

ỉw ḫry-ḥbt ᶜ3 n(y) B3stt, ỉty, nb·n, Nfrty rn·f

There is a great lector-priest of Bastet, o Sovereign, our Lord, by the name of Neferty. (Neferty Pet. 9 f.)

ỉw ỉt ỉm ḥnᶜ bdt

There was barley there along with emmer. (Sinuhe 84)

§101. Negation

Negations were accomplished in two ways in Egyptian: 1) by negative particles, and 2) by means of negative auxiliary verbs (i.e. verbs meaning "to not do"). The negative auxiliary verbs (§164–166; 175–80) have special functions and are not used to negate "simple statements of fact." The negative particles were used to negate non-verbal sentences with adverbial comment, verbal sentences (whose affirmative counterparts are *ỉw sḏm·f*, *ỉw sḏm·n·f*, *ỉw sḏm(w)*, and *ỉw·ỉ šm·kwỉ*), and existential "there is / are" sentences (§100).

There are two negative particles in Middle Egyptian: *n* and *nn*. *Nn* negates nominal elements, and *n* is used primarily with verbal elements. The particle *n* is cognate to the Semitic negation *lā*: "not," e.g. Arabic لا (*lā*) "no, not"; Hebrew לֹא (*lō*) "no, not."[2] The negative particle always stands at the beginning of the clause or sentence.

With the possible exception of the construction *n sp* + prospective *sḏm·f* ("he never heard," §110), all of the negated clauses may be used either as main clauses or as subordinate clauses of circumstance. One must judge by context which clauses are main clauses and which are subordinate.

§102. Negation of Non-verbal Sentences with Adverbial Comment

Sentences of the pattern *iw* + Topic + Adverbial Comment (§10) are negated by *nn* (which may be preceded by *mk*). The particle *iw* is not used. The word order is *Nn* + Topic + Adverbial Comment. If the topic is a pronoun, the dependent series is used. E.g. the negation of *iw·f m st·f* "it is in its place" is *nn sw m st·f* "it is not in its place." (Or, as a circumstantial clause, "..., it not being in its place.")

Exx.

nn wi im
I am not there. (*Lesest.* 50, 5–6)

nn s(y) m ib·i
It was not in my heart. (Sinuhe B223–24)

§103. Negation of Existential Sentences ("There is / are no...")

The usual construction begins with *nn wn* "there is / are no...." Quite often just *nn* without *wn* is used. Quite rare, but identical in meaning is *n wnt*. (This expression can be found in the dictionaries under *wnt*, and need not be learned at this point). Note that when possession is involved (e.g. a suffix pronoun, the genitival *n(y)*, or the dative *n*), one can often better translate with the English "does / did not have ..." etc.

Sentences with *nn wn* are always main clauses, but when just *nn* is used, the clause may be either a main or a circumstantial clause: "..., there being no...."

Exx.

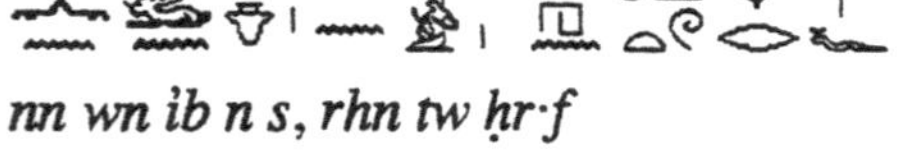

nn wn ib n s, rhn tw ḥr·f
There is no heart to a man so that one might rely on it. *Or better*: No one has a heart that might be relied on. (*Lebensm.* 121)

[2]The connection of *nn* is less certain. Its Late Egyptian counterpart is *bn*, which might be cognate to Semitic *bal* "not."

nn wn pḥwy·fy
There is no end of it. *Or*: It has no end. (*Lebensm*. 130)

nn isf<t> m ẖt·i
There is no falsehood in my innermost being. (BD ch. 18)

§104. Negation of Nouns: "Without..."

Nouns and noun phrases could also be negated with *nn*. In these cases, the best translation is usually "without." Frequently the noun that is being negated takes a suffix pronoun to add clarity, but this is often redundant in English.

Exx.

(I plundered all their people as captives) 

... mnmnt iry nn ḏrw
... and their cattle without limit. (*Rb* 57, 13–14)

(I crossed over) 

... m wsḫt nn ḥmw·s
... in a barge without a steering oar" (lit. "not [having] its steering oar" Sinuhe R 38).

§105. Negation of the Infinitive: "Without (doing)..."

In place of an ordinary noun, an infinitive may follow *nn* with the meaning "without (doing)." This construction is not uncommon, especially when the actor is the same as that found earlier in the clause. It functions like a circumstantial clause, but, of course, without a subject.[3]

Ex.

( [§110] )

(n sp sin<n>·f rssy[4]*), Bik ꜥḥ·f*[5] *ḥnꜥ šmsw·f nn rdit rḫ st mšꜥ·f*
(He never even hesitated), the Falcon (the heir apparent) flying off with his retinue (i.e. his personal body-guard), without letting his troops know it. (Sinuhe R 20 f.)

[3]There are some cases of *nn* + infinitive as main clauses that mean "There was no (doing)...." These sentences are certain, but not terribly common outside of a few literary texts.

[4]The term *rssy*, later *rsy*, basically means "quite," "entirely," and after negations "(not) at all." Here it has been translated as "(not) even."

[5]This is a circumstantial clause, but note that the word order is Noun + circumstantial *sḏm·f*.

§106. Negation of the Verbal Clauses & Predicate Adjectives

The two basic verbal negations (corresponding to affirmative statements of fact) are *n sḏm·f* (past time!) and *n sḏm·n·f* (present time!). The *sḏm·f* and *sḏm·n·f* forms are *not* the circumstantial forms. These clauses may be either main or subordinate clauses of circumstance. The sequence of tenses is often the key factor in determining clause type. In particular, negated verbal clauses conveying (relative) present time that occur in a past time context are almost certain to be circumstantial clauses.[6] (Of course, in the case of prior action in a circumstantial clause, the relative past tense construction is required.)

Predicate adjectives are negated by means of this construction as well. The required form of "adjective verb" (a verbal form of the adjective) is used, and it is treated just as any other verb. The tense distinctions are not always as clear-cut as in negated verbal clauses.

§107. Past Time: "He did not Hear..." / "He was not Heard..."

1) Active Voice ***N Sḏm·f*** **"He did not Hear":** This construction corresponds to the affirmative *ỉw sḏm·n·f*. Note that it does not use a *sḏm·n·f* form, but rather a *sḏm·f*. The reason for this is that the form in question is the "old indicative" form, which was a past tense form in Old Egyptian.[7] The use of the old indicative forms is quite limited in Middle Egyptian, and it is common only in this fossilized construction. In subordinate clauses of circumstance, *n sḏm·f* is the negative counterpart of circumstantial clauses formed with the circumstantial *sḏm·n·f* forms, and can be translated "because he did not hear," "although he did not hear," etc. or less specifically, "he not having heard."

To say "I do not know," one used the verb *rḫ* "to learn" in this past time negation. (This corresponds to the use of the stative and past tense *ỉw sḏm·n·f* in the affirmative.)

With adjectives, the time reference is usually past. There may be a few exceptions which seem to refer to the present.[8]

The stems of the old indicative *sḏm·f* forms from the mutable and irregular verbs are as follows:

3rd Weak: no gemination— *gmỉ·f*, sometimes (rarely) with *y*: *h3y·k*; *ỉrỉ*, *ỉrỉ*

2nd Gem.: no gemination— *qb*

ỉỉ / ỉw: mostly *ỉw*; much less common: *ỉỉ*

ỉnỉ: *ỉnỉ*

rdỉ: mostly with *r*: *rdỉ*, but sometimes without *r*: *dỉ*

[6] I.e. if they were main clauses, they would be in the "present tense," but as subordinate clauses, they relate circumstances contemporary to their time context.

[7] Cf. E. Doret, *The Narrative Verbal System of Old and Middle Egyptian* (Geneva: 1986), pp. 27–28.

[8] E.g. Peas. B2, 103.

wnn: no gemination— *wn*

m33: *m3·ỉ*; also with *n*[9]: *m3n*

Exx.

n sḏwy·ỉ ḥm n ḥry-tp·f. n smr·ỉ. n sḥqr·ỉ. n srmỉ·ỉ. n sm3·ỉ. n wḏ·ỉ sm3.

I did not slander a servant to his master. I did not inflict pain. I did not cause hunger. I did not cause weeping. I did not kill. I did not order to kill. (BD Ch. 125 Intro)

ḏd·ṯn m3ꜥt r·ỉ m-b3ḥ Nb-r-ḏr ḫr-nt(y)t (§114) *ỉrỉ·n·ỉ m3ꜥt m T3-mrỉ, n šnt·ỉ nṯr, n ỉw sp·ỉ ḥr nsw ỉmy-hrw·f*

May you tell the truth about me in the presence of the Lord-of-all[11] because I did justice in Egypt, not having denounced a god, nor with a fault of mine having come out concerning a king in his day. (BD Ch. 125, Address to gods)

With an adjective/verb:

n bdš ḥr·ỉ m-ḥ3t b3k

I was not faint-hearted in face of the work. (My face was not faint in front of the work.) (Sinai 90, 15)

2) Passive Voice ***N Sḏm·tw·f*** **"He was not heard":** This Middle Egyptian construction replaced the older *n* + *sḏm(w)·f* passive construction (a few examples can be found in early texts, see §115, second example). The verb form is a passive of the "old indicative" formed with the passive suffix *·tw*. As with its affirmative counterpart, the time reference is *past*. The clause may be main or subordinate.

Ex.

n ỉnỉ·t(w) n·ỉ ꜥqw

The rations have not been brought to me. (P. BM 10549 4)

§108. Present Time: "He does not Hear..." / "He is not Heard..."

1) Active Voice ***N Sḏm·n·f*** **"He does not Hear," "He cannot Hear":** This construction

[9]Probably not a different form, but a different writing influenced by pronunciation only.

[10]The writing *sm3m* indicates that original *sm3* was then pronounced *sm*, the *3* having been dropped. The standard practice in transliterating is to follow the earlier writing.

[11]An epithet of Osiris.

is formed with a *sḏm·n·f* form, possibly derived from the old indicative forms, but this is not certain. Whatever the form might be, the tense is *present* (relative to the context) in spite of the *·n* suffix (otherwise the "past tense" marker). As with the other negated clauses, these may be either main or subordinate. When this construction occurs in past time contexts, it is almost always in a circumstantial clause. Sometimes this construction has the meaning "cannot hear."

The *sḏm·n·f* forms used in this construction are identical (in written form) to all the other *sḏm·n·f* forms: no gemination in the 3rd weak or the 2nd gem. roots.

Exx.

n rdì·n·k n·ì db3w n mdt tn nfrt
You do not give me compensation for this fine speech. (Peas. B1 318)

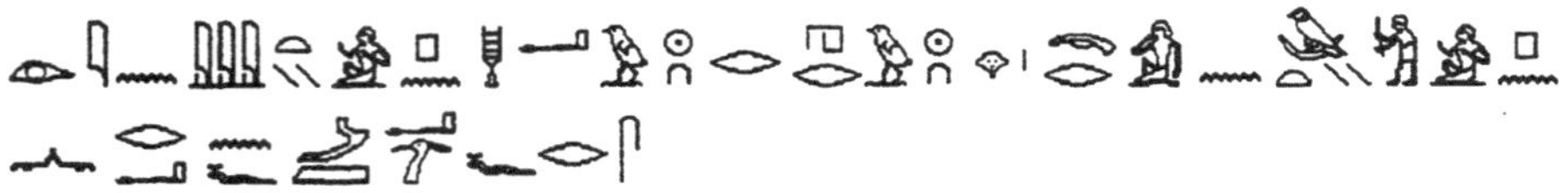

ìrì·ìn (§131) *sḫty pn ꜥḥꜥw {10} r hrw 10 ḥr spr n Nmty-nḫt(w) pn, n rdì·n·f m3ꜥ·f r·s*
Then this peasant spent a period of[12] ten days petitioning to this Nemty-nakhte, but he did not give his attention to it. (Peas. B1 31 f.)

With adjective/verb:

n nḏm·n n·f ḫtḫt ìm
A reversal thereof ("therein") is not pleasant for him. (*Lesest.* 93, 10 ff.)

2) Passive Voice *N Sḏm·n·tw·f* **"He is not Heard":** The passive is formed with the suffix *tw*.

Ex.

[. . .] m (§24) *rḫt n(y) ntìw* (§111) *sw3(w)* (§82), *n rḫ·n·tw m3ꜥt r grg*
[You have heard of events] consisting of the knowledge of those who have passed on, but one cannot tell the difference between fact and fiction. (Literally: "but fact cannot be ascertained from fiction." West. 6, 23 f.)

§109. Future Time: *Nn sḏm·f* "He will not Hear..." *Nn sḏm·tw·f* "He will not be heard"

The negative counterpart of *ìw·f r sḏm* "he will hear" is formed with the negative particle *nn* + prospective *sḏm·f* form. It has been claimed that his construction was used for negative wishes, but this does not seem to be the case. Note that negative wishes and negative purpose clauses ("in

[12]The Egyptian uses the preposition *r* "(amounting) to," "as long as."

order not to do ...") require a different type of negation (§§164, 175).

With adjectives, this construction is also used for future time. The examples of ***nn*** + adj. that are clearly not future should probably be analysed as nominal constructions (§103): "What I did upon earth was not a trifling thing."[13] (Or more literally, "It was no trifle (namely) what I did on earth.")

Exx.

nn dỉ·n ᶜq·k ḥr·n, ỉn bnšw n(y) sb3 pn, n ỉs ḏd·n·k rn·n

We will not let you enter past us—so say the doorposts of this gate—unless[14] you say our names. (BD ch. 125 Address to gods)

nn ỉhm dpt{w}·k. nn ỉwt ỉyt m ḥt·k

Your boat will not be held back. No harm will come to your mast. (Peas. B1 56 f.)

With adjective/verb:

nn šrỉ rn n(y) s m ỉrt·n·f[15]

A man's name will not be lessened through what he has done. (Merikare 10, 2–3)

§110.  ***N sp* + Prospective *sḏm·f* "He never heard..." "It was never heard"**

The verb *spỉ* "to remain over" (presumably in the "old indicative" form after *n*) is followed by a clause beginning with a prospective *sḏm·f* form, either active or passive, with the meaning "never." (Of course, the verb *spỉ*, when not used in this construction, also occurs with its original meaning "to remain over, to survive.") One can translate "he has never heard" and "he had never heard," depending on the context. This construction can also be used with future time reference: "He will never hear...."

Exx.

n sp h3ỉ mỉt(y)·f ḥr ḫ3st tn ḏr rk nṯr

One like it had never come down from this desert since the time of the god. (RB 76, 9 f.)

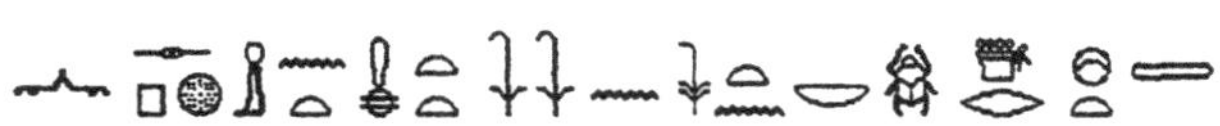

n spỉ ỉnỉ·t(w) mỉtt nn n nsw nb ḫpr(w)[16] *ḏr p3wt t3*

The like of this had never been brought to any king who existed since the primeval time of the earth.

[13]The example is from Ptaḥḥotpe 640: *nn šrỉ ỉrt·n·ỉ tp t3*.

[14]One of the meanings of *n ... ỉs* is "unless."

[15]*Ỉrt·n·f* is a relative verb form, here used as a noun meaning "what he has done."

[16]*Ḫpr(w)* is a participle (§121, da) "who existed."

(*Rb* 53, 3–4)

§111. *Nty* The relative adjective "That, which, that which, who"

The relative adjective *nty* is a *nisba* adjective, and is declined as expected, although occasionally plurals and feminine forms use the masc. sing. *nty*.

TABLE 10: THE RELATIVE ADJECTIVE

	Masculine	Feminine
Singular	*nty*	*nt(y)t*
Plural	, *ntiw*	*nt(yw)t*

The basic meaning is "who," "that," "which." Like all adjectives, the relative adjective *nty* can modify a preceding noun (its antecedent) *or* it can stand alone as a noun meaning "the one who," "the ones who," "those who," "that which," "whatever." The relative adjective is used mostly in cases where the antecedent is definite (i.e. it would be preceded by "the" in English), but also in a few cases which would seem to be indefinite (cf. §38, where the antecedent is almost always indefinite). The meaning of the relative adjective is broader than the English equivalents, and when place is involved, it can be translated "where," "wherever," etc.

The Egyptian relative adjective is not related to the Semitic relative markers *ʾšr*, *ʾš*, and *ša*, but its use is similar in a general manner.

§112. *Nty* + Adverbs / Adverbial Phrases

Whether *nty* modifies an antecedent or stands on its own as a noun ("the one who is … / those who are"), an adverb or adverbial phrase may follow. This may consist of an adverb (e.g. *im* "there," *ꜥꜣ* "here," etc.), a prepositional phrase, a stative form, and circumstantial clauses, verbal and non-verbal (with adverbial comments). When the relative adjective is used as a noun (and not referring to an antecedent) its gender and number are those required by the context: *nty ḥnꜥ·f* "the one who is / was with him," *nt(y)t m-bꜣḥ·f* "she who is in his presence." Note the euphemism for the deceased: *ntiw im* "those who are there" (i.e. in the world of the hereafter).

In the simplest construction, and by far the most common, *nty* refers directly to a specific antecedent about which some information is related: *pr·f nty m niwt ḥnꜥ ḏꜣtt·f nt(y)t m sḫt* "his house which is in the city along with his estate that is in the country."

Somewhat more convoluted are cases in which the information related is not *directly* about the antecedent, but rather about something or someone *indirectly* connected with the antecedent. For example, *st tn nt(y)t sn·s m sš* "that woman whose brother is a scribe."[17] The use of the suffix pronoun *·s* after *sn* "brother" is necessary to determine the particular relationship—"possession." Thus the English relative pronoun required is the genitive "whose" rather than "who." Note that in such cases, the relative adjective agrees in gender and number with the antecedent, regardless of the associated noun that follows. (E.g., in the previous example, *nt(y)t* agrees with *st* although followed by the masculine noun *sn*.)

In this type of relative clause, the nominal element following *nty* may be a pronoun. In this case, the *dependent pronoun series* is used, except in the expression *bw nty* X *im* "the place where X is." In that phrase, we find the forms *nt(y)·f* and *nt(y)·k* (the *y* is sometimes omitted): *bw nty·f im* "the place where he is" and *bw nt(y)·k im* "the place where you are."

Exx.

nṯrw nbw ntiw m pt, ntiw m tꜣ, di·sn iri nb·i ꜥnḫ(w), (w)ḏꜣ(w), s(nbw) rnpt ḥḥ m ꜥnḫ, (w)ḏꜣ, s(nb)
All the gods who are in heaven and who are on earth—may they let my Lord, l.p.h., spend a million years in life, prosperity, and health! (P. BM 100567 5–6)

[...] m rḫt n(y) ntiw swꜣ(w) (§82 ff.)
[...] consisting of the knowledge of those who have passed on. (West. 6, 23)

nṯr ꜥꜣ, di·k iwt n·i bꜣ·i m bw nb nty·f im
O great god, may you let my *ba* come to me from any place where it might be. (BD ch. 89)

nḥm·k Nbsny m-ꜥ nṯr pwy nty ḥr·f m ṯsm inḥwy·fy m rmṯ
May you rescue Nebseny from the hands of that god whose face is (that of) a dog and whose eyebrows are (those of) a human. (BD ch. 17)

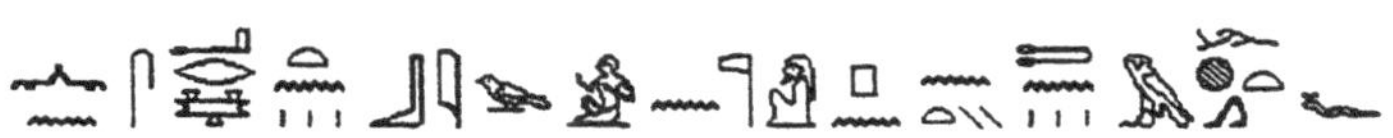

nn sꜥr·tn bi<n>·i n nṯr pn nty tn m-ḫt·f
You will not raise up a misdeed of mine to that god in whose following you are. (BD ch. 125 confession)

Verbal clauses may refer directly or only *indirectly* to the antecedent, and there may be an accusative relationship (e.g. "the bread and beer *that* I gave you") or much more often another

[17]Here there is a non-verbal circumstantial clause following the relative adjective. Literally, "her brother being a scribe."

type of relationship (e.g. "the book *from which* the scribe read," "the steering-oar *with which* he guided the boat"). The exact relationship is determined by the use of "resumptive pronouns" and "resumptive prepositions" such as *ỉm·f* "with it," "in it," "from it"; *ḥr·s* "on it," "on account of it," etc. The use of verbal clauses after *nty* is quite limited because there existed an Egyptian verb forms that specifically expressed the relative idea "that, which, who, etc." (§157–62). Both *sḏm·f* and *sḏm·n·f* forms occur after *nty*. The *sḏm·f* forms are the circumstantial forms, as are presumably also the *sḏm·n·f* forms. Negative verbal constructions after *nty* are somewhat more common than affirmative ones. Of course, *n* + the old indicative forms are used.

Exx.

wn(w) (§§35, 72) *r·ỉ, wpw r·ỉ ỉn Šw m nwt·f twy n(y)t bỉꜣ{t} n(y) pt*[18] *nty wp·n·f r n(y) nṯrw ỉm·s*

May my mouth be opened, may my mouth be unlocked by Shu with that iron adze of his with which he opened the mouths of the gods. (BD ch. 23)

... *st-ḥmt 20 m* (§24) *nfr(w)t ... nty (!) n wp·t(w)·sn m msỉt*

... 20 ladies, that is beautiful women, ... who have not been opened in giving birth (West. 5, 9 f.)

§113. *Nt(y)t* "that which is..."

The fem. sing. form of the relative adjective *nt(y)t* can stand on its own as a noun meaning "that which is" / "what is." In negative expressions it can be translated "nothing": *nn nt(y)t nn st ỉm·f* "There is nothing that is not in it." Quite common is the phrase *nt(y)t nbt* "everything that is," "whatever is..." E.g. *pr·ỉ ḥnꜥ nt(y)t nbt ỉm·f* "my house and everything that is in it."

§114. *Ḥr nt(y)t* "because"

Egyptian writers tended not to say "because" specifically, as they preferred the less precise circumstantial clause. However, in cases where it was essential to be more specific, the phrase *ḥr nt(y)t* "because" could be employed. Other similar expressions (*ḏr nt[y]t, m-ꜥ nt[y]t*) will be learned later as vocabulary items.

Exx.

ḏd·ṯn mꜣꜥt r·ỉ m-bꜣḥ Nb-r-ḏr ḥr nt(y)t ỉr·n·ỉ mꜣꜥt m Tꜣ-mry

May you tell the truth about me in the presence of the Lord-of-All because I did justice in Egypt. (BD ch. 125, Address to gods)

[18]The term *bỉꜣ n(y) pt* "metal from heaven" denotes meteoric iron.

... *ḥr nt(y)t tw m rḫ*
(Do not be arrogant) because you are a learned man (Ptaḥ. *Lesest.* 37, 10)

§115. *R nt(y)t* / *Ḥr nt(y)t* "to the effect that" in Letters

A typical Egyptian letter is structured as follows: 1) "(title and name of writer) speaks to (title and name of recipient)"; 2) a series of wishes involving prayers to the gods for the recipient's good health, etc.; 3) the body of the letter begins with such phrases as "This is a communication to inform my lord, to the effect that. . . ." In informal letters the preambles may be dismissed and the body begins directly *r nt(y)t* or *ḥr nt(y)t* "to the effect that." Also, these phrases may be used within the body of a letter to introduce a new topic. (Again, in more formal letters there may be such a phrase as "a(nother) communication to the effect that. . . .") The letter may end with some such phrase as: *nfr sḏm·k* "May your hearing be good." (Probably *nfr* is the prospective of the "adjective verb" followed by the infinitive.) The idea being something along the lines of "may you hear this letter in good health."

Exx.

r nt(y)t hꜣw nb n(y) nb·i ꜥ.w.s. ꜥḏ(w), wḏꜣ(w), m st·sn nbt m ḥst n(y)t Spdw Nb iꜣbtt, ḥnꜥ psḏt·f, nṯrw nbw
(This is a communication to my lord, l.p.h.,) to the effect that all the affairs of my lord, l.p.h., are safe and sound and in proper order[19] through the favour of Sopdu, Lord of the East along with his Ennead[20] and all the gods. (P. Kahun, pl. 29)

ḥr nt(y)t n gm(w) (§107, 2) *nꜣ n(y) ḫrdw*
(This is a communication to my lord, l.p.h.,) to the effect that those children have not been found. (P. BM 10567)

§116. *Nt(y)t* "that" after verbs of knowing & seeing

This use is not terribly common and is here included only for future reference. It is used only with verbs of knowing and seeing, and *not* with verbs of speaking / saying.

Ex.

[19]Literally, "being in all their places."
[20]A group of nine gods.

mtn rḫ·n·ṯn nt(y)t ỉr ḫt nbt ddt[21] *sr nb, nḏs nb r ḥwt-nṯr m tpy n(y) šmw·f, n nḏm·n n·f ḫtḫt ỉm*
Now you know that as for anything that any official or any commoner gives from the best of his harvest to the temple (for contracted mortuary services), a reversal thereof (i.e. of the terms of the contract) is not pleasant for him. (*Lesest.* 93, 10 ff.)

VOCABULARY IX

Ỉwnw n. loc. Heliopolis

ỉn "... so says" (introduces the speaker following a quotation)

ỉnḥ "eyebrow"

ỉt (masc.) "barley" (also the generic word for "grain")

ꜥqw "loaves, rations"

ꜥḏ "to be safe" (of persons and things)

wnḏwt n. fem. collective "people," "fellow human beings"

, , *Wsỉr* n. div. Osiris

bdt (later *bty*) "emmer" (a type of wheat)

pꜣwt tꜣ "primaeval time of the earth"

Pḫr-wr the Euphrates River

, *psḏt* "ennead" (group of nine gods)

mꜣꜥ "temple" (of head); *rdỉ mꜣꜥ r* "to pay attention to"

, *mỉty* (*nisba*) "which is like," "a thing like it"

mḥty (*nisba*) "northern"; *mḥt(y)w* "Northerners"

mḏḥ "to hew" (wood, stone); "to build" (ships). Cf. ? Semitic, e.g. Hebrew חצב (*ḥṣb*) "to hew" (stone, wood)

nḏm "pleasant," "sweet," "charming" cf. Semitic *nꜥm* "pleasant"

r (to act, do injury / injustice, etc.) "against" (a person) ("*r* of opposition")

rḫ "a learned man," "a scholar"

rsy (*nisba*) "southern"

rk "time," "era," "age"

hꜣw (place) "vicinity," "neighbourhood"; (time) "time," (of king) = "reign"

ḥsỉ "to praise," "honour," "favour" Cf. ?? Semitic *šbḥ* "to praise," "laud"

[21]*Ddt* is the imperfect relative *sḏm·f* (§159) form of *rdỉ*: "that [a subject] gives," modifying *ḫt nbt*.

ḥst "praise," "favour," (divine) "grace"

ḥqꜣ-ḥwt "local ruler," "mayor"

ḫt (masc.) "wood"; "tree"; "stick"; "mast"

ḫry-ḥbt "lector-priest" (lit. "one with the ritual book")

swꜣ (intrans.) "to pass," "to pass by," "to pass away" (die). Cf. Semitic *šwr*: Hebrew שור (*šwr*) "to journey"; Arabic سار (*sāra*) "to move on, go away, travel"

swt (enclitic particle) "however," "but"

sp "time," "matter," "deed," "misdeed," etc. (consult dictionary)

spỉ "to remain over," "survive"

spr "to petition," "appeal," "make petition"; *spr ḥr* "make a petition against" (a person)

sn-nw "companion," "partner" (from "second")

sḏr "to sleep," "lie down," "spend the night (doing)"

špsy "noble," "splendid," "costly," "elegant," "luxurious" (of gods): "august"

špssw "precious things," "luxuries," "riches," "wealth"

šnt (a variant of *šnṯ*) "to revile," "denounce"

šspt (collective) "cucumbers"

n. loc. *Kpny* (also spelled *Kbn*) Byblos (an Egyptian "colony" in Lebanon)

grg "falsehood," "lie"

Tꜣ-mrỉ "Egypt"

Tꜣ-nṯr "God's Land" (designation of far-off lands)

tnw "number"

ṯsm "dog," "hound"

ḏt fem. "eternity," "for ever"

ḏw "mountain"

ḏr prep. "since" (temporally); *ḏr-nt(y)t* "because"

ḏrw "limit," "boundary" (concrete and abstract)

EXERCISE IX

(A) Reading Passage: Clauses are aligned to indicate parallel structures and indented lines are subordinate clauses. The clause structure here presented is a suggested interpretation, but in some cases other analyses are possible.

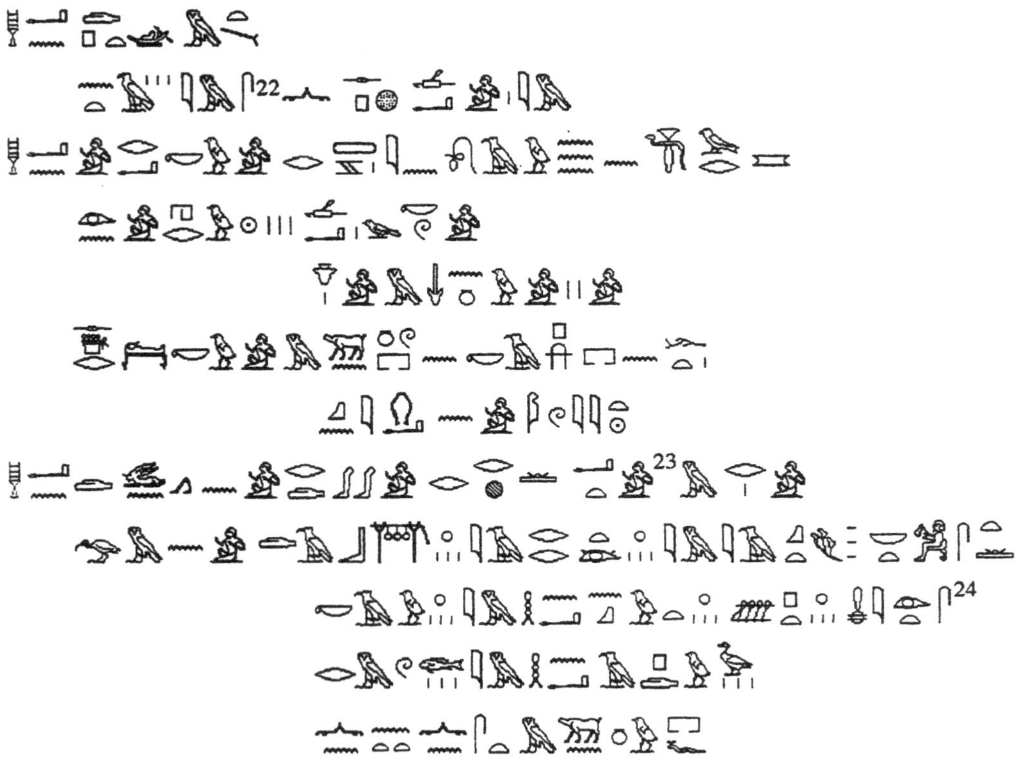

(B) Transliterate and Translate. Additional vocabulary is to be found in the dictionary.

1) 

2) 

3) 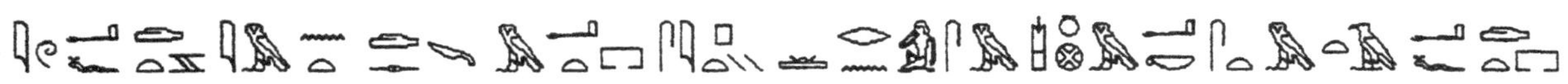

[22]This is an example of "fronting," i.e., the general topic is placed in clause-initial position. "Fronting" gives a slight shift of focus to the topic. The phenomenon can usually be imitated in English translation, but the words "As for,..." may be required.

[23]*Dit·i* is the fem. sing. prospective relative form of *rdi* (with 1st sing. suffix as subject) used on its own as a noun: "that which I might put" / "what I might put" (§§157; 160).

[24]Here translate *mi* "as if." The verb *iri* "to do, produce" here implies "cultivation."

4) [hieroglyphs]
5) [hieroglyphs]
6) [hieroglyphs]
7) [hieroglyphs]
[hieroglyphs]
8) [hieroglyphs]
9) [hieroglyphs]
[hieroglyphs]²⁵
[hieroglyphs]²⁶ [hieroglyphs]²⁷ [hieroglyphs]
10) [hieroglyphs]²⁸
[hieroglyphs]
11) [hieroglyphs]
12) [hieroglyphs]
[hieroglyphs]
13) [hieroglyphs]

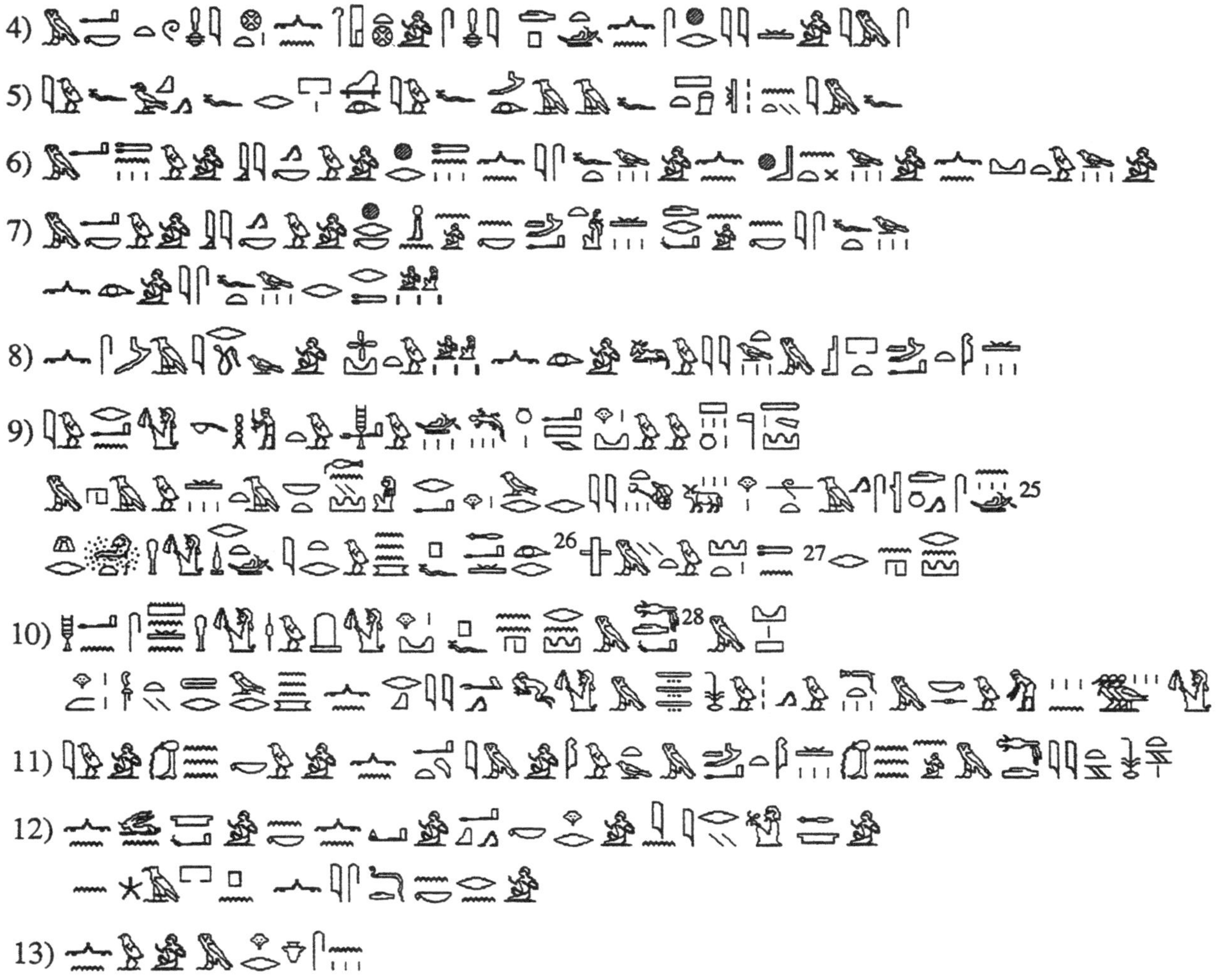

(C) Parse from section (B):

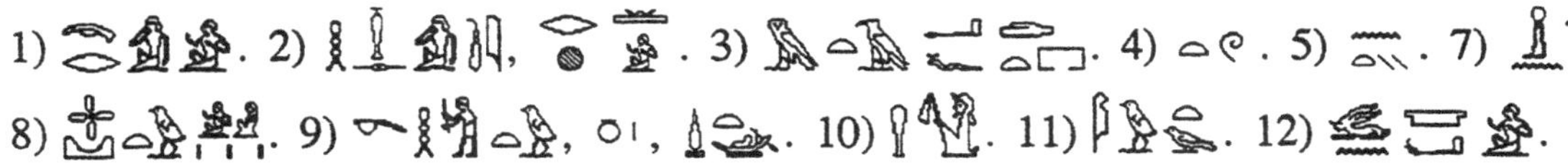

1) [hieroglyphs]. 2) [hieroglyphs], [hieroglyphs]. 3) [hieroglyphs]. 4) [hieroglyphs]. 5) [hieroglyphs]. 7) [hieroglyphs].
8) [hieroglyphs]. 9) [hieroglyphs], [hieroglyphs], [hieroglyphs]. 10) [hieroglyphs]. 11) [hieroglyphs]. 12) [hieroglyphs].

---

²⁵§41, 2: The determinative normally precedes the suffix pronoun, but placing it after allowed a more pleasing spacing here.
²⁶*Iry* is a stative (cf. §87) or a participle (§117 ff.), here in the sense "that occurs" (i.e. "that is produced").
²⁷A false archaism for *tn*.
²⁸*Šd* a passive participle (§121, 2b) "one that is carved out...."

LESSON 10

§117. The Egyptian Participle

The participle is an adjective derived from a verbal root. It possesses all of the features of adjectives and some features of verbs. It is not a conjugated verb form (i.e. it does not form a unit in conjunction with a subject as is the case with the *sḏm·f* and other forms). The participles do not convey the information that a specific action was done (or is or will be done), but that someone or something is the "doer" of an action or the "undergoer" of an action (in the passive voice). The meaning is literally: "the one who does" (or "that did," or "will do," depending on the particular participle used).

Students familiar with Biblical Hebrew should note that the Egyptian participles, although generally similar in function to their Hebrew counterparts, do not convey the notion of ongoing or progressive action (which in Egyptian is expressed by *ḥr* / *m* + infinitive, §§58–60).

§118. The Basic Uses of the Participle

The participle is used exactly like any other adjective:

1) It can **modify a noun** (qualifier): "stinging criticism" ("stinging" is a participle in English) *s3 sḏm(w)* "a hearing son," i.e. "a son that listens" or "an obedient son."

2) It can **stand on its own as a noun**: *sḏm(w)* "hearer," "one who hears," which as a technical term is the Egyptian word for "judge." The participle is very commonly used to express occupations ("one who does . . .") and as such corresponds to words formed with the English suffix -er/-or: "teacher," "supervisor," "actor," "singer." The word *sš* "scribe" is almost certainly a participle ("writer"). When used this way, the participle is often followed by the seated man or woman determinative. The use of the participle as a noun is not, however, limited to occupations: e.g. *ḏd m3ꜥt* "speaker of truth" or "one who tells the truth."

3) The participle can be used as the **predicate adjective** (§44). This use is most common with verbal roots meaning "to rejoice," "to be happy," and the like, but also with descriptive verbs, such as "to be crooked," "to be hidden," "to be tilted," etc. It is also used with transitive verbs with the meaning "he is one who does. . . ." As always with the predicate adjective, the adjective (here a participle) begins the sentence, without the particle *ỉw*—although *mk* may precede it. The participle as predicate adjective does not agree in gender and number with the subject (§44). The subject, if a pronoun, is from the dependent pronoun series. They may also take the exclamatory -*wy* ending "How . . . !" This use—although not exceedingly frequent—is probably more common than generally held.

Since participles are adjectives (derived from verbal roots) and can serve as predicate adjectives, the distinction between adjectives and verbs is often a very fine one indeed. Of course, this is not unlike the situation with English participles used as predicate adjectives: "That's disgusting!" (with a participle) parallel to "That's awful!" (with an adjective).

Ex.

ḥʿ(w) sw ỉm r sprw (§121, 1a) *nb*

He is more joyous over it (literally "therein") than any other petitioner. (Ptaḥḥ. 270)

§119. Adjectival Features of the Participle

Participles, like all adjectives, express gender and number and are declined exactly like other adjectives (and nouns). As usual, only the feminine marker *t* is consistently written out. When they are used as modifiers they follow the noun and must agree in gender and number. When they are used as predicate adjectives they are always masc. sing. regardless of the gender or number of the subject (§44). The feminine singular forms may be used as abstract nouns meaning "thing that..." "what (is) ..." or "something that..." (§21, 2).

§120. Verbal Features of the Participles

Participles, like other verb forms, express voice: active and passive. They also express tense / mood: past, present, and prospective (a future equivalent [active voice only] involves a different form, §125). Like other verb forms, participles may have a direct or indirect object (dative): 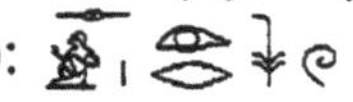 *s ỉr sw* "the man who made it." 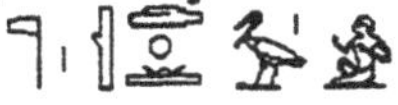 *nṯr qd b3·ỉ* "the god who formed my *ba*."

§121. Forms of the Participle

There are three basic types of participles in Middle Egyptian: imperfect, perfect, and prospective. Each type has both active and passive counterparts (thus a total of six forms). The strong verbs hardly differentiate any of these forms in writing, and one must deduce which form is required based solely on context. Even with the anomalous verbs, where one can differentiate between imperfect and perfect forms, one must usually determine whether the active or passive form is required by the meaning demanded by the context. Usually the voice is obvious, at least after some consideration (e.g. "I am one who was praised in the palace"—and not *"one who praised in the palace"). Sometimes parallel statements may contain forms from the mutable verbs that corroborate the determination of the particular form. For instance, in a tomb inscription, one might suppose that in the phrase "I am one who..." the speaker employed the perfect participle. This may be corroborated by the occurrence of non-geminating 3rd weak (i.e. perfect) participles later in the inscription. However, the tomb owner may have considered his actions as on-going or timeless and therefore used imperfect participles.

1, a) Imperfect Active Participle

The imperfect[1] participle conveys relative present time. The masc. sing. sometimes has an ending in *-w* or *-y*, but mostly it is not indicated. Otherwise the participle is declined exactly like other adjectives (and nouns). E.g. *bꜣ ꜥnḫy* "a living *ba*"; *ꜥnḫw* "the living" (i.e. "those who live"), or when in direct address (the vocative): "you who are alive."

The forms for the various verb classes are listed below. Note that the "gemination" in the participle is completely unrelated to gemination found in the "suffix conjugation." In other words, here, as elsewhere, gemination does not mean anything *in and of itself*. Particular forms either have it or do not have it. Nevertheless, its presence or absence is significant. Thus, although gemination is found in imperfect participles (and not in perfect participles), gemination in no way is a marker of "present tense."

Strong Verbs: all consonants— *sḏm* "hearing, listening," "(one) who listens"

3rd Weak: with gemination— *hꜣꜣ* "who goes down"

2nd Gem.: with gemination— *ḫnnw* "brawlers" (i.e. "ones who cause a disturbance")

ii / iw: *ii* "that comes"

ini: *inn* "who brings"

rdi: without *r*; with reduplication: , , *dd* "who gives / puts / places / causes"

wnn: with gemination— *wnn(w)* "(those) who are"

mꜣꜣ: with gemination— *mꜣꜣt* "(she) who sees"

Anomalous: *irr*, *ir(r)* "who does." When written with only one *r*, the second *r* is included in parentheses in transliterations.

Exx.

As an adjective:

ꜣḫ sḏm n sꜣ sḏmw
Listening is good for a son who listens (or "an obedient son"). (Ptaḥḥ. 534)

As a noun:

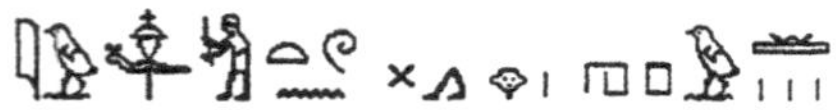

iw ḫsf tw n[2] *swꜣ ḥr hpw*
One punishes him who passes over the laws. (Ptaḥḥ. 90)

[1] I.e. the action is not "completed." The term "imperfective" is used in the standard grammars, but is confusing.

[2] The phrase *ḫsf* + the preposition *n* = "to punish" requires the dative, not a direct object (i.e. it means something like "to deal out punishment *to* (a person)."

1, b) Imperfect Passive Participle

The masc. sing. passive forms often end with *w*. This may reflect a *u*-vowel (cf. the Semitic passive participle: *katūb*.) This ending is more commonly written than that of the active forms. The passive forms usually look identical to their active counterparts, and the voice must be determined from the context (usually quite obvious—temples, for instance, are built, but do not build). The occurrence of gemination is identical to that of the active forms.

Ex.

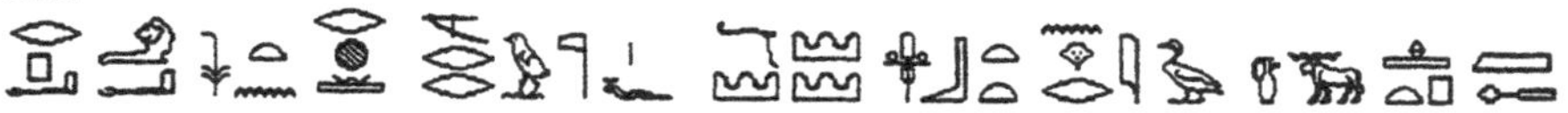

ỉry pᶜt, ḥ3ty-ᶜ, rḫ-nsw, mrrw nṯr·f, ỉmy-r smy(w)t ỉ3bt(yw)t Ḫnm(w)-ḥtp s3 Nḥrỉ (§41, 1), *m3ᶜ ḫrw*
Hereditary prince, count, royal acquaintance,[3] beloved of his god, the overseer of the Eastern Deserts, Khnum-ḥotpe, son of Neḥri, justified. (*Rb* 67, 12)

ỉr(r)t nbt n[4] *nsw*
all the things that are done for a king (West. 12, 2)

2, a) Perfect Active Participle

These forms express relative past time. Masc. sing. forms sometimes end with *w*. E.g. *ỉr m3ᶜt* "the one who did justice," *st ḏdt ḥr·s* "the woman who spoke about it."

Strong Verbs: all consonants— *sḏm* "hearing, listening," "(one) who listened"

3rd Weak: no gemination— *h3* "who went down"

2nd Gem.: no gemination— *qb* "that was cool"

ỉỉ / ỉw: both roots occur *ỉỉ*, var. *ỉy*; *ỉw* "that came"

ỉnỉ: *ỉn* "who brought"

rdỉ: usually with *r* *rdỉ*; more rarely without *r*: *dỉ* "who gave / put / placed / caused"

wnn: no gemination— *wn(w)* "which was"

m33: no gemination— *m3t* "(she) who saw"

Anomalous: *ỉr*, *ỉr* "who did" The latter writing is identical to the less full writing of the imperfect participle (*ỉrr*)

Exx.

ḏd mdw ḥr ỉrtt n(y)t msỉt ṯ3y
Words recited over the milk of one who has given birth to a male child. (P. Ebers 69, 7)

[3]Perhaps *rḫ* is the passive participle, "who is known" in a bound construction.

[4]The "negative arms" *n* is not infrequently used in hieratic texts for the dative *n*—but *not* for the genitival *n(y)*.

ḥʿ nṯr ꜣbḫ(w) (§87) *m ir sw*
the flesh of the god (i.e. the deceased king's body) having been united with the one who made him (Sinuhe R1, 8 ff.)

2, b) Perfect Passive Participle

The passive forms generally correspond to their active counterparts, apart from the bi-consonantal class. These forms sometimes have an ending *y*, possibly vocalic (cf. the Semitic passive participles with *i*-vowel: *katība* "written"). E.g. *mi gmyt m sš* "like what was found in writing." Occasional forms with *w* ending are also attested.

Some bi-consonantal roots exhibit gemination of the second consonant. These forms need not be committed to memory, but this section should be noted for future reference: e.g. *wḏḏt* "what had been decreed"; *rḫḫy* "one who is known" (the tense may be present tense in the English translation); *ḫmmy* "which are unknown"; *šꜣꜣt* "which had been ordained"; *ḏddt* "what was said."

This form of the participle occurs in the epithet *di ʿnḫ* "given life" used after the king's name in the royal titulary (§69).

Exx.

rḫ ir(ryw)t (§121, 1b) *m dgm m* (§24) *gmyt* (§121, 2b) *m sšw iswt m* (§24) *ꜣḫt n rmṯ(w)*
(Title of a medical text): Knowledge of what is made from the castor oil plant—as found in (literally "as something that was found in") the writings of antiquity, being something of benefit to people. (P. Ebers, 47, 15 ff.)

iw·i mi s itw m ʿḫḫw
I was like a man who had been overpowered by darkness. (Sinuhe B. 254)

3, a) Prospective Active Participle

There is no gemination in the prospective participles of 3rd weak and 2nd geminating classes of verbs. These forms and their passive counterparts therefore tend to look like the perfect participles, but the tense is relative future or else they express the optative mood "who should do," "that ought to happen" or "what is desirable to happen." Some scholars have denied their existence, but they are fairly widely accepted these days. *mst* "she who will give birth."

Exx.

ḫsf iw ḫr irt iy(w)t
The one who should punish crime is committing offences. (Peas. B1, 102–3)

3, b) Prospective Passive Participle

The prospective passive participles are indistinguishable from their active counterparts in written form, but the passive meaning is required. The fem. sing. sometimes ends with *ti*, e.g. *ḏd·ti* "what might be said."

Ex.

m ꜥm(w) (§166) *ib·k ḥr ḏd·ti n·k*

Do not be neglectful concerning that which might be said to you. (Ptaḥḥ, 153)

§122. Translations of the Participle

There are three basic translations of participles.

1) The English **participle** "the living god."
2) As a **profession**: "baker," "singer," "scribe," etc.
3) A **relative clause** "which creeps upon the earth," "one who works," "he who comes," "that moves," "that which was found," etc.

The English relative clause is often the best translation. The Egyptian participle does *not* constitute a relative clause in Egyptian, but this is a convenient way to translate it.

§123 Extended use of the Passive Participles

The passive participles are not infrequently followed by a "complementary direct object," that is, what would normally be the direct object if an active verb form had been used. For example in the phrase *bw irw ḫrw im* "the place where the sound was made," the noun *bw* "place" is modified by the perfect passive participle *irw* "which was done," and the thing that was done is then specified, here *ḫrw* "sound." The whole phrase is then wrapped up with the resumptive *im* "there." When the "complementary direct object" is a pronoun, the dependent series is used. The demonstrative pronouns (e.g. *nn*) may also occur as "complementary direct objects."

The passive participle in these cases refers to its antecedent *indirectly*. The use is generally similar to that of *nty* with indirect reference to the antecedent (§112, end). The "resumptive" pronouns, the dative ("to whom ..."), and other words (e.g. *im* "where," "in which," "with which," etc.) may also be used. In translating, one may usually use the passive voice, but the "complementary direct object" should be made the subject of the phrase in English (since it is impossible in English to say: **"the place that was made the sound there"). Resumptive words, although essential to the Egyptian, are redundant in English. For instance *w3t šm(y)t ḥr·s* must be translated as "the road that is walked upon" or "the road that one / they walk on" (or more formally, "the road upon which one walks"), since **"the road that is walked upon it" is impossible in English.

Particularly common is the phrase introducing a person's secondary name or nickname. In this expression, the dative is required: *PN_1 ḏdw n·f PN_2* "Name$_1$, who is called Name$_2$." (Literally "Name$_1$ to whom is said 'Name$_2$.'")

Some of these constructions can, it must be admitted, seem quite convoluted. For instance,  *rꜥ mꜣꜣw ḫt nbt m stwt·f* must be translated as "the sun, by whose rays all things are seen," in which *rꜥ* "sun" is modified by the imperfect passive participle *mꜣꜣw* "is seen," when in fact it is not "the sun" that is seen, but rather "all things."[5] Actually, the problem is *not* that the Egyptian is so convoluted, but rather the fact that English is incapable of such phrases as: **"the sun which is seen—things—by its rays." Note that the "complementary direct object" may also be left out: "the sun by whose rays one sees" for the impossible English **"the sun which is seen by its rays." Such constructions are notoriously difficult for beginning students, and only with time and repeated exposure does this use come to "feel" natural.

English actually allows a similar use, but only with a handful of verbs such as "to give," cf. "the player who was given the highest award of the season." (The *award* and not the *player* was given, but the passive form grammatically refers back to the *player*.) Egyptian allows this with almost any verb (even intransitive verbs of motion[6]), and goes one step beyond the English use, since the reference can be *indirect*—as if one could say: **"the peasant who was given food to his wife" for "the peasant whose wife was given food."

Exx.

Sꜣt-Spdw, sꜣt Šft, ḏd(y)t n·s Tỉ
Sit-Sopdu, daughter of Šaftu, called Teti (P. Kahun, 12, 8)

ꜥḥꜥ·n sḏm·n·s ḫrw ḥsy šmꜥw, ḫbt, wꜣg,

ỉr(r)t nbt n nsw m tꜣ ꜥt ... wn·ỉn·s (§131) *ḥr dbn tꜣ ꜥt,*

n gm·n·s bw ỉrw st ỉm
She heard the sound of singing, music-making, dancing, and ⸢celebrating⸣—everything that is done for a king—in the room ... She was going (all) around the room, but she could not find the place where it was done. (West. 12, 1–3)

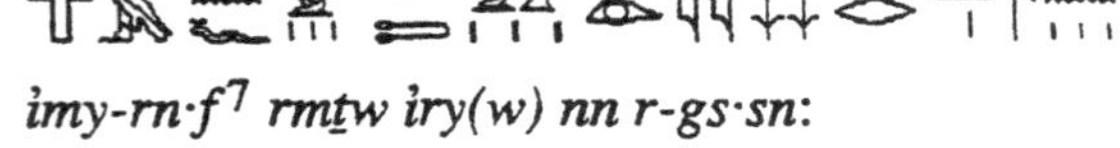

ỉmy-rn·f[7] *rmṯw ỉry(w) nn r-gs·sn:*

[5]Alternately, one could supply a subject in the translation: "by whose rays we see."
[6]E.g. "the road that is walked upon ..."
[7]The term *ỉmy-rn·f* "list" is a compound word of a sort that seems quite illogical to English speakers, since by our

List of persons in whose presence[8] this was made: (followed by the names of witnesses to a legal document) (P. Kahun, 12, 13)

§124. Passive Participle + Noun (bound construction) or with Genitival *n(y)* + Noun

Very frequently the passive participle occurs in a bound construction with a following noun. Examples such as *mrr(w) nb·f* "the beloved of his lord," (or "one who is / used to be loved by his lord"),[9] but the construction with the genitival *n(y)* + noun also occurs: *ḥss(y) n(y) mwt·f* "one who is / used to be praised by his mother."

§125. *Sḏm·ty·fy*, *Sḏm·ty·sy*, and *Sḏm·ty·sn* Future Active Participles

These forms are a limited set of future active participles, and are only used when referring to individuals in the 3rd person: "he," "she," "it," "they." There are no passive counterparts. They are formed with the following suffixes:

Masc. Sing.	*·ty·fy*, var. *·ty·f(y)*, *·t(y)·fy*, *·t(y)·f(y)*
Fem. Sing.	*·ty·sy*, var. *ty·s(y)*, *t(y)·sy*, *t(y)·s(y)*
Plural	*·ty·sn*, var. *t(y)·sn*

The forms from the mutable verbs are as follows:

3rd weak: no gemination *ỉr·ty·s(y)* "she who will make"

2nd gem.: gemination *mꜣꜣ·ty·fy* "who will see"

ỉw / ỉỉ: "to come" *ỉw·ty·sn* "who will come"

rdỉ "to give" with *r* *rdỉ·ty·f(y)* "he who will give"

wnn "to be" *wnn·t(y)·sn* "those who will be"

The *sḏm·ty·fy* forms are adjectival (as are also the true participles), but their use is somewhat more limited, as they are not used as predicate adjectives. As well, they are not used in the construction known as the "participial statement" (§134). All the other uses, however, are identical to those of the participles. There is some overlap with the prospective participles.

The more abbreviated writings tend to look exactly like the abbreviated writings of passive *sḏm·f* forms with *·tw*. In practice, there is little confusion, since the use of the *sḏm·ty·fy* forms (adjectival) is quite different from that of the passive forms (e.g. statements of fact,

---

logic it should mean: "that which is in his name," but probably originated from a colloquial phrase meaning "his name's in it."

[8]Literally "at whose side."

[9]A phrase *mrr nb·f* might hypothetically contain the active participle: "one who loves his lord," but this would not be said, since it is the feelings of the "lord" that are important, and not the feelings of the subordinate.

circumstantial clauses, purpose clauses). Only the use of the circumstantial clause as a relative clause with indefinite antecedent (§38) would be similar, but the context should leave no doubt (e.g. is the required voice active or passive? Is the required tense relative present or future?).

Exx.

ḫnms·tn wd (§121, 2a) *sp nfr ḏd·ty·f(y) n·ỉ nhy n(y) md(w)t nfr(w)t*

a friend of yours who has made a fine achievement who will tell me a few fine words (Neferty, Pet. 7)

ḏd·k ḫt tnw, ỉḫ[10] *ḏd srw sḏm·ty·sn: nfrwy prw n(y) r·f!*

You should say things of distinction, then the officials who will hear will say: "How fine are the declarations[11] of his mouth!" (Ptaḥḥ, 625–27)

§126. Possession

In general, the dative (the preposition *n* "to, for") is used in the sentence with adverbial comment: *ỉw n·ỉ X* "I have an X" (literally "there is an X [belonging] to me.") Other expressions sporadically occur. They are not terribly common, but they were not necessarily rarities in the language, and should be noted.

Ex.

mk bꜥḥ rn·ỉ, mk r ḫrd qn ḏd(w) (§121, 1b) *r·f: ỉw·f {ỉw·f}*[12] *n msdw·f*

Behold, my name[13] stinks, yes, more than a strapping child about whom is said: "He belongs to his rival.[14]" (*Lebensm.* 99–101)

1) *N(y) sw X* "He belongs to X"

When the thing or person "possessed" is a pronoun, the genitival adjective *n(y)* can be used as the predicate adjective to mean "he belongs to X." The dependent pronoun series is used, and as any other predicate adjective (§44), *n(y)* is invariable in gender and number. With the 3rd person sing., a writing with the "tongue" sign *ns* is quite common: *n(y)-sw*, *n(y)-sy*. Several common personal names involve this construction, and it was also occasionally

[10]A particle indicating sequence or consequence, "then," "so."

[11]Literally, "that which has come forth."

[12]The second *ỉw·f* is an error (dittography). Note how this is indicated in the transliteration.

[13]In Egyptian (as in the Semitic languages) "name" has a rather broad range of meanings, and often means "reputation," and the like.

[14]I.e. his father's rival. In other words the child is said to be born of adultery.

used to indicate measurements (English usage involves "being [a measure]," but other languages, as Egyptian, involve "having [a measurement].")

Exx.

n(y) wi Rᶜ
I belong to Rēᶜ. (*Lesest.* 47, 11)

N(y)-sw-Mnṯw
He-belongs-to-Montu (a man's name)

2) *Ntf X* "X belongs to him"

The independent pronouns followed by a noun are occasionally used to mean "to him belongs ..." or "... belongs to him." At first sight such sentences might seem to mean "he is X" (cf. the AB type nominal sentence, §56, 1), and indeed, they are structurally identical, but the meaning will be impossible in context. For instance, it is not difficult to decide between: **"You are gold." and "Gold belongs to you."

Ex.

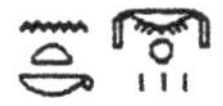

ntk nbw
Gold belongs to you. (Urk. IV 96, 6)

3) *N·f ỉmy X* "X belongs to him"

The phrase *n·f ỉmy* (*n·k ỉmy*, etc.) is composed of the dative unit *n* + suffix pronoun, followed by the *nisba* derived from the preposition *m*. In this construction *ỉmy* serves as the predicate adjective (whose rules are in full force, e.g. the subject is the dependent pronoun, when not a noun).

Exx.

n·k ỉmy ḥḏ
Silver belongs to you. (Urk. IV 96, 7)

n·k ỉm(y) s(y) mitt ṯsmw·k
It (Canaan) belongs to you—a thing like your dogs. (Sinuhe B 222)

§127. *n·f ỉmy* "Of His" / "His Own"

A noun may be followed by the phrase *n* (dative) + suffix pronoun + *ỉmy*. The writings are sometimes abbreviated: *n·k ỉm(y)*. Sometimes the use is that of the partitive "of them."

Exx.

ỉw smsw n·sn ỉmy r ỉrt wr mꜣw m ỉwnw
The eldest of them will serve as the Greatest of Seers (i.e. the high priest of Rēʿ) in Heliopolis. (West. 9, 11 f.)

tꜣ ḥꜣt n·n ỉmy
this vanguard of ours (Urk. IV 650, 5)

§128. AB Nominal Sentences

The simple nominal sentence in which element A is simply followed by element B (without any connecting words), known as the "AB nominal sentence," was introduced in §56, 1. This sentence pattern is used in the following cases:

1. A is an independent pronoun (*ỉnk*, *ntk* etc.) and B is a noun.
   ỉnk Wr ỉr (§121, 2a) *šsp·f*
   I am the Great One who made his light. (BD 147)
2. A is an interrogative pronoun, e.g. , *pw-tr*, *ptr*, later variant *pty* "who?"; "what?". In this case, B is commonly a dependent pronoun.
   pty rf sw Who, then, is he? (BD, *passim*.)
3. A is a name and B is *rn·f*, *rn·s*, etc.
   N(y)-s(w)-Ptḥ (§§41,1; 126, 1) *rn·f* Nisu-Ptaḥ is his name. (Often as subordinate clause: "whose name is Nisu-Ptaḥ," or "Nisu-Ptaḥ by name.")
4. A is *rn* "name" and B specifies the name.
   rn n(y) mr pn Wn-tꜣ-Wꜣt The name of this canal is "Opening-the-way" (*Rb* 46, 4–5)

§129. Bi-partite Nominal Sentences with *pw*

The demonstrative pronoun *pw* ("this") is used invariably (i.e. it does not agree in gender and number) in the two-element construction *X pw*, meaning "it is X," "this is X," or "he / she / it is X," "they are X." This construction is a special type of AB nominal sentence, but differs somewhat from these. Most importantly, *pw* "it" takes position B, but it is the topic, while the noun in slot A is the comment. (I.e. the speaker is talking about B, and A is what is said about B.) The term bi-partite is used because the sentence consists of two components (A and B). Some scholars refer to *pw* as the "copula" (a linking word like the verb "to be" in English). It is not the copula, but is almost identical in meaning and function with French *ce* in the sentence *C'est moi*.

If a pronoun fills position A, it must be of the independent series. Note that *pw* must come immediately after the first word (or words in the case of a compound or bound construction), and modifiers of element A (such as adjectives, participles, and noun phrases introduced with the genitival *n(y)*, etc.) may continue after the *pw*. When element A consists of a bound construction, this is treated as an indivisible unit that is followed by *pw*. (I.e. nouns in the bound construction cannot be broken up with an intervening word.)

Negations of these sentences are formed with the particle *n* or the compound negative ... *n ... is*. Occasionally *pw* is left out in negated sentences.

Exx.

pw tr rf sw? snf pw pr m ḥnnw n(y) Rᶜ m-ḫt wꜣ·f (§75, 2) *r irt šᶜd(w) im·f ḏs·f*

What then is it? It is the blood that came forth from the phallus of Rēᶜ after he started to make incisions upon his own person. (BD ch. 17)

Pty sy tꜣ Rd-ḏdt? ḏd·in (§131) *Ḏdi: ḥmt wᶜb pw n(y) Rᶜ Nb Sꜣḫbw, iwr·ti m ẖrdw 3 n(y) Rᶜ Nb Sꜣḫbw*

"Who is she—this Redjedet?" Then Djedi said: "She is the wife of a *wᶜb*-priest of the Temple of Rēᶜ, Lord of Saḫbu, who is pregnant with the three children of Rēᶜ, Lord of Saḫbu." (West. 9, 8 ff.)

ḏd·in·sn (§131) *ḫft Ḥm·f: n ntf pw m mꜣᶜt, ity, nb·i. ḏd·in Ḥm·f: ntf pw m mꜣᶜt*

Then they said to (literally "before") His Majesty: "It is not really[15] him (is it)? O sovereign, my lord!" Then His Majesty said: "It is really him." (Sinuhe B1, 268 ff.)

n sꜣ·i is

(He) is not my son. (*Les.* 84, 16)

§130. Bi-partite Nominal Sentences with Other Demonstrative Pronouns

The construction is identical to that with *pw*, the only difference being that the demonstrative force is retained ("this" as opposed to the sense "it," "he," "she" of *pw*). The pronoun *nn* "this" is especially common in this type of sentence.

[15]"In truth."

Ex.

dpt mt nn
This is the taste of death. (Sinuhe B1, 22)

§131. The *Sḏm·in·f* "Then he heard" and Related Constructions

There are two sentence particles that introduce statements concerning events contingent upon previous circumstances (whether the circumstances are made explicit or not): *ḫr*, and *k3*. The idea behind these particles is: (if such and such is the case), "then ..." and they can usually be translated with "then" (in this sense of the word).

There also existed a special verbal stem used involving these particles and a third, *in*, as "infixed" elements. The resulting forms are known as the *sḏm·in·f*, *sḏm·ḫr·f*, and *sḏm·k3·f*. All of these relate things as events "contingent" upon previous circumstances, events, actions, etc.[16] Only the *sḏm·in·f* is common, and it is used extremely often in narrative tales, for instance in introducing changes in speakers in a conversation: "then [speaker 1] said: ..." "Then [speaker 2] said: ..." For translation purposes, one may render the *sḏm·in·f* (and the other contingent forms) as "then he heard," etc.

The sentence construction using these forms is never introduced by *iw* or *mk*. The "bare initial" *sḏm·in·f* begins a new main clause, but relates it to previous circumstances. Clauses beginning with *sḏm·ḫr·f* may be secondary main clauses (e.g. following conditional clauses: "If ..., then he will hear ..."). But such uses are rarely found outside of medical texts.

Also common in narratives is the use of the *sḏm·in·f* form of *wnn* "to be" *wn·in·f* to introduce non-verbal sentences with adverbial comments. The full range of adverbial comments are encountered:

wn·in [subject] + prepositional phrase

wn·in [subject] + adverb

wn·in [subject] + *ḥr* + infinitive

wn·in [subject] + stative

The forms of the *sḏm·in·f* in mutable and irregular verbs are in need of more study (there may be even more than one form involved), but are generally as follows:

3rd weak: without gemination *iri·in·sn*

***iw* / *ii*:** the stem *iw* is used: *iw·in*

***rdi*:** almost always with initial *r*; never with gemination: *rdi·in·f*

***wnn*:** without gemination *wn·in·f*

[16] The function of these forms has been dealt with in depth by Leo Depuydt in his valuable study: *Conjunction Contiguity Contingency* (Oxford University Press: 1993).

The forms of the ***sḏm·ḫr·f*** are possibly built on a different stem as shown by the forms of the 2nd geminating verbs and *wnn* "to be."[17]

3rd weak: without gemination *ỉri·ḫr·k*

2nd gem.: *mꜣꜣ·ḫr·k*

rdỉ: with initial *r*; without gemination: *rdỉ·ḫr·k*

wnn: almost always with gemination *wnn·ḫr·f*, but also rarely without gemination: *wn·ḫr·f*, which seems to be: 1) a form related to the prospective *sḏm·f*; 2) a form related to the *sḏm·n·f* past form

Exx.

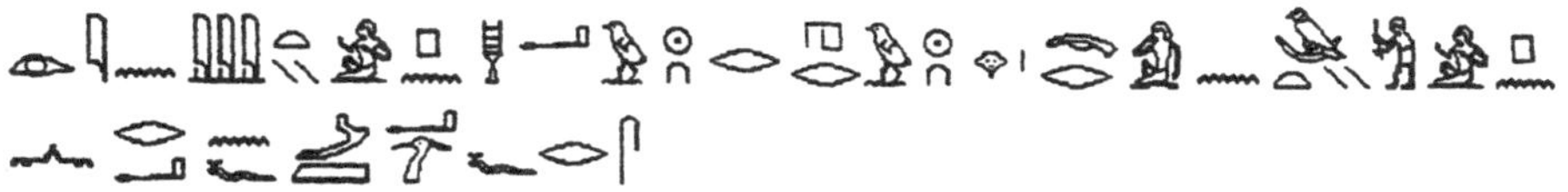

ỉri·in sḫty pn ꜥḥꜥw {10} r hrw 10 ḫr spr n Nmty-nḫt(w) pn, n rdỉ·n·f mꜣꜥ·f r·s

Then this peasant spent a period of[18] ten days petitioning to this Nemty-nakhte, but he did not give his attention to it. (Peas. B1 31 f.)

wn·in sḫty pn ḥr rmyt ꜥꜣw (§97)*wrt n mr n(y) ỉryt r·f*

Then this peasant was crying very greatly because of the pain of that which was done to him. (Peas. B1 24 ff).

wn·in ib n(y) Ḥm·f nfr(w) n mꜣꜣ ḫnn·sn[19]

Then His Majesty's heart was happy at seeing how they rowed. (West. 5, 14–15)

VOCABULARY X

ꜣḫw "skills," "expertise," "craft"

ỉyt "mishap," "incident," "trouble," "offence," "wrongdoing" (i.e. unfavourable things that happen or are committed—literally "that which has come," cf. English "event," "outcome" for a similar, but less negative, semantic development)

[17]But it is also possible that the contingent verb forms are a single conjugation, but that they distinguish relative tense and mood (e.g. *sḏm·n·f* for past tense, and have prospective forms, etc.). The apparent differences in form might then be shown to be differences in tense (e.g. *sḏm·in·f* forms would be related to the *sḏm·n·f* forms). In any case, there are obviously too many discrepancies to simply consider the contingent *sḏm·f* forms as part of the other *sḏm·f* conjugations.

[18]The Egyptian uses the preposition *r* "(amounting) to," "as long as."

[19]The direct object of *mꜣꜣ*, *ḫnn·sn*, is a second tense form and means "how they row."

ỉw "crime," "wrongdoing," "injustice," "misconduct"

ỉmy-rn·f "list of names"

ỉnỉ "to bring"; "to attain," "reach" (a goal, etc.)

ỉrt sing. fem. "eye"; the dual is possibly masculine, *ỉrwy*?

ỉs adj. "old," "ancient" Cf. Hebrew יָשָׁן (*yāšān*) and Ugaritic *yṯn* "old"

ỉswt "ancient times," "antiquity"

ỉṯỉ, var. *ỉtỉ*; infin. *ỉṯt*, *ỉtt* "to take," "take away," "overcome," and various idioms to be looked up in the dictionary

ỉdbwy: *ỉdb* "river-bank"; as dual "the Two Banks" = Egypt

ꜥpr "to equip"; in the stative: "to master" (a craft, etc., i.e., "to be equipped with" the required knowledge and experience)

wꜣ adjective: "far," "distant," "long ago";
verb: "to fall" *r* "into (a condition)," *wꜣ r* + infinitive "to start (doing)"

wpỉ "to open"; *wpỉ* *r* *r* + person: "to address" (a person)

wr mꜣw "Greatest of Seers" (title of the high priest of Rēꜥ in Heliopolis)

mr adj. "sick," "painful"; noun: "pain," "ailment"

mr "canal"

mty "straightforward," "exact," "correct"; "faithful," "loyal"

n This writing is sometimes used in hieratic texts for the preposition *n*, but almost never for the genitival *n(y)*.

nḫt(w) "strength," "force," "power"

, var. *rmỉ* "to cry"

rḫ nsw "royal acquaintance" (a title)

ḥꜣty "heart," "thought"; variant pl. *ḥꜣtyw* (not **ḥꜣt ỉbw*!)

ḥꜥ "flesh"; pl. *ḥꜥw* "body"; with suffixes: "~self"; "(so-and-so), in person"

ḥꜥỉ "to be joyous," "rejoice"

, *Ḥꜥpy* Nile, *ḥꜥp ꜥꜣ* "high Nile"; as god: Ḥaꜥpy

ḥmt "craft," "art"

ḥmww "artisan," "artist"

ḥsỉ, *ḥsy* (infin. without *t*) "to sing"

ḥḏ ḥr "cheerful" (literally "bright of face")

ḫt noun fem. "fire"

ḫn "phrase," "utterance," "speech"; "matter," "affair"; *ḫn nfr* "a kind word"

ḫsf "to oppose," "thwart," with *ḥr* + infinitive: "to prevent (someone) from doing (something)"; with the preposition *n*: "to punish"

ẖt noun, fem. (sometimes masc.) "belly," "abdomen," "womb"; the belly was considered the seat of emotions: "innermost being"

ẖnỉ "to row" (a boat)

Ḫnm(w) The god Khnum

s3q "to pull (oneself) together," "to be collected" (of mind), "composed"

sb in the expression *sb n(y) sḏt* "burnt-offering"

sb3 "to teach" (can take two direct objects: "to teach a person a thing")

smsw "eldest" (of persons) Note the crook at the bottom of the staff.

srwd (from *srwḏ*; *s*-causative) "to strengthen"; "to perpetuate" (offerings to the gods)

sḏt "fire," "flame"

šdỉ "to dig out," "cut out," "carve (out)"; "remove"

qnỉ adjective and verb "to be brave," "strong," "sturdy," etc. Cf. ? Semitic *dnn*: Ugaritic *dnn* "to be strong, powerful"; Akkadian *danānu* "to be strong, powerful

grg "to establish," "re-establish," "found"; "to prepare"

ṯnỉ, *tnỉ* "to distinguish" (one thing *r* "from" another); "to be distinguished," "elevated" (of actions, speech, character, etc.)

ṯnw, *tnw* "distinction," "eminence"

ṯst "troops"

dbn "to go around," "circulate," "travel around"

dgỉ (transitive) "to hide" (something); (intransitive) "to be in hiding", "to be hidden"

ḏ3 "fire-drill" (an implement to start fires)

ḏf3w "provisions," "sustenance," "abundance"

, abbreviated *ḏd mdw* "words to be recited" (*ḏd* is the infinitive [§57, 7] literally "the saying of words"): a phrase to introduce the text of rituals, incantations, and lines of dialogue of divinities in dramatic performances or on temple walls accompanying illustrations (the speaker is identified by the agent particle *in* "by")

EXERCISE X

(A) Reading Passage: Note that some words are somewhat abbreviated or slightly "miswritten"—as is normally the case in original texts.

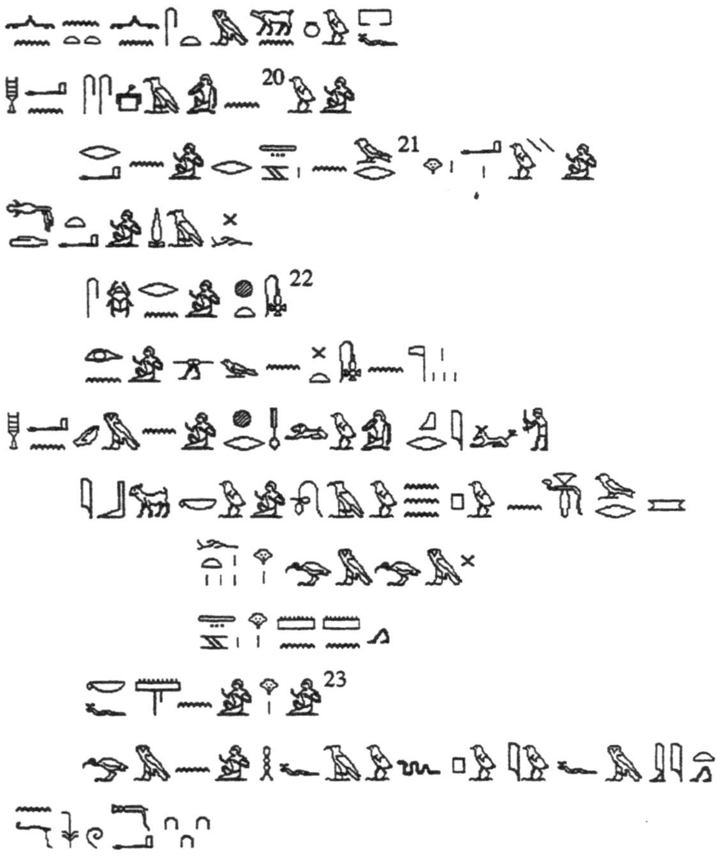

[20]The subject has been omitted either through error or because it was considered unnecessary (§140).

[21]The subject of *wr* (fruit and vegetables) was probably omitted since it is clear from the context. English requires the use of a "dummy" subject: "because there was so much...." Alternately, *wr* might be analysed as a noun meaning "excess," "large amount."

[22]Note to advanced readers: The *sḏm·n·f* forms may be 2nd tense forms used in a reciprocal construction (§152). They have usually been analysed as circumstantial *sḏm·n·f* forms standing parallel to preceding clauses of the *ꜥḥꜥ·n sḏm·n·f* construction (§95).

[23]The *sḏm·n·f* forms may possibly be 2nd tense forms used in a reciprocal construction (§152). They are here presented as parallel clauses (§95).

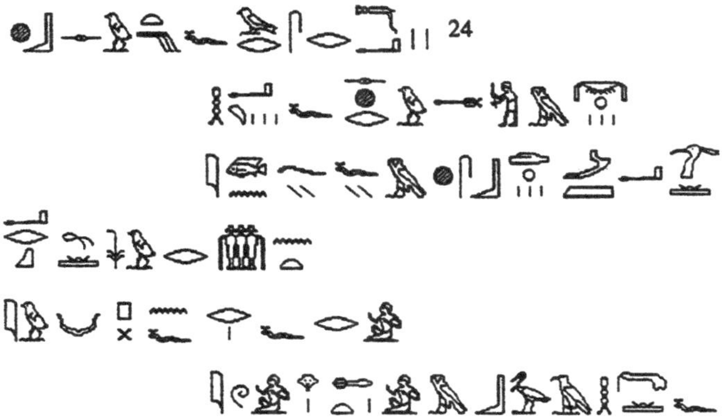

(B) Transliterate and Translate. Much of the new vocabulary must be looked up in the dictionary. A couple of writings are not exactly as found in the dictionary or vocabulary.

1) An address to the king who, as plentiful provider, is the source of much happiness:

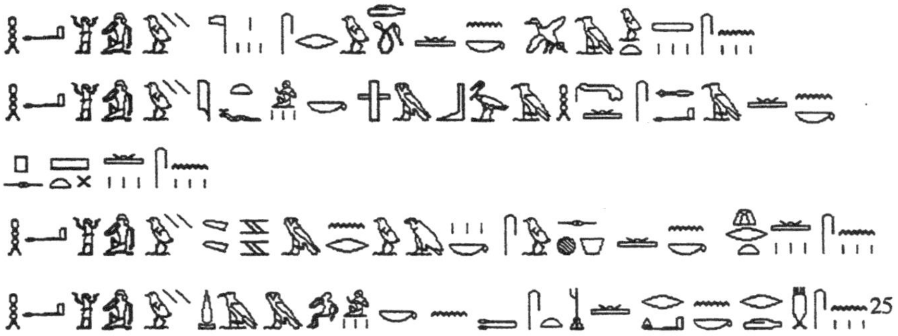

2) On the nature of art and rhetoric:

3) A self-laudatory tomb inscription:

[24]This is another case of "fronting" a noun to the head of the sentence (topicalization).

[25]*Rd* is a variant writing of 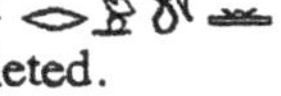 *rwḏ*.

[26]The second *n* is to be deleted.

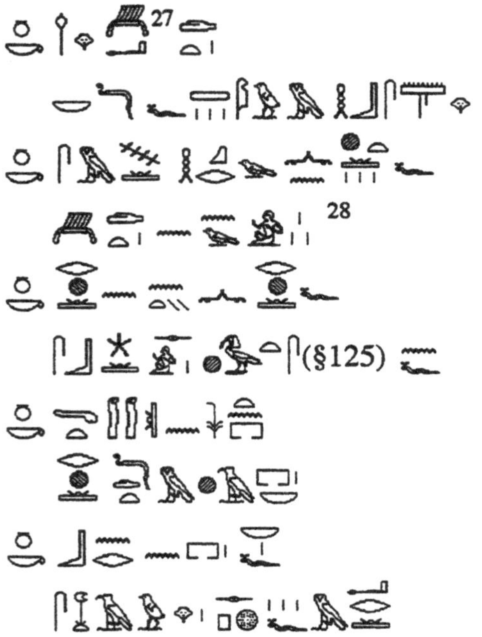

4) 

5) Said of the king who is identified with deities:

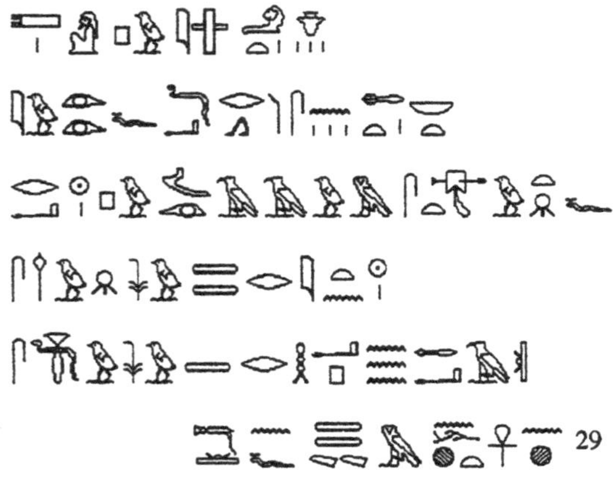

(C) Parse from *(B)*:

1) 

2) 

[27]The "arm" sign is a determinative.

[28]The last word is an abbreviated writing of *nḏsw*.

[29]Perhaps this clause forms an explicatory sentence (§148), but it could just as well be a circumstantial clause, and should be so translated for the purposes of this exercise.

3) 

4) 

5) 

LESSON 11

§132. The Possessive Article "My," "Your," "His," etc.

From the demonstrative pronoun (definite article) series *p3*, *t3*, *n3* were derived *nisba* forms which take personal suffixes (originally meaning something like "the one of + his" [etc.]): e.g.  *p3y·f*,  *t3y·f*, 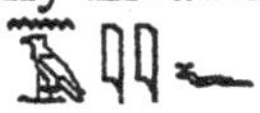 *n3y·f* "his." These are placed before the noun, and agree with it in gender and number. As with the plural definite article  *n3*, the plural form *n3y·* is used for both masc. and fem. nouns; earlier examples use genitival *n(y)*:  *n3y·f n(y)* + plural noun, but later examples have just  *n3y·f* + plural noun. The possessor is indicated by the appropriate suffix pronoun: e.g.  *p3y·f it, t3y·f mwt, ḥnꜥ n3y·f sn(w)t nb(w)t* "his father, his mother, together with all his sisters." This is the normal way of indicating possession in Late Egyptian, but these forms were already in use in colloquial Middle Egyptian, and are to be found in every-day documents of the Middle Kingdom and some literary works, but not in monumental inscriptions. Other examples:  *p3y·i pr* "my house,"  *n3y·s n(y) ẖrdw* "her children."

§133. Fronting of Nouns with  *ir* "As for..."

In verbal sentences, a noun or a noun phrase could be placed at the head of the sentence, thereby making it the topic or focal point of the sentence. The particle  *ir*, derived from the preposition  *r* "towards," "regarding," can also introduce nominal elements at the head of a sentence of almost any type. In this capacity, *ir* can be translated by the English: "As for X, ..." Subsequent conjugated verb forms, if they occur, require the appropriate suffix pronouns as subject.

The "fronted" topic is often the same as the subject of the verb, but this construction does not place particular emphasis on the topic as the "doer" of the action. (For this type of construction, see §134 ff.) Sometimes a subject was fronted because it was modified by one or more lengthy qualifiers; the whole unit could then be referred to by a single suffix pronoun, thus avoiding confusion. This construction is found in wisdom literature, but is particularly common in medical, magical, and didactic texts, especially when the speaker wished to point out something or clarify a term or name. The construction is not common, however, in narratives (except, perhaps, in quotations).

Exx.

ink sf, rḫ·kwi dw3w. pw tr rf sw? ir sf, Wsir pw. ir dw3w, R^c pw, hrw pwy n(y) sḥtm ḫftyw·f n(y)w Nb-r-ḏr im·f ḥn^c sḥq3·tw (§75, 2) *s3·f Ḥr*
"I am Yesterday, and I know Tomorrow." Who then is it?[1] As for "yesterday," it is Osiris. As for "tomorrow," it is Rē^c on that day of destroying his enemies—(i.e., those) of the Lord-of-All [Osiris] along with his son Horus' being installed as ruler. (BD ch. 17)

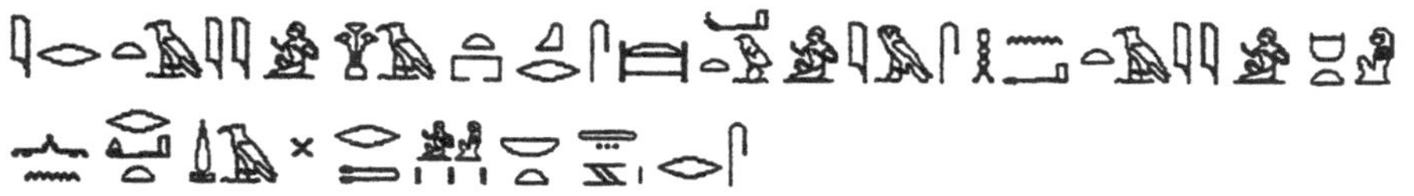

ir t3y·i ḥ3t qrs(t)·tw·i[2] *im·s ḥn^c t3y·i ḥmt, nn rdit d3 rmṯ(t) nbt t3 r·s*
As for my tomb in which I will be buried with my wife, there will be no permitting any person to interfere[3] with it. (Les. 91, 4–5)

§134. The "Participial" Statement

This construction, rather inappropriately known as the "participial statement," uses the perfect and imperfect participles and the 2nd prospective *sḏm·f* forms. It is used to highlight the "doer" of the action and is comparable to English "It is he who hears." Structurally, this is a type of "fronting," but the particle *in* specifically introduces the fronted noun as the "doer," as opposed to the non-specific use of the particle *ir* "as for." The particle *in* is no doubt the same particle used to introduce the "agent" in passive clauses. (And just as *ir* is an initial form derived from the preposition *r*, *in* is likely related to the preposition *n*).

Forms of the perfect and imperfect participles are used for past and present time, respectively. The 2nd tense prospective *sḏm(w)·f* forms (§138)—and *not* the prospective participles—are used for future time reference. Only examples with *active* participles / 2nd prospective *sḏm(w)·f* forms are known. The participle is always in the masc. sing. form and does not agree in gender and number with the "doer."

[1]This is a "gloss"—a type of commentary—on the text. First the gloss asks who the speaker in the main text is, then proceeds to supply the answer. Many beautiful, poetic parts of the Book of the Dead are riddled with such glosses, sometimes compounded with alternate glosses, which are introduced by *ky ḏd* "another saying...." The esoteric explanations of the more or less straightforward text often seem nonsensical to the modern reader. Here the speaker in the original text was claiming to have mastery over time. The writers of the glosses, however, were more concerned in identifying the speakers and relating their statements to mythical incidents. By contrast, glosses in the medical texts often supply important definitions of difficult technical terminology.

[2]*Qrs(t)·tw·i* is a (passive) relative form (§162 that modifies *ḥ3t* "tomb" and means "that I will be buried."

[3]The expression *d3 t3 r* + thing means "to interfere with." Here *nn* + infinitive must begin a main clause (unlike §105).

In the case of the future construction with the *sḏm(w)·f* forms, a 3rd person suffix pronoun must serve as the subject of the *sḏm(w)·f* form. The suffix pronoun agrees in gender and number with the noun introduced by *ỉn*. The 2nd prospective forms are dealt with in §138 and §188.

The three constructions are as follows:

Past	+ DOER + PERFECT PARTICIPLE (It is X who heard.)
Present	+ DOER + IMPERFECT PARTICIPLE (It is X who hears/is hearing.)
Future	+ DOER + 2nd PROSPECTIVE *SḎM(W)·F* (It is X who will hear.)

If the "doer" is a pronoun, the **independent pronoun series** is used *without* introduction by *ỉn*. There may be some morphological connection between the particle *ỉn* and the preformative element of the independent pronouns (i.e., the *n* of *ntf*, etc. may be related to the particle *ỉn*).

The interrogative pronoun *m* var. , "who?" can be used in this construction. Earlier texts write out *ỉn m* fully, but the two became fused as a single word *nm* "who." The Late Egyptian writing is , cf. Coptic ΝΙΜ (*nim*) "who?"

Exx.

ḏd·ỉn Ḏdỉ: ỉty,ʿnḫ(w) (w)ḏꜣ(w) s(nbw), nb·ỉ, mk nn ỉnk ỉs ỉnn n·k sy. ḏd·ỉn Ḥm·f: ỉn m rf ỉn(w)·f (§138) *n·ỉ sy? ḏd·ỉn Ḏdỉ: ỉn smsw n(y) pꜣ ẖrdw 3* (§66) *nty m ẖt n(y) Rdḏdt ỉn(w)·f n·k sy.*

Then Djedi said: "O Sovereign, l.p.h., my Lord, Behold, it is, in fact, not I who is bringing it to you." Then His Majesty said: "Well, who will bring it to me?" Then Djedi said: "It is the eldest of the three children who are in the womb of Redjedet who will bring it to you." (West. 9, 5 ff.)

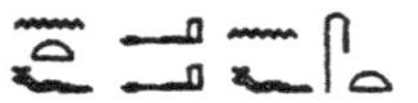

ntf dd n·f st

He is the one who was giving it to him. (Peas. B1 85–86)

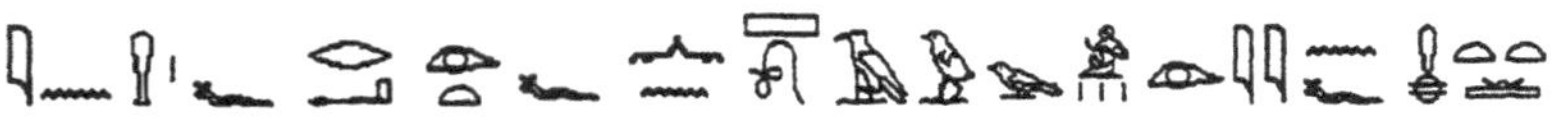

ỉn Ḥm·f rdỉ ỉr·t(w)·f; nn šwꜣw ỉry n·f mỉtt (§123)

It is His Majesty who had it done; there is no commoner for whom the like has been done. (Sin. B308 ff.)

§135. Tri-partite Nominal Sentences with *Pw*

The bi-partite nominal sentence with *pw* (§129) was expanded in a special way to permit the speaker to say "X is Y." The bi-partite element actually forms the core of the construction. As with the bi-partite sentence, *pw* ("this, it") is the grammatical subject, but it is followed by another noun in apposition that specifies what "it" refers to. E.g. *Y pw X* would mean literally, "It, namely X, is a / the Y." In other words, *Y pw* is the bi-partite core of the sentence. The pronoun *pw* is modified by X, which stands in apposition to it. In translating, it is customary to simply make *X* the subject in English, and *Y* the predicate (i.e. "X is a Y."). On a structural level, the Egyptian construction bears some resemblance to the French *L'état, c'est moi*.

Exx.

dmỉ pw ỉmnt

The West is a harbour.[4] (Lebensm. 38)

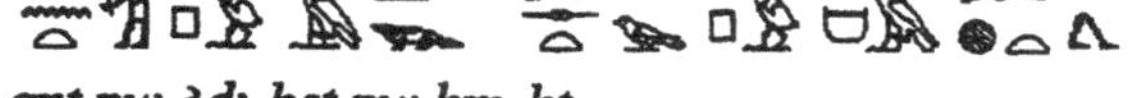

qnt pw ꜣd; ḫst pw ḥm-ḫt

Aggression is valour; retreating is cowardice. (*Les*. 84, 3–4)

§136.  *Šmt pw ỉr(w)·n·f* A Narrative Past Tense Construction

A very common narrative construction, used almost always with verbs of motion, is a special bi-partite nominal sentence in which the first element is the infinitive of the verb in question, which is modified by  *ỉr(w)·n·f*, a past relative *sḏm(w)·n·f* form (§161): "which / that he did." The subject of *ỉr(w)·n* is, of course, any noun or a suffix pronoun (only the third person occurs). The sentence  *šmt pw ỉr(w)·n·f* literally means "it is a going that he did," but this is normally translated "then he went," "and so he went," or simply "he went."

The construction is never preceded by *ỉw* or *mk*, but the sentences constitute main clauses. The *šmt pw ỉr(w)·n·f* construction introduces new action in the narrative, and is frequently followed by one or more sentences of the *sḏm·ỉn·f* construction to convey subsequent actions. (Other sentence types may, of course, follow the *šmt pw ỉr(w)·n·f*.) This construction may be followed by subordinate *sḏm·n·f* circumstantial clauses that relate prior events. The construction is extremely common in the tales.

A passive construction with  *ỉry*, the perfect passive participle, is encountered, but it is very rare: 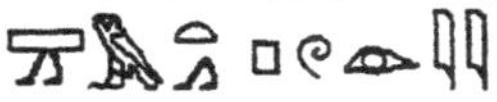 *šmt pw ỉry* literally "It is a going that was made...."

Exx.

prt pw ỉr(w)·n nn nṯrw, sms·n·sn Rdḏdt m pꜣ ḫrdw 3

These gods went out, having delivered Redjedet of these three children. (West. 11, 3–4)

[4]This is a poetic reference to the deceased person's tomb in the necropolis.

š3s pw ir(w)·n t3 wb3yt r int n·s ikn n(y) mw. ꜥḥꜥ·n it·n sy msḥ. š3s pw iry r dd st n Rddt in p3y·s sn
The maid went to get herself a basin (lit. "a drawing") of water. A crocodile seized her. A trip was made to tell this to Redjedet by her (the maid's) brother. (West. 12, 17–20)

§137. Conditional Sentences

The "if" clause of conditional sentences is most commonly introduced by the particle *ir* "if," which is nothing more than the initial form of the preposition *r* "as for" (§133). Conditional sentences are easily distinguished from the "fronted nominal phrase" by the presence of a *sḏm·f* verb form directly after *ir*. (The only words that commonly intervene between *ir* and the *sḏm·f* form are *grt* "now, however, but," and *swt* "but, however.") The "if clause" (known as the protasis) comes first and is followed by the "then clause" (known as the apodosis). The "then clause" may be of a variety of main clause sentence types including the prospective in a wish or exhortation ("you are to do ..."), an imperative (a command: "do ..." §145), a future tense: *iw·f r sḏm* ("he will ..."), or a *sḏm·ḫr·f* ("then he will ..."), the last of these being found mostly in medical texts.

§138. The Second Tense Prospective *Sḏm(w)·f* Forms

Since the particle *ir* is a form of a preposition, one rightly expects the phrase to follow to be nominal in grammatical function. Nominal phrases with verbal meaning are regularly formed by the use of a nominal form of the verb. Since we are dealing with a conjugated nominal form, two well known possibilities are readily at hand, 1) the prospective *sḏm·f*, and 2) the "second tense" *sḏm(w)·f* (§147). Prospective *sḏm·f* forms do indeed occur after *ir* in conditional sentences (*ir di·tw* "if [...] is given"; *ir grt m3n·k* "if, however, you should see...." The 2nd tense *sḏm·f* forms (§147) probably also occur, but rarely: *ir gmm·k* "if how you find it is...."

Somewhat more common, however, are forms of the "second tense prospective *sḏm(w)·f*."[5] A *w*-ending is found in the 2nd tense prospective forms with most verb classes, but as always, this ending is usually not written. At this point, only the use of these forms in the conditional sentence and the "participial statement" (§134) need be considered (most of the time it is impossible to distinguish between the two forms—even in conditional sentences). (Superficially the 2nd prospective forms appear to be identical to those of the circumstantial *sḏm·f*. Their functions, however, are quite distinct. The circumstantial is adverbial; the 2nd prospectives occur where nominal forms are required, and indeed, their negations are clearly nominal [§177].)

[5]For this verb form (and its bibliography), see Pascal Vernus, *Future at Issue. Tense, Mood and Aspect in Middle Egyptian: Studies in Syntax and Semantics* (New Haven, 1990), pp. 29–53. The *name* of this form—although quite a mouthful—has no meaning, and students are warned not to attempt to *understand* why it bears this name.

The Second Tense Prospective *Sḏm(w)·f*

3rd weak: without gemination *ỉr ỉrỉ·k* "if you make"

2nd gem.: with gemination *ỉr mꜣꜣ·k* "if you see"

ỉw/ỉỉ: the stem *ỉw*; with no *t*: *ỉw*

ỉnỉ: with no *t*: *ỉn(w)·f*

rdỉ: with initial *r*: *rd(w)*

wnn: with gemination *ỉr wnn·k* "if you are. . . ."

Only very rarely does one encounter a *sḏm·n·f* form after *ỉr* in conditional sentences. These may be translated "if I had . . ." or "if only I had. . . ." This use is for "unfulfilled conditions" (i.e. the action was not done). Examples are not likely to be encountered until advanced stages of study.

Exx.

ỉr ỉqr·k, grg·k pr·k, mrỉ·k ḥmt·k m ḫnw, mḥ (§145) *ẖt·s, ḥbs sꜣ·s*

If you are prosperous, you should establish your home; you should love your wife therein; fill her belly, clothe her back. (Ptaḥḥ. 325–27)

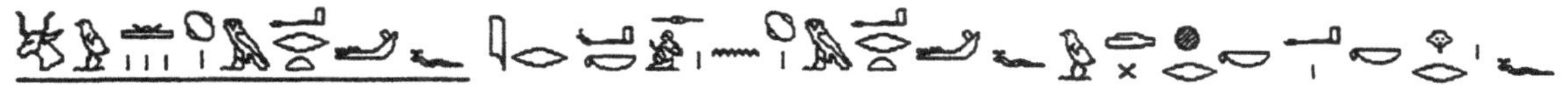

šsꜣw ḥsb m ꜥrt·f:[6] *ỉr ḫꜣỉ·k s n ḥsb m ꜥrt·f wdỉ·ḫr·k ꜥ·k ḥr·f . . .*

Treatment of a fracture in his jaw: If you examine a man for a fracture in his jaw, you are to place your hand upon him . . . (examination procedure and observations follow). (Ed. Sm. 8, 22 ff.)

§139. Conditional Clauses Without *ỉr*

Much less common than circumstantial clauses introduced by *ỉr* "if" are clauses with bare initial prospective *sḏm·f* forms conveying the sense "should X happen, Y would occur," etc. Usually the "should" clause precedes the "would" clause, but this is not always the case. Examples are not particularly common.

Ex.

wḏ·tw n·f dbꜣ st, dbꜣ·f st

[6]Underlining indicates *rubrics* in the original. Titles, headings, the opening words of new sections, etc. were often written in red ink.

Should he be ordered to repay it,[7] he would repay it. (Peas. B1 48-49.)

A pair of "should" clauses using prospective *sḏm·f* forms serves as the Egyptian equivalent of "whether he did X or whether he did Y." The overall use is reminiscent of French *soit ... soit*, which uses the subjunctive.

Ex.

mꜣ·sn pt, mꜣ·sn tꜣ, mꜥkꜣ ib·sn r mꜣw

Whether they looked at the sky or whether they looked at the land, their hearts were braver than (those) of lions. (Sh. S. 29)

§140. The Omission of the Subject

It has been noted in various places that the subject could be omitted when it was obvious, or that perhaps it was simply a less full writing that the reader was to fill out as required by the grammatical context. Of course, there is also the phenomenon of pure scribal error (leaving out the subject by mistake). All three types of omission are probably attested. It seems likely that the cases of omission of the first person suffix in the construction *ꜥḥꜥ·n·(ỉ) rdỉ·kwỉ*, the suffix, probably the vowel *-i*, was simply to be supplied by the reader. The explanation as a scribal error—although scribes were notoriously sloppy at times—should be suggested only as a last resort. The case of the omission when the subject is obvious may be more complicated.

In the *ꜥḥꜥ·n sḏm·n·f* construction, subsequent clauses are usually parallel clauses beginning with a *sḏm·n·f* verb form. There are, however, cases of a subjectless, tenseless (?) verb form. One might have thought the infinitive a possible candidate, but in the following example the infinitive of the second form would be *sꜥqt*. Perhaps this is simply the circumstantial form with subject omitted.

Ex.

ꜥḥꜥ·n ꜥꜣ<g>·f (§96) *ꜥt·f nb(t) ỉm·s, nḥm ꜥꜣw·f, sꜥq r ḏꜣtt·f*

He beat his every limb with it, took his donkeys, and brought (them) into his estate. (Peas. B23 ff.)

In other instances, there seems to be a special subjectless ending of the *sḏm·n·f* that resembles a *nisba* ending: *·ny*. In most, if not all, examples of this ending, the subject is in the 3rd person.

Ex.

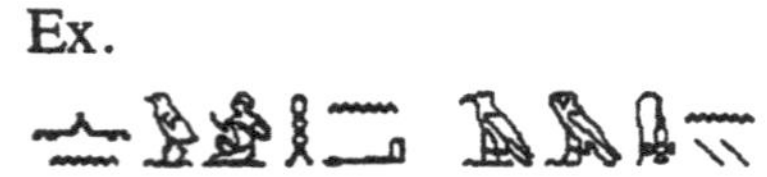

nn wỉ ḥnꜥ(w) (§97), *ꜣm·ny*

I was not with (them) when (they) burned up. (Sh. S. 130)

[7]In the phrase *dbꜣ st*, *dbꜣ* is the imperative: Should he be ordered: "Repay it!" Egyptian frequently employs a direct quotation in such cases.

§141. The Omission of the Object

Not at all infrequent is the omission of the direct object when this was clear from context. English generally will require the use of the appropriate pronouns in such cases. In the case of the omission of the object of prepositions, there may have been an adverbial ending *(w)* attached to the preposition. Cf. both of the examples in the preceding section. In the first example a pronoun referring to "donkeys" is not present, and in the second example, the object of the preposition was left off.

§142. The Vocative *Pw*

Although it has been stated in various places that there was no specific vocative case, Egyptian used either context or certain particles to indicate direct address to the listener or reader. In the case of the address to the living (in funerary inscriptions), one must supply "you," whether the vocative particle *i* "O!" has been used or not: e.g. "All scribes, officials, priests of Temple X, (you) who live upon the earth ... you should say (offerings of various sorts)."

There is another vocative particle *pw*, which is actually nothing other than the demonstrative adjective "this" in a specialized, and highly idiomatic use. This fairly rare use of *pw* is found in direct speech between individuals of distinction or high rank. It seems from the contexts to be quite formal or high-flown, and not a part of ordinary conversation among common people. It does occur, however, in religious texts. The use can be distinguished from the demonstrative meaning since it occurs only in direct address. The context of direct address will also normally preclude an interpretation as a bi- or tri-partite nominal sentence.

Ex.

nḏ-ḫrt s3 nsw pw
Greetings, o prince! (West. 7, 26 f.)

§143. *Sḏm·f pw*: "This means that he hears" etc. in Explanations

The pronoun *pw* could be used to form a variety of bi-partite nominal sentence frequently used in explanations. There are two nominal *sḏm·f* forms that occur in this construction, but only the prospective "that he hears," etc. has been learned at this point. The sentence is a bi-partite nominal construction, meaning literally "it is that he hears," more closely rendered by the French *c'est qu'il....* The translation "this means that" is often the best in English. The second tense *sḏm·f* forms (§147 ff.) also occur in this construction and they regularly mean: "this is *how* he hears," or "thus he hears" (indicating manner—examples will be presented in §149).

Ex. with prospective *sḏm·f* form:

... ỉr·n ꞽInpw s(w)t·sn hrw pwy n(y) "mỉ (§145) rk[8] ỉm." ... ỉr grt hrw pf "mỉ rk ỉm," ḏd Wsỉr pw n Rʿ: "mỉ rk ỉm!"

..., Anubis having made their places on that day of "come out of there."[9] ... Now as for "that day of 'come out of there,'" it means that Osiris says to Rēʿ: "Come out of there!" (BD ch. 17)

§144. *'Ink pw*: in Explanations

A variety of sentences, verbal and non-verbal, can be introduced by the independent pronoun + *pw*. In place of the independent pronoun, there may be a noun or name. These constructions are typically used in explanations, but are often impossible to translate adequately in English. Colloquial English uses: "It's like this, ...," but written English has no convenient equivalent. Sometimes one may translate: "It so happened that...."

Ex.

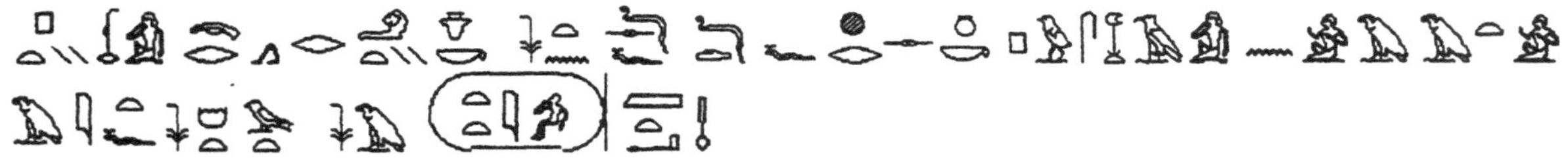

"pty spr (§121, 2a) r ḥꜣty·k?" nsw ḏs·f ḏd·f ḫr·s: "ỉnk pw sḫꜣ·n·ỉ mwt-mwt·ỉ, mwt ỉt·(ỉ) Ḥmt-nsw wrt, mwt nsw, Tỉ, mꜣʿt ḫrw."

(The queen said:) "What is it that has come into your heart?" The king himself said to her: "I was remembering my grandmother, (my) father's mother, the Great Wife of the King, the King's Mother, Teti, justified." (Urk. IV 27, 12–15)

§145. The Imperative (Commands and Instructions)

The imperative is the verb form that is used to tell the hearer or reader to do something, either as a command or as instruction. It is more direct than the prospective *sḏm·k*, *sḏm·ṯ* or *sḏm·ṯn* in an exhortation: "you should listen / ought to listen / are to listen." The second person is inherent in the form, so no subject is expressed. There is no distinction between masc. and fem. forms in the writing, but there may have been distinct forms (as in the Semitic languages). The plural may have had a *ū*-ending in Middle Egyptian, but the *w* is almost never written out. Plural strokes are fairly common on plural forms. Adjectives (or "adjective verbs") can be used in the imperative, especially when part of a compound, e.g. *ḥḏ ḥr·k* "be cheerful" (literally, "be bright of face").[10]

The forms from the mutable and irregular verbs are as follows. It should especially be noted that some "irregular" verbs use different roots in the imperative.

[8] *Rk* is a particle commonly used after imperatives. It can be translated as "then" or the like, but is often best left out of the translation.

[9] This is a difficult passage—so difficult that it required explanation even by the ancient Egyptians! (And even the explanation is not very convincing.)

[10] One might take this as a prospective *sḏm·f* in a wish-type statement, but the negative equivalents (§166) clearly show these to be imperatives.

3rd weak: without gemination *ỉrỉ* "make, do"

2nd gem.: without gemination *qb* "be cool"

ỉỉ / ỉw: uses a different root—, , , *mỉ* "come"

rdỉ: uses a different root— *ỉmỉ* var. , , , "give, put, cause."

wnn: ??

m33: with and without gemination *m3*, *m33* "see"

In addition to *šm* "go," there is also an imperative from a different root *ỉs* "go," which is especially common in the phrase *ỉs ỉn*... "Go, get...!" (Both forms are imperatives.)

Although a given imperative form may—in isolation from its context—appear to be very similar to an infinitive or a participle (since none of these have subjects), the grammatical context and above all the context of communication (discourse) and the meaning in context make it fairly straightforward to recognize imperatives. Imperatives, of course, occur only in *direct address*, and in contexts where one person (speaker or writer) tells another person (or the reader) to do something. Thus imperatives are quite common in didactic literature ("If you are in this situation, do this...") and in technical treatises, such as medical texts: ("Mix with beer, let stand exposed to sunlight during the day and to the dew at night for 4 days. Have him drink it for 3 days.") Imperatives also occur in letters: ("Send the leather that I wrote to you about without delay.") Imperatives do not occur in narratives, except in direct quotations of speech addressed to third parties. (E.g. the king ordering his troops to advance, etc.)

Two enclitic particles are not uncommon in commands: *m* "please" and *rk* "now." The latter has its origin in the preposition *r* with 2nd masc. sing. suffix and is akin to *rf* "then." Both occur immediately following the imperative form.

Ex.

ḏd·ỉn s3 nsw Ḥr-dd·f: ỉty, ꜥnḫ(w) (w)ḏ3(w) s(nbw), Nb·ỉ, ỉw ỉn·n·ỉ Ḏdỉ. ḏd·ỉn Ḥm·f: ỉs, ỉn n·ỉ sw

Then Prince Ḥar-dedef said: "O sovereign l.p.h., my Lord, I have brought Djedi." Then His Majesty said: "Go, bring him to me." (West. 8, 7–9)

mỉ rk ỉm

"Come out of there!" (BD ch. 17)

mỉ, m, ỉb·ỉ
Please come, o my heart! (Adm. p. 105)

§146. Polite Requests ("Have X be done...")

Polite requests make use of the passive voice and sometimes, although not always, this may have served as a means of distancing oneself out of deference: i.e. it would correspond to English "might X be done," as opposed to the more direct "do X." The construction consists of *ỉmỉ*, the imperative of *rdỉ*, "to cause, let" + 1st prospective *sḏm·tw·f* forms (cf. §75, 1).

Exx.

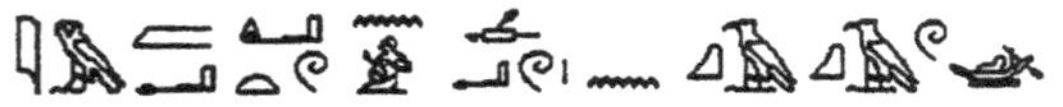

ỉmỉ dỉ·tw n·ỉ wꜥ n(y) qꜣqꜣw
Let one of the barges be given to me. (West. 8, 3.)

ỉmỉ sspd·tw tꜣ šspt nt(y)t m pꜣ š
Have the summer house that is in the garden prepared! (West. 2, 8 f.)

VOCABULARY XI

ỉmỉ var. , imperative form: "give, put, cause." Less common: and

ỉmnt "the West" Cf. Semitic *ymn*: Hebrew יָמִין (*yamīn*) "right-hand side"; "south"; Arabic يمن (*yaman*) "right-hand side"

ỉnpw the god Anubis

ỉs imperative form: "go"

ꜥt "limb," "part" (of the body)

, *wꜣḥ* "to put down," "lay down," "set down"; "apply (a remedy), and many idiomatic meanings to be looked up in the dictionary

wbꜣyt "maid" (a servant)

, *Wsỉr* Osiris

p(ꜣ)qt "fine linen"

pẖrt "prescription," "remedy" (medical)

m (enclitic particle after imperative forms) "please"

mỉ imperative form: "come"

mwt-mwt "grandmother" (even when referring to one's paternal grandmother)

nḏ "to ask," "enquire"; "seek advice" *nḏ-ḫrt* (compound verb, but *ḫrt* may be separated by the subject) "to greet"; as noun masc. *nḏ-ḫrt* "Greetings!"

rk an enclitic particle similar to *rf*, but used especially when addressing a person (i.e. in the second person) and is fairly common after imperative forms

ḥꜣt-ꜥ "beginning"; *ḥꜣt-ꜥ m* "Here begins (the book of ...)" Used as the opening lines of a book or chapter in a compilation of texts. Do not confuse with *ḥꜣty-ꜥ* "governor," "count," etc.

ḥbs "to clothe" (a person); "to cover"

ḥm-kꜣ "*ḥm-kꜣ*-priest," "*kꜣ* priest" (a category of priest who supervised the funerary cult of the deceased and supplied [under contract!] offerings to the deceased person's *kꜣ*)

ḥr-ꜥwy "immediately"; occasionally with the singular *ḥr-ꜥ*.

ḥsb "fracture" (in bone)

ḥsmn "natron" (a naturally occurring sodium carbonate [$Na_2CO_3 \cdot 10H_2O$] used in embalming and as a cleaning agent); identically written words (also read *ḥsmn*) mean "bronze" and "amethyst"

ḫꜣi, abbreviated "to examine" (a patient); "to measure"

st-ḥr "care," "charge," "supervision" in the expression *ẖr st-ḥr* "in the care of (a person)," "under (a person's) supervision"

siꜣ "to perceive"; as noun "prognostication" (a way of predicting the health of a patient)

spr "to arrive" *r* "at"; "to reach" with *r* + person; transitive "to reach" (a place)

sf "yesterday"

smsi (*s*-causative) "to deliver" (a woman in childbirth)

snḏm (*s*-causative) "to make happy"; "to sit, be seated"; "dwelling-place"; "home" Cf. Semitic *nꜥm* "pleasant, comfort," etc.

sḥqꜣ (*s*-causative) "to install as ruler," "to make (someone) a ruler"

, var. *sḫtm* (*s*-causative) "to destroy"

sspd (*s*-causative) "to prepare," "to make ready," "to supply" *m* "with"

st(w)t "shooting pains"

sdm "to apply (cosmetics, medicines) to the eyelids"

š "garden"

š3s "to travel," "go," "make a trip"

šs3w "treatment" (medical)

qrs "to bury"; noun "burial"

qsn "painful," "troublesome," "difficult," "nasty"; as a noun "pain" Cf. Hebrew קָשָׁה (*qāšā*) "difficult, hard, severe"; Arabic قسا (*qasā*) "to be hard, harsh, cruel"

gr(w) "also," "too"; "still"

grg "to establish," "found"; *grg pr* "set up a household" (start a family)

grt "moreover"; "however"; "now"

gs "to anoint"

gs-tp "migraine headache" (literally "half the head") The Greek and Latin names from which "migraine" derives (*hēmikrania*, *hemicrania*) are very likely loan-translations from Egyptian.

dw3w "tomorrow"; "morning"

db3 from earlier *ḏb3* "to restore," "repay," "replace"

dmỉ "town"; "harbour"

dmỉ "to touch"

dg3ỉ (also *dgỉ*) (final weak) "to see," "look at"; also with prep. *n* "look at" Cf. Semitic: Hebrew דָּגוּל (*dāgûl*) "visible; distinguished"; Akkadian *dagālu* "to see"

ḏ3tt "estate"

EXERCISE XI

(A) Reading Passage:

(B) Transliterate and translate. Look up new signs and additional vocabulary in the sign list and dictionary.

1) Words addressed to a judge:

2) Ḥepdjefa's exhorations to his *ḥm-k3*-priest:

Medical Texts

3) 

4) 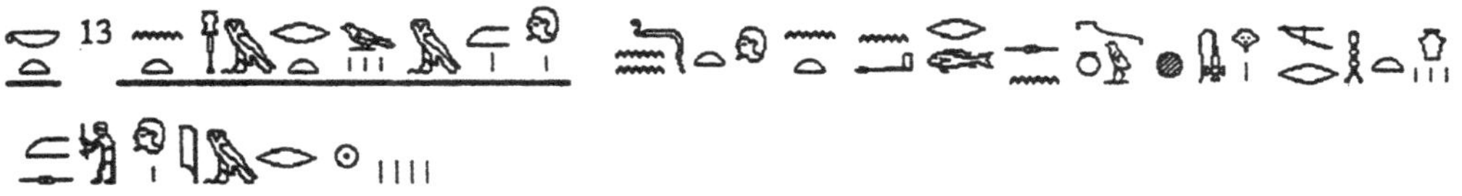

5) 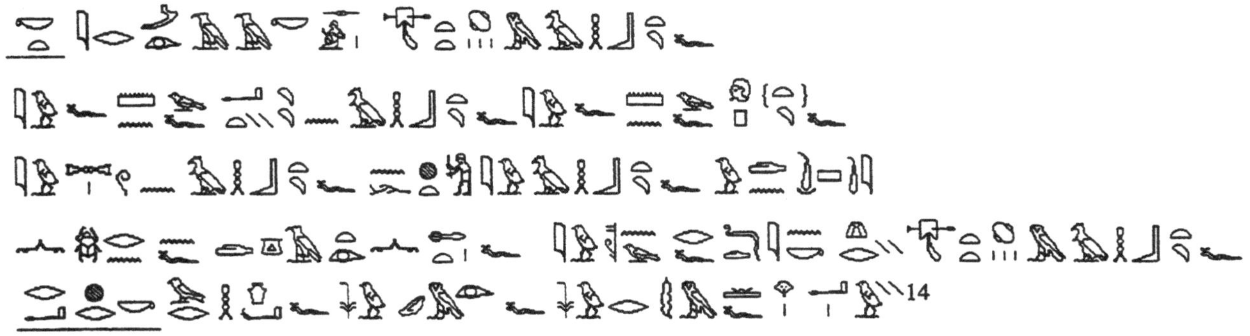

[11] 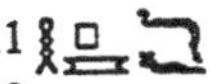 is the tomb owner's name. The determinative was omitted because he is depicted in the tomb scene.

[12] A m. pl. *sḏm(w)·n·f* relative form (§161) "which I have put under contract. . . ."

[13] The word  *pḫrt* "prescription" is alluded to in this common abbreviated heading of a medical text.

[14] This text consists of four sections: presenting symptoms, examination / observation, diagnosis, and treatment. Unlike fuller cases, there is no formal prognosis, but this is implied in the section on treatment.

6) [hieroglyphs] [15][hieroglyphs] [16][hieroglyphs]
[hieroglyphs] [17][hieroglyphs]
[hieroglyphs] [18][hieroglyphs] [19][hieroglyphs]
[hieroglyphs]

7) [hieroglyphs]
[hieroglyphs]

(C) Parse from *(B)*:

1) [hieroglyphs]

2) [hieroglyphs], [hieroglyphs]

3) [hieroglyphs]

4) [hieroglyphs]

5) [hieroglyphs], [hieroglyphs], [hieroglyphs], [hieroglyphs]

6) [hieroglyphs], [hieroglyphs], [hieroglyphs], [hieroglyphs]

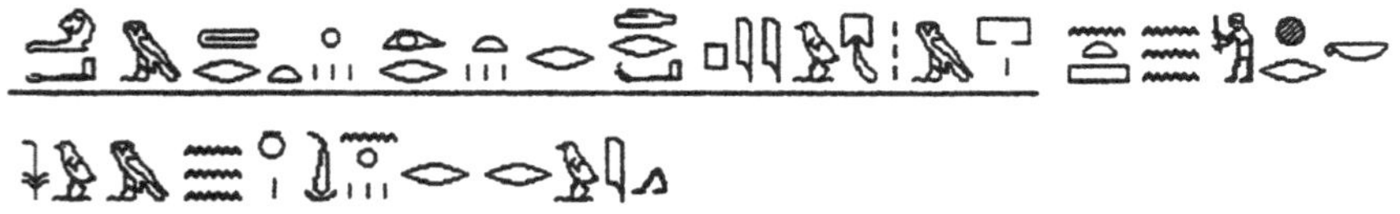

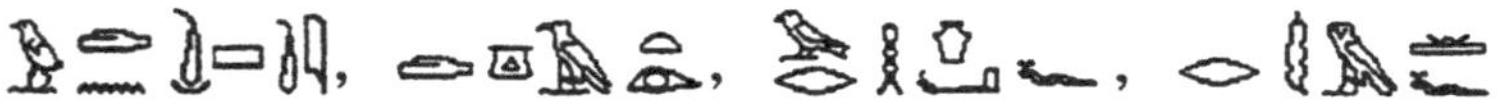

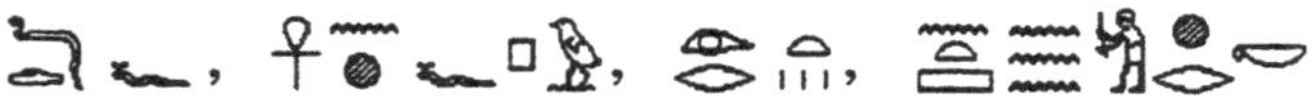

[15]*Mss·tw·f*: a relative verb form that modifies the noun immediately preceding it and has the meaning "that he is born."

[16]What the newborn says is, of course, not a word, but a sound made by healthy infants. (Cf. English "Waaaaahhhhhh.")

[17]Another sound "*umbii*," which resembles the Egyptian word for "no" *m-bỉꜣ*.

[18]This is an abbreviated title, based on the previous one.

[19]The *n* is either the genitival *n(y)* in an elliptical expression "(as that) of" or the preposition *n* "to" in the sense of "sounds like."

LESSON 12

§147. The Second Tense Forms

The Egyptian language possessed a series of verb forms that function grammatically as nominal elements and convey the meaning "the way (or the situation under which) something is done," or in elliptical constructions "thus something is done."[1] Most scholars refer to this form as the "emphatic *sḏm·f*" or "emphatic *sḏm·n·f*" but these terms should be strictly avoided, because they confuse the forms with one of their several functions.[2] The term "emphatic" is misleading in that it falsely implies that the verb form is somehow emphatic. Lately some scholars have taken to referring to this form as "the nominal form," but this is confusing, since the prospective *sḏm·f* is also a nominal form. The term "second tense form," although not at all descriptive, and somewhat confusing in that tense or time are not involved, is nevertheless fairly widely used, and universally understood by Egyptologists, since it is the accepted term in Coptic grammar. As with the names of the other Egyptian verb forms, the "second tense" should be recognized as a label that does not *mean* anything (i.e. "second" has no bearing here, nor is the idea of "tense" particularly involved).

Like other Egyptian verb forms, the second tense forms distinguish at least two tenses (proper): relative present: *sḏm·f*[3] and relative past: *sḏm·n·f*.[4] There is also the possibility that there were

[1] With regard to this verb form, J.B. Callender coined the term "manner nominalization," which is fairly apt, but not inclusive enough. The term is not widely used, in any case. For the classical treatment of the subject, see H.J. Polotsky, "Egyptian Tenses," *Proceedings of the Israel Academy of Sciences*, vol. II no. 5 (1965), pp. 1–25; and especially, Polotsky, "Les transpositions du verbe en égyptien classique," *Israel Oriental Studies*, vol. VI (1976), pp. 1–50. These articles are best left for a later stage. In older theories of the verbal system (such as that found in Gardiner, *EG*), this form was identified (partially) as the "imperfective *sḏm·f*" form thought to be used in cases of repeated action and the like. The term and the supposed use have been almost universally abandoned.

[2] That is, the so-called "emphatic construction," which is termed the "explicatory sentence" in this work. It should be noted that many scholars use the term "the emphatic" interchangeably with regard to the *form* and to its *use* in the so-called "emphatic construction" (§148). This misuse of terminology should be understood but not emulated by students.

[3] And the passive *sḏm·tw·f*, and very likely in the *sḏmw·f* passive, as well. The possibility of a second tense for the latter has not, to my knowledge, been proposed elsewhere.

[4] Some scholars do not recognize the existence of the second tense *sḏm·n·f*, since the form cannot be differentiated from other *sḏm·n·f* forms in the writings. The existence of the different forms is based on analogy with the *sḏm·f* forms and functions, and on the syntax of the *sḏm·n·f* itself. The syntax of verbs of motion provides the strongest evidence for a differentiation of the *sḏm·n·f* forms. Sentences with bare, initial *sḏm·n·f* (i.e. no *iw* or other introductory word) *from verbs of motion* occur: *iy·n·i m niwt·i* ("Out of my town have I come." [an explicatory construction]) But a hypothetical **iw iy·n·i m niwt·i* ("I came from my town." [as a simple statement of fact]) never occurs. Instead we find *iw·i iy·kwi m niwt·i* "I have come from my town" (the stative §88). With verbs that do not designate motion, both bare initial (i.e. no introductory word or particle) *sḏm·n·f* [explicatory] and *iw sḏm·n·f*

second tense prospective forms, too, but the evidence is not conclusive (§138). As elsewhere with the Egyptian conjugated verb, the forms express relative time only. Note especially that in some cases the second tense *sḏm·f* form can have past time reference. Second tense forms *never* follow the particle *iw*. The particle *mk* may, however, precede the explicatory construction (§148).

1) **The second tense *sḏm·f* forms** from the mutable and irregular classes of verb are as follows:

3rd Weak: has gemination— *hȝȝ*, *ir(r)·k*, *irr·k*
2nd Gem.: has gemination— *qbb·f*
ii*/*iw "to come": only the root *iw*— *iw·s*
ini "to bring": has gemination— *inn·k*
rdi "to give": no *r*; has gemination— , *dd·f*
wnn "to be": has gemination— *wnn·f*
mȝȝ "to see": has gemination— *mȝȝ·ṯ*

In particular, the "defective" writing *ir(r)·k*—which looks like a circumstantial or prospective *sḏm·f* form—should be noted. The form of *rdi* should also be carefully learned. Otherwise, the rule is gemination for all classes that can have gemination.

The passive second tense *sḏm·f* forms are formed from the active base followed by the passive marker *·tw*: *irr·tw·f* "how it is made" or "where it is done," etc.

2) **The second tense *sḏm·n·f* forms** never have gemination. The writings of the form are identical to those of the circumstantial *sḏm·n·f*. The forms from the mutable verbs are as follows:

3rd Weak: , *iri·n·k*
2nd Gem.: *qb·n·f*
ii*/*iw "to come": only the root *ii*— *ii·n·s*
ini "to bring": *in·n·k*, *ini·(n)·k*
rdi "to give": with *r* , *rdi·n·f*
wnn "to be": *wn·f*
mȝȝ "to see": *mȝ·n·ṯ*

The *sḏm·n·f* form of *ini* "to bring" is often written with just one *n*: . This looks like the circumstantial (but *not* the 1st prospective) form. On the other hand, the form with two *n*'s ( ) looks identical to the present-time second tense *sḏm·f* form. Also, the *sḏm·n·f* form of *wnn* ( ) "to be" is written identically to its 1st prospective form. The tense should be clear from the context, and grammatical context will indicate whether a circumstantial or a second tense form is required.

The passive forms of the second tense *sḏm·n·f*, unlike the passive counterparts of the

---

[simple (non-explicatory) statements of fact] constructions occur.

circumstantial *sḏm·n·f* (§35), are formed by the suffix *tw*, which is placed on the active base:  *rdỉ·n·tw·f* "where it was placed."

§148. The Explicatory Sentence Construction

The most widely recognized use of the second tense forms is in the explicatory sentence construction. The term "explicatory sentence" derives from the fact that the speaker is not presenting something as a simple statement of fact, but is explicating the details surrounding an action. Or, in other words, what would be the "adverbial modifier" in a statement of fact becomes the "adverbial comment." (I.e. not: "she is making bread in the house" [adverbial modifier], but rather "(where) she is making bread is in the house" [adverbial comment].) The concepts of "when," "where," "how," and "why" are inherent in the meaning of the second tense forms, but in typical Egyptian fashion, the exact notion is not specified, and it is left to the reader/hearer to make the appropriate connection. This construction is usually known under the unfortunate term: the "emphatic construction." The construction is not particularly "emphatic," but rather puts a certain highlight on the circumstances (time, location, manner, condition, state, purpose, cause, etc.) occurring when an action takes or took place. In the explicatory sentence, the speaker wishes to relate not that an action took (or takes) place, but rather to fill in the details surrounding the action—to *explain* the circumstances.

The construction is *never* preceded by *ỉw*, but occasionally it is preceded by *mk*. It is crucial to note that in this construction, the second tense verb form (as a nominal form) and the subject (and other words that constitute the phrase) together form the *topic* of the sentence, and the *comment* is adverbial. The adverbial comment can consist of any one of the following: an adverb, a prepositional phrase, a circumstantial clause, a stative form, a purpose clause (with prospective *sḏm·f* [§74] or *r* + infinitive [§57, 2]), or a noun phrase used "adverbially" (§79).[5] This information is summarized as follows:

Topic (nominal)	***Comment*** (adverbial)
second tense form + subject (etc.)	adverbial element: adverb prepositional phrase circumstantial clause stative purpose clause noun used adverbially

[5]Purpose clauses are actually noun phrases used "adverbially."

The explicatory sentence essentially works as follows. The underlined portion corresponds to the adverbial comment in the Egyptian.

How/where/when/why/to whom/ the action is done is (according to the explicatory circumstances).

topic	**adverbial comment**

gm·n sw wpwtiw	*ḫr w3t.*
(Where) the messengers found him	was on the road. (Sinuhe 38)

topic	**adverbial comment**

pḥ·n·sn sw	*r tr n(y) ḫ3wy*
(When) they reached him	was at night-time. (Sinuhe 39)

One of the main clues by which the explicatory sentence can be recognized is that the verb form is a "bare, initial" form (i.e. there is nothing in front of it). This is particularly true for *sḏm·n·f* forms, which are written identically to their circumstantial counterparts. The following is the key question to ask: is a given clause a circumstantial clause beginning with a *sḏm·n·f* indicating action prior to that of the main clause (which precedes it), or is it a new explicatory sentence beginning with a second tense form? In the case of the passive forms, there is no confusion since the circumstantial clause would require a *sḏm(w)·f* passive form, and the explicatory sentence would require the second tense *sḏm·n·tw·f* form.

It has been learned that with simple statement of fact and literary constructions, verbs of motion are not used in the *sḏm·n·f* form (cf. §§31, 88, 92, 136). The explicatory sentences, however, regularly contain second tense *sḏm·n·f* forms of verbs of motion.

Ex.

ii·n·i ʿ3 r nis r·k m wpwt n(y)t it·i Ḫ(w)fw m3ʿ-ḫrw

Why I have come here is to summon you on a mission of my father, Ḥufu, justified. (West., 20–21)

Here the speaker indicates the purpose of his visit. The other adverbial elements (*ʿ3* "here" and *m wpwt...* "on a mission") serve as adverbial *modifiers* and not as the adverbial *comment* (or predicate). The adverb *ʿ3* "here" modifies *ii·n·i* "I have come," and *m wpwt* modifies the infinitive phrase *r nis* "to summon."[6] As indicated by the underlining, the adverbial comment consists of the adverbial element in question and *all* of its modifiers, including adverbial

[6] The phrase *r·k* "to you" is also adverbial, although this is not apparent from the translation.

modifiers. Theoretically one might take *ˁ3* "here" as the adverbial comment, but the sense is poor, and as frequently, one must rely on the context—what the speaker was most likely explaining.

The highlighting of the adverbial element is accomplished by making the action and the doer of the action (as a unit) the topic of the sentence, while the comment consists of any type of adverbial element. The focus is thus shifted from the doer and the deed to the circumstances: the motivations for, time, and manner in which the deed was done. In other words, the speaker uses the explicatory construction in order to explain to the listener *how*, *when*, *where*, and *why* the action took place, and not simply that it did (or does) take place. Since the focal point is on the adverbial element, the explicatory sentence cannot highlight the subject or the direct object of the sentence.[7] Note that some verbs are used almost exclusively in explicatory sentences for semantic reasons. For example, the verb *gmỉ* "to find" is only rarely found in basic statements of fact since usually the speaker wished to relate the condition in which something was found—or the place where / time when something was found—rather than simply stating that something was found.

In English we can shift the focus onto the explicatory details in several ways:

1) With qualifiers:[8] E.g. "just as the day was dawning," "precisely because she hated it," "on that very night," "with only his hands," "right through it."
2) With intonation: "She came *two hours late*."
3) With word order (Topicalization[9]): "With her axe she chopped them up." "Panting, he hurried back to his car."[10]
4) With the "cleft sentence" construction:[11] "It was with great difficulty that we got home."
5) By translating the second tense form as "where I found it was..."; "how I found it was..."; "why I have come here is to..."; "when I came here was...; and otherwise as required by context. This is actually a fairly literal way of translating the explicatory sentence. It is not, however, a translation technique used on a regular basis by most Egyptologists. Note that in Egyptian the meaning of the second tense form was broader

[7]To highlight the subject, the "participial statement" (§ 134) was used. To make the subject (less often the direct object) the topic of the sentence, it could be placed in sentence initial position (fronting), usually preceded by *iw*, *mk*, or *ỉr*.

[8]The extreme lack of such qualifiers in Egyptian can be explained by the very existence of the explicatory construction.

[9]I.e. shifting the key phrase to the head of the sentence.

[10]Joyce Carol Oates, *Wonderland*. The phenomenon can be termed "topicalizing," i.e. making a certain word or phrase the general topic of the sentence. Some linguists call it "thematicization," making it the theme ("jumping-off place") of the sentence.

[11]I.e. the normal structure is "broken" into two clauses (instead of "X does..." we have "It is X that does..."). The cleft sentence is common in French, but in English it is extremely forceful, somewhat tortuous, and can be clumsy. Its overuse in a translation can spoil elegant Egyptian verse. There are, however, times when it is the best alternative, but it should be used sparingly. Also, one should never, as some scholars erroneously do, refer to the Egyptian explicatory constructions as "cleft sentences." The Egyptian explicatory sentence is not a cleft sentence.

than the English equivalents, which must be more specific ("when," as opposed to "how," or "why").

The Egyptian explicatory construction is used frequently and, despite the notions of many scholars, it is not particularly "emphatic" in the usual sense of the word, but rather indicates a shift in focus. Translations should indicate the special focus, and, as much as possible, sound natural in English. In translating the explicatory construction, one should first try using a qualifier such as "precisely," "only," etc. If none are appropriate, then the adverbial element might be placed at the head of the sentence. Finally, as a last resort, the cleft sentence construction or italics may be used. The Egyptian explicatory sentence is fairly subtle, and overly "emphatic" translations should be avoided.

Exx. (The adverbial comment is underlined in the transliterations.)

ỉw swt mꜣꜥt r nḥḥ. hꜣꜣ·s m-ꜥ ỉr(r)·s(y) r ḫrt-nṯr.

"Justice, however, is for all eternity. It goes down with one who does it right into the cemetery." (Peas. B1 307–8)

dm·tw rn n(y) ḥwrw ḥr nb·f

The name of a poor man is mentioned only on account of his lord. (Peas. B1 20.)

gmm·k sw šm·f ỉw·f ḥr ḏbꜥw·k[12]

You find it *moving back and forth under your fingers*. (Ebers 40, 1)

gm·n·f sw ḥr prt m sbꜣ n(y) pr·f

He found him just as he was going out the door of his house. (Peas. B1 34–35)

By way of example, the last sentence has as its basic meaning and structure: "The circumstance under which he found him (was) as he was going out the door of his house."[13] The basic meaning of the second example may be something like: "The reason why a poor man's name gets mentioned (is only) because of his lord." (I.e. otherwise he is not important enough to be mentioned by name.)

§149. The Independent Use of the Second Tense Forms

Some scholars have rejected the existence of the second tense forms because in some cases the forms occur with no adverbial element that could serve as the comment. In almost all of these instances, however, the verb can be translated on its own as "how someone did something." In

[12] *Šm·f* and *ỉw·f* are circumstantial clauses, lit. "... it going (and) it coming.'

[13] The verb *gmỉ* "to find" very often is used in the explicatory construction, no doubt because the speaker wished to relate when, where, the condition in which, or circumstances under which a person or object was found.

other words, the second tense forms occur (as verbal nouns with subjects) outside of the explicatory sentence with other functions, but with similar meanings (i.e. they do not *always* have to have an adverbial comment because they are not *always* used in the explicatory sentence pattern). Some examples of a distinct use are in the abbreviated "caption" or "journal entry" style of writing. This is sometimes the case in the titles of spells in magical / ritual texts involving instructions:  *ṯss sw s ḥr gs·f [ỉ3by]* "How a man raises himself up from his [left] side." (CT III 199a) This use is less common than the simple infinitive ("Rising up from the left side.")

In captions to monumental reliefs one can often translate "Thus, I ..." E.g.  *dỉ·n·(ỉ) n·k t3w nb(w)* "Thus, I have given to you all lands." This is a caption illustrating the delivery of bound prisoners to the king. (Although the dative, as an adverbial, can serve as the adverbial comment, the sense—as well as the fact that the direct object follows the dative—suggest the independent use as the most likely here.)

The *sḏm·f pw* construction (§143) that is often used in explanations can employ second tense verb forms, often with the sense "this is how...." It is also used in the typical colophon that ends literary works:

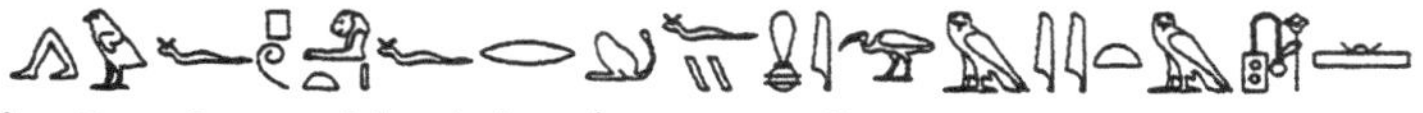

ỉw·f pw ḥ3t r pḥ(wy)·fy mỉ gmyt m sš

This is how it goes, (from) beginning to its end as found in writing. (Sh. S. 186–87)

§150. The Second Tense Forms as Objects of Prepositions

Because the second tense forms are nominal, they (with their subjects and associated words, e.g. their direct objects) can serve as noun phrases indicating the way something was done, the attending circumstances, or the time of an action. The second tense forms often occur after prepositions in this capacity. The meaning of the prepositions is normally that found with other nouns, e.g. *ḥr mrr·f sw* "on account of how (much) he loved him," *m-ḫt spr·n·f* "after he had reached." In these cases, an adverbial element may not be present. It is uncertain whether adverbial elements, when present, are highlighted or not. It is possible that at least in some cases they are.[14] Cf. the common phrase *ỉrr·f mỉ mrr·f* "He does just as he pleases."[15] (This is an explicatory sentence whose comment consists of a preposition + a second tense *sḏm·f* form.)

Ex.

prt pw ỉn s r mrr·f m ẖrt-nṯr

[14] It is possible that adverbial elements, although not essential to the construction, when present, are always to be stressed. Such clauses would not be simple statements of manner, but rather complete explicatory constructions in their own right.

[15] Literally, "The way that he acts is in accordance with the way that he desires."

It is the going out by a man from the necropolis according to the manner he wishes. (CT II, 47)

§151. The Second Tense Forms as the Direct Object of Verbs

Similarly, the second tense forms can occur as the direct object of verbs. The meaning almost always involves "how" or "the way that" (someone does/did something). That is, they are treated as manner nominalizations.

ib n(y) Ḥm·k r qbb n[16] *m33 ḫnn·sn*
Your Majesty's mind will be refreshed at seeing how they row.[17] (West. 5, 15)

mri·n·f wi rḫ·n·f qnn·i
He loved me because he knew how brave I was.[18] (Sinuhe B1, 105 ff.)

§152. Reciprocal Sentences (The *Wechselsatz*)

Although not often discussed in introductory courses, and not universally recognized, two clauses containing second tense verb forms could be placed together to create a reciprocal sentence. Such sentences are far from rare, and are indeed a favoured literary device. The fact that the couplet is the basic mainstay of Egyptian verse may account for the large number of this sentence type in such narrative verse works as the tale of Sinuhe. Many of the grammatically difficult couplets in that work will probably be better analyzed as reciprocal sentences, but the final word has not been said on the matter. Also quite common are such formulaic devices as *ʿnḫ* (god X); *ʿnḫ* (person Y) "As god X lives, so lives person Y!" (i.e. eternally and in good health).

In this construction there is no adverbial element serving as comment. Structurally, this is an AB nominal sentence.[19] The basic meanings include the following:

- "How A happens is how B happens."
- "Just as A happens, so B happens."
- "Just when A happened, B happened."
- "No sooner did A happen than B happened."[20]

[16]The negative arms are here used as a variant writing of the preposition *n*. *M33* is the infinitive, and *ḫnn·sn* is the object of *m33* "seeing."

[17]The context is of a rowing exhibition performed by women as a royal entertainment.

[18]The whole sentence is an explicatory sentence explaining *why* the ruler loved him. Both *mri·n·f* and *qnn·i* are second tense forms, but they function differently, the latter being the direct object of *rḫ·n·f*.

[19]I.e. element A is simply juxtaposed to element B without any linking words: A = B.

[20]From the basic meaning: "When A happened is precisely when B happened." This construction uses *sḏm·n·f* forms in both clauses.

Exx.

ḫpr·n tr n(y) msyt sꜣḥ·n·i r Dmi Ngw.

Just as supper time arrived I reached Cattle-town. (Sinuhe 66–67)

rdi·n·i wꜣt n rdwy·i m ḫd dmi·n·i ꞽnbw-Ḥqꜣ.

No sooner did I set out[21] going north than I reached the Ramparts-of-the-Ruler.[22] (Sinuhe 72–73)

Sometimes, however, two explicatory sentences occur in what may appear to be the reciprocal construction. E.g. *pr·n·sn r pt m bikw / pr·n·i ḥr ḏnḥwy·sn* "As falcons they ascended to the heavens; upon their wings I ascended." In this case, the two clauses probably do not constitute a true reciprocal sentence, but are two complete explicatory sentences loosely bound by meaning and form. It is sometimes difficult to distinguish between the reciprocal construction and the explicatory sentence in which the second clause is the adverbial comment (§148). In the former case the clauses are virtually simultaneous: "No sooner did she hear this than she told her father." In the latter case, the *sḏm·n·f* form expresses prior time: "Only *after* she had heard this did she tell her father." Only context and judgement can determine which is meant.

§153. The *ʿḥʿ·n sḏm·n·f* Construction

The *ʿḥʿ·n sḏm·n·f* and related constructions (§§90–96) are actually a specialized type of explicatory sentence. The *ʿḥʿ·n* is a second tense form used impersonally (the subject was normally omitted because it is merely the non-specific "it"). Since this construction requires an adverbial comment, it is therefore not surprising that the *sḏm·n·f* form following *ʿḥʿ·n* is the circumstantial *sḏm·n·f* or *sḏm(w)·f* passive (which are adverbial forms), and that pseudo-verbal constructions (noun + *ḥr* + infinitive; noun + stative) also occur. However, the adverbial comment of this construction must contain some form derived from a verbal root. Other types of adverbial comments (such as ordinary prepositional phrases) cannot occur in this construction. (Thus, a hypothetical ***ʿḥʿ·n·f m pr* is impossible.)

The sentence type has its origins in a literary device meaning roughly: "How it arose (was) with his having heard. . . ." Translations, however, should simply treat these as literary past tense constructions: "He heard."

§154. The *Sḏmt·f* Form

The rather rare form with suffixed *t* is very well attested in two constructions. Gardiner and

[21]Literally "gave the road to my feet."

[22]The couplet could not read: "I set out going north only after I reached Ramparts-of-the-Ruler" (with the second line as a circumstantial clause serving as adverbial comment), since the speaker obviously had to set out on the journey *before* reaching his next destination. An alternate reading of the first line as an expository sentence "I set out *going north*" is not very satisfactory, but even worse, it leaves the second line a virtual impossibility.

others have also posited a third use of the *sḏmt·f* in a narrative construction (*EG* §406), but the examples are not very convincing, and most of them are probably infinitives of third weak verbs used as narrative infinitives (§57, 7). The morphology is uncertain. The form may be akin to the *sḏm·in·f* type forms (§131), but the evidence is scant. The 3rd weak class exhibits no gemination, but examples from 2nd geminating verbs are too scarce to ascertain. In its use after prepositions it is clearly nominal in nature and this is corroborated by its mode of negation (§180). Examples of the forms from the third weak verbs are less certain because their infinitives also contain *t*'s, and are therefore ambiguous. With strong verbs, however, the only possible alternative is a defective writing of the passive with *tw*. Both active and passive forms of the *sḏmt·f* are encountered and the passive forms look identical to the feminine singular of the perfect passive participle (§121, 2b), e.g.  *iryt*. Examples of the passive forms are not common, and those cited in Gardiner, *EG* § 404 should suffice for future reference.

§155. The *N Sḏmt·f* Construction "...before he (has / had) heard"

N sḏmt·f functions in a manner identical to the circumstantial *sḏm·f*. The most common use is as a circumstantial clause meaning "before he heard," or in past contexts "before he had heard." But like the circumstantial *sḏm·f*, *n sḏmt·f* can also follow the introductory particle *iw*. In these cases the construction is a main clause meaning "He has / had not yet heard." Here as elsewhere, tense is relative to the context.

Exx.

ꜥḥꜥ·n·i ḥr irt wꜥw r ḏbꜣ·f ... iw·i m šri n irt·i ḥmt

I was serving as a soldier in place of him [speaker's father] ... when I was a lad, before I had taken a wife. (Urk. IV 2, 15)

... mḥy·i ḥr msw·s sdw m swḥt mꜣw ḥr n(y) Ḫnty n ꜥnḫt·sn

..., but I am sorry for her offspring who were crushed in the egg [i.e. killed as unborn children] and who saw the face of the Crocodile before they had (even) lived. (Lebensm. 77–80)

iw n mrt irt·f

His eye had not yet been afflicted. (Gardiner, *EG* §402)

§156. The *Sḏmt·f* Forms as Objects of Prepositions

The *sḏmt·f* forms (and the phrase that follows it) can serve as the object of the prepositions *r* "until" and *ḏr* "since," "until," "from the time that" and also "before." It is possible that *sḏmt·f* forms also occur after the prepositions *m-ḫt* "after," *m* "when," *mi* "like," and *ḫft* "when." However, the only examples after these prepositions are from third weak verbs and these are probably infinitives (with *t* ending).

Ex.

m gfn(w)[23] *sw r skt·f ẖt·f, r ḏdt{i}*[24]*·f ỉỉt·n·f*[25] *ḥr·s*
Do not dismiss him until he has poured out his heart,[26] until he has told (you) what he has come about. (Ptaḥḥotpe 265 ff.)

VOCABULARY XII

wꜥ im "one of them" (literally: "one therefrom")

wpwt "mission," "business"

wpwtyw n. pl. (*nisba* from *wpwt*) "envoy," "agent"

m-ḥr-ỉb "among"

n(y) rmṯt nbt "public"

Nmty-nḫt A man's name

, *nḥḥ* "forever" "eternity," also in the expressions *r nḥḥ* "forever," and *r nḥḥ ḏt* "for ever and ever."

r-wꜣt "path," perhaps "beginning of the path"

ḥwrw "poor man," "humble man"

ḥr-ḫw[27] "except"

ḥqꜣ "ruler"

ḥḏ "to be bright"; *ḥḏ tꜣ* "the day dawns" (literally "the land becomes bright")

ḫꜣm "to bend (the arm)" as a gesture of respect

ḫni "to land" (of flying, falling things); "to stop (at a place)"; "to rest" (at a place) (also of resting for refreshment) Cf. Semitic *nwḫ* e.g. Hebrew נוח (*nwḫ*) "to rest," "to settle," "to stop (at a place)"; Ar. نوخ (*nwḫ*) "to halt for a rest"

[23]*M* is the imperative (command) form of the negative verb "do not" (§166) and *gfn(w)* is the "negatival complement" (the form of the verb that occurs in conjunction with the negative verbs).

[24]The writing of the *t* of the *sḏmt·f* with the "tall *t*" group is unusual.

[25]*Ỉỉt·n·f* is the *sḏmw·n·f* relative form, with the feminine singular standing on its own with the "neuter" idea.

[26]Literally, "wiped out his belly."

[27]The writing with three *ḫ* signs for *ḫw* is a "sportive plural" writing. Cf. the writing **sss* for *sw* and **tt* for *ty* (a "sportive dual").

ḫdỉ "to sail north"; "to travel north," "to travel downstream"

sm3-t3 "juncture" "fork" (of a road). The meaning is not entirely certain.

sk "to wipe out" (pots, etc.); *sk ẖt* "pour out one's heart" (literally "wipe out one's belly")

sd (from older *sḏ*) "to break," "to crush," "to smash"

qbb "to be refreshed," "to be cool"; also as an adjective "cool"

tr "time," "season"

ṯsỉ "to raise up," "lift up," "get up"

dmỉ "to reach" (a place); "to touch"

ḏb3 "compensation," "payment"; *r-ḏb3* "in place of"; "in stead of"

EXERCISE XII

(A) Review from the Special Reading Passage, Lesson VII

(B) Reading Passage

[28]

(C) Transliterate and translate

1) Meeting a man who lives a life of ease (fictional narrative):

2) A plot to trick a peasant (fictional narrative):

[29]

3) A royal canal inscription:

[28]This sentence is notoriously difficult. Read: *in ẖt ḥwḥ n·i s(y)*. The construction can hardly be anything but the participial statement (§134). *H̱t* here can only mean "mast." *Ḥwḥ* is possibly the imperfect active participle of *ḥwỉ* "to strike." If so, it is unusual in reduplicating the first consonant (one expects *ḥww*). This is perhaps because it is doubly weak, with *w* as its second root letter. The nuance conveyed by the use of the imperfect participle is unclear, but possibly involves repeated action "was battering." Another possibility is that the writing with two *ḥ* signs is a "sportive dual" writing that should be read *ḥwy*. (Cf. the writing of *ty* with two *t* signs—e.g. *pḥtt* as a not uncommon writing of *pḥty*.) If so, this could be a perfect participle. Whichever participle it is, it is followed by a dative. The sentence ends with the 3rd fem. sing. dependent pronoun *s(y)* "it," which must refer to *nwyt*, the only feminine noun in the vicinity.

[29]The tense is uncertain. One expects present/future/modal: "you must not ..." "you had better not ..." "so that you do not...." It is possible that the Egyptian semantics required a past circumstantial clause "without your having done...."

4) 

5) 

6)  (§§57, 7; 79; 152; *iri šmt* = "to travel" Peten is a place name.)

(D) Parse from *(C)*:

1) 

2) 

3) 

5) 

LESSON 13

§157. The Relative Verb Forms—An Overview

Egyptian has a set of verb forms, known as the relative verb forms, which closely resemble the participles and are almost certainly derived from them. The relative forms are used, among other things, to form relative clauses ("the man whom I met"; "the woman whose sandal broke"; "the papyrus from which the lector priest read"). These forms are conjugated in the normal manner, but they function grammatically as adjectives. As with adjectives, if they modify an antecedent, they must agree in gender with it. Presumably they also agreed in number, but this is not indicated in the writing apart from the use of plural strokes. Masculine forms may have a *w*-ending, especially if the subject is a noun—the *w* is extremely rare with suffix pronouns. Feminine forms have the expected *t* ending. Both the masculine and feminine endings are normally placed before the determinative.

Many of the uses of these forms are identical to those of the participles—in fact the presence or absence of a subject is the main key in determining whether one is dealing with a participle or a relative verb form. The only use of the participle that is impossible with the relative verb forms is that of predicate adjective (§118, 3). As other adjectives, the relative forms have two basic functions:

1) They modify nouns: *st rḫt·n·i* "a woman that I know";[1] *r-pr qd(w)·n Ḥm·f* "the temple that His Majesty built."
2) They can stand on their own as nouns: *sḏmw n·f sḏmw* "one to whom the judges listen" (relative form + dative + plural subject); *ḏdt·n·f* "what he said," *ḏd(w)t·n·f* "the things that he said."

There are four relative forms derived from the perfect, imperfect, and prospective participles, and there is a past relative that contains the past-tense marker *·n*. These are referred to as the perfect, imperfect, prospective, and the *sḏm(w)·n·f* relative forms.

Learning to recognize the relative forms takes time and practice. Sometimes they occur together with participles, and one might attempt to parse a relative form as another participle, but relative forms will always have a subject. Some of the forms may provide a clue to the correct analysis, especially when a feminine form is involved, when the masculine *w* is actually written out, or when plural strokes are present. Nevertheless, in most cases, the best way to distinguish a relative form from a circumstantial form in a circumstantial clause is to compare the meaning of

[1] As has been seen on previous occasions, the verb *rḫ* "to learn (of)" requires a past tense (or stative) form to convey the sense "to know."

the two: which analysis works better? The independent use (especially of the 3rd fem. sing. meaning "that which [a person] did") can often be recognized when they occur in places requiring nouns, e.g. after prepositions or as direct objects of other verbs.

An important clue arises in the case of transitive verbs that lack a direct object when one would otherwise expect one. This is because when a relative form modifies an antecedent, that antecedent is precisely what would otherwise have been the direct object. (In other words, in Egyptian—rather like English—one does not say **"the man that I know him" but rather "the man whom I know.") Thus, in a situation where the direct object *seems* to precede the verb form that it must be associated with, one is likely dealing with a relative form. (The relation is not, however, that of a true direct object.) Students should examine the examples in the following section, attempting to locate a direct object in its expected position (after the subject). For instance, in §159, what do the official and commoner give? ("anything from the best of their harvest"). And whom do the two kings love? ("their true servant," the tomb owner).

When the relative forms stand alone as nouns (without an antecedent) they are self-referential: "What His Majesty said: ... (quotation follows)."

§158. Perfect Relative Verb Form

This form is derived from the perfect participle (§121, 2a), and its appearance is identical to it. There is no gemination in either the 3rd weak or 2nd geminating classes of verbs (e.g. *mr(w)·f* "whom he loved"). The form expresses past time (relative to its context). This form was early on replaced by the *sḏm(w)·n·f* relative form (§161) and is fairly rare in Middle Egyptian.

ᶜḥᶜ·n ỉr(w) mỉ wḏt nbt Ḥm·f

(It) was done in accordance with all that His Majesty had commanded. (West. 5, 13)

ptr ḏdt n·ỉ Nb·ỉ? ỉḫ wšb·ỉ st.

What did my Lord say to me? Then I might respond to it. (Sinuhe, 565)

§159. Imperfect Relative Verb Form

The imperfect relative expresses present time (relative to its context). Like the imperfect participles (§121, 1a), there is gemination in both the 3rd weak and 2nd geminating classes of verbs. Some contexts tend to favour the use of these forms, and in particular, they are found in the tomb owner's self-laudatory inscriptions, of the following sort: "I am one that the king favoured and one whom everyone loved."

Exx.

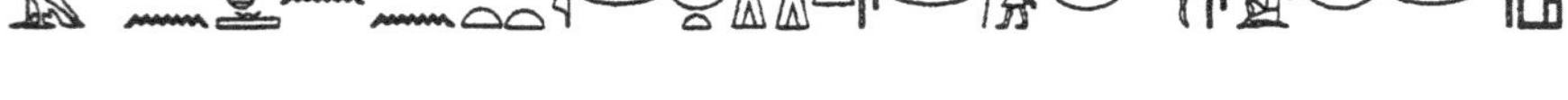

mṯn rḫ·n·ṯn nt(y)t ỉr ḫt nbt ddt sr nb, nḏs nb r ḥwt-nṯr m tpy n(y) šmw·f, n nḏm·n n·f ḫtḫt ỉm
Now you know that as for anything that any official or any commoner gives from the best of his harvest to the temple (for contracted mortuary services), a reversal thereof (i.e. of the terms of the contract) is not pleasant for him. (*Lesest.* 93, 10 ff.)

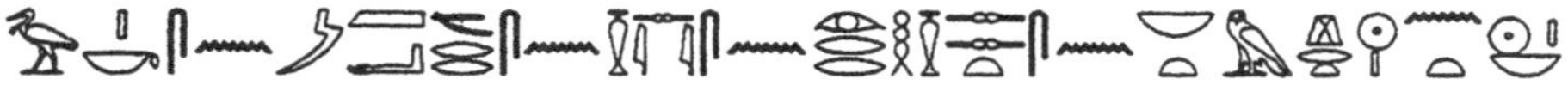

bꜣk·sn mꜣꜥ, mrr·sn, ḥsy·sn, irr ḥsst·sn nbt m ḫrt hrw n(y)t rꜥ nb
Their (referring to two kings) true servant, one whom they love, one whom they have favoured, one who does everything that they favour in the course of every day. (*Lesest.* 81, 14 ff.)

§160. Prospective Relative Verb Form

The prospective relative verb forms closely resemble the prospective participles (§121, 3a) from which they derive. There is no gemination in 3rd weak or 2nd geminating classes of verbs. The feminine singular sometimes has a writing with the group *tỉ* rather than a simple *t*. The modal meanings of the prospective are the expected ones: "that one might do," "that one ought to do," "that one could do," "that one should do," and so on. Sometimes they are best translated by the English future rather than with a modal force. Since there were no future relative forms, it is logical that the prospective—the closest available form—would be used.

ꜥḥꜥ·n dwn·n·ỉ rdwy·ỉ r rḫ dit·ỉ m r·ỉ
I stretched my legs to find out what I might put in my mouth.

§161. *Sḏm(w)·n·f* Relative Verb Form

The relative with past-time reference is the *sḏm(w)·n·f* relative form. Like all *sḏm·n·f* forms there is never gemination in any of the verb classes. The feminine ending occurs *before* the *n* of the past tense: *ỉit·n·f ḥr·s* "that about which he has come."

m gfn(w)[2] *sw r skt·f ẖt·f, r ḏdt{ỉ}·f ỉit·n·f ḥr·s*
Do not dismiss him until he has poured out his heart,[3] until he has told (you) what he has come about. (Ptaḥḥotpe 265 ff.)

mk nn n(y) ḫt r ḏrw ḫtm(w)·n·ỉ m-ꜥ nn n(y) wꜥbw ḫr st-ḥr·k
Look, all of these things that I have put under contract with these *wꜥb*-priests are under your

[2] *M* is the imperative (command) form of the negative verb "do not" and *gfn(w)* is the "negatival complement" (the form of the verb that occurs in conjunction with the negative verbs). (See §§165–66.)

[3] Literally, "wiped out his belly."

supervision. (*Lesest.* 92, 12 f.)

§162. Passive Relative Verb Forms

The passive of the various relative forms is formed with the suffix ·*tw*. These forms are not universally recognized by scholars since no examples with *w* (masc. sing.) or *t* (fem. sing.) have been found. In the case of the feminine, the two *t*'s probably were not separated by a vowel (e.g. **sadmattuf*), and the *t* would therefore have only been written once.

ir t3y·i ḥ3t qrs(t)·tw·i im·s ḥnᶜ t3y·i ḥmt, nn rdit d3 rmṯ(t) nbt t3 r·s
As for my tomb in which I will be buried with my wife, there will be no permitting any person to interfere[4] with it. (Les. 91, 4–5)

ky si3 ẖrd hrw mss·tw·f
Another prognostication of a child on the day that he is born. (*Les.* p. 57, 18)

§163. The *Šmt pw ir(w)·n·f* Construction

The literary narrative construction that was introduced in §136 can now be fully appreciated. It is essentially a bi-partite sentence with *pw* with an infinitive in the first slot "It is a going," and with a *sḏm(w)·n·f* relative form modifying the infinitive: "It is a going that he did." The construction is generally translated "then he went," "and so he went," or simply "he went."

§164. Negation of Wishes and Exhortations

As was seen in §109, *nn* + prospective *sḏm·f* is the negation of the future statement of fact. Negative wishes and exhortations require the use of an auxiliary "negative verb." There are two such negative verbs,  *tm* and  ,  *imi*. The auxiliary verbs themselves mean "to not do." The negative verb is conjugated as the prospective and it is followed by a nominal form of the verb (the "negatival complement") that conveys the verbal idea. Negative wishes and exhortations use the negative verb  *imi*. It is important to avoid confusion with the imperative of *rdi*:  *imi* "give!"; "put!"; "cause!" The prospective form of *imi* is *imi*, e.g.  *imi·k ir(w)* "you should not do," "you must not do," "may you not do." The modal idea of the wish or exhortation comes from the fact that *imi* is conjugated as a prospective form.

Note that when the subject is a noun, it *follows* the negatival complement, apparently because the negative verb was bound to the negatival complement.

[4]The expression *d3 t3 r* + thing means "to interfere with." Here *nn* + infinitive must begin a main clause (unlike §105).

Adjectives can be used in this type of sentence. The adjective is then used as the "adjective verb" and occurs as the negatival complement after *ỉmỉ* (cf. the first example, below).

Purpose clauses are negated with the other negative verb, *tm*. These negations will be dealt with in §175.

Exx.

ỉmỉ·k wsr(w) m ẖt·s m rn·k pwy n(y) Wsr-r·f.
May you not be mighty within her womb in that name of yours: "Mightier than he." (West. 10, 9)

ỉmỉ mꜣꜣ(w) rmṯ. ỉmỉ wʿr(w) ỉb·sn
May people not see. May their hearts not flee. (Destruction of Mankind, 5)

§165. Negatival Complement

The negatival complement is probably nominal, but is distinct from the infinitive (§166). In later middle Egyptian, the negatival complement is replaced by the infinitive. There is a *-w* ending, probably vocalic, that is sometimes encountered, but it is usually not written. The forms of the negatival complement are as follows:

3rd Weak: no gemination— *hꜣw*, *ỉr(w)*
2nd Gem.: with gemination— *ẖnn(w)*
ỉỉ/ỉw "to come": only the root *ỉw*— *ỉw(w)*
ỉnỉ "to bring": no gemination— *ỉn(w)*
rdỉ "to give": with *r* and no gemination— , *rdỉ(w)*
wnn "to be": with gemination— *wnn(w)*
mꜣꜣ "to see": with gemination— *mꜣꜣ(w)*

The negatival complement resembles very closely the "conditional" *sḏm·f* (§138) or the Prospective II (§138). The connection, if any, is uncertain, but it is an interesting fact that all are nominal.

§166. Negative Commands

In English, when one wishes to make a negative command, one negates the auxiliary verb "do": "do not" or "don't," and the following infinitive conveys the actual meaning ("don't go"). In Egyptian, commands use the imperative of the negative verb *ỉmỉ*: *m* "don't" followed by the negatival complement. Note that the adjective verb may occur as the negatival complement in this construction.

Exx.

m ꜥꜣ ỉb·k ḥr rḫ·k. m mḥ ỉb·k ḥr-nt(y)t tw m rḫ

Don't be proud ("big of heart") on account of your knowledge. Don't be conceited on account of the fact that you are a learned man. (Ptaḥḥ. 52–53)

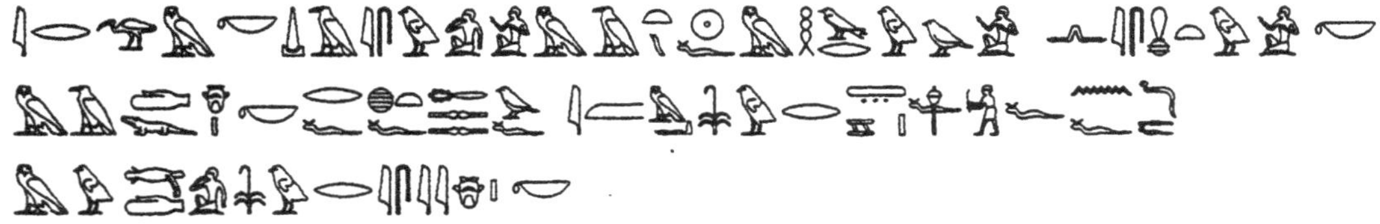

ỉr gmỉ·k ḏꜣỉsw m ꜣt·f, m ḥwrw, n ỉs mỉtw·k, m ꜣd(w) ỉb·k r·f ḫft ẖss·f. ỉmỉ sw r tꜣ, ḫsf·f n·f ḏs·f. m wšd sw r ỉsy ỉb·k.

If you encounter a disputant in action,[5] an inferior man—hardly your equal—do not be savage hearted towards him in proportion to how weak he is. Leave him alone so that he may oppose himself on his own! Don't answer him so that your heart might be at ease. (Ptaḥḥ. 74–78)

§167. Questions

Questions can be divided into two types, those that evoke a yes/no answer (questions for corroboration: "Did you eat the figs?") and those that ask for specific information (questions for specification: "When did you eat the figs?" "Who ate the figs?" and so on). The former are quite straightforward, but the latter involve a number of fairly rare words that are probably best dealt with as vocabulary items at a later stage. The general pattern and function of interrogatives will be presented as will the more useful interrogative words.

§168. Questions for Corroboration

Most commonly questions for corroboration are introduced by the interrogative phrase  *ỉn ỉw*. Practically any sentence type may follow *ỉn ỉw*, even those that do not allow the use of the sentence particle *ỉw*. There is no change in the word order after *ỉn ỉw* (unlike English, where such questions are marked by inversion of subject and verb: "you are going" vs. "are you going?"). Existential questions ("is there?" / "are there?") can begin *ỉn ỉw wn* NOUN or *ỉn ỉw* NOUN. With verbal sentences, a commonly found pattern is: *ỉn ỉw* NOUN (= Topic) *sḏm·f* (the suffix pronoun refers back to the topic). The use of the enclitic particle *rf* ("now," "then") is fairly common in questions for corroboration.

Exx.

ỉn ỉw wn twꜣ mrrw n šꜣ(w) n(y) tp-ḥr(y)?

[5]Literally "in his moment."

Is there a lowly man who is loved to the extent of the master? (Sinuhe, 265–66)

in iw k3 mri·f (§38) *ʿḥ3 pry?*
Is there a bull (i.e. a challenger) who wants to fight the champion? (Sinuhe, 269)

in iw nṯr ḫm(w) (§85) *š3t·n·f* (§157, 2)*?*
Does god not know what he has ordained? (Sinuhe, 274)

in iw ii·n·t r sn ẖrd·i pn?
Is it in order to kiss this child of mine that you have come? *Readingbook* p. 115

in iw m3ʿt pw p3 ḏd iw·k rḫ·ti ṯs tp ḥsq(w)
Is it true, this talk of your knowing how to attach[6] a severed head? (Westcar 8, 12–13)

Much less common are questions introduced by 𓇋𓈖 *in* without 𓇋𓅱 *iw*. There seems to be little if any difference. The negative word *nn*, and less often *n*, can introduce questions that expect a "yes" answer (cf. "Is he not human, after all?"). For this sense, English often employs a positive question followed by a negative tag question: "You are coming, aren't you?" There is also a negative question pattern that is introduced by *in nn* + prospective *sḏm·f* that means: "Won't he hear?"

Exx.

iw·i grt rḫ·kwi nb n(y) ḏ3tt tn. ny s(y) (§126) *imy-r pr wr Rnsy s3 Mrw. ntf grt ḫsf ʿw3 nb m t3 pn r ḏr·f. in ʿw3·tw·i m ḏ3tt·f? ḏd·in Nmty-nḫt pn: in p3 pw ḫn n(y) mdt ḏdw rmṯ(w): dm·tw rn n(y) ḥwrw ḥr nb·f?* (§159)
"Moreover, I know the owner of this estate. It belongs to the high steward Rensi, son of Meru. He, moreover, is the one who punishes robbers in this entire land! Shall I be robbed on his estate?" Then this Nemty-nakhte said: "Is this the phrase of speech (i.e. "proverb") that people say: 'The name of a poor man is mentioned only on account of his lord.'?" (Peas. B, 15 ff.)

[6] Literally "Is it true, this saying: you know how to attach...."

ỉn nn rf dỉ·k sw3·n ḥr w3t?
Won't you let us pass by upon the road? (Peas. B, 8–9)

§169. Questions for Specification

Questions for specification employed a number of interrogative words that are best treated as vocabulary items. We have already seen examples of *m* "who" or "what" in the "participial statement" after the particle *ỉn* (§134). We have also seen the phrase *pw-tr* and *ptr* "who" or "what" that is used in bipartite nominal sentences (§128, 2). Much less common are the interrogative words *sy*, *ỉšst*, and the combined *sy-ỉšst*, all "what."

Some interrogative phrases are formed with the aid of prepositions, e.g. *ḥr m* "why" (literally "on a account of what"), and *mỉ m* "how" (literally "like what"). In questions involving these and other adverbial phrases or words (e.g. *ṯn* "where") the explicatory sentence construction with the second tense verb forms are normally used. (English translations do not need to shift the focus, since the interrogatives do that sufficiently.)

Exx.

pḥ·n·k nn ḥr sy ỉšst?
Why did you reach this (place)? (Sinuhe, 108)

wnn ỉrf t3 pf mỉ m m-ḫmt·f, nṯr pf mnḫ?
How, then, is that land without him (the deceased king), that beneficent god? (Sinuhe, 127)

Ptr ỉrt·n·k ỉr tw r·k?
What is it that you have done that one should act against you? (Sinuhe, 387)

ỉr·tw nn mỉ m n b3k thỉ·n ỉb·f ḫ3s(w)t ḏrḏry(w)t
How can this be done for a servant whose heart has gone astray to foreign lands? (Sinuhe, 433)

msỉ·s ỉrf sy nw, Rdḏdt?
Now when[7] is she supposed to give birth—(this) Reddjedet? (Westc. 9, 15)

[7]Literally "what time?"

VOCABULARY XIII

 *ȝt* noun, fem. "moment"; "instant";  *m ȝt·f* "in his moment" = "in action"

,  *imi* Negative verb ("to not do") (§164)

 *imyt-pr* "transfer of title" (a legal term, literally "that which is in the house")

 *imy-sȝ* "attendant"

 *in iw* Question particle (§168)

 *is*, var.  *isy* "to be light" (of weight and of frivolity); "to be at ease"

 *išst* interrogative pronoun "what"

 *whi* "to fail"; "to be thwarted"

 *wšd* "to respond to"; "to speak to"

 *bw-ḥwrw* "evil"

 ...  *pri* ... *m ḫt* "to go up in flame"

 *mty n(y) sȝ* "phylē controller"; as position "phylē controllership"

 *mtrw* "witnesses" (a legal term)

 *mdw iȝwt* "staff of old age" referring to a son who supports an aged parent

 *nḫt-ḥr* "violent man"

 *Nni-nsw* Heracleopolis Magna (Ahnas) This was the capital in the 9th and 10th Dynasties.

 *ḥȝ* (preposition) "behind"

 *ḥdi* "to injure"

 *ḫft-nt(y)t* "in view of the fact that," "since" (cf. *ḥr-nt(y)t* §114)

 *ḫmt* in the expression:  *m-ḫmt* + suffix (or following noun) "without"; "in (a person's) absence"

 *ẖrt hrw n(y)t rᶜ nb*  *m ẖrt hrw n(y)t rᶜ nb* "in the course of every day"

s3 r·s "let it be revoked" (said of superseded legal documents—literally "away with it!")

s3 "a phylē (of priests)"; "regiment," "company" (of troops) Phylē is a Greek word meaning "division" that was also used of the divisions within the Egyptian priesthood of a temple

s3w "protection" (by means of amulets or spells)

sy (interrogative pronoun) "what" (precedes the noun); "who" *sy išst* "what"

š3 (bi-consonantal) "to ordain"; "to order"

š3(w): *n š3w n(y)* "to the extent of"; "in the capacity of"

q3b "interior"; "intestines"; *m q3b* "in the midst of" Cf. Semitic *qrb* "intestines"; "interior"

qnbty n(y) w "district magistrate" ("magistrate of the district")

km (bi-consonantal) "to complete"; "to come to a total of," "to total up to"

tni "to grow old"

dns (adjective) "heavy"; "serious"

dhn "to appoint" (a person to an office)

d3tt "estate" The reading of the word is not entirely certain. It might be read *sp3t* "district," "nome"

EXERCISE XIII

(A) Reading Passage

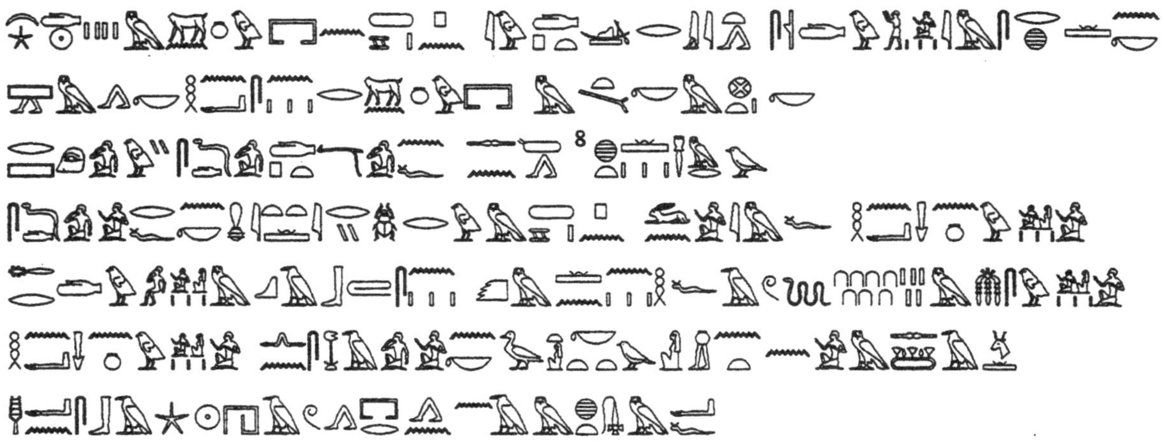

(B) Transliterate and translate

1) A transfer of a priestly office and property (similar to a will):

Note the Geneology

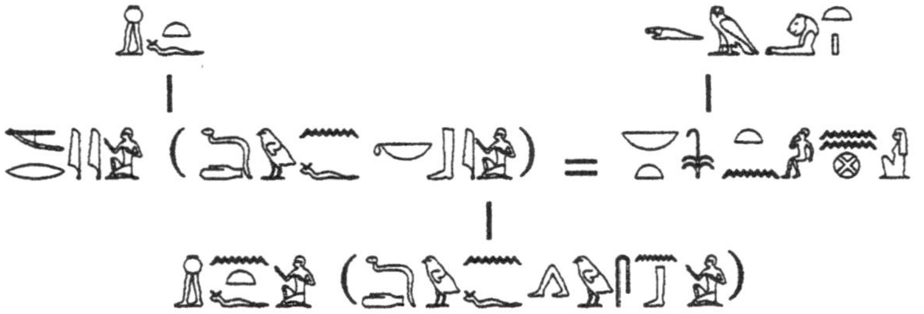

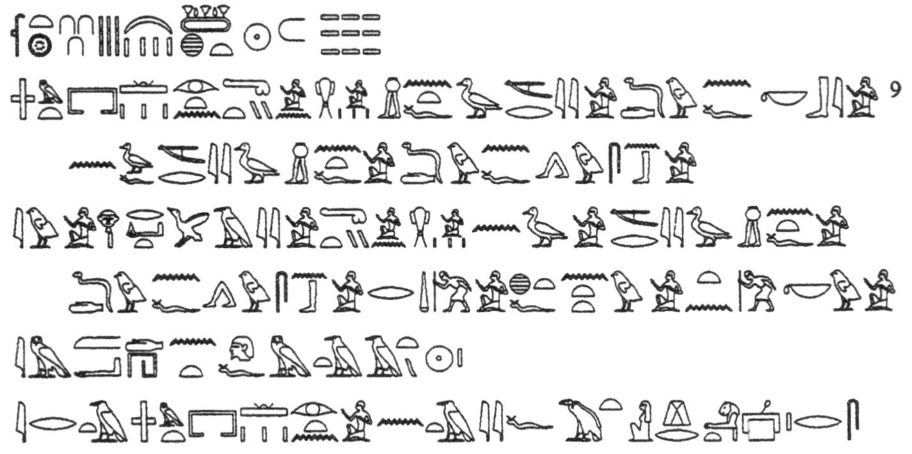

[8]One expects *snì·n*. Perhaps there was some confusion since the final consonant of the verb was *n*. (Cf. the writing of the *sḏm·n·f* form of *ìnì*: *ìn·f*.)

[9]Cf. §41, 1.

 [10]

(The names of the witness follow at this point.)

2) 

3) 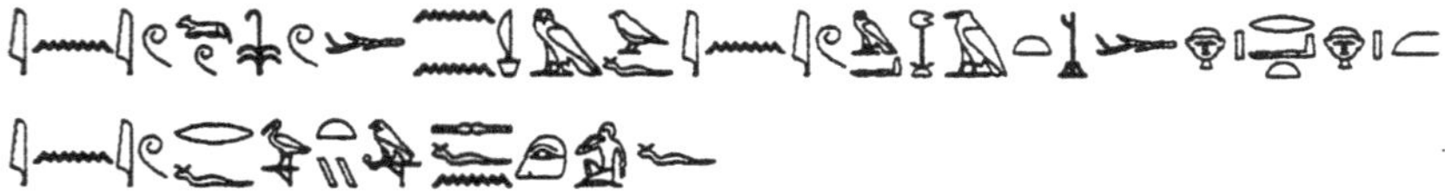

4) 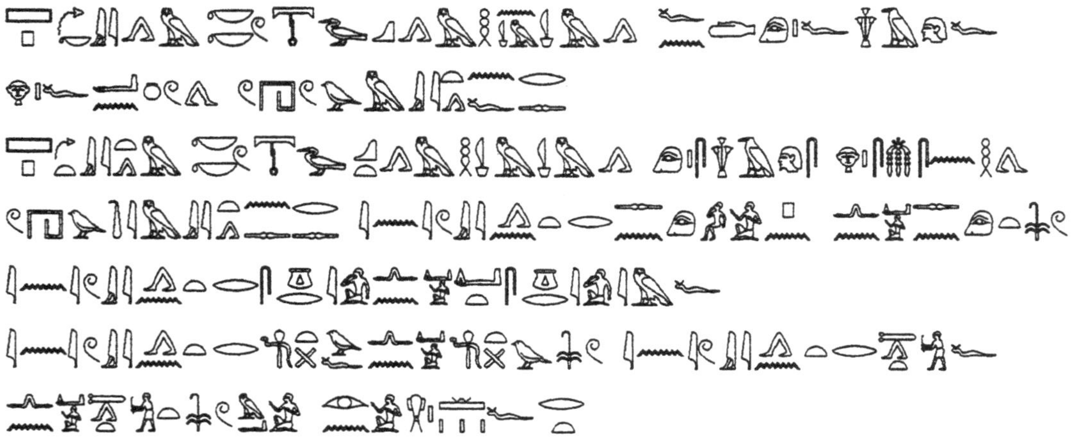

(C) Parse from (B)

1) 

2) 

4) 

[10] *Ḥwt Mdt*, if that is the correct reading of the hieratic signs, is an otherwise unknown place name.

LESSON 14

§170. Less Common Classes of Verbal Roots

The main classes of verbal roots were introduced in §28. There are, however, several less commonly encountered verb classes. The following classes are attested:

Quadri-consonantal Roots Many are reduplicated roots, e.g. *mnmn* "to move quickly, quake"; *gmgm* "to crash, break." Some have four strong root letters: *wsṯn* "to stride." Also in this group are *s*-causatives of tri-consonantal roots: *sḥtp* "to please, satisfy."

Third Geminating Roots These roots have the same third and fourth root letters: *spdd* "to supply." This class also includes *s*-causatives of 2nd geminating verbs: *sqbb* "to make cool." These verbs are strong verbs and all forms always indicate all four consonants.

Fourth Weak Roots These have been encountered earlier, and as was seen, some take *t* in the infinitive, but others do not. This is also the case with *s*-causatives of 3rd weak roots: *smsy* "to cause to give birth," *sṯst* "to raise." Gemination is not found in the 2nd tense *sḏm·f* forms of this class.

Quinqui-consonantal Roots All verbs of this class involve reduplicating roots: *ḥb3b3* "to waddle"; *swtwt* "to go for a walk." Also in this class are verbs with the preformative element *n*-, which may be a fossilized remnant from an earlier stage of the language: *nftft* "to leap."

§171. *ʼIrỉ* as an Auxiliary Verb

The verb *ỉrỉ* "to do" can be used in any of its forms in conjunction with infinitives of less commonly used verbs, and certainly with the less common verb classes that had more than the normal three consonants. This periphrastic use allowed the speaker (or reader) to avoid conjugating the rarer roots and to use the familiar forms of *ỉrỉ*. This use is common in Late Egyptian, but rare examples do occur in Middle Egyptian:

Ex.

ỉw ỉb·f ỉrỉ·f dbdb
His heart pounds. (P. Ebers 42, 9–10)

Verbs of motion sometimes also occur in this periphrastic construction.

Ex.

ỉrt·ỉ šmt m ḫntyt
I travelled south. (Sinuhe, B 5–6)

§172. *Ḫpr* as an Auxiliary Verb

The verb *ḫpr* "to happen" can be used as an auxiliary verb followed by various constructions, nominal and verbal, with the sense "it happened" or "it will come to pass," and the like. The past-tense 2nd tense form *ḫpr·n*, like *ꜥḥꜥ·n*, does not require a subject. The prospective form *ḫpr* may have as its subject a noun-phrase headed by another prospective verb form ("it may happen that he will hear").

Exx.

ḫpr·n rs, nn wỉ ḥnꜥ(w)
Now, it happened that I was not among them. (Sh. S. 130)

ḫpr ỉs ỉwd·k (§71) *tw r st tn*
Indeed, it shall happen that you separate yourself from this place. (Sh. S. 153)

§173. The Auxiliary Verb *Pꜣ(w)* "To Have Done in the Past"

There was an auxiliary verb , , , *pꜣ(w)* or *pꜣ* "to have done in the past." It occurs in a variety of forms, including the participle and the relative verb forms. The verb *pꜣ* is conjugated normally and is followed by the infinitive. In almost no cases can it be translated literally into English. In a few cases, it may cover the semantic ground of English "used to do." The verb *looks* like the demonstrative *pꜣ* "this," "the," but it is quite easily distinguished from this in its use. The negation *n pꜣ·f sḏm* can be translated "he has never heard."

Exx.

ḏd·ḫr·sn: ỉw mfkꜣt m ḏw r nḥḥ, ỉnm pw wḫꜣ(w) r tr pn. ỉw pꜣ·n sḏm mitt
Then they said: "The (quantity of) turquoise in the hill is infinite, but it's a fact that the colour is faded in that season." We used to hear things like that. (Sinai 90, 11)

n sp pꜣ·tw ỉrt st ḏr hꜣw nsw-bity Snfrw, mꜣꜥ ḫrw
It had never been done since the reign of Snofru, justified. (Sinai 139, 10–11)

nfr st r pꜣyt (fem. sing. perfect active participle) *ḫpr*
They were more beautiful than what had previously existed. (Gardiner, *EG* §484)

§174. Other Auxiliary Verbs

Several verbs function similarly to *ꜥḥꜥ·n* in what are basically explicatory sentences. The original meaning would have been: "so how it turned out was...." The verbs in question are *ii* "to come," *pri* "to go out," and *ḏr* "to end up."

Exx.

ꜥḥꜥ·n·s gr·ti, nn ẖnt. ii·n ḥḏ·n·s pꜣy·s rmn
She stopped still, without rowing. This is the way she ended up ruining her side (of the rowing). (West. 6, 3–4)

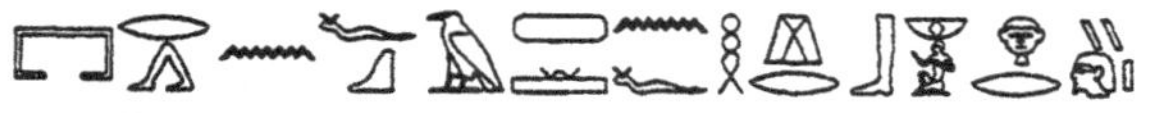

pr·n fqꜣ·n·f ḥry-ḥbt ḥry-tp
So it turned out that he rewarded the chief lector-priest. (West. 6, 14)

The verb *ḏr* can also be found in the *sḏm·in·f* form:

Ex.

ist rf ir pꜣ mw iw·f m mḥ 12 ḥr iꜣt·f, ḏr·in·f mḥ 24 r-sꜣ wdb·f
Now as for that water that had been 12 cubits deep straight across (literally "upon its back") it then ended up 24 cubits deep after being folded over.[1] (West. 6, 10–12)

§175. Negation of Purpose Clauses

Purpose clauses ("in order that he might do") are negated by the use of the negative verb *tm*, var. , , (and not by the negative verb *imi*, as are wishes). Like the other negative verb, *tm* is conjugated as the particular form required, here the prospective, and it is followed by the negatival complement (§165). If the subject is a noun, it follows the negatival complement.

Since *tm* is a bi-consonantal root, it does not have a distinct prospective form. The negative purpose clause occurs after the main clause, just like its affirmative counterpart. Such clauses may be translated by such phrases as "so that something might not happen," "in order that something not happen," or "lest something happen."

[1] The text refers to a feat of magic in which half of the water in a pool is "stacked" upon the other half.

The verb *tm* also occurs as an ordinary verb meaning "to be complete," "finished," and is not rare in the stative as a modifier meaning "complete." It also occurs as a derived noun meaning "everything," "the universe." There is also a verb *tm* (perhaps the same verb) that means "to perish, fail, cease." (This is actually the origin of the negative verb *tm*.) The negation *n tm·f* means "he did not fail (to do)." The use of *tm* as the negative verb, however, is by far the most common.

Ex.

m k3hsw ḫft wsr·k, tm spr(w) bw-ḏw r·k

Do not be harsh in proportion to how powerful you are, so that evil not reach you. (Peas. B1, 213–14)

§176. Negation of Prospective Forms as Direct Objects of Verbs and Objects of Prepositions

Prospective forms may begin clauses that serve as direct objects ("that clauses") of verbs of speech, perception, and causation (§75, 1) and as objects of prepositions (§75, 2). The negations of these functions are accomplished by means of the negative verb *tm*.

Exx.

iw wḏ·n Gb, it Wsir, tm·i wnm(w) ḥs

Geb, the father of Osiris, commanded that I not eat excrement. (Ḥarḥotpe 396–97)

sgr q3 ḫrw r tm·f mdw

Silencing the loud-mouth so that he may not speak. (Siut I, 229)

§177. Negation of Conditional Sentences

The second tense *sḏm(w)·f* (§138) form (and the regular prospective *sḏm·f*, when it occurs here) was negated by use of the negative verb *tm*. The prospective of *tm* may also be used in less explicit conditional clauses without *ir* (§139) ("should such and such be the case").

Ex.

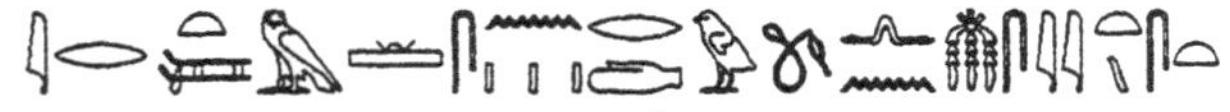

ir tm·sn rdw nn msy{t}·s{t}[2]

If they do not grow, then she will not give birth. (P. Med. Berlin vs. 2, 4-5)

[2] The two *t*'s are superfluous. The 3rd fem. sing. suffix *·s* is commonly written *st* in Late Egyptian.

§178. Negative Infinitives

As was seen in §105, the infinitive could follow the nominal negation *nn* with the meaning "without doing something." With this expression, the speaker could state the doer of some action did not carry out a certain other action. The infinitive itself could, however, be negated directly to yield a meaning like "the not doing of something." The negative infinitive can be used anywhere a noun can be used: as the object of a preposition, as the direct object of a verb, as a caption and in any sort of nominal phrase.

As with the other uses of the negative verb, *tm*, itself, is placed in the infinitive form, and it is followed by the negatival complement.

Exx.

ky n(y) tm rdi͗(w) wnm kk(w)t i͗t m mẖr: ḥs gḥs, rdi͗(w) ḥr ẖt m mẖr, sẖr(w) i͗nbw·f, s3tw·f ḥr i͗tnw·sn ḥr mw. tm rdi͗(w) pw wnm·tw i͗t

Another (treatment) for not letting *kkt*-animals eat grain in the barn: Excrement of gazelle, placed upon a fire, after its walls and floor and also their ˹hiding places˺ have been swept over with water. This is how to prevent the grain from being eaten. (Ebers, 98, 6–9)

ḏd·i͗n Ḥm·f "pty st, Ḏdi͗, tm rdi͗(w) m3n·i tw?" ḏd·i͗n Ḏdi͗ "ni͗sw pw i͗y, ʾIty,ʿnḫ(w) (w)ḏ3(w), s(nbw). ni͗s (§57, 7?) *r·i—mk wi͗ i͗y·kwi͗*"

Then His Majesty said: "What is this, Djedi, not letting me see you?" Then Djedi said: "The one who comes is one who has been summoned, o Sovereign, l.p.h. I was summoned—(and) see, I have come!" (West. 8, 10 ff.)

i͗w wḏ·<n> n·i Ḥm·f tm ḏh<n>(w) t3 n sr nb ʿ3 r·i

His Majesty commanded me not to touch my head to the ground for any official greater than me. (Gardiner, *EG*, p. 425)

§179. Negative Participles and Relative Verb Forms

The negative verb *tm* can occur as any of the participles, including the future active *sḏm·ty·fy* forms. As expected, the negatival complement follows immediately after it. The functions are exactly as those of affirmative participles, except for the use as predicate adjective. They are translated according to the context as "who did not do," "who ought not to do," "one who will not do," etc. The negative verb *tm* also occurs as the passive participle. Since *tm* is a bi-consonantal root, its perfect passive form is *tmm*, e.g. *tmmt mꜣꜣ(w)* "that which has not been seen" or "that which was not seen."

Exx.

ink sḏmw r wn-mꜣꜥ, tm {ꜥ} nmꜥ(w) n nb ḏbꜣw

I am a judge ("one who listens") in the true sense, one who does not show partiality to the owner of bribes. (*Les.* 79, 18–19)

in ib sḫpr nb·f m sḏm, m tm sḏm(w)

It is the heart that turns its owner into one who listens (or) one who does not listen. (Ptaḥḥ. 550–51)

ir grt fḫ·t(y)·fy sw tm·t(y)·f(y) ꜥḥꜣ(w) ḥr·f, n sꜣ·i is, n msi·t(w)·f n·i is

Moreover, as for anyone who will displace it (a boundary stele) and who will not fight for it, he is not my son, he was not born to me. (Les. 84, 15–16)

tmmt bs(w) wr-mꜣw ḥr·s

"a thing into which (§123) the chief of seers (the high priest of Heliopolis) has not been initiated" (*ZÄS* 57, 2*)

The negative verb can also be conjugated as a relative form. Examples are not numerous, but their occurrence is certain.

Ex.

nn st nbt tmt·n·(i) ir(w) mnw ims

There is not any place where I did not make monuments. (Louvre C15)

§180. The Negative Verb *Tm* in Other Verb Forms

The negative verb *tm* can occur as a number of other forms, including *sḏmt·f* (§154) and *sḏm·ḫr·f*. There is one possible example of the *sḏm(w)·f* passive (§35), but this is difficult to explain, since *n sḏm(w)·f* otherwise occurs (§§107, 115). Here as elsewhere, the verb *tm* itself assumes the desired form and is followed by the negatival complement. As always, if the subject is a noun, it follows the negatival complement.

Exx.

ir sp ḥnꜥ·f wꜥw, r tmt·k mn(w) ḫrt·f

Deal with him alone until you are not troubled by his affairs. (Ptaḥḥ. 465–66)

tm·ḫr·s ḫpr(w) m ḥsb(w)t
Then it will not turn into worms. (Ebers 52, 5)

imi ḫsf·tw n·f m iȝt·{t}f[3] *n(y)t*[4] *ḥwt-nṯr m sȝ n sȝ, iw<ʿ> n iwʿ, ptḫ(w)* (§86) *ḥr tȝ, nḥmw ʿqw·f, ḏrf·(f), wʿb(w)t·f, tm(w) sḫȝt* (§§57, 165) *rn·f m r-pr pn*
May he be driven from his temple office (and) from son to son, from heir to heir, he having being cast upon the ground, his offering loaves, his title-deeds, and his meat-offerings having been withdrawn and his name not being remembered in this temple. (*Les*. 98, 11–14)

§181. Rarer Modes of Negation: *Nfr n* & *Nfr pw*

There are two expressions involving the root *nfr*, which has as one of its meanings "finished," "completed," and perhaps occurs as a related word for "zero."

In the negative phrase var. *nfr n*, *nfr* is a predicate adjective followed by the dative. The writing of the dative with negative arms was no doubt influenced by the negative sense of the phrase. The rare Middle Egyptian examples seem to have an infinitive following the dative. It may be translated "happens not to" and the like. This expression was probably already quite archaic in Middle Egyptian. It was more widely used in Old Egyptian.

Exx.

iw·ṯn r ḏrp n·i m nt(y)t m ʿ·ṯn. ir nfr n wnn m ʿ·ṯn, iw·ṯn r ḏd m r·ṯn.
You will offer to me from that which is in your hands. If it happens that nothing is in your hands (literally "if it happens that there not be [anything]), then you will say with your mouths ... (Cairo 20003)

A second expression consists of *nfr pw* + noun, meaning "there is (are) not..." When an infinitive is used in the noun slot, it can be translated in such ways as "there was not even the offering of a lamp there," or "there is nothing to use." A variation consists of *nfr pw* + a *sḏm·f* form of unknown variety (with past tense meaning). One expects a nominal form, and it may be the prospective.

[3]The *t* following a feminine word (particularly if there is a suffix pronoun attached) is far from rare. This is actually because of phonetic reasons. The final *t* of feminine words without suffix pronoun was dropped in pronunciation. The extra *t* before the suffix is to indicate that the *t* was retained before suffixes.

[4]*Nṯ* is for *n(y)t*.

Exx.

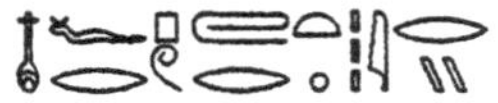

nfr pw pḫrt ỉry
There are no prescriptions for it. (Adm. 4, 11–12)

nfr pw smnḫ ꜥꜣ, wpw-ḥr pꜣ ỉt n(y) nn ḫny(w)t, ỉw·f m ꜥt ḥr ḫtm·sn
There is nothing of use here, except that barley of those dancing girls which is in the room under[5] their seal. (West. 11, 23)

§182. The Ancient Negation W

A mode of negation so rare that even advanced scholars may not encounter an example is the word *w*, meaning "not." The particle is placed after the prospective *sḏm·f*. The use is restricted to prohibitions.

Ex.

srw(ỉ)·ṯn w mꜥḥꜥt tn[6] m st·s tn r nḥḥ
You shall not remove this funerary monument from this its place for all time. (Cairo 20539, i. *b* 20)

§183. The Negative Relative Adjective *ỉwty*

There existed a negative counterpart of *nty* that is far from rare, and occurs in a number of expressions, as well as being used freely on its own with the meaning "that not." The word is written *ỉwty* and the reading is known from the Old Egyptian writing *ỉwt(y)* "that not." When used on its own as a noun (without antecedent) meaning "one who is not" or "one who has no..." the writing *ỉwt(y)w* also occurs. The negative relative adjective declines exactly like *nty* (or any other adjective, for that matter).

1) *ỉwty* + noun + suffix: "which has no..." / "without a..." In this use, possession is denied. The use is very common. It can modify an antecedent, or stand alone as the head of a nominal phrase ("he who has no...." When modifying nouns, it can additionally be translated "lacking a," "devoid of," "having no," or "...-less."

[5]Note that the Egyptian idiom is to be "upon one's seal," as opposed to the English, which requires "under one's seal."
[6]*Ṯn* is for *tn*.

Exx.

mḏ3t ỉwt(y)t sšw·s
a papyrus without writing (Ebers 30, 7)

ntk ỉt n(y) nmḥ, hỉ n(y) ḫ3rt, sn n(y) wḏꜥt, šndyt n(y)t ỉwt(y)w mwt·f
You are the father of the orphan, the husband of the widow, the brother of the divorced woman, the apron of him who has no mother. (or "of the motherless") (Peas. B1 62–64)

2) *ỉwty + sḏm·f*: "who does not..." The particular *sḏm·f* form is not certain, but it is possibly the circumstantial *sḏm·f*. Examples are not uncommon.

Ex.

kf3-ỉb ỉwty pḫr·f ḏd m ẖt·f ḫpr·f m ṯsw ḏsf
The trusted man who does not circulate speech from his belly ("gut feelings") becomes a leader, himself. (Ptaḥḥ. 234–37)

3) *ỉwty* + adverbial phrase is not very common. Translations vary, depending on the type of adverbial expression. The adverbial phrases are similar to the comments of non-verbal sentences.

Ex.

ỉ3t ṯwy (for twy) n(y)t 3ḫw ỉwt(y)t sqdw ḥr·s
that mound of the spirits upon which there are no travellers (literally "that there are no travellers upon it") (Gardiner, *EG* §203, 1)

3) Various fixed idioms: *ỉwty n·f* This idiom means "one who has nothing." It is literally "one with (things) not belonging to him." ***ỉwty sw*** is similar to the previous idiom, but *sw* would seem to be the subject of *ỉwty* (as a type of predicate adjective), the whole meaning something like "he who is nothing." Quite common is the curious expression *nt(y)t ỉwt(y)t* (and *ỉwt[y]t nt[y]t*) "that which exists and that which does not exist." This means "absolutely everything."

Exx.

ink ḫnms n nḏsw, bnr (ỉ)m3t n ỉwty n·f
I am a friend to the poor, graciously pleasant (§48) to the pauper. (*Les.* 80, 22 ff.)

ỉmy-r pr wr, nb·ỉ, wr n(y) wrw, sšmw n(y) ỉwtt nt<t>
O high steward, my lord, greatest of the great, director of all that isn't and all that is (or "absolutely everything"). (Peas. B1 53–54)

VOCABULARY XIV

 *ỉs* "after all," "indeed," "even"

 *ꜥ3* "greatness"

 *bỉnr*, variant of *bnr* "dates"

 *mt*, variant of *mwyt* "urine"

 *mnỉ* (infinitive without *t*) "to moor" (ship); "to bring to port"

 *nḏsw* "poverty"; "low status"

 *ḥs* "excrement"

 *ḥknw ḥknw*-oil (a sacred oil)

 *ḥḏt* "the White Crown" (of Upper Egypt)

 *ḫntw, ḫnt(w)* (adverb) "before," "beforehand"; "previously"; "earlier"; (adjective?) "previous"; "former"

 *ḫ3yt* "heap" (of corpses)

 *s3tw* "floor"; "ground"

 *sbt* variant of *sbṯ* "to laugh" *m* "at"

 *sp* "venture," "undertaking"

 *sft* variant of *sfṯ* "to slaughter" (animal)

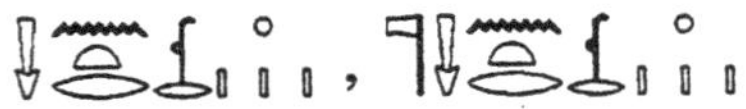 *sntr* variant of *snṯr* "incense"

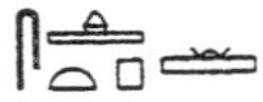 *sḥtp* (*s*-causative) "to satisfy"; "to please"

 *sš3* variant of *šs3* "to be wise"; *rdi šs3* "to inform" (a person) *m* "of," "acquaint" (a person) *m* "with"

 *sšmw* "conduct"; "behaviour"

 *qni* "embrace"

 *qnbt* "court" (of law)

 *k3* "bull"

 *gs-pr* "temple"

 *d3r* "to control" (one's temper, etc.);  *d3r ib* "to get control of oneself"

EXERCISE XIV

(A) Reading Passage

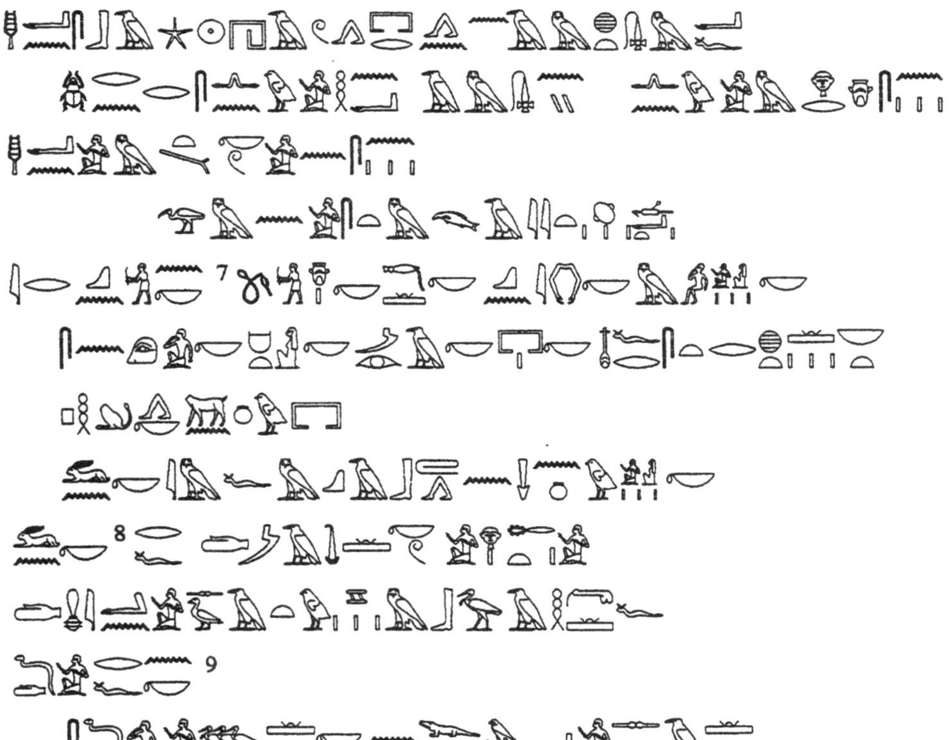

[7]Emend the text to read: *ir qni·k* or transliterate: *ir qn·{n}k*.
[8]At this point, some confusion over the pronouns begins. Here the scribe must have intended *wn·k(wi)* and cf. §98.
[9]Emend the text to read: *ḏd·i n·f*.

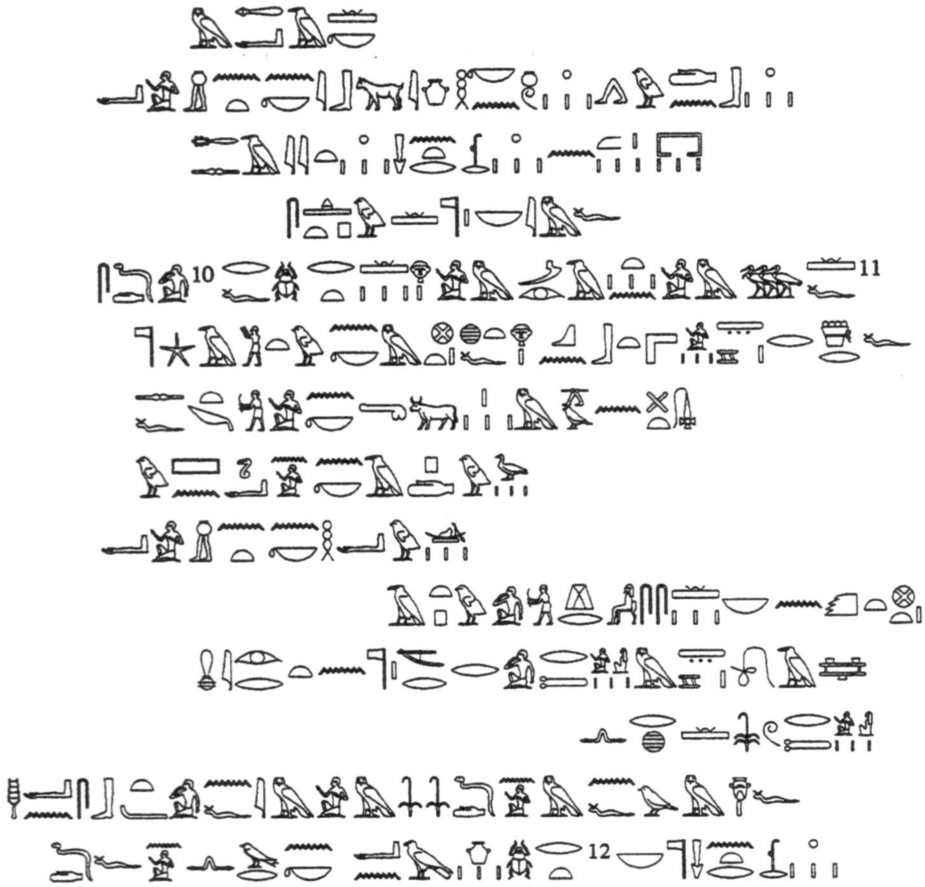

(B) Transliterate and translate

1. 
2. 
3. 
4. Advice to the poor man:

[10]Supply a 1st person sing. suffix pronoun here.
[11]Emend the text to read *b3w·k* rather than *b3w·f*.
[12]*Ḫprt* participle "that which is produced" = "products."
[13]The verb *wn* is possibly in the circumstantial form: "for when the end comes about...."

5) 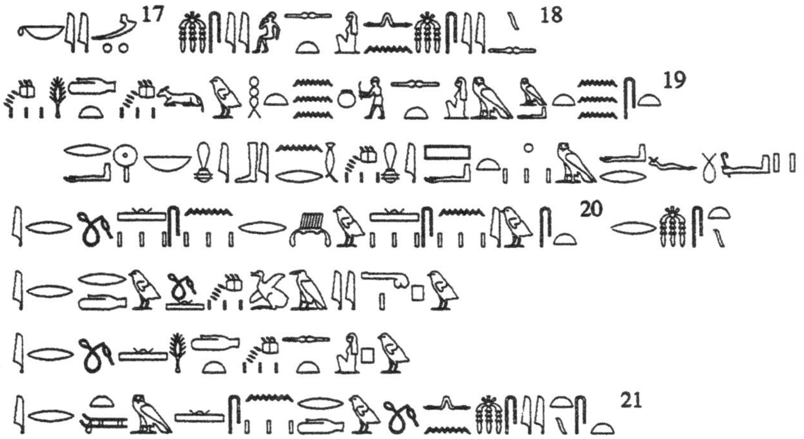

(C) Parse from *(B)*:

1) 

2) 

3) 

4) 

5) 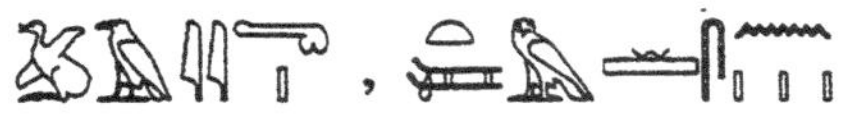

[14]This refers to the master's former status. Here *rḫ* is almost "to seek out." Note that *n·k* is the dative.
[15]Here *ḫt* means "wealth."
[16]"They" must refer to the gods.
[17]Read *m33*. This is an infinitive that here means "way of seeing."
[18]Cf. §139, 2nd example.
[19]The writing *s{t}* is for *s*.
[20]The writing *s{t}* is for *s*.
[21]The writing *s{t}* is for *s*.

LESSON 15

§184. Negations in the Explicatory Sentence

There are four types of negation that occur in explicatory constructions. Their use is determined by whether the action took place or not, and by the speaker's assertions concerning the validity and occurrence or non-occurrence of circumstances.[1] Some of these negations are quite rare, and the differences in meaning are quite subtle by comparison with English, where such precision is not normally encountered. The reason that there are four types of negation stems from the fact that various elements can be negated: the verbal idea, the connection between the action and the circumstances, and the circumstances themselves.

The general situations are outlined in the paragraphs immediately following. They are summarized in the chart, below, and are dealt with in somewhat greater detail in the subsequent paragraphs of this section.

1. The subject does not do a particular action and the speaker wishes to point out the reasons or circumstances surrounding the non-action (or to enquire about the circumstances, etc.). (The verbal idea is negated.)
2. The subject does something and the speaker wishes to point out that certain hypothetical reasons or circumstances of which a hearer might conceive are not valid. (The connection between the verbal idea and the circumstances is negated.)
3. The subject does something and the speaker wishes both to point out what is maintained as the true reason or circumstances and to deny certain hypothetical ones. (The connection between the verbal idea and *some* of the circumstances is negated.)
4. The subject does something and the speaker wishes to point out that certain circumstances did not arise at all, or that the action was done precisely because a certain circumstance did not occur. (The circumstances themselves are of a negative nature.)

[1]Following M. Gilula, (review article), *Journal of Egyptian Archaeology* 56 (1970), pp. 209, 210, except for the fourth situation.

ACTION DONE	ACTION NOT DONE
1.	Circumstances are treated as valid: 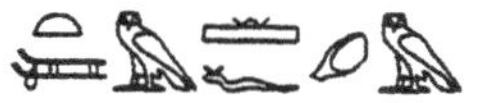 *tm·f sḏm(w)* + adverbial element
2. Hypothetical circumstances are denied:  /  *n sḏm·n·f is* / *n sḏm·f is* + adverbial	
3. Some circumstances are validated, others denied: 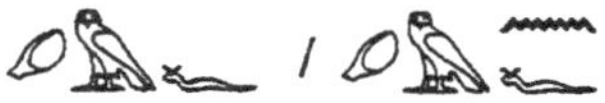 + adverbial +  + adverbial	
4. Action done *while* or *because* certain circumstances did not occur: 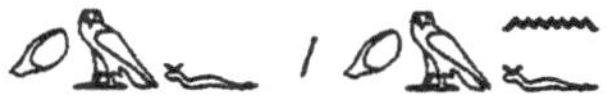 + 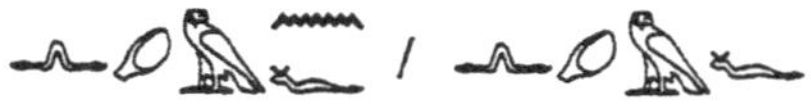 (a negated circumstantial clause serves as adverbial)	

1. The negative verb  *tm* (+ negatival complement) is used in its second tense forms and is followed by the adverbial element. In this case, it is the verbal idea itself that is being negated. The passives were formed by means of the infix *tw*, but no certain examples of *tm·n·(tw)·f sḏm(w)* have been discovered.

Exx.

tm·k tr sḏm(w) ḥr m

Why, then, do you not listen? (Peas. B1, 180.)

tm·tw rdỉt rḫt·sn ḥr wḏ pn r tm sꜥšꜣ mdwt

An enumeration of them has not been put on this stele just so as not to have too many words. (Urk. IV, 693.)

2. It is not the subject's action that is denied in this construction, but the supposed reasons or circumstances surrounding the action. Since the explicatory sentence is essentially non-verbal, the ... *n*...*ỉs* negation is used to deny the connection between the topic (the second tense form and associated words) and the comment (the adverbial element).

It is of importance to note that the *sḏm·(n)·f* forms after the *n* are the second tense forms and not the old indicative forms encountered in the *n sḏm·n·f* and *n sḏm·f* constructions[2] (§§106–8). **Therefore, in contrast to these, the time reference of *sḏm·f* is present and that of *sḏm·n·f* is past.**

Ex.

šm·n·k ꜥnḫ·k. n šm·n·k ỉs mwt·k

You have departed *being alive*. You have *not* departed *being dead*.[3] (Pyr. 833a)

3. This construction differs from the second only in that certain circumstances or reasons are first affirmed before others are denied. In both cases, the negation is the connection between the topic (2nd tense + its subject) and the adverbial comment. The construction *n* + 2nd tense *sḏm·(n)·f* + *ỉs* would deny all the following adverbial elements. Therefore the sentence begins as a normal affirmative explicatory construction, but the particular adverbial element that is denied is preceded immediately by *n ỉs*.

Ex.

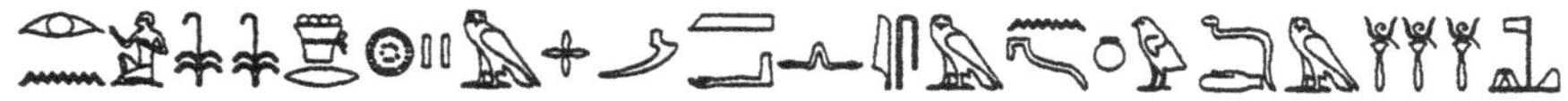

ỉrỉ·n·ỉ nn (sic) *ḏr sp sn m wn-mꜣꜥ n ỉs m nw ḏd(w) m ỉꜣwt*[4] *ḫrt-nṯr*

I did all—all— of these things in actual fact, and not just as what is said out of the duty of the necropolis. (Petrie, *Dendereh*, pl. X[5])

4. In this type of sentence, the speaker is not denying a link between the topic and the adverbial comment. Here the adverbial element itself conveys a negative situation. In fact, the speaker is making a connection between an action that is / was done and negative or non-existent

[2]These negations negate the verbal idea. Here the verb is affirmative because the action took place. The constructions appear similar, but are very different in function.

[3]The speaker does not wish to say that the deceased has not departed, but rather that the deceased has departed, but did not do so as a dead person.

[4]The original is written with a rare variant sign that appears as the cursive *w* with three strokes on the top.

[5]Cited by Gilula, *op. cit.*, p. 211.

circumstances, the point being that the action took place *while* or *because* the conditions mentioned were not present. Negative circumstantial clauses (which are adverbial) can serve as the adverbial element in a normal affirmative explicatory construction. The negation of the circumstantial clause is that dealt with in §§107–8.

Ex.

iri·n·i nn n ḫs·i ḥr ib

I did these things for I was not the least bit incompetent. (or "precisely because I was not incompetent.") (Urk. IV, 933)

§185. Non-enclitic Sentence Particles

There were a number of non-enclitic sentence particles in Egyptian. Most familiar at this point are the particles of this variety learned early on: *iw* and *mk*. These are the two least obtrusive particles. Others are considerably more emphatic. Of course, the particle *iw* is never used when one of the stronger sentence particles is used. The most important ones are listed below.

1)  *isṯ* later ,  *ist* and  *isk* and  *sk*, and the archaic (or archaistic)  *sṯ*: One of the uses of this particle that is normally claimed is that of marking a clause of time or circumstance (e.g. Gardiner, *EG* §119, 2). However, rather than marking a subordinate circumstantial clause, this particle may have meant something like "That was when ..." or "Now at the time, ..." with full main clauses following.

Sometimes the force is closer to that of *mk* "lo!"—to use an archaic expression. If "behold" is avoided as a translation of *mk*, then one can perhaps tolerate the translation "behold" for this use of *isṯ*. Like *mk*, *isṯ* is followed by the dependent pronoun series.

The phrase 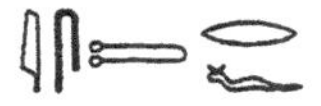 *isṯ rf* is fairly common in prose narratives and can usually be translated simply as "now."

Exx.

isṯ wi ḫd·i r nḏ-ḫrt r ḫnw pf wr n(y) Ḥm·f

See me as I travelled downstream to make greetings at that great court of His Majesty's. (Lesest. 74, 12–13)

2) The particle 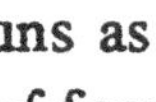 *k3* "next," "then" introduces what comes next in a sequence. It can form phrases with nouns as well as introduce verbal sentences, including the participial statement (§134). The *sḏm·f* form used is the prospective. Like the particle *iw*, *k3* may be followed by a suffix pronoun. Both *k3 sḏm·k* and *k3·k sḏm·k* constructions occur.

Exx.

kꜣ sꜣ·k, kꜣ sꜣ·f, kꜣ wꜥw ỉm·s<n>[6]

Next your son, then his son, and then one of them. (West. 9, 14)

ỉr m-ḫt hꜣỉ{w}[7] *nḏs r pꜣ š mỉ n(y)t-ꜥ·f n(y)t rꜥ nb, kꜣ·k ḫꜣꜥ·k pꜣ msḥ n(y) mnḥ r-sꜣ·f*

Now after the commoner has gone down to the pool according to his daily routine, you are then to throw that wax crocodile after him. (West. 3, 2 ff.)

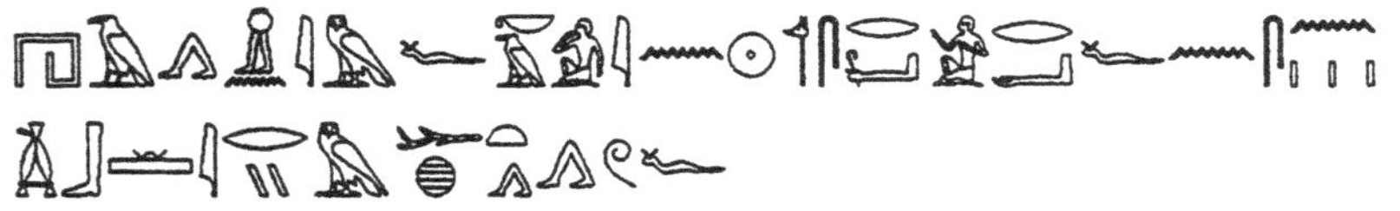

hꜣỉ ỉnỉ ỉm·f, kꜣ ỉn Rꜥ-wsr rdỉ(w)·f[8] *n·sn ḏbꜣ ỉry m-ḫt ỉw·f*

Go down and take some of it, then it will be Reꜥ-woser who will give them its replacement after he has returned. (West. 11, 25 ff.)

3)  *ḫr* , var.  , "then," "now," "thus," "further," is not very common before sentences with adverbial predicates, but it is not uncommon introducing verbal sentences. The construction *ḫr* + NOUN + stative is attested. It is most frequently followed by the prospective *sḏm·f* to form optative statements: "then you should do," etc. It can also be used in sentences that express the result of some previous act "then he will do...." The construction *ḫr sḏm·f* occurs, but the suffixed *ḫr·f sḏm·f*, *ḫr* NOUN *sḏm·f*, and *ḫr·tw sḏm·tw·f* are far more common.

Exx.

ḫr·tw tḫb·tw·f m bỉt. wt ḥr·s, snb·f ḥr-ꜥwy.
ỉr grt tmm·f ḥr stꜣw·f,
wt·ḫr·k sw ḥr ꜥd nrꜣw, sft, tỉḫwy nḏ(w),

6 This is a defective writing of the 3rd plural suffix. It is not very common, but it is very well attested (§187).
7 The *w* is probably nothing more than a "space-filler," not uncommon in hieratic texts.
8 The form is a second tense prospective (§188).

ỉr hq ẖr·f, ḫr·k tmt·k
sw m ⸢q3w⸣ n(y) ḥmt w3ḏt.
ỉr m-ḫt ḫr·k wt·k sw m ftt n(y)
dbyt ḥr 3bḫt

Then it (a wound) should be irrigated with honey and bandage over it (the honey) so that he recovers immediately. If, however, it closes up over its secretions, you are then to bandage it with[9] ibex grease, (pine) oil, and ground peas. If it ⸢breaks out⸣ (from) under it, then you should dust it with the powder of green ⸢glass flux⸣. Now later, you then bandage it with the fibres of the *dbyt*-plant on top of *3bḫt*-liquid. (P. Ebers 70, 14, ff.)

4)  *ḫr m-ḫt* "now after," "now later," "now afterwards" is commonly used in prose narratives. Almost any sentence type may follow. There are two basic uses: 1) "Now, after someone did something ..." or "Now, after many days had passed ... 2) "Now later ..." In the latter case, *ḫr m-ḫt* is used on its own without qualification. This usually indicates the beginning of a new section in the narrative, and the phrase is therefore commonly written in red ink.

 *ỉr m-ḫt* occurs with little or no difference in meaning. Here *ỉr* is nothing more than the initial form of the preposition *r*, and *m-ḫt* is actually a fronted nominal element (§133). The combined form also is not infrequently encountered:  *ḫr ỉr m-ḫt*.

Exx.

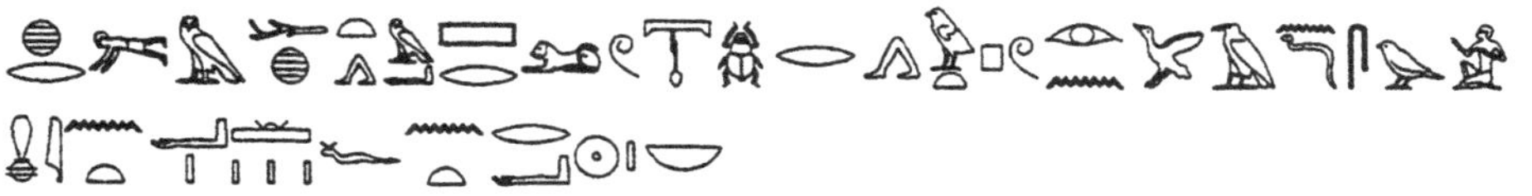

ḫr m-ḫt mšrw ḫpr(w), ỉwt pw ỉr(w)·n p3 nḏs mỉ n(t)-ꜥ·f n(y)t rꜥ nb

Now after evening had arrived, the commoner went according to his daily routine. (West. 3, 10 ff.)

ḫr ỉr m-ḫt, gsw·ḫr·k sw m mrḥ<t>, tmtm ⸢ỉbnw⸣. ḫr ỉr m-ḫt ḥr-s3 nn, srwḫ·k sw m mrḥ<t> bỉt, nḏm·f

Now afterwards, you then anoint him with oil sprinkled with ⸢alum⸣. Now later, after this, you are to treat him with oil and honey in order that he be relieved. (P. Med. Berlin 52)

5) Although not involving a sentence particle, but functioning rather like *ḫr m-ḫt* are other adverbial or nominal phrases of time. These are encountered in narrative texts. Not uncommon is the phrase *wꜥ m nn hrw* "one of those days."

[9]Literally "over it," since the physician was to apply the bandages on top of the medical preparation.

Ex.

wʿ m nn hrw ḫpr(w), ʿq pw iri·n qnbt n(y)t ẖnw r pr-ʿ3, ʿnḫ(w), (w)ḏ3(w), s(nbw), r nḏ ḫrt

One of those bygone days, the magistrates of the royal court entered the palace, l. p. h., to make greetings. (Neferty 1–2)

6) *smwn* "probably," "certainly" is not a very common sentence particle. It can be followed by the suffix pronoun.

Ex.

ḏd·in nsw bity Nb-k3 m3ʿ-ḫrw: smwn msḥ pn <n>ḥ3(w)

Then the King of Upper and Lower Egypt, Neb-ka, justified, said: "This crocodile certainly has become terrifying." (West. 4, 1)

7) *nḥmn* "surely," "indeed," if followed by a pronoun, requires the dependent pronoun series. It is not very common.

Ex.

nḥmn wi mi k3 n(y) wḏw m ḥr-ib ky idr

Indeed I am like a bull of the ⌜range⌝ in the midst of another herd. (Sinuhe 261)

§186. Enclitic Particles

A number of enclitic particles have already been encountered. These particles are placed as early as possible in the sentence, usually they are the second or third word of a sentence. Examples already familiar are *rf*, *rk*, *grt*, *swt*, etc. Other important enclitic particles are listed below.

1) *is* "indeed," "even," "after all," "in fact"

Ex.

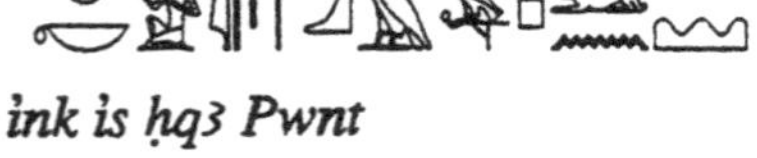

ink is ḥq3 Pwnt

I am the Ruler of Punt, after all. (Sh. S. 153)

2) *ms* "surely," "indeed," or sim. The exact meaning is not certain.

Ex.

mk ms sy šm·ti

Now look, she has gone off. (West. 12, 22 f.)

3)  *ḥm* "to be sure," "surely," indeed.

Ex.

ḫr ḥm nfr wꜣḥ-ib nḥm[10] *wỉ m-ꜥ mt*

Now good, indeed, is the mercy that has rescued me from the hand of death. (Sinuhe 435 f.)

4)  *tr* "indeed," "certainly," or sim., is rather rare in statements, but quite common in questions (cf. §128, 2).

Exx.

n ỉnk tr smꜣ·f

I am certainly not an associate of his. (Sinuhe 255)

tm·k tr sḏm(w) ḥr m

Why, then, do you not listen? (Peas. B1, 180)

§187. Defective Writing of the Third Plural Suffix Pronoun

Occasionally one encounters a defective writing of the 3rd plural suffix pronoun as ·*s* instead of the expected ·*sn*. This is perhaps because of a dropping or nasalization of the *n*.

Ex.

ỉst ḫtm·n nꜣ n(y) rmṯw dmỉ pn ḥr·s<n>

Now the people had locked up this town on them. (I.e. the town gates were locked, and some citizens were left outside, with the enemy troops advancing.) (Urk. IV 658, 5)

[10] Note the play on words between *ḥm* "surely" and *nḥm* "to rescue."

VOCABULARY XV

3ḫt "uraeus" (the serpent on the royal crown—said to overpower the enemy)

ỉwd "to separate" *X r Y* "X from Y"

ỉm3w "tent"

ỉs-ḥ3q "easy prey" (a military expression along the lines of the English hunting metaphor "sitting ducks"—literally: "a 'go and plunder!'")

wn m3ʿ "actual truth"; *m wn m3ʿ* "in actual fact"

wt "to bandage"; *wt ḥr* + medical preparation "to bandage with"

bw wr "the greater part"

Psḏntyw "the new moon (festival)"

mmy "giraffe"

mšrw "evening" Probably cognate to Semitic: Aramaic רַמְשָׁא (*ramšā*) "evening"; Arabic مساء (*masāʾ*) "evening"; Akkadian *mušu* "evening"; Hebrew אֶמֶשׁ (*ʾemeš*) "yesterday"

mty "exact"; *r mty* "exactly"

n(y)t-ʿ (Noun fem.) "custom, habit," "routine"

nwy "water"

nb-ỉr-ḫt "Lord of Action" (said of king) literally "the Lord who does things"

r-ʿ-ḫt "war"; "combat"

rdỉ m ḥr "to command"; "call to (one's) attention"

rḏ3yw "melee," "time of battle"

ḥb "festival"

ḫt (preposition) "throughout," "through" and as adverbial comment "pervading"

ḫkrw "panoply" (of war accoutrements)

ḫr(y)t "obligation" (of a person); "requirement"; "possessions, belongings"

sbỉt (fem.) "load," "cargo"

sqr-ꜥnḫ "captive"

Stḫ the god Sutekh (Seth)

šn(w) "net"

Qi-na (a place name), written in New Kingdom style group writing

Qdš Kadesh, a city on the Orontes River

tišps (a spice)

tmm "to close up (abnormally)" (said of wounds)

tmt "to sprinkle," "to dust" (with a powder)

ṯmꜣ-ꜥ "strong of arm," "strong-armed"

ḏꜥmw "electrum" (a gold-silver alloy)

EXERCISE XV

(A) Reading Passage

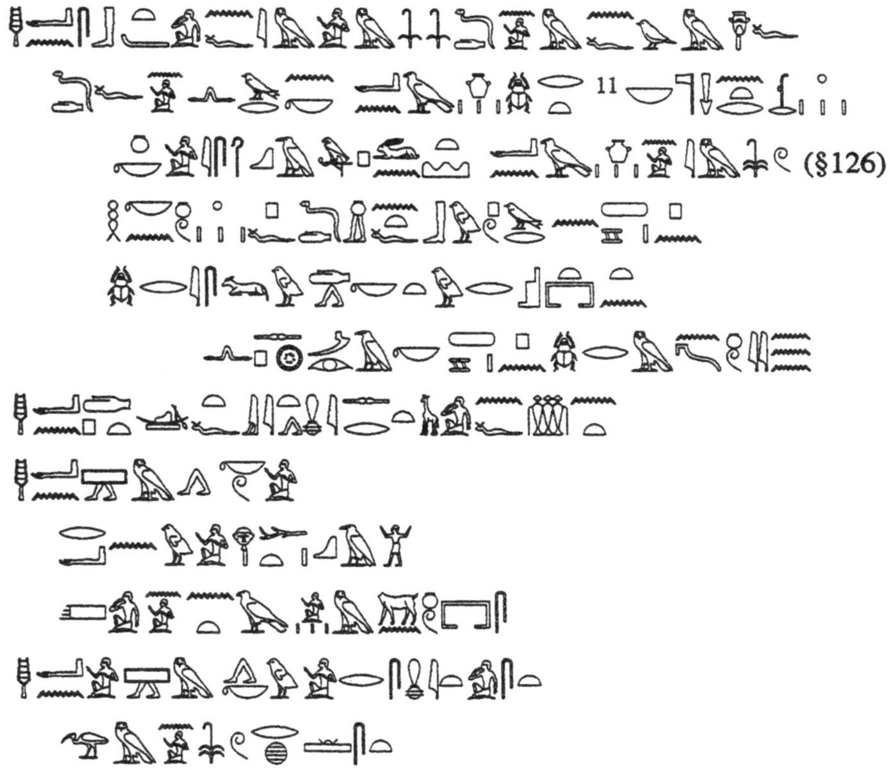

11 *Ḫprt* participle "that which is produced" = "products."

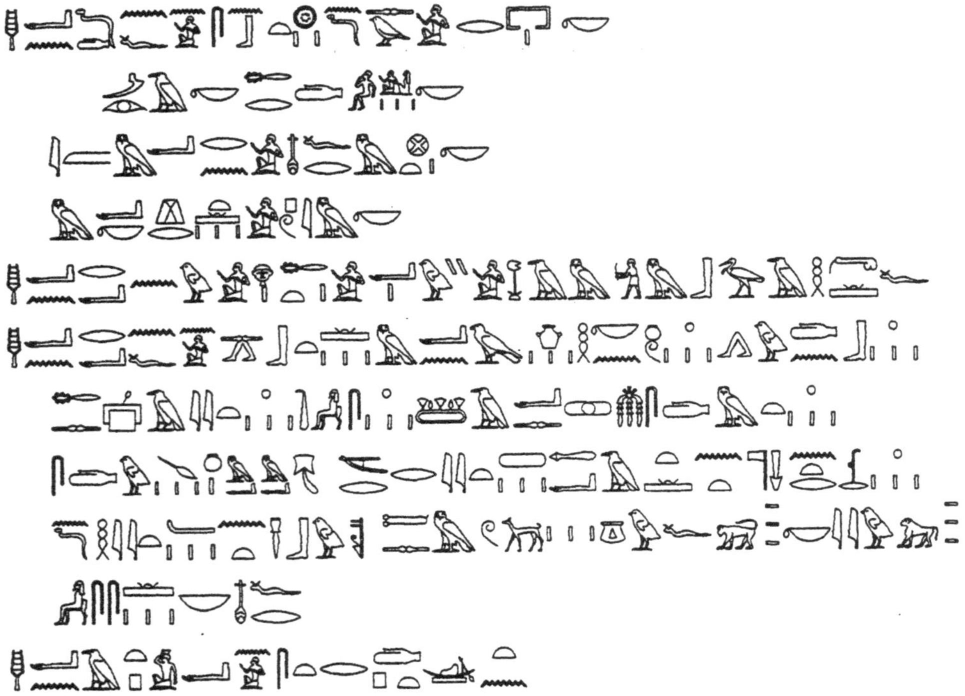

(B) Transliterate and translate the following narrative passage from the Annals of Thutmose III: "The Attack and Siege of Megiddo."

Context: The rulers of Canaan had united in a coalition along with their northern neighbours and had been resisting Egyptian control over the region. The text begins with the Egyptian king's order to carve the records of his military campaigns and to list the booty (including severed hands) plundered. The first campaign began at the very end of year 22 in Thutmose III's reign (ca. 1480–1470 B.C.E.). Having passed the fortress at the Egyptian border, within a few days (now early year 23) the troops reached the town of Gaza, which the Egyptians have renamed: What-the-Ruler-Took. The troops move northwards to the Carmel ridge, where the king consults his officers concerning the route of march. In spite of the officers' advice to take the safer road, the king's will prevails, and they take the more direct, but dangerous route through a narrow pass. The troops swear not to break ranks, and the king vows to lead the way. They pass through without encountering the coalition troops. This the king declares a victory. The troops praise the king. The king waits for the rear of the army. The van reaches the Megiddo plain at noon. The troops are commanded to prepare their weapons and to steel themselves for battle. The king rests in his tent and rations are distributed to the troops. The scouts later report that the "coast is clear." The annals continue with the following text.

1 

 (§§ 41, 1; 57, 7)

 (a few signs lost) (§35)

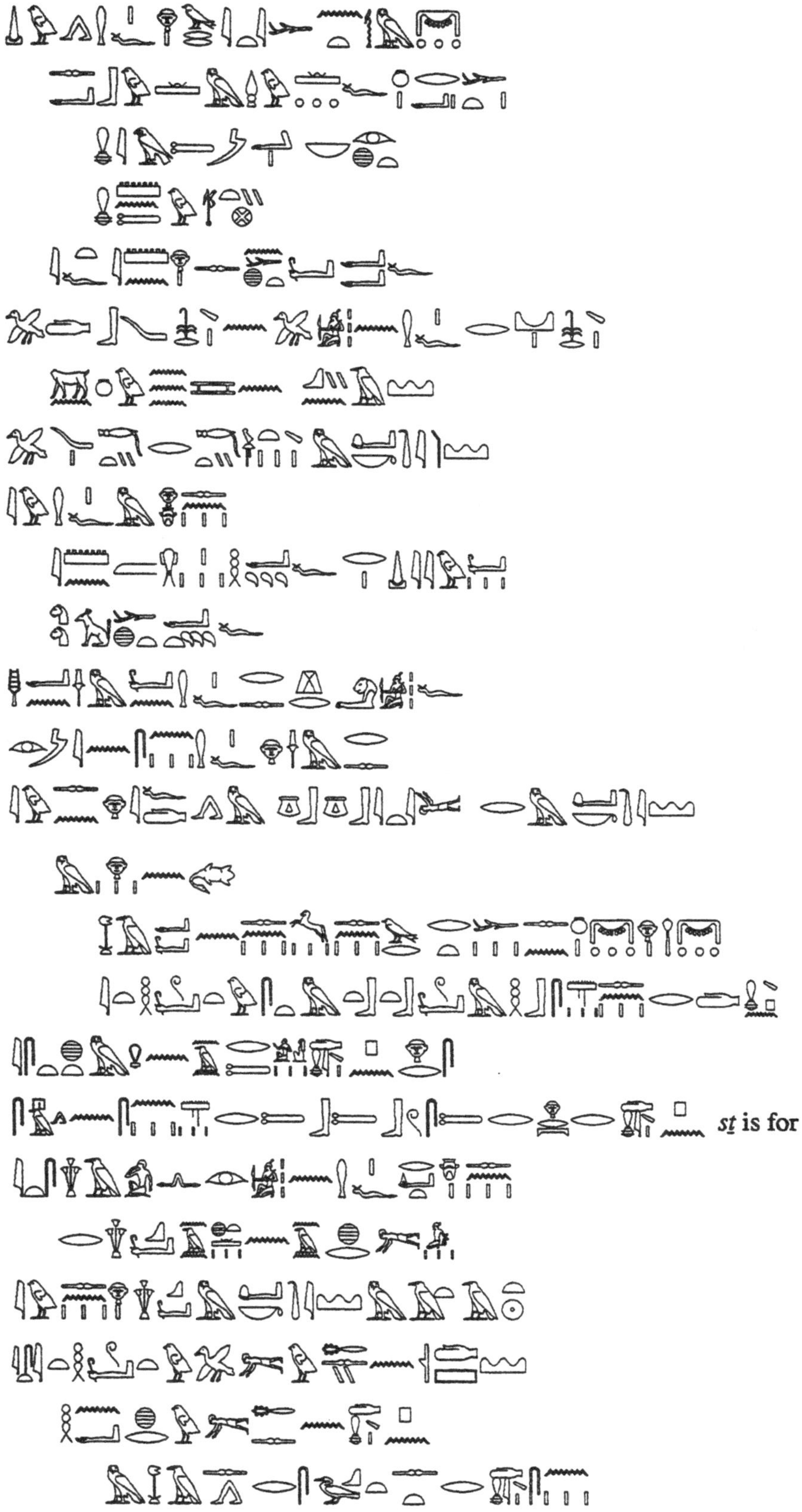

sṯ is for *st*

 (§91 or §86)

(approximately one line damaged)

(C) Parse the following words and phrases from Exercise XV *(B)*. The numbers refer to the line number.

4. 

5. 

7. 

8. 

13. 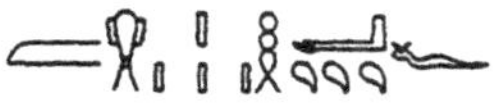

20. 

26. 

29. 

33. 

39. 

41. 

LESSON 16

§188. Second Tense Prospective *Sḏm(w)·f* Forms and Their Uses

The forms of the 2nd tense prospective *sḏm(w)·f* were introduced in §138, where they were encountered in conditional clauses somewhat more frequently than the regular (or modal) prospective *sḏm·f*. The 2nd tense prospective forms were also encountered in the "participial statement" (§134) where they seem to occur consistently (rather than the modal 1st prospective *sḏm·f*). The uses of the two prospective forms is apparently not exclusive to either type in most instances, and it is very likely that the two were in the process of merging during the Middle Kingdom. Not all the subtleties have been fully worked out yet, but the general outlines of these two forms is emerging.[1]

The two prospective forms had a couple of distinctions. The 1st prospective *sḏm·f* was almost exclusively modal ("ought to do," "should do," "may one do," or "is likely to do"); the 2nd tense prospective *sḏm(w)·f* tends to be closer to a true future (i.e. it overlaps with the *ỉw·f r sḏm*). The 2nd tense prospective *sḏm(w)·f* forms are future ***2nd tense*** forms, and are used in places that one expects 2nd tense forms to be used: in explicatory sentences, after prepositions, and as the direct objects of verbs. In particular, the prospective explicatory sentence (with bare initial 2nd tense prospective *sḏm(w)·f*) contrasts with the simple future *ỉw·f r sḏm* in the same way that *mrr·f* + adverbial contrasts with *ỉw mrỉ·f*. Since both prospectives are nominal, they also occur in virtually any spot that a noun might be used (for instance, they may head a noun phrase that serves as the subject of a verb).

1) Examples of 2nd tense prospective *sḏm(w)·f* forms in explicatory sentences:

ỉw·f r smr m-m srw. rdỉ(w)·tw·f m-q3b šnyt
He will be a companion among the officials. In the midst of the courtiers shall he be placed. (Sinuhe B 280–1)

[1]The 2nd tense prospective forms were posited for Old Egyptian by Hans J. Polotsky as early as 1969. The morphology of the form in Old Egyptian was noted by Elmar Edel some years before that. Important work on the subject was undertaken by James P. Allen (e.g. *The Inflection of the Verb in the Pyramid Texts (Bibliotheca Aegyptia*, vol. 2) [Malibu: 1984]). Further work was done by Pascal Vernus, whose book *Future at Issue* (New Haven: 1990) provides additional evidence and a good bibliography on previous studies of this form. In some works the term "future active *sḏm(w)·f*" is used. The examples in this section were all presented by Pascal Vernus in *Future at Issue*, but the translations are my own.

ỉr sḏm n·ỉ bꜣ·ỉ ỉwty btꜣ, twt ỉb·f ḥnꜥ·ỉ. ỉw·f r mꜥr. rdỉ(w)·ỉ pḥ·f ỉmnt mỉ nty m mr·f, ꜥḥꜥ·n ḥry-tꜣ ḥr qrs·f.
If my guiltless (§183) soul listens to me, it will agree with me (literally "its mind[2] will be in accord with me"). It will be fortunate. I will make it reach the West just like one who is in his pyramid with a survivor having attended to his burial. (Lebensm. 39–43)

2) Example of the 2nd tense prospective *sḏm(w)·f* after prepositions:

dd·k st r hꜣw snf
You place it just so that the blood flows. (Ebers 88, 19)

§189. Parenthetic Expressions for "So He Said," "So She Will Say," etc.

In addition to using a verb of speech (especially *ḏd*) there were several parenthetic expressions to indicate the speaker. These phrases normally follow the first part of the quotation, and often occur in the middle of the quotation. Examples involving the use of the particle *ỉn* "so says," were introduced in Lesson 9 (§109, Exercise B, 12). With *ỉn* the time is regularly present.

Similar in function is *ḫr*. It is used with present and past time reference. It can take *tw* "one" as a quasi-passive "so they say."

kꜣ is also used, but always has future time reference.

Exx.

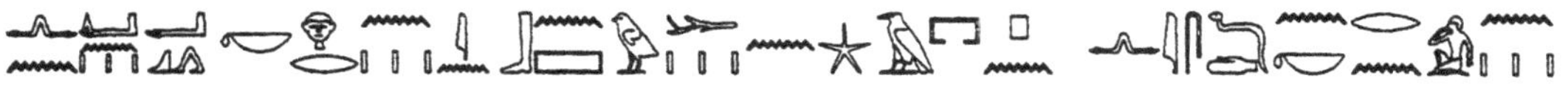

nn dỉ·n ꜥq·k ḥr·n—ỉn bnšw n(y) sbꜣ pn—n ỉs ḏd·n·k rn·n
We will not let you enter past us—so say the doorposts of this gate—unless[3] you say our names. (BD ch. 125 Address to gods)

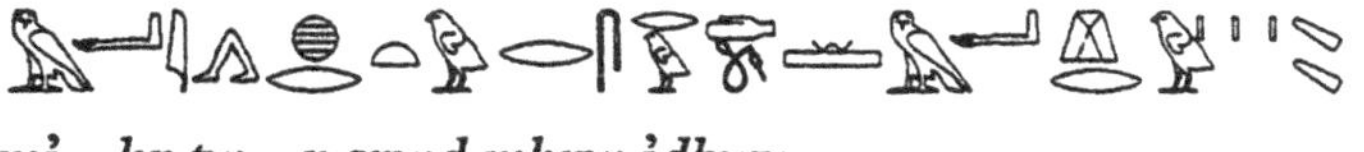

mỉ—ḫr tw—r srwd mḫrw ỉdbwy
"Come," they say, "in order to make flourish the affairs of the Two Banks!" (Urk. IV 1075 ff.)

mk wỉ, kꜣ·k
"Here I am," so you shall say. (Gardiner, *EG* p. 348)

In the Coffin texts, later Middle Egyptian hieratic, and the Book of the Dead, there is a

[2]The man and his soul have been arguing—definitely of different minds on the question of death.
[3]One of the meanings of *n … ỉs* is "unless."

peculiarly written *nisba* (?) form:  *ḫr(y)·fy*, var. . The *fy* is difficult to account for. The phrase is followed by a dependent pronoun or a noun, or both (e.g. *ḫr(y)·fy sn nṯrw* "so the gods say"—literally "so they, namely the gods, say"). For the plural, both *sn* and *st* are attested.

Exx.

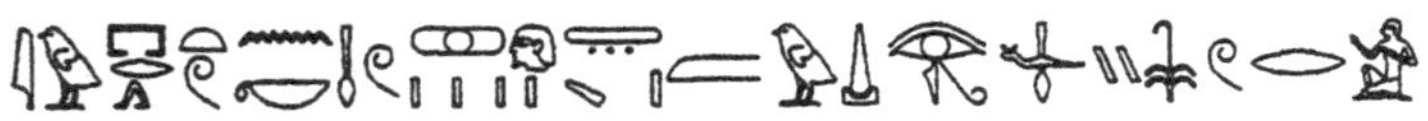

ỉw prỉ·tw n·k ḫrw tp tꜣ m wḏꜣ, ḫr(y)·fy sw r·ỉ
"Invocation offerings come forth to you upon the earth from the *wedjat*-eye," so he said to me. (BD chapter 125)

ḏd·n·f n pꜣy·ỉ ỉt: "ỉw·ỉ r <r>dỉt n·k tp ḥnꜥ fꜣt wꜣwꜣ nb n·k ỉmy," ḫr(y)·fy sw
(Scribe PN) said to my father: "I will give you the ⌜principal⌝ together with the accrual of all the ⌜interest⌝ owing (literally "belonging") to you," so he said. (P. Kahun 2, 22)

§190. Verbs Following the Genetival *N(y)* "Such as the King Gives," etc.

The 2nd tense verb forms were used after the genetival *n(y)* to form a type of relative clause. The meaning may have been something like "fine food such as the king gives" from "fine food of how the king gives (it)." The use is not common, and tends to be limited to a few more or less set phrases in high-flown speech. With the verb *wnn*, the form *wn* is the *sḏm·n·f* form, and *wnn* is the *sḏm·f* form. The latter often has future time reference.

Exx.

ḫt nbt nfrt n(y)t šsp Ḥm·f
all sorts of fine things such as His Majesty receives (Urk. IV 707)

wnm·k špssw n(y) dd nsw
You are to eat delicacies such as the king gives. (West. 7, 21)

ꜥnḫ·n m ṯꜣw n(y) dd·f
We live only by means of the air that he (the king) gives. (*Readingbook* 52, 7)

m ḥwn·k n(y) wn·k ỉm·f
in your youthful vigour such as you (once) were in (Urk. IV 497, 10)

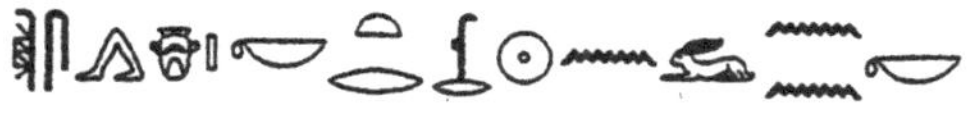

šms ib·k tr n(y) wnn·k
Follow your heart for the time of however long you live (i.e. "as long as you live"). (Ptaḥḥ. 186)

§191. The Genetival *N(y)* before Prepositional Phrases

In a few idiomatic expressions, the genetival adjective precedes a prepositional phrase. The most common consists of *n(y) ḫr nsw* "which are with the king." This expression is used of things received *from* the king, and also quite abstractly with favour and honour "of the king."

Exx.

imꜣḫy n(y) ḫr nsw
one honoured by the king (Gardiner, *EG* p. 121)

iw·i ḫr ḥswt n(y)t ḫr nsw (honorific transposition!) *r iwt hrw n(y) mni*
I was in the favour of the king until the day of mooring (dying) arrived. (Sinuhe B. 310)

§192. *M-* Preformative Nouns

One of the Afro-Asiatic noun formations involves the preformative element *m-* attached to a word root. As in the Semitic and other Afro-Asiatic languages, the *m-* preformative nouns are frequently of place and instrument (i.e. *place* where something is done, *instrument* with which something is done). It is also used for such things as chests and boats. The *m-* preformative element is frequently written *m*. Eg. *mḫr* "low-lying land" (from *ḫr* "under"); *mḫtmt* "sealed chest" (from *ḫtm* "to seal").

§193. Abstract Nouns—Idioms with *Bw* and *St*

Quite a number of abstract nouns were formed with *bw* "place" and *st* "seat." *Bw* is modified by an adjective, and *st* is used as the first element in bound constructions. With *bw*, idioms are generally listed under the second element in the dictionaries. With *st*, most are listed under *st*. Exx. *bw mꜣʿ* 'truth"; *bw nfr* "good, goodness"; *st ʿ* "blow, strike (of gods against people)"; *st ḥr* "supervision." The following are not in the main entry of Faulkner's dictionary:

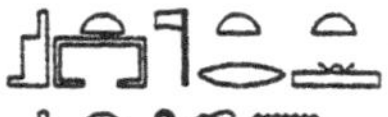 *st nṯryt* "divine state"
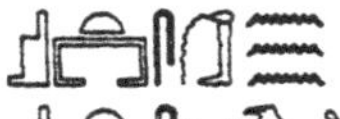 *st swʿb* "purity, cleanliness"
 *st skꜣ* "ploughing"
 *st štꜣw* "mysteries"

§194. Colourful Idioms as Nouns

The Egyptians created a number of colourful idioms based on phrases or even sentences that are used as nouns or noun phrases. The historical narrative of Exercise 15 contained the expression *is ḥ3q* "easy prey" (literally "go and plunder!"). Of a similar nature are *iw·f ꜥ3·f* "a man on the rise" (literally "no sooner he comes than he becomes great"—a reciprocal sentence [§152]) and *h3i·i ini·t(w) n·i* "a free for all" ("should I go down, it would be brought to me"). Nominal phrases following the *m* of predication also occur.

Ex.

ꜥnḫt n(y) Kmt m (§24) *h3y·i ini·t(w) n·i*

The grain of Egypt is (now) a free for all. (Admonitions 6, 9)

(. . .), šny(w)t m tp-ḥr-m3st

(The palace was still . . .), the courtiers (sitting) with head-on-knee (i.e. in mourning). (Sinuhe R10)

§195. The Reflexive Dative

The dative is not uncommon in commands and exhortations. The exact force is difficult to convey in the translation, but in the original it may have implied a feeling of connection between the speaker and the person receiving the command. In English one can say "Get yourself some food before it's all gone!" But **"Go for yourself to your home!" is hardly possible. In such cases, the dative is best left untranslated. The reflexive dative after the imperative *looks* like a second person *sḏm·n·f*, but this possible reading must be ruled out by context (i.e. present time, one person speaking to another, etc.).

Ex.

ir n·k iwt r Kmt, m3·k Ḫnw ḫpr(w)·n·k (§161) *im·f*

Come back to Egypt so that you may see the royal court where you used to be. (Sinuhe 399 f.)

§196. *'Iw* + Adjective (Stative)

This construction appears to be an impersonal use of the stative. There is no antecedent, and the 3rd masc. sing. stative form, generally unmarked, follows directly after *iw*. The construction is similar to the following, but with no pronoun or demonstrative: *iw n3 wr(w) r·i* "This has become too much for me!" (Lebensm. 5)

Ex.

ỉw qsn(w) r·f wn r·f
It is painful for him to open his mouth. (Or: It is too painful for him to open his mouth. (Ed. Sm. 3, 3)

ỉw šw(w) m ꜥq-ỉb
There is a lack of a confidential friend. (Lebensm. 123–24)

§197. The Offering Formula

Funerary steles and cenotaphs bear a formulaic text that was to be read out by persons visiting the site. The texts sometimes request that visitors offer food or whatever they have upon them to the soul of the deceased. If the visitors had nothing, then they were encouraged to read the offering formula. One text states that it does not take much effort—unlike running—and that one's breath is not consumed by reading, and that it is a kindness that will not go unrewarded! The offering, whether material (bread, beer, etc.) or spiritual (spoken words), was made to the person's *kꜣ*, which required nourishment. The least inconvenience to the visitor was to say simply *ḫꜣ m t ḥnqt n kꜣ n(y) PN* "a thousand loaves of bread and (jugs) of beer to the *kꜣ* of PN!"

The formula occurs with many variations, but most are fairly similar. They all start with the phrase *ḥtp dỉ nsw* "an offering that the king makes," in which *dỉ* is the relative verb form. The word *nsw* is placed first as an honorific transposition. In the Middle Kingdom version of the formula, the name of one or more gods follows immediately after *ḥtp dỉ nsw*, but it is clear that the idea was that the king was to make a general offering to one or more gods, who in turn would provide the *kꜣ* of the deceased with specific "invocation offerings" known as *prt-ḫrw* (literally "what comes forth [at] the [god's] voice"). Note the abbreviated writing of the offerings: *t* "bread," *ḥnqt* "beer," *kꜣ* "beef," *ꜣpdw* "fowl," *šs* "alabaster (vessels)," and *mnḫt* "clothing." The formula is generally as follows: *ḥtp dỉ nsw* God_1, God_2 *dỉ·sn prt-ḫrw* (and other offerings) *n kꜣ n(y) PN* "An offering that the king gives (to) God_1 and God_2, so that they will make (offerings) to the *ka* of PN." Sometimes the formula itself is abbreviated by leaving out the *dỉ·sn* (or *dỉ·f* if only one god is mentioned). One may then translate: "An offering that the king makes (to) Osiris: invocation offerings of...."

ḥtp dỉ nsw Wsỉr, Nb ꜣbḏw: prt-ḫrw t, ḥnqt, kꜣ, ꜣpdw, šs, mnḫt, ḫt nb(t) nfr(t) wꜥb(t) ꜥnḫ(t) (§159) *nṯr ỉm n kꜣ n(y) mwt·f mrt·f* (§158 or §124) *Nb(t)-ỉwnt, mꜣꜥ(t) ḫrw, nb(t) ỉmꜣḫ* (Stele British Museum 557)
An offering (to) Osiris, Lord of Abydos: invocation offerings of bread, beer, beef, fowl, alabaster, clothing, and every fine and pure thing upon which a god lives to the *kꜣ* of his beloved mother, Nebet-iunet, justified, possessor of eminence.

The following is a fairly elaborate Middle Kingdom offering formula.

ḥtp dỉ nsw Wsỉr, Nb Ḏdw, nṯr ꜥꜣ, Nb Ꜣbḏw,

dỉ·f prt-ḫrw kꜣ, ꜣpdw, šs, mnḫt, snṯr, mrḥt, ḫt nb(t) nfr(t) wꜥb(t) ddt (§159) *pt, qmꜣt tꜣ, ỉnnt ḥꜥp, ꜥnḫ(t) nṯr ỉm*

n kꜣ n(y) rḫ nsw mꜣꜥ, mry·f (§124) *n(y) st-ỉb·f, ỉrr* (§121, 1a) *ḥsst* (§159) *Nb Tꜣwy m ḫrt-hrw n(y)t rꜥ nb, ỉmy-r pr ḥsb rmṯw, S-n(y)-wsrt-snbw* (sportive plural writing of the stative), *mꜣꜥ ḫrw nb ỉmꜣḫ, ỉr(w)·n* (§161) *Nbt-ỉwnt, mꜣꜥt ḫrw*

An offering that the king gives (to) Osiris, the Lord of Busiris, the Great God, the Lord of Abydos,

that he might make invocation offerings of bread, beer, beef, fowl, alabaster, clothing, incense, oil, and every fine and pure thing that heaven gives, that the earth produces, that the Nile brings, and upon which a god lives

to the *kꜣ* of the true king's acquaintance, his beloved of his affection, the one who does what the Lord of the Two Lands praises in the course of every day, the Superintendent of the House of Enumerating People, Senwosret-sonbu, justified, possessor of eminence, whom Neb-iunet, justified bore (literally "made"). (Stele British Museum 557)

§198. The Late Egyptian Set of Pronouns *Tw·ỉ, Tw·k,* etc.

From the Seventeenth Dynasty on, a new series of pronouns comes into use as the subject of sentences with adverbial comment. Not all of the forms are attested before Late Egyptian. This series is the normal one for sentences of this type in Late Egyptian.

TABLE 11: THE LATE EGYPTIAN PRONOUNS

	Gender:	Common	Masculine	Feminine	
Singular	1st Pers.	*twỉ*			"I"
	2nd Pers.		*twk*	*twt*	"You"
	3rd Pers.		*sw*	*sy*	"He"/"She"/"It"
Plural	1st Pers.	*twn*			"We"
	2nd Pers.	*twtn*			"You"
	3rd Pers.	*st*			"They"

The 3rd fem. sing. *sy* was later replaced with *sw*. There is also an impersonal pronoun (quasi-passive) *tw·tw* "one."

Ex.

sw ẖr tꜣ n(y) ꜥꜣmw; tw·n ẖr Kmt

He holds the land of the Asiatics; we hold Egypt. (Tab. Carnarvon, 7)

§199. Late Egyptian Writing Conventions

Since a number of Middle Kingdom literary works are known only from later New Kingdom copies, students of Middle Egyptian must eventually become familiar with the conventions of Late Egyptian. The best way to do this is, of course, to learn Late Egyptian, which is actually easier to read than Middle Egyptian (once the writing conventions are learned).

First, in order to indicate that a *t*-ending was pronounced (e.g. before the suffix pronouns), it is often written as *tw*, thus appearing like a passive verb form. For the same reason, *t* is also written twice (once before the determinative and once after). Exx. *ḫt·f* "his possessions"; *r ḫnt·n* (§ 154) "until we rush off."

Writings tend to be fuller, with more *w*'s and *y*'s written out, even where not expected. Compounded determinatives are also much more frequent. Exx. *ẖry* for ME *ẖr* "under"; *šms* "follow" (imperative).

The introduction of Late Egyptianisms is a common feature. Examples include the use of the negative particles *bn* for *nn* and *bw* for *n*. Occasionally *bw* occurs where one expects an original *nn*. In general, there tends to be great confusion with the use of the Middle Egyptian negative particles *n* and *nn*, and they are often interchanged.

Exx.

bw sḏm·n Wrd-ỉb sẖbꜣ(w)t·sn

but the Weary-of-Heart (Osiris) does not hear their cries.

bw ỉy ỉm (One expects *nn* in the original Middle Egyptian.)

There is no one who has returned from there.

There is also a tendency to write the 2nd masc. sing. suffix as if it were the 1st common sing. stative: *·k{wỉ}* for *·k*.

Ex.

šmsw ib·k wnn·k{wi}
Follow your heart as long as you live (literally "are").

Other peculiarities include superfluous *t*'s, which often serve as "space fillers," especially over the walking legs determinative. Dots also occur as space fillers. In a similar way, the seated man determinative is sometimes thrown in where it is not needed. (It was little more than a dot in some manuscripts.)

§200. Further Reading

Serious students who have reached this point in their studies of Egyptian have, it may be assumed, expended a great deal of time and much effort. Although reading Egyptian texts will not feel natural for years (if ever), there is an undeniable satisfaction in the ability to read—first-hand—the fascinating literature and to have direct access to the culture of this ancient society. The time and effort required to learn Egyptian may have been great, but the time and effort to maintain and to expand one's capabilities is minimal by comparison. There is no better way to keep and sharpen one's skills than by reading texts.

Highly recommended is the Westcar Papyrus, (A.M. Blackman, *The Story of King Kheops and the Magicians* [Reading: J.V. Books, 1988]), but it also available in A. de Buck, *Egyptian Readingbook* (Chicago: Ares Publishers, 1977) a reprint from the 1948 edition. One could start with the new section beginning at 4, 17 ff. (one could also start earlier, at 1, 17, but the text is badly damaged and there are many lacunae and this section is not found in all the translations). The story and characters (the magician Djedi, Prince Hardedef, Redjedet, and her husband Ra-woser) will be quite familiar to those who have studied the examples of this book carefully, and the plot will all fall into place. Good translations of this text and other literary texts can be found in Miriam Lichtheim, *Ancient Egyptian Literature*, Vol. 1 (Berkeley: 1973), pp. 216–22 and in W.K. Simpson, editor, *The Literature of Ancient Egypt* (New Haven: 1973). The translations in Lichtheim and Simpson do not, however, always conform to the grammar as presented here (especially with regard to the explicatory sentence, and occasionally the voice was changed for no apparent reason).

The Eloquent Peasant is another tale that has many simple passages, but it also contains lengthy verses in very flowery language that modern readers are apt to find somewhat tedious. The abridged version in de Buck is therefore recommended.

The Book of the Dead, although containing some beautiful passages is in many places difficult to understand, both grammatically and culturally. Above all, E.A.W. Budge's publications of this (or any text) should be treated with great caution, as his transliterations and translations are wholly unreliable.

Still a useful collection of Egyptian texts is Kurt Sethe, *Ägyptische Lesestücke zum Gebrauch im akademischen Unterricht* (Hildesheim: Georg Olms Verlagsbuchhandlung, 1959) a reprint of the original edition. This collection contains a variety of texts, including an abridged version of Sinuhe,[4] magical and medical texts, mortuary / autobiographical texts, legal documents, etc. Finding translations of the texts may be difficult. This is also the case for some of the texts in de Buck. Apart from the Eloquent Peasant, the texts in de Buck's work are generally not as interesting than those in Sethe's collection with the exception of some of the historical texts (Gebel Barkal stele). De Buck's book does, however, include formal royal inscriptions of various types.

All of the hieroglyphic publications mentioned here are hand written, and the signs are not always easily recognized, but they will serve as an introduction to Egyptian texts as they have been published in modern times. With the advancement of new technology we are moving into the age of electronic Egyptian and hieroglyphic word-processing—an amazing way to transmit the works of the ancient scribes. But beyond preserving these ancient works in modern formats is the necessity of preserving humanity's recovered knowledge of Egyptian language, literature, culture, science, and art. All who have studied this language are transmitters—in a greater or lesser extent—of this priceless heritage.

VOCABULARY XVI

 *ꜣḫ* "spirit" (said of the dead)

 *ỉqr* "worthy man"; sarcastically "a goody-goody/good-doer"

 *ꜥnw* "again"

 *wnḫ* "to put on (clothing)"

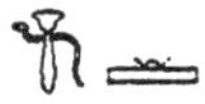 *wꜣḏ* "fortunate," "happy"; "fresh"; "hale"

 *bꜣgỉ* (4th weak) "to be lazy"; "to be tired"; *bꜣgỉ ỉb* "to be half-hearted"

 *bỉꜣ* "a marvel," "miracle" (also said of luxury goods)

 *bnt* "harp"

 "to destroy," "to fall to ruins"; "to obliterate"

[4] A recent translation can also be found in J.L. Foster, *Thought Couplets in The Tale of Sinuhe* (Frankfurt am Main: Peter Lang, 1993).

mr "pyramid"

mhỉ (3rd weak) + *ỉb* "to be forgetful"; "to forget"

ms "to deliver"

rnpy (4th weak) "to be young, youthful"

ḥn "to hurry," "rush" (to a place)

ḥsỉ (infinitive without *t*)"to sing"

ḥsyw "singer" (the participle of *ḥsỉ*)

ḥknw "praise" (to god)

ḥḏ-tꜣ "dawn"; "daybreak"

ḥdỉ "to destroy"; "to injure"; "to disobey" (the heart)

ẖdy "annihilation"; "destruction"

ẖt "generation"

sꜣḥ "to endow" *m* "with"

sḏdwt "quotations"; "literary works"

šꜣw "fate"

tp "person"

EXERCISE XVI

(A) Reading Passage

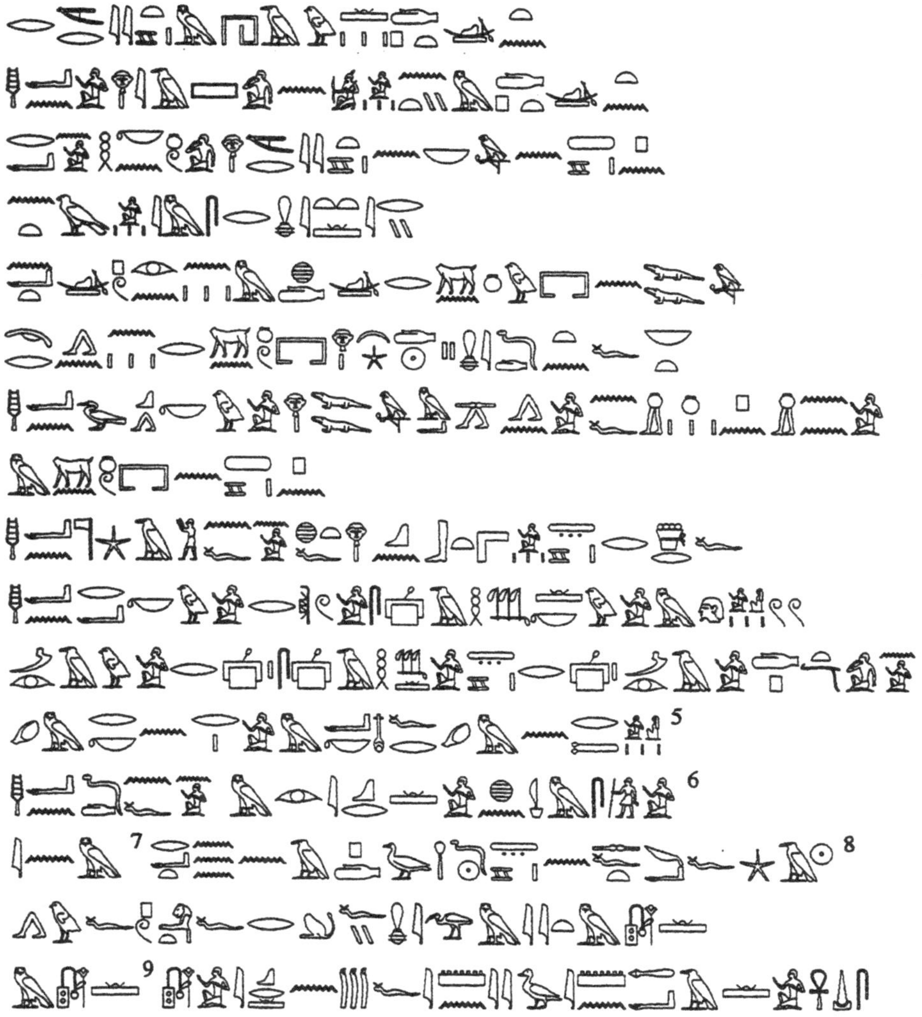

[5]With this line, the "shipwrecked sailor" ends his story. In this literary work, the story is told by an official who was trying to cheer up a colleague after a royal mission had gone terribly wrong. The main narrator tells a story of a disaster that happened to him, and how good had come from it. Nested within this story, it will be recalled, is the story told by the serpent to cheer up the shipwrecked sailor himself. The serpent's story was thus a story-within-a-story-*within-a-story*! The rest of the text (before the colophon: "Thus it has come [to an end] ...") is the response of the troubled colleague. The story fails to put the colleague in a good frame of mind, and he tells the "shipwrecked sailor" to stop trying to cheer him up. The text is difficult at this point and includes a pessimistic proverb.

[6] *M ir(w) iqr* would seem to mean something like: "Don't be a goody-goody!"

[7]This is an interrogative participial statement (§134).

[8]This proverb (or witty saying) is difficult. First, the form of *rdit* is difficult. One expects the 2nd tense prospective form *rdi(w)*, perhaps the *t* was a writing error for *w*. The phrase *n(y) sft·f* modifies *3pd*—or else it could be a dative *n* followed by the independent use of the prospective relative "to one that he will slaughter." The general sense is that his is a hopeless cause.

[9]The second *m sš* is probably not a case of dittography, but is more likely the *m* of predication: "being a document of...."

(B) Transliterate and translate the following poem:

A Song of Death and the Pleasures of Life.

The author begins with a parody of the harper's songs, which glorify the life beyond. This author is less sure and questions the utility of building monuments that will crumble and even casts doubt on the state of the "blessed dead," given a lack of first-hand evidence! The author is a master of sarcasm, making points with great power. He also exhibits a superb sense of humour. Note, however, that this is a New Kingdom copy, and contains a number of "corruptions" presented in §199.

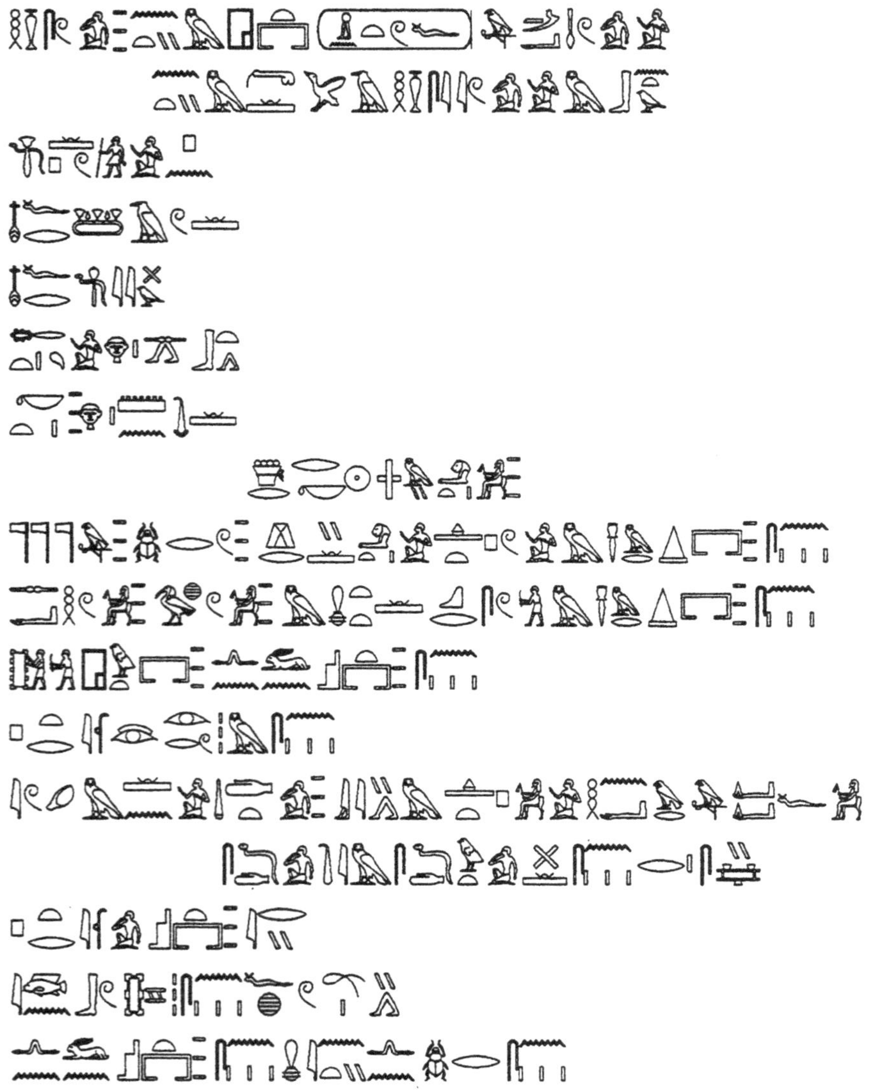

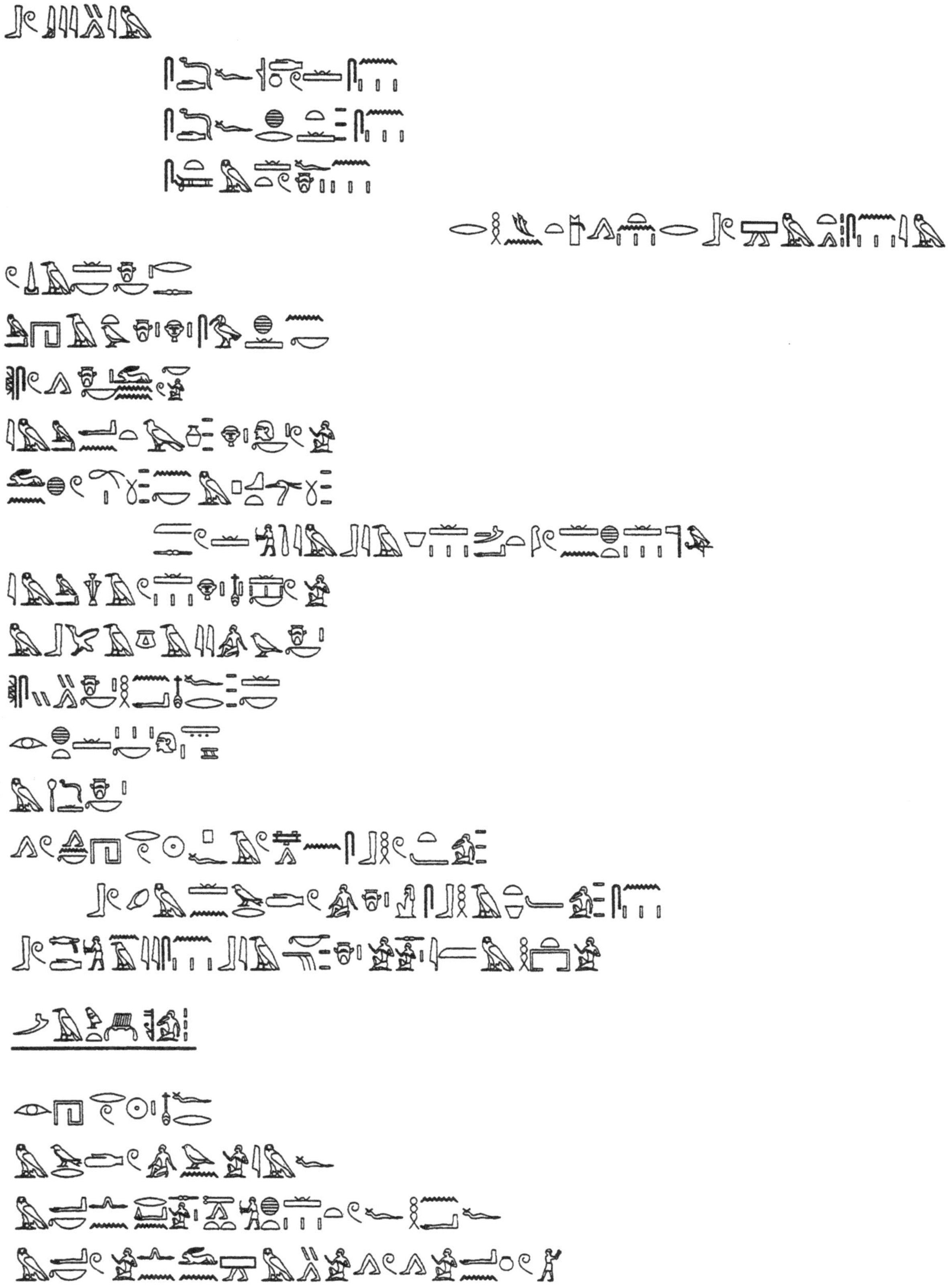

Notes to the Poem

1)  here means "funerary chapel."

2) *bnt*: emend to read . The scribe apparently was thinking of the word *bỉnt* "badness."

6)  is a determinative.

7) The plural strokes on *kt* are for semantic reasons, *ḫt*, to which it refers, being a collective noun.  is a phonetic determinative in this late writing of .

9) *Ḥtpw*: the  sign is superfluous.

12) *Ptr* is for *pw tr* "what(?)." *Ỉrw* is probably a perfect passive participle. The idiom *ỉrỉ m* is "become," "happen to," or "turn into."

13) Imhotep and Hardedef were famous Old Kingdom sages.

14) *Rsy* for *rssy* "so much."

18) The original must have had .

21) *Stm* is a miswriting; emend to . The copyist had a bit of trouble here. He must have thought the line was *sm·tw ỉb·n* "so that our minds might be relieved," but then discovered that the text read *sm·f ỉb·n*, and wrote in the *f* (leaving the erroneous *·tw*).

24) *Mh3t* is for older *mhỉ* (this is New Kingdom group-writing). The *t* may or may not be correct. If it is superfluous, then it might be another imperative. The lines can be read differently: a) *mh ỉb ḥr·s. 3ḫ n·k.* (with an impersonal construction §46) or b) *mht-ỉb ḥr s3ḫ n·k.*

29) The idiom *rdỉ ḥ3w ḥr* means "to go beyond," "add to," "exceed." Here, perhaps even "maximize."

32) The idiom *ỉrỉ ḫt* means "to be active."

34) The subject of *ỉw* is *hrw*.

35) The "weary-hearted one" is an epithet of Osiris.

36) Read *n3y·sn ỉ3kb(w).*  is for  *ḥ3t* "tomb."

40) The idiom *ỉrỉ hrw nfr* means "to celebrate" (said of banquets and special holidays)

41) *N·ỉ* is perhaps correct, the idea being something like: "Don't get tired on me, now!"

42) The original probably had . *N s* is the dative.

43) Read simply *mk* and not *mk wỉ*. The meaning of *šm* and *ỉw* are very specific here.

KEY TO EXERCISES I–XVI

This key is to be used to provide quick feed-back on one's progress. The exercises should be completed *before* consulting the key for maximum benefits. When mistakes are discovered, the student should then try to see where the "wrong turn" was made. Note, however, that in some cases differences may not be mistakes, but rather different interpretations. In obvious cases two or more translations have been provided.

This key was not intended to replace the instructor, and it is hoped that instructors will examine students' work covered by this key (corrected or not) in order to address problems that may have arisen or to confirm or reject a possible reading suggested by the student.

Lesson I

1) to another man

3) Another thing is there.

5) The man speaks to another.

Lesson II

1) This scribe speaks to this woman.

3) See, the scribe hears this plan.

5) Look, the sun is in the sky.

7) See, the boat is in the water when the sun shines forth in (or "from") the horizon.

9) The man hears another plan in the city.

Lesson III

1) Look, the steward's daughter is on her maid-servant's donkey.

3) Rē^{c} crosses the sky in his great bark.

5) The Lord of the Two Lands is in joy over this great construction project.

7) See the mother of your servant in her little house, her children with her. (*Or* "See, the mother of your servant is in her little house, her children being with her.")

9) Our lord send his servant to another city concerning this construction project.

Lesson IV

2) How sweet is the taste of honey! It is finer than anything in this land!

4) A son who listens to his father when he is a child is good. (*Or* "Good is a son who listens to his father when he is a child.") How well it goes for him with this advice in his heart every day.

6) I am a *ḥm-nṯr*-priest who does not know the taste of misfortune.

7) Slaves of great strength are given to you together with kind-hearted female slaves.

9) How great is this house of yours! It is rich in all sorts of fine things.

Lesson V

1) All the property of this temple was in good order when the *ḥm-nṯr*-priest ordered its inspection. (*Or* "that it be inspected")

3) (As caption) Arrival of His Majesty to slay the enemy of vile Kush. (As narrative infinitive) His Majesty arrived to slay the enemy of vile Kush.

5) I am one who is dearly beloved in the heart of his lord, who is generous to all the people of his town. (*Or* "who was …")

6) The servant loaded it for his master after he had ordered that it be done for him.

8) He said it to him after sitting down upon his great throne.

Lesson VI

2) The wife of this loud-mouthed peasant is making 13 loaves of bread and 8 jugs of beer to take to him and her children in the fields.

4) Look, he is talking to your daughter!

6) Amen-nakhte was eating a little bread and drinking beer, the third hour of evening having arrived.

7) He slayed 8 lions by shooting in the twinkle of an eye.

8) The *wᶜb*-priest saw the goddess in the pool bathing herself, she having laid her garments on the ground.

Lesson VII

1) Look, it is good for people to listen. (*Or* "listening is good for people.") *Or*, Look, it is good to listen to people.

3) The children of the chief *ḥm-nṯr*-priest were brought to me that I might inform them of this fine thing.

5) His Majesty came that he might eliminate corruption in this land in its entirety and that he might let one town discover its boundary from (that of) another.

7) He predicted this to me saying: "A ship will come from home. You are to go with them (back) home so that you might die in your town." (*Or* "so that you might go (back) home and so that …")

9) They were fleeing headlong to Megiddo with faces of fear, having abandoned their horses and chariots of gold and silver.

Lesson VIII

1) One of these donkeys filled its mouth with a shoot of Upper Egyptian barley.

3) She had a chest filled with clothing brought to him.

6) The rivers of Egypt will[1] have turned dry so that the water can be crossed on foot. One will search for water for the boats in order to sail (on) it, its course having become a sand-bank.

Lesson IX

1) Look, I have been appealing to you, but you do not listen to it. I will go so that I might make an appeal concerning you to Anubis.

3) There is a box of flint there in the room called "Inventory" in Heliopolis. Look, it is in that box.

5) He enters the house of Osiris. He sees the mysteries that are in it.

7) Here I am come before you, having brought justice to you, having driven out injustice for you, and not having done wrong against people.

9) I had many pine ships constructed upon the mountains of God's Land in the vicinity of the Lady of Byblos, they being placed upon carts, with oxen drawing (them) as they travelled before My Majesty in order to cross that great river that occurs between that land and Naharên.

11) I am pure, there being no part of me devoid of righteousness, for I have bathed in the southern pool.

Lesson X

2) The limits of art have not been attained. There is no artisan who has mastered his craft. Fine speech is more hidden than green-stone. (Yet) it is found with slave-girls at the grind-stone.

4) You are Ḥaꜥpy who makes the meadows green, who re-establishes the ravaged tracts.

Lesson XI

1) Hereditary nobleman, Count, Supervisor of *ḥm-nṯr*-priests, Ḥepdjefa says to his *kꜣ*-priest: "Look, all of these things that I have placed under contract with (*or literally* "in the hands of") these *wꜥb*-priests are under your supervision. Now look, it is a man's *kꜣ*-priest who perpetuates his things and who perpetuates his funerary offerings."

2) Book of conjuring migraine headaches: Strip of fine linen, placed around his head.

6) Here begin the prescriptions that are made to drive fleas from the house: You are then to sprinkle it with a natron-water (solution) in order to drive (them) out.

Lesson XII

1) He found him lying on a mat at the threshold of his wall, a slave at his head anointing him, and another massaging his feet. (This sentence describes *how* he found him, and one could also translate "how

[1] The context requires a future context. Otherwise, this sentence could be translated: "the rivers of Egypt have gone dry."

he found him was ..." but since this sentence type is the one normally used with *gmi* "to find," no particular focus is needed in the English.)

2) Then this Nemty-nakhte said to his retainer: "Go get me a sheet from my house." Then it was brought to him immediately. He spread it out at the fork at the head of the path. Its fringe was resting right in the water and its hem right over the barley. This peasant walked along the public road. Then this Nemty-nakhte said: "Be so good, peasant, as to not walk upon my cloth!" (Literally: "Do well, peasant, so that you have not tread upon my cloth!")

4) I returned serving him as an alert one with absolutely no loss having occurred in my troops. (It is possible, but less likely that the focus begins with *ḥr šms·f m spd-ḥr*.)

6) I travelled at night. No sooner did the day dawn than I reached Peten. (*Or* "I reached Peten just as the day was dawning.")

Lesson XIII

1) (Geneology: Grandfather is Intef [no nick-name]. His son is Mery, called Kebi. Mery's son is named after the grandfather: Intef, but is called Iusonbu.)

Regnal year 39, 4th month of Inundation, day 19.

Transfer of title that the phylē controller Mery—called Kebi—son of Intef made for his son, Intef—called Iusonbu—son of Mery.

I am giving my phylē controllership to my son, Intef—called Iusonbu—son of Mery to be my staff of old age in view of the fact that I have grown old. Let him be appointed from this moment.

As for the transfer of title that I made for his mother previously, let it be revoked.

As for my house that is in the estate of Hut-medet, it is for my children who were born to me by the daughter of the attendant of the district magistrate Sobek-em-hēt, Nebet-neni-nisu, together with all that is in it.

List of witnesses in whose presence (literally "at whose side") this transfer of title was made.

3) Do the scales go wrong? Does the balance tilt to one side? Now does Thoth show mercy?

Lesson XIV

2) Wrongdoing has never brought to port its venture, for when the end comes around, justice prevails.

4) If you are a poor man, serve a wealthy man so that all your conduct will be fine with the god. Do not find out for yourself (his) former poverty. May you not be arrogant concerning him because of what you know of him from former times. Respect him in view of what has accrued to him. Wealth doesn't just come on its own. It is their law for the ones that they love.

Lesson XV

No key is provided as the exercise is relatively straightforward, unlike exercise XVI, for which the entire text is translated.

Lesson XVI

Song that is in the chapel of Intef, justified, which is in front of the singer with the harp.

Fortunate is this nobleman.
Good is fate.
Good is anihilation!

One generation passes on;
Another one remains,
(As) since the age of the ancestors.
The gods who existed before are at rest in their pyramids.
The nobles and the spirits, likewise, are buried in their pyramids.
Those who built chapels—their places are no more.
What has become of them?

I have heard the sayings of Imhotep and Hardedef,
Cited by their quotations so much.
What are their places (now)?
Their walls have fallen to ruins.
Their places are no more—as if they had not existed.

There is no one who has returned from there,
That he might tell of their condition,
That he might tell of their circumstance,
That he might soothe our hearts,
Until we rush off to the place where they go.

May your heart be glad therefore.
Be forgetful of it—(it's) good for you!
Follow your heart as long as you exist.
Place myrrh upon your head.
Dress yourself up in fine linen,
Anointed with a true marvel fit for a god (literally "of a god's things")

Increase your happiness.
Don't be half-hearted.
Follow your heart and your happiness.
Be active on earth.
Don't disobey your heart.

That day of wailing comes to you,
But the Weary-Hearted hears *NOT* their wailing!
Their mourning has not retrieved a man's heart from there—from the tomb.

Refrain:

Celebrate the day.
Don't get weary of it on me.
Look, it is not permitted for a man to take his things with him.
Look, there is no one who has gone who has returned again.

EGYPTIAN VOCABULARY

This vocabulary list contains some 1200 entries and includes only the vocabulary used in this book, although it may still prove useful for reading simpler texts. Note that suffixes and other sub-word level word elements (morphemes) are not listed here, but rather in the **Grammatical Index**. Suffixes, prefixes, and infixes must be learned thoroughly, but one may consult the verb charts for a number of these morphemes. The feminine ending *t* is treated as a suffix and therefore feminine forms are not listed in strict alphabetical order, the feminine form following the basic masculine form (e.g. *ḫt* "thing" is at the beginning of its section because it consists of the root letter *ḫ* + *t*, whereas the masc. word *ḫt* "tree" (the *t* being a root letter) is listed after *ḫsf*). *Nisba* derivatives from feminine words are listed directly after the feminine form (e.g. *sḫty* follows the sequence: of *sḫ*, *sḫt*, *sḫty* and would not follow the root *sḫt* "to weave"). Words are also generally listed together with those written with the same signs, even if the alphabetic order is broken. These conventions are standard in Egyptian lexicons.

ꜣ

ꜣ (particle) that follows *ḥwy* in polite requests **please** (§73)

ꜣt (n. f.) **moment, instant**; *m ꜣt·f* **in one's moment, in action**; *m km n(y) ꜣt* **in the blink of an eye**

ꜣw (adj.) **long, extended**; *ꜣw ib* **happy**; *ꜣw ḏrt* **generous** (i.e. always extending the hand to help others)

ꜣw (n. m.) **length**; *r ꜣw·f* **in its entirety**; *r ꜣw* **in their entirety** (§80)

ꜣwt (n. f.) **length**; *ꜣwt ib* **happiness, joy**

ꜣbi (vb. 3rd weak) **to long**; **desire** with infin. "to do"

ꜣbw (n. m.) **elephant**

ꜣbḫ (vb.) **to mix** *m* **"into"** (ingredients of medicines), **mingle, join**, *m* **"with,"** *ḥnꜥ* **"with," unite** *n* **"to"**
Cf. ? West Semitic *ꜥrb* "to mix" (e.g. Hebrew עֶרֶב (*ꜥēreḇ*) "mixture"

ꜣbḫt (n. f.) a liquid, perhaps **solution** if derived from *ꜣbḫ*

, *ꜣbd* (n. m.) **month**

ꜣbḏw (place name) **Abydos**; *Nb ꜣbḏw* **Lord of Abydos** (an epithet of Osiris)

 *3pd* (n. m.) **bird** (a generic term); cf. ? Semitic: Hebrew צִפּוֹר (*ṣippōr*) "bird"; Arabic عصفور (*ʿuṣfūr*) "sparrow, small bird"

 *3m* (vb. bi-cons.) **to burn up** (said of persons in a fire)

, var.  *3ḥt* (n. f.) **field** (specifically agricultural land)

 *3ḫ* (adj.) **good, useful, beneficial; glorious;** (adj. f.)  *3ḫt* **something beneficial, a useful thing**

 *3ḫ* (n. m.) **spirit** (said of the dead); pl. 

 *3ḫt* (n. f.) **uraeus** (the serpent on the royal crown—said to overpower the enemy)

 *3ḫw* (n. m. pl.) **skills, expertise, craft**

 *3ḫt* (n. f.) **inundation** (a season §69)

 *3ḫt* (n. f.) **horizon**

 *3ḫty* (m. s. *nisba*) **who is from the Horizon**

 *3qi* (vb. 3rd weak) **to perish**

 *3t* < *3yt?* (vb. bi-cons.) **to be white, to be pale;**  **to be pale of face** (said of frightened persons)

 *3tp*, see *3ṯp*

 *3ṯp*, later  *3tp* (vb.) **to load** *m* **"with"**; *ḥr* **"with"**

 *3d* (vb. bi-cons.) **to be aggressive, savage;**  *3d ib r* + person **to be cruel to (a person);** (n. / infin.) **agression**

 *i*, ,  *y*

 *i* (vocative particle) **O (you)!**

 *i3t* (n. f.) **back**

,  *i3t* (n. f.) **office** (e.g. one's position in a temple, etc.); **duty; function** can refer to the royal office, i.e. kingship

 *i3t* (n. f.) **mound**

 *i33w* (n. m. pl.) **reeds**

 *i3w* (n. m.) **old age**

iꜣw (n. m.) **praise;** *rdi iꜣw n* **to give praise to** (a god)

iꜣby (*nisba*) **left, left-hand**

iꜣbty (*nisba*) **eastern**

, *iꜣbt(y)t* (n. f. *nisba*) **the East**

iꜣrrt (n. f. pl.) **grapes**

iꜣš (vb.) **to call out; to summon**

iꜣqt (n. f. pl. or collective) **vegetables, greens** cf. Semitic *wrq* "greens"

iꜣkb (n. m.) **mourning;** pl. **wailings**

ii and *iw* (anomalous verbs; infinitives: *iit* and *iwt*) **to come, arrive; return.** These two related verbs are not exactly interchangeable, and usually a particular form prefers one root over the other. *ii·ti* (stative) **Welcome!** (§99); As an auxiliary verb **to come out (doing / having done)** (§174); *iw·f ꜥꜣ·f* (idiomatic phrase §194) **a man on the rise**

iyt (n. f.) **harm; mishap; incident; trouble; wrongdoing** (i.e. unfavourable things that happen or are committed—literally "that which has come," cf. English "event," "outcome" for a similar, but less negative, semantic development)

iw (sentence particle) 1) used to begin a statement of fact; 2) used to form circumstantial clauses when the topic is a pronoun (§§9, 10, 15, 16)

iw **island** Cf. Hebrew אִי (*ʾî*) "island"; "coast"

iw See under the root *ii* **to come**

Iw-snb (man's name) **Iusonbu**

iw (n. m.) **crime, wrongdoing, injustice, misconduct**

iwyt (n. f.) **wrongdoing**

iwꜥ(w) (n. m.) **heir**

iwf (n. m.) **meat**

Iwnw (place name) **Heliopolis**

iwr (vb.) **to conceive** (a child), **become pregnant** Possibly cognate to Hebrew הָרָה (*hārā*); Ugaritic *hr(r)*; and Akkadian *arû*, all "to conceive," "become pregnant"

 *iwḥ* (vb.) **to moisten**

 *iwsw* (n. m.) (hand-held) **scales; balance** (fig. of justice)

 *iwty* (negative relative adj.) **which is not;**  *iwt(y)w* **one who is not** (for the uses see §183)

 *iwt(y)t* (neg. rel. adj. f.) **that which does not exist;**  *nt(y)t iwt(y)t* (and  *iwt[y]t nt[y]t*) **absolutely everything** (literally "that which is and that which is not")

 *iwd* (vb.) **to separate** *X r Y* **"X from Y"**

 *iwdnb* (n. m. pl.) a type of incense (?)

 *ib* **heart, mind** Cf. Semitic *lb*, *lbb* heart, mind

 *ib* (vb. bi-cons.) **to think, suppose**

 *ibi* (n. m.) **laudanum** (?) (an aromatic resin)

 *ibnw* (n. m.) **alum** (?)

 *ip* (vb. bi-cons.) **to count, assess;** (n. m.) **accounting**

 *ifd* (vb.) **to flee**

 *ifd* (n. m.) **sheet, rectangular piece of cloth**

 *im* (adverb) **there, therein, therewith, therefrom** (§54)

,  *im3t* (n. f.) **charm, kindliness, graciousness**

 *im3w* (n. m.) **tent**

, var. 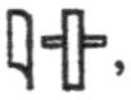, ,  *imy* (*nisba*) **which is in** (from the preposition  *m)*

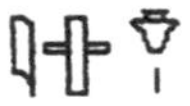 *imy-ib* **favourite**

 *imyw-b3ḥ* (*nisba* of compound prep.) **(those) who are in the presence** (of a god); **(those) who lived before, (those) who came before; ancestors**

,  *im(y)t-pr* **transfer of title to an estate** (a legal term, literally "that which is in the house")

, ,  *imy-r*[1] **overseer, superintendent,**  *imy-r pr* **steward,**  *imy-r pr wr* **high steward;**  *imy-r sm(yw)t i3bt(yw)t* **overseer of the eastern deserts**

[1]The word is always written as an abbreviation. Note that some scholars transliterate *mr* or *imy-r3*. These are not considered standard in the Anglo-American practice.

 *ỉmy-rn·f* (n. m.) **list of names**

 *ỉmy-ḥ3t* (*nisba* of compound prep.) **former; previous; which / who was before; of olden times; forerunner;** pl.  *ỉmyw-ḥ3t* **those of former times; ancestors; predecessors**

 *ỉmy-ḫt* (*nisba* of compound prep.) **one who will come after;** pl. *ỉmyw-ḫt* **those of later times, future generations**

 *ỉmy-s3* (n. m.) **attendant**

 *ỉmỉ* var. ,  (vb. imperative of *rdỉ*) **give, put, cause** (§ 145) Less common writings:  and 

 ,  *ỉmỉ* negative auxiliary verb ("to not do") negates: wishes and exhortations (§164); the imperative  *m* (§166)

 *ỉmytw* (prep.) **between;** *ỉmytw X r Y* **between X and Y**

 *ỉm3ḫ* (n. m.) **honour, veneration;**  *nb ỉm3ḫ* **possessor of eminence, honoured lord**

 *ỉm3ḫy* (*nisba* m.) **one who is honoured; revered one**

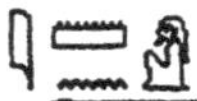 *Ỉmn* (divine name) **Amun**

 *Ỉmn-m-ḥ3t* (king's name) **Amenemḥēt** (the nomen of a number of kings in the Twelth and Thirteenth Dynasties)

, abbrev.  *Ỉmn-nḫt* (man's name) **Amen-nakhte**

 *ỉmn* **right hand,** which is cognate with Arabic يمن (*yaman*) right-hand side; south and Hebrew יָמִין (*yamin*) right hand; south

 *ỉmnt* (n. f.) **the West**

 *ỉmnty* (*nisba*) **western**

 *ỉmr* (vb.) **to be deaf**

 *ỉn* 1) in passive constructions, the agent particle: **by,** also expresses means: **through;** 2) , **"(...)," so says (speaker X)** parenthetically introduces the speaker following a quotation (cf. §109, exx.; §189); 3) in the participial statement (§134) emphasizes the doer of the action: **It is so-and-so who (did** ...)."

 *ỉn ỉw* (question particle) (§168)

 *ỉn-m* (interrogative pronoun) **Who?** (§134)

ini (anomalous 3rd weak; infinitive *int*) **to bring; get, acquire; to attain, reach** (a goal), and many other idioms. (This is not a "verb of motion.") Note that the *sḏm·n·f* forms are written *in·(n)·f* and *in·n·f*.

inw (n. m. pl.?) **tribute; gifts; goods** (often cocerns trade goods) The word is a passive participle "the things that have been brought back."

Intf (man's name) **Intef**

inb (n. m.) **wall**

Inpw (divine name) **Anubis**

in-m See under *in*

inm (n. m.) **colour; skin**

inn (1st com. pl. indep. pron.) **We** (§56); **X belongs to us** (§126, 2)

inr (n. m.) **stone**

inḥ (n. m., usually dual) **eyebrow**

, var. , *ink* (1st sing. indep. pron.) **I** (§56); **X belongs to me** (§126, 2)

ir (particle) 1) **As for...** (§133); *ir m-ḫt* **Now after, now later, now afterwards;** 2) **If...** (in conditional sentences §137)

, var. , *iry, ir(w)* (*nisba*) **thereto, connected to, associated with** (§54); **its; their** (§55) *m st iry* **in their (proper) place(s), in good order;** *mitt iry* **its likeness, something like it**

iry (m. s. *nisba*) **companion, associate;** pl. *iryw* **crew** (of ship)

iry-ꜥꜣ (n. m.) **door-keeper**

iry-pꜥt (n. m.) **hereditary nobleman** (This is an abbreviated writing. *Iry* is the *nisba* adjective of *r* = "one belonging to" and the *pꜥt* was the social stratum of the nobility usually translated "the patricians.")

irt (n. f.) **eye;** the dual is possibly masculine, *irwy*?

, *iri* (vb. 3rd weak) **to do; make; carry out** (a project, activity, etc.), **undertake; to spend** (time); **to act, serve** *m* **"as"; to beget, engender** (children); as auxiliary verb (followed by the infinitive) (§171)

irf (enclitic particle) **then, now** (often left untranslated)

 *irtt* (n. f.) **milk**

 *ihm* (vb.) **to linger, lag; to be held back**

 *ihmt* (n. f.) **confinement**

,  *iḥ* (n. m.) **ox; cow** (generic); (n. f.) *iḥt* **cow**

 *iḫ* (sentence particle) + prospective *sḏm·f* in polite requests (often from a superior to an inferior, parent to child, etc.) **Please;** (subordinating particle) **then; so**

 *is* (enclitic particle) **after all, indeed, even; in fact** (§186, 1);  + *sḏm·n·f* **unless he hears**

 *is* (vb. imperative) **go!** *is in* **Go, get...!** (§145)

 *is-ḥ3q* (nominal colloquial phrase §194) **easy prey** (a military expression along the lines of the English hunting metaphor "sitting ducks"—literally: "a 'go and plunder!'")

 *is* (adj.) **old, ancient** Cf. Hebrew יָשָׁן (*yāšān*) and Ugaritic *yṯn* "old"

,  *ist* (n. f. collective) **crew** (of ship); **gang** (of workers)

 *iswt* (n. f.) **ancient times, antiquity**

 *is*, var.  *isy* (vb. bi-cons. or 3rd weak) **to be light** (of weight); **frivolous; to be at ease**

 *isft* (n. f.) **injustice; wrongdoing; crime; falsehood; chaos**

 See under *isṯ*

 *isṯ* var. ,  *ist* (sentence particle) **Now;** *isṯ rf* **Now** (§§100; 185, 1) Other variants:  *isk*,  *sk*, and the archaic (or archaistic)  *sṯ*

 *išst* (interrogative pronoun) **what?** (§169)

 *iqr* (adj.) 1) **excellent, dependable, reliable, worthy, trusty;** 2) **prosperous, wealthy** Cf. Hebrew יָקָר (*yāqar*) "precious, highly esteemed"; Arabic وقور (*waqūr*) "dignified, venerable"

 *iqr* **worthy man;** sarcastically a **goody-goody; cheer-monger; "nice guy"**

 *ikn* (vb.) **to draw** (water). Derived noun: **drawing** (i.e. the water that is drawn)

 *it* (n. m.!) **barley** (also the generic word for "grain")

 *it* (n. m.) **father** (the *f* is not pronounced!). Note that  can also stand for *it·i* **my father** and  can be read *it·f* **his father** (especially in reference to a god). Plural , 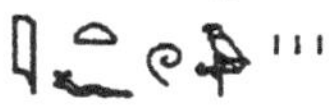 *itw* "ancestors"

, , ,  *Ỉty* (n. m.) **Sovereign** (a title of the king)

 *itn* (n. m.) **the sun; the solar disk**

 *itnw* (n. m. pl.) **hiding places (?); holes (?)**

 *itrw* (n. m.) **river, the Nile**

 *itḥ* (vb.) **to pull, draw; to drag up** (people)

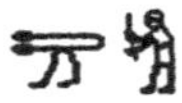 *iṯi*, var. 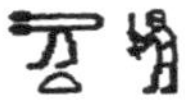 *iṯi*; (vb. 3rd weak infin. 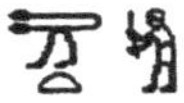 *iṯt*, 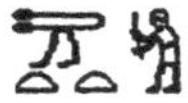 *itt*) **to take, take away, overcome, overpower**

 *idb* (n. m.) **river-bank;** as dual 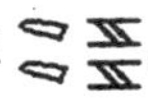,  *idbwy* **the Two Banks** (Egypt)

 *idr* (n. m.) **herd**

 ᶜ

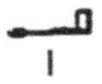 ᶜ (dual  *ᶜwy*) **arm, hand;** 2) ᶜ **condition, state** (e.g. of a person's health); 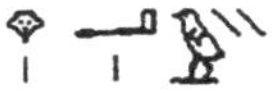 *ḥr-ᶜwy* (adv.) **immediately;** occasionally with the singular  *ḥr-ᶜ*;  *n(y)t-ᶜ* (n. f.) **custom, habit, routine**

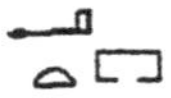 *ᶜt* (n. f.) **room** (of a building)

 *ᶜt* (n. f.) **limb, part** (of the body)

, *ᶜ3* (adj.) **great, large, grand;** (adj. vb.) *ᶜ3 ib* **to be proud; arrogant**

 *ᶜ3* (n. m.) **greatness**

 *ᶜ3* (adv.) **here**

,  *ᶜ3* (n. m.) **donkey**

 *ᶜ3* (n. m.) **door;**   *iry-ᶜ3* **door-keeper**

 See under *pr ᶜ3* in the entry *pr* "house"

,  *ᶜ3w*, *ᶜ3(w)* (adv.) **greatly** (§ 97)

 *ᶜ3m* (n. m.) **Asiatic** (i.e. the people living to the north and east of Egyptian borders)

 *ᶜ3g* (vb.) **to thrash, beat**

 *ᶜw3i* (vb. 4th weak) **to steal** (property); **to rob** (a person); active participle  *ᶜw3(w)* **robber;** passive participle **robbery victim** Perhaps cf. Semitic *ᶜwl* "to act unjustly," e.g. Hebrew עָוֶל (*ᶜāwel*) "injustice";

Arabic (*ʿāla*) "to oppress"

ʿpr (vb.) **to equip, provide** *m* **"with";** in stative + direct object **to have mastered** (skill, craft, etc., i.e., "to be equipped with" the required knowledge and experience)

, *ʿfdt* (<*ʿfḏt*) (n. f.) **box, chest**

ʿm (vb. bi-cons.) **to swallow, devour;** *ʿm ib ḥr* **to be neglectful concerning, forgetful about, negligent with**

ʿmʿm (vb.) **to anoint** uses the dative *n* (a person)

ʿn, var. *ʿnw* (adj.) **beautiful, pleasant**

ʿnw (adv.) **again**

ʿnn (vb. 2nd gem.) **to turn back; to go backwards; to face backwards**

ʿnḫ (vb.) **to live** (exist); not in the sense to live (in a place), which is *ḥmsi* in Egyptian; *ʿnḫ(w), (w)ḏ3(w), s(nbw)* (stative) **may he live long, prosper, and be healthy!** or **l.p.h.** (§§82, 99); *ʿnḫw ḏt* (stative) **may he live forever;** feminine *ʿnḫ·ti ḏt* **may she live forever** (§99)

ʿnḫw (m. pl. participle) **the living, those who live**

ʿnḫt (n. f.) **grain**

(n. m. dual)*ʿnḫwy* **ears**

ʿntiw (n. m.) **myrrh**

ʿrt (n. f.) **jaw**

ʿrf (n. m.) **sack, bag**

ʿrq (vb.) **to be bent up, curved**

ʿrqy (n. m.) **last day of the month**

ʿḥ (n. m.) **palace**

ʿḥ3 (vb.) **to fight; to wage war**

ʿḥʿ (vb.) **to stand up;** in stative **to be standing;** *ʿḥʿ r* **to rise up against;** *ʿḥʿ n* **to attend to** (a person); *ʿḥʿ ḥr* **to attend to** (a matter)

ʿḥʿ·n auxiliary verb that introduces narrative past sentences (§90 ff.) Rarely written .

, *ʿḥʿw* (n. m.) **period; span of time; lifetime**

ꜥḥꜥw (n. m. pl.) **ships**

ꜥḫḫw (n. m.) **darkness**

ꜥḫi (vb. 3rd weak) **to fly, fly off**

ꜥš (n. m.) **pine** (so-called "cedar" of Lebanon)

ꜥš (n. m.) **groan**

ꜥšꜣ (adj.) **many, numerous;** (of people) **rich** *m* **"in/with"** (things). (The plural strokes are a semantic determinative.) Cf. (?) Semitic *ǵṯr* Hebrew עשר (*ꜥšr*) "to be rich"

, *ꜥq* (vb. bi-cons.) **to go in** with *m* (a place); with *r* **"to a person";** *ḥr* **"by"** (a door), **"past"** (a person); of sun **to set;** *ꜥq-ib* **intimate friend; confidant**

, *ꜥqw* (n. m.) **loaves; provisions; rations**

See under *ꜥḏ*

ꜥd (n. m.) **grease**

ꜥḏ, var. *ꜥd* (vb.) **to be safe** (of persons and things); *ꜥḏ wḏꜣ* **to be safe and sound** (of persons and property)

𓅱, 𓏲 *w*

, , *w* (n. m.) **district**

w an extremely rare negation used in prohibitions (§182)

wꜣ (adj.) **far, distant, long ago;** (vb. bi-cons.) **to fall** *r* **"into** (a condition)"; *wꜣ r* + infinitive **to start** (doing)

, *wꜣt* (n. f.) **road, path; side; course** (of a river); *rdi wꜣt n rdwy·fy* **to set out** (on a trip—literally "give the road to one's feet"

wꜣw (n. m.) **wave** (of ocean)

wꜣwꜣ (n. m.) **"interest"** (on a loan)

, , *wꜣḥ* (vb.) 1) **to put down; lay down; apply** (a remedy); **set aside; put away; lay aside, discard;** 2) **to endure; to live long; to be patient**

wꜣḥ-ib (compound vb.) **to be kind, patient;** (compound n. m.) **mercy, kindness, benevolence**

w3s (n. m.) **ruin(s)**

W3st (place name) **Thebes**

W3sty (*nisba*) **the Theban** an epithet of Montu

w3g (vb.) exact meaning unknown, perhaps "**to celebrate**" or "**to exult**"

w3ḏ (adj.) **green, fresh;** *iwf w3ḏ* **raw meat; fortunate; hale** cf. Semitic *wrq* "green," "foliage" e.g. Hebrew יֶרֶק (*yereq*) "green"; Arabic ورق (*wariq*) "green," "verdant"

w3ḏ (n. m.) **green-stone** (a green semi-precious stone), almost certainly **malachite**

w3ḏ-wr (n. m.) **the sea** (lit. "the great green one")

w3ḏb see under *wḏb* **river bank**

wi (n. m.) **mummy case**

wi (1st sing. dep. pron.) **me** (or **I** after particles taking the dependent pronoun)

wi3 (n. m.) **sacred bark** (ship used by gods)

wꜥ, *wꜥt* (adj. / noun) **one; individual** *wꜥ ... ky* **one... other,** *wꜥ ... wꜥ* **one...other** (§66); *wꜥ m* (partitive) **one of** (a group); *wꜥ nb* **everyone;** (adj.) **unique, sole**

wꜥi (vb. 3rd weak) **to be alone**

wꜥw (n. m.) **soldier**

wꜥb (adj.) **pure;** (vb.) **to purify (oneself), to bathe;** also with dependent pronoun **to bathe oneself**

wꜥb (n. m. *or* infin. of preceding) **purification**

wꜥb (n. m.) ***wꜥb*-priest**

wꜥb(w)t (n. f. pl.) **meat-offerings**

wb3yt (n. f.) **maid** (a servant)

wbn (vb.) **to shine** (said of the sun)

wpi (vb. 3rd weak transitive) **to open** (objects, regions, women in childbirth); *wpi r r* + person: **to address** (a person) In religious or mortuary texts, *wpi r* "opening the mouth" refers to the ceremony performed with an adze which was thought to render the deceased's mouth useful again.

wpw-ḥr (compound preposition) **except; except for; apart from** *wpwt* (n. f.) **mission, business**

wpwtyw (n. m. pl., *nisba* from *wpwt*) **envoy, agent**

wn (vb. bi-cons.) **to open**

wnwt (n. f.) **hour;** and general **time; moment**

, *wnm* (vb.) **to eat, consume** (of food, and also figuratively)

wnn (vb. anomalous 2nd gem.) **to be** The verb *wnn* is not normally used in statements of fact or circumstantial clauses (e.g. §§10, 44), except when used as the stative. It is used in wishes (§72), purpose / result clauses (§74), and in explicatory sentences (§148 ff.). It is also used in the participle (§117 ff.) and infinitive (§57). *iw wn* **there is / there are** (§100); *nn wn* **There is / are no....** (§103). Also *nn* plus noun is used for **There is no** (§103). *n wnt* **There is / are no....** (§103)

, *wn-m3^{c}* (n. m.) **reality, actual truth; true existence;** *m wn-m3^{c}* **in very truth;** *r wn-m3^{c}* **in actual fact; in very deed; in the true sense**

wnḫ (vb.) **to put on** (clothing)

wnḏwt (n. f. collective) **people, fellow human beings**

wr (adj.) **great;** abbreviated , and as noun **great one, ruler** (of a foreign land); in titles **chief,** etc.; *imy-r pr wr* **high steward** Cf. (?) the Semitic roots *rbb*, *rb$^{\supset}$* great.

wr m3w **Greatest of Seers** (title of the high priest of Rē^{c} in Heliopolis)

, *wrt* (n. f. s.) **greatness;** (adv.?) **very** (§97)

wrryt, var. *wrr(y)t* (n. f.) **chariot;** exceptionally **wagon**

wrḥ (vb.) **to anoint**

wrd < *wrḏ* (vb.) **to be weary, tired;** may have sense of "dying"; *Wrd-ib* **the Weary-hearted** (an epithet of Osiris)

whi (vb. 3rd weak) **to fail, to be thwarted** *m* **"in"** an undertaking

wḥm (vb.) **to repeat** (an action); **to report;** *wḥm* + infin. **to (do) again;** *m wḥm* (adverbial) **again;** *m wḥm-^{c}* **again**

wḥmyt (n. f.) exact meaning unknown, perhaps **howling**

wḫt (n. f.) **darkness**

wḫ3 (n. m.) **an incompetent person, a fool**

wḫ3 (vb.) **to fade** (colours); **to empty out; purge** (the body)

, , *Wsir* (divine name) **Osiris**

, var. *wsr* (adj.) **strong, powerful, mighty; wealthy, rich**

See under *S-n(y)-Wsrt* (man's name) **Senwosret**

, *wsḫ* (n. m.) **width** Cf. ? Semitic *ws*ᶜ, e.g. Arabic (*ws*ᶜ "to be wide")

wsḫt (n. f.) **barge** (i.e. a wide-bodied boat)

wstn (vb. 4-cons.) **to stride; to travel freely**

wšb (vb.) **to answer; reply; respond** *n* **"to"**

wšn **to wring the neck; sacrifice** (birds)

wšd (vb.) **to respond to; to speak to**

wt (vb. bi-cons.) **to bandage;** *wt ḥr* + medical preparation **to bandage with / over** (i.e. the medications or other substances [including raw meat] are applied to the skin and bandages are wrapped over them)

wṯs (vb.) **to make an accusation**

wdi (vb. 3rd weak) **to put, place; plant** (trees); **throw;** and in several idiomatic expressions, e.g. *wdi sp* **to carry off an achievement; to carry out a venture** Cf. Semitic *wdy*: יָדָה (*yādā*) "to shoot, throw, cast down"

wdb < *wḏb* (vb.) **to fold over**

wdf (vb.) **to delay, stall**

wdn (vb. / adj.) **to be heavy; grevious; oppressive**

, , *wḏ* (vb. bi-cons.) **to command, order, decree** Cf. Arabic وصى (*wṣy*); Hebrew (with metathesis) צָוָה (*ṣāwā*) "to order, command, decree"

, , *wḏ* (n. m.) **command, decree**

wḏt (n. f.) **command; order**

, *wḏ* (n. m.) **stele, monumental inscription**

wḏ3 (adj.) **sound, in good condition, prosperous;** *wḏ3 ib* **to be glad, happy**

wḏ3(t) (n. f.) ***wedjat*** **eye** (the uninjured eye of Horus)

,  *wḏꜣ* (vb.) **to go, set out, proceed** (cf. Semitic **wḏy*, e.g. Hebrew יָצָא (*yaṣā*) "to set out, go forth")

 *wḏꜥ* (vb.) 1) **to judge;** 2) **to cut (cord); to cut off (head); to be separated** (lips of a wound)

 *wḏꜥt* (passive participle, f. s.) **divorced woman**

 *wḏw* (n. m.) meaning uncertain **range** (?); **roving herd** (?); or perhaps a misreading of a word *ḥww* that refers to cattle, but whose meaning is also not certain

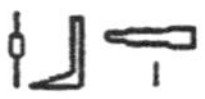 *wḏb*, var.  *wꜣḏb* (n. m.) **river bank**

 *b*

 *bꜣ* (n. m.) **the ba; soul** (a part of a person's spiritual and physical being, often depicted as a bird, and thought to have the ability to leave the body after death for visits among the living)

 *bꜣw* (n. m. pl. of previous) 1) **might, power;** 2) **souls**

 *bꜣt* (n. m.) **shoot,wisp, ear** (of grain); **bush**

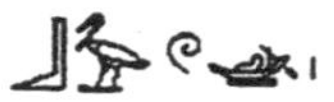 *bꜣw* (n. m.) **galley** (a type of boat that was propelled by oars). In the Westcar Papyrus, a small version must be involved.

,  *bꜣḥ* in ,  *m-bꜣḥ* (compound prep.) **before, in the presence of** (used of an audience with the king, or when ushered in before the gods)

 *Bꜣstt* (divine name) **Bastet**

 *bꜣk* (vb.) **to work;** in stative *bꜣk(w) m* + precious metal **wrought in** gold, silver, etc. (i.e. overlaid in gold, etc.)

 *bꜣk* (n. m.) **work, labour**

 *bꜣk* (n. m.) **servant**

 *bꜣkt* (n. f.) **female servant**

 *bꜣgi* (4th weak) **to be lazy; to be tired;**  *bꜣgi ib* **to be half-hearted**

 *bit* (n. f.) **honey**

 *bity* (n. m. *nisba*) **King of Lower Egypt**

 *biꜣ* (n. m.) **a marvel, miracle** (also said of luxury goods)

,  *biꜣw* (n. m.) **mining-region**

 *biꜣ n(y) pt* (n. m.) **iron** (meteoric)

 *bin* **bad**

 *binr* See under *bnr* **dates.**

 *bik* (n. m.) **falcon** (also used as an designation of the king: **the Falcon**)

 *bꜥḥ* (vb. or adj.) **to stink, reek**

 *bw* (n. m.) **place**

 *bw wr* (phrase) **the greater part**

Bw can be used as the first element of compound expressions for abstract words (§193):

 *bw mꜣꜥ* **truth**

 *bw nfr* **good, goodness**

 *bw-ḥwrw* **evil; crime**

 *bw-ḏw* **evil**

 *bw* (Late Egyptian negation particle §199), generally equivalent to Middle Egyptian  *n*. Occasionally *bw* occurs where one expects an original  *nn*.

 *bn* (Late Egyptian negation particle §199), generally equivalent to Middle Egyptian  *nn*, but sometimes also  *n*.

 *bnt* (n. f.) **harp**

 *bnwt* (n. f.) **grindstone, millstone** (used to make flour)

 *bnr* (adj.) **sweet, pleasant** (of taste; of a person's disposition)

, var.  *bnr* (n. m. pl.) **dates**

 *bnš* (n. m.) **doorpost**

 *bs* (vb. bi-cons.) **to introduce; to initiate** *ḥr* **"into"** (mysteries)

 *bdt* (later *bty*) (n. f.) **emmer** (a type of wheat)

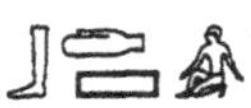,  *bdš* (vb.) **to become faint, weak;** *bdš ḥr* **to be fainthearted**

p

pt (n. f.) **heaven(s), sky**

var. , hieratic: *p3* (m. s. demonstrative / definite article) **this; the** (§78)

, , , *p3(w)* or *p3* (vb. bi-cons. or 3rd weak) **to have done in the past; used to** (§173)

, *p3wt* (n. f. pl.) **offering loaves**

p3wt (n. f.) **primaeval time;** *p3wt t3* **primaeval time of the earth**

p3qt, *p(3)qt* (n. f.) **fine linen**

pyw (n. m. pl.) **fleas**

pw 1) particle following a noun in bi-partite or tri-partite nominal sentence (§§129, 135) **It is... / They are...** 2) *sḏm·f pw* (§143) in explanations **It means that he will hear. / This is how he hears.** 3) *ink pw* in explanations (§144); 4) archaic demonstrative adjective **this** (§78); 5) a rare vocative particle **o!** (§142)

, *pw-tr*, *ptr*, later variant *pty* **Who...?; What...?** (§128)

pwy (m. s. demonstrative) **this; that** (§78) archaic

Pwnt (place name) **Pwenet** (otherwise known as **Punt**) the source of luxury spices and aromatic substances, probably the Somali coast

pf (var. *pf3*, *pfy*) (m. s. demonstrative adj.) **that** (§78)

pn (m. s. demonstrative adj.) **this** (follows the noun, and agrees in gender with it). Sometimes it is better translated **that**. (§78)

pr (n. m.) **house, household; temple** (of gods); **palace** (of king); *pr-nsw* **palace** (lit. "house of the king"); , , *pr ˁ3* **palace** (literally "great house"—this is the origin of the word "pharaoh," although the use as a term for the king was a New Kingdom development; , *pr-ḥḏ* **treasury**

prt (n. f.) **winter** (a season §69)

pri (vb. 3rd weak) 1) **to go / come out** *m* **"from,"** *ḥr* **"through"** (a door); 2) **to ascend, go up** *r* **"to"**; *pri ... m ḫt* **to go up in flames;** 3) as auxiliary verb **to turn out that...** (§174)

prt-ḫrw (compound noun) **invocation offerings** (§197)

pry (n. m.) **champion; hero**

, *pḥ* (vb. bi-cons.) **to reach; attain** (a status); **end up** (doing)

for words written with this logogram, see also *kfꜣ*

pḥwy (n. m. dual) **end** (concrete and abstract); **bottom; hind quarters**

, ; *pḥty*; var. *pḥty* (*tt* for *ty*: sportive dual) (n. m.) **might, power** (of god, king), **strength**

pẖr (vb. trans.) **to circulate;** (intrans.) **to travel around; to pervade**

Pẖr-wr (place name) **the Euphrates River**

pẖrt (n. f.) **prescription, remedy** (medical)

psšt (n. f.) **portion, share**

, *psḏt* (n. f.) **ennead** (group of nine gods)

Psḏntyw (n. m.) **the new moon; new moon festival**

pty See under *pw-tr* **Who...?; What...?** (§128)

Ptn (place name) **Peten**

ptr See under *pw-tr* **Who...?; What...?** (§128)

ptḫ (vb.) **to cast to the ground**

, *pds* (n. m.) **box, chest**

f

fꜣi (vb.) **to raise, lift up;** *fꜣi ṯꜣw* either with "wind" as direct object **to sail \ run before the wind** (catching up the wind) or else with "wind" as subject **the wind picks up; accrue** (interest on a loan)

, *fnd* < *fnḏ* (n. m.) **nose**

, *fḫ* (vb. bi-cons.) **to loosen** (threads, stiches, hair, clothing); **to displace** (monuments); **to destroy; to fall to ruins; to obliterate**

fqꜣ (vb.) **to reward**

ftt (n. m.?) **fibres, lint**

m

m (vb. imperative) *m* + negatival complement **Don't, Do not** (This is the imperative of the negative auxiliary verb *imi* [§§165, 166].)

m (enclitic particle after imperative forms) **please**

m var. , (interrogative pronoun) **who?** *in-m* **Who?** (§134); *ḥr m* **why?** (literally "on a account of what"); *mi m* **how?** (literally "like what," §169)

m (prep.) 1) **in, inside;** 2) **by means of, with** (instrument); 3) **from, out of; into** (with verbs of motion—the meaning depends very much upon the verb used); 4) **being; namely; as** (*m* of predication [§24]); 5) (made) **of** (material); (worked) **in, with** (material); **being made of**; 6) **of** (partitive [§66], "one of a group"). Its form before suffixes is *im*· Note that to express "with" persons and things one used the preposition *ḥnꜥ*. Egyptian *m* is cognate with West Semitic *ba/bi*, e.g. Hebrew בְּ (*bᵊ*) "in," "with" (by means of); Arabic ب (*bi*) "in," "at," "with" (by means of)

, *m-ꜥ* (compound prep.) **in the hand; in the possession** (charge) **of; by the hand of; with (a person); because of; from the hand of**; *ḫpr m-ꜥ* **to happen to** (a person)

, *m-m* (compound prep.) **among** (people)

mt, variant of *mwyt* (n. f.) **urine**

See under *imꜣt* **charm.**

, *mꜣꜣ* (vb. irregular 2nd gem.) **to see, to look at, to regard** with prep. *m* **"as"** Perhaps cf. Sem. *ꜣmr* cf. Akkadian *amāru* "to see"; Ugaritic *ảmr* "saw"

mꜣi (n. m.) **lion;** pl. , *mꜣw*

mꜣꜥ (n. m.) **temple** (side of the head); *rdi mꜣꜥ (r)* **to pay attention (to); give (one's) attention (to);** and literally, **to put (one's) temple to** (a wall to eavesdrop)

, *mꜣꜥ* (adj.) **true, just, fair, right, correct; innocent** (as legal term)

, abbrev. , *mꜣꜥ ḫrw* / (fem.) *mꜣꜥt ḫrw* (epithet of deceased) **justified, vindicated** (I.e. in the trial court of the hereafter, the deceased has been declared innocent, and is admitted to the hereafter.)

, , , , *mꜣꜥt* (n. f.) **justice; truth; order;** and as a goddess (and various writings) *Mꜣꜥt* **Maꜥat** *mꜣw* (adj.) **new**

mꜣwt (adj. f.) **something that is new, a new thing** (§21, 2); *m mꜣwt* **again, anew, afresh** (literally "as a new thing")

mi (prep.) **like**

mi m (interrogative) **how** (literally "like what," §169)

min (n. m.) **today**

mit(y) (adj./n. m. *nisba*) **(one) which is equal; one like (it); likeness**

mitw (n. m., prob. *nisba*) **(one's) equal**

mitt (n. f. *nisba*?) **likeness; a thing like;** *mitt iry* **something like it**

mi (vb. imperative) **come!** (§145)

mꜥr (adj.) **successful, fortunate**

mꜥḥꜥt (n. f.) **cenotaph; funerary monument**

mꜥkꜣ (adj.) **brave**

See under *mk* **Look; See**

mw (n. m.) **water** Cf. Arabic ماء (*māʾ*), Hebrew מַיִם (*mayim*), Akkadian *mû* "water."

mwt (n. f.) **mother;** *mwt-nsw* **Mother of the King, King's Mother** Prob. cf. Sem. *ʾimm*, *ʾumm*, *ʾēm* "mother"

mwt-mwt (n. f.) **grandmother** (even when referring to one's paternal grandmother)

mbi (sound) **"umbii"** (a sound that a new-born infant might make—but sounds like Egyptian *m-biꜣ* "No!")

mfkꜣt (n. f.) **turquoise** (stone)

mmy (n. m.) **giraffe**

mn (vb. bicons.) **to endure; to be enduring; to be firm; to remain** *m* **"in";** *r mn m* **down to (time); as far as (distance)**

Mn-ḫpr-Rꜥ (king's name) **Men-kheper-Rēꜥ** (Thutmose III of the Eighteenth Dynasty)

mn (vb. bicons.) **to be sick, suffer; to suffer in** (a body part); **to suffer from** (an illness) *mn* (n. m.) **sick man; pain**

mnt (n. f.) **sickness, illness, pain**

mnỉ (vb. 3rd weak, infinitive without *t*) **to moor** (ship); **to bring to port;** *mnỉ sp* **bring (one's) venture to port** (i.e. achieve a goal successfully); *hrw n(y) mnỉ* **day of mooring** (a euphemism for death)

mnỉt (n. f.) **mooring post**

, *mnw* (n. m., s. or pl.) **monument(s)**

mnmn (vb. quadri-cons. intransitive) **to quake, shake** (of earth)

mnmnt (n. f. sing. collective) **cattle**

mnḥ (n. m.) **wax**

mnḫ (adj.) **beneficent; potent** (of king); **dependable, trusty** (of officials); **excellent**

Mnṯw (divine name) **Montu** (a god of war)

, , See under *imy-r* **overseer.**

mr (n. m.) **canal**

mr (adj.) **sick, painful;** (n. m.) **pain, ailment**

mr (n. m.) **sick man**

mr(w)t (n. f. pl.) **pains;** *mr(w)t m gs tp* **migraine headache pains**

mr (n. m.) **pyramid**

mrỉ (vb. 3rd weak) **to love, like;** less common variant

Mry (man's name) **Meri**

mryt (n. f.) **shore, bank; quay**

Mryt, var. *Mrt* (woman's name) **Merit**

Mrw (man's name) **Meru**

mrwt (n. f.) **love;** *n mrwt* + 1st prospective form **in order that** (§75, 2)

mrryt (n. f.) **lumps** ?

mrḥt (n. f.) **oil; fat**

mhỉ (vb. 3rd weak) + *ỉb* **to be forgetful; to forget**

mḥ (vb. bi-cons.) **to fill** with *m* **"with"**; in stative **to be full** *m* **"of"**; *ḫr* **"of"**; *mḥ ỉb* **to be conceited**

mḥ (vb. bi-cons.) **seize, grasp** *m* + person; **take** (into detention) (for a crime)

mḥ (n. m.) **cubit** measure of ca. 52.3 cm

mḥ (fem.) (participle) in ordinal numbers from 10 and higher, *mḥ* follows the noun and the cardinal number follows this (§67)

mḥy (vb. 3rd weak) **to feel sorry** *ḥr* **"about," to concern oneself with, to worry about**

mḥty (m. s. *nisba*) **northern;** *mḥt(y)w* **Northerners;** *mḥty-ỉmnt* **North-west**

mḫ3t (n. f.) **balance; scales** (This type of balance had a stand.)

mḫtmt (n. f.) **sealed chest**

mẖr (n. m.) **barn, storehouse**

mẖr (n. m.) **low-lying land**

mẖrw (n. m. pl.) **affairs; dealings; business**

ms (vb. bi-cons.) **to transport** (booty); **to deliver**

ms (enclitic particle) **surely; indeed** (meaning not certain) (§186, 2)

msỉ (vb. 3rd weak) **to give birth; bear** (a child); **fashion** (statues)

msw (n. m. pl., prob. participle) **offspring; children** (usually plural)

msyt (n. f.) **supper**

msnḥ (vb. 4-cons.) **to turn backwards; to rotate around**

msḥ (n. m.) **crocodile** Cf. Arabic تمساح (*timsāḥ*) "crocodile"

msṯpt, *mstpt* (n. f.) **portable shrine**

msd < *msḏ* (vb.) **to hate; dislike;** participle **rival, adversary**

msdmt (n. f.) **eye paint** (black)

mšꜥ (n. m.) **soldiers, troops, army; crew, gang;** **military expedition**

mšrw (n. m.) **evening** Probably cognate to Semitic: Aramaic רַמְשָׁא (*ramšā*) "evening"; Arabic مساء (*masāʾ*) "evening"; Akkadian *mušu* "evening"; Hebrew אֶמֶשׁ (*ʾemeš*) "yesterday"

, var. ,  *mk* (deictic particle) **Look; See** (§§17; 39; 40)

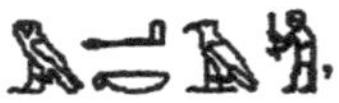,  See under *mꜥkꜣ* **brave**

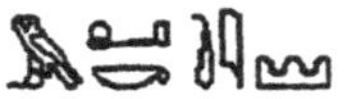 *Mkti* (place name) **Megiddo** (a town in Canaan)

,  *mt* (vb. bi-cons.) **to die; to perish** (ships) (Cf. Semitic *mwt* "to die.")

,  *mt* (n. m.) **death**

, 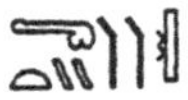 *mty* (adj.) **straightforward, exact, correct; faithful, loyal;**  *r mty* **exactly;** *hrw ... r mty* **the exact day of...**

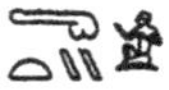 *mty* in  *mty n(y) sꜣ* (n. m.) **phylē controller;** as position **phylē controllership**

 *mtrw* (n. m. pl.) **witnesses** (a legal term)

, var.  *mṯ, mt* Equivalent of *mk* used when addressing a woman. (§40)

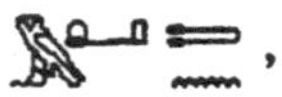, var.  *mṯn, mtn* Plural equivalent of *mk*. (§40)

 *mdw* (vb. 3rd weak, infin.  *mdt*) **to speak;** *mdw n* **speak to** (a person); *mdw ḥnꜥ* **have words with** (a person), **dispute, contend** (with a person); (n. m.) **speech**

 *mdt* (n. f.) **speech, word, words; thing, matter;** *ḥr mdt n(y)t* (a person) **on (account of) the word of** (a person)

 *mdw* (n. m.) **staff, rod;**  *mdw iꜣwt* **staff of old age** referring to a son who supports an aged parent

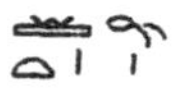 *mḏꜣt* (n. f.) **papyrus roll; book** *mḏꜣt n(y)t* ... **Book of...** (used as title)

 *mḏḥ* (vb.) **to hew** (wood, stone); **to build** (ships). Cf. ? Semitic, e.g. Hebrew חצב (*ḥṣb*) "to hew" (stone, wood)

n

 *n* (negative particle) **not** (negates various verbal forms and the predicate adjective,  *n sḏm·f* **He did not hear** (§§106, 107);  *n sḏm·n·f* **He does not / cannot hear** (§108);  *n sp sḏm·f* **He never heard** (§110);  + *sḏm·n·f* **unless he hears;** *n ... is* negation of nominal sentences **not at all** (§129)

, hieratic var.  *n* 1) (prep.) the dative: (give, say) **to** (someone), (do something) **for** (someone); 2) (going) **to** (a person); 3) **because (of)**; 4) **belonging to** (§126); 5) *n·f imy* **X belongs to him** (§126, 3); 6) *n·f imy* **of his; his own** (§127) Cf. West Semitic *l-*, e.g. Hebrew לְ (*lᵊ*) and Arabic لِ (*li*) both "to," "for"

n (1st pl. dep. pron.) **us** (after particles requiring the dependent pronoun, **we**) (§39)

nꜣ / *nꜣ n(y)* (pl. demonstrative / definite article) **these; the** (§78)

n(y) (genitival adjective, m. s.) **of** (§22, 1b); *n(y)-sw*, *n(y)-sy* **he / she belongs to...** (§126, 1)

, *n(y)w* (genitival adjective, m. pl.) **of** (§22, 1b)

n(y)wy (genitival adjective, m. dual.) **of**—very rare (§22, 1b)

n(y)t / *n(yw)t* (genitival adjective, f. s. / pl.) **of** (§22, 1b)

n(y)t-ꜥ (n. f.) **custom, habit, routine**

n(y)ty (genitival adjective, f. dual.) **of**—very rare (§22, 1b)

ny (a sound) **"nyaah"** (the sound of a baby's cry)

niwt (n. f.) **city**

niwty (*nisba*) **local, of the city**

nis (vb.) **to summon;** also with prepositions *nis n* + person, *nis r* + person **to summon** (a person) or **to make summons to**

nꜥr (n. m.) **catfish**

nw (pl. demonstrative) **this; these** (§78) archaic

nw (n. m.) **time**

nwt (n. f.) **adze**

nwy (n. m.) **water**

nwyt (n. f.) **wave**

See under *ink*

nb (adj.) **all, every, any, all kinds of;** *ḫt nbt* **everything;** *ḫt nbt nfrt* **all sorts of fine things;** *s nb* **everyone;** *ḥr nb* **everyone;** , *rꜥ nb* **every day** (The variant is not to be misread as **hrw nb*!)

Note that although *nb* is an adjective (and therefore follows the noun it modififes), it cannot be used as a predicate adjective, nor as a noun on its own.

, , *nb* (n. m.) **lord, master; possessor, owner; the Lord** (i.e. the king), which is also written

; *nb-ir-ḫt* **Lord of Action** (said of kings and gods; literally "the Lord who does things"); *Nb-r-ḏr* **the Lord-of-all** (an epithet of Osiris); and especially as the first element in bound constructions: e.g. *nb pr* **the owner (lord) of a house;** *Nb-T3wy* **Lord of the Two Lands** (an epithet of the king)

nbt (n. f.) **lady; possessor, owner**

t3 Nbt Kpny **the Lady of Byblos** (epithet of a Canaanite goddess)

Nb(t)-iwnt (woman's name) **Nebet-iunet**

Nbt-Nni-nsw (woman's name) **Nebet-Neni-nisu**

Nbsny (man's name) **Nebseny**

, (n. m.) *nbw* **gold**

*Nbw-k3w-R*ᶜ (royal name) **Nebkaurēᶜ** (prenomen of Amenemḥēt II)

npnpt (n. f.) **hem, selvage**

nf (n. m.) **nonsense, foolishness**

nf n(y) (pl. demonstrative adj.) **those** (§78)

nfr (adj.) **good, fine, fair, nice, kind; happy**

nfrt (adjective as an abstract noun §21, 1) **a good thing; good** (also in plural)

nfr (negative word) in var. *nfr n* and *nfr pw* (for these extremely rare negations, consult §181)

Nfrty (man's name) **Neferty**

nftft (vb. 5-cons.) **to leap**

nm (interrogative pronoun) **Who?** (§134)

*nm*ᶜ (vb.) **to show partiality; to be partial; to be one-sided**

nmḥ (n. m.) **orphan**

Nmty-nḫt(w) (man's name) **Nemty-nakht** (this name was formerly read as Djehuty-nakht)

nn (negative particle) **not** Negates nouns: **without a...; not having a...** (§104). Before infinitives: **without (doing)** (§105). Negates existential sentences **There is / are no...** (§103); *nn sḏm·f* **He will not hear** (§109).

nn n(y) or *nn* (demonstrative, pl.) **these** (§78) (Note: *nn (ny)* precedes the noun.); as a demonstrative noun: **this**

Nnỉ-nsw (place name) **Heracleopolis Magna (Ahnas)** This was the capital in the 9th and 10th Dynasties.

nnm (vb.) **to err; go wrong**

nrw (n. m.) **fear; dread; awe** (Suggestion: *nrw* followed by a reference to the king should not be "his fear," but rather "the fear of him" [i.e. in foreign lands])

nrꜣw (n. m.) **ibex**

nhy n(y) (noun phrase) **a little** (of something), **some, a few**

nhw (n. m.) **loss**

nhm (vb.) **to shout**

Nhrn (place name) **Naharên** (country around the great bend of the Euphrates)

nḥꜣ (adj.) **terrifying; terrible**

nḥbt (n. f.) **neck**

, var. *nḥm* (vb.) 1) **to rescue, save;** 2) **to take away, carry off; to take out; to withdraw** This verb has developed in two different directions from the semantic field of "taking out": on the one hand "taking away (property, etc. from a person" and on the other hand "taking a person out of a dangerous situation—rescuing." Cf. Arabic حمل (*ḥml*) "to bear, carry, take"; stem VIII (*iftaꜥala* stem) "to carry off, take away."

nḥmn (sentence particle) **surely, indeed** (§185, 7)

Nḥrỉ (man's name) **Neḥri**

, *nḥḥ* (n. m.) **forever, eternity;** also in the expressions *r nḥḥ* **forever,** and *r nḥḥ ḏt* **for ever and ever**

(abbrev. in names) *nḫt* (adj.) **strong, mighty; victorious; stiff** (of joints); *nḫt ḥr* **violent, violent man;** *nḫt ꜥ* **strong of arm**

nḫt(w) (n. m.) **strength, force, power; victory;** *nḫt(w) ꜥnḫ* **the force of life**

ns (n. m.) **tongue** Cf. Hebrew לָשׁוֹן (*lašōn*); Arabic لسان (*lisān*) "tongue"

See under *imy-r* **overseer**

 *n(y)-sw*, 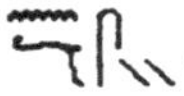 *n(y)-sy* See under *n(y)* **of** (§126, 1)

 *N(y)-sw-Mnṯw* (man's name) **Nisu-Montu**

 *nsw* commonly abbreviated to  **king** Bound constructions regularly involve hororific transposition (§41, 1), e.g.  *sš nsw* **royal scribe.**  *nsw bity* **King of Upper and Lower Egypt;**  *ḥtp dỉ nsw* **An offering that the king gives** (offering formula, §197)

 *nsyt* (n. f. *nisba*) **kingship**

 *nšny* (n. m.) **storm**

 *nqwt* (variant of *nqꜥwt*) **notched sycamore figs** (i.e. the ripened figs, which have been processed by being notched on the tree)

 *ngw* (n. m.) **long-horned bull / ox**

 *nty* (m. s. relative adj.) **that, which; that which; who** (§§111, 112)

, ,  *ntiw* (m. pl. relative adjective) **(those) who are / were;**  *ntiw ỉm* **those who are there** (i.e. in the world of the hereafter), a euphemism for the dead

 *nt(y)t* (f. s./pl. relative adj.) **that, which; that which; who; that which exists; that which is; she who is** (§§112, 113); (conjunction) **that** (after verbs of knowing & seeing §116); 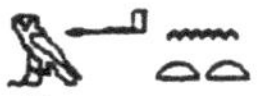 *m-ꜥ nt(y)t* **seeing that;**  *r-nt(y)t* **to the effect that** (introduces the body of a letter §115);  **because; on account of the fact that** (§114); **to the effect that** (in letters §115);  *ḏr-nt(y)t* **because, since**

 *ntf* (3rd m. sing. indep. pron.) **He** (§56); **X belongs to him** (§126, 2)

 *nts* (3rd f. sing. indep. pron.) **She** (§56); **X belongs to her** (§126, 2)

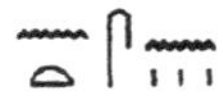 *ntsn* (3rd com. pl. indep. pron.) **They** (§56); **X belongs to them** (§126, 2)

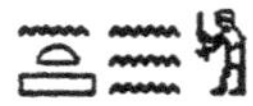 *ntš* (vb.) **to sprinkle**

 *ntk* (2nd m. sing. indep. pron.) **You** (§56); **X belongs to you** (§126, 2)

 *ntṯ* (2nd f. sing. indep. pron.) **You** (§56); **X belongs to you** (§126, 2)

 *ntṯn* (2nd com. pl. indep. pron.)**You** (§56); **X belongs to you** (§126, 2)

 *nṯr* (n. m.) **god** In bound constructions it is written first, but read second (honorific transposition §41), e.g.  *ḥm-nṯr* **the *ḥm-nṯr*-priest;** pl.  *ḥmw-nṯr*

 *nṯrt* (n. f.) **goddess**

 *nḏ* (vb. bi-cons.) **to ask, enquire; seek advice**  *nḏ-ḫrt* (compound verb, but *ḫrt* may be separated by the subject) **to greet;** (n. m.) *nḏ-ḫrt* **"Greetings!"**

 *nḏm* (adj.) **pleasant, sweet, charming;** (adj. vb.) **to recover, be relieved** (from medical conditions) cf. Semitic *nʿm* "pleasant"

 *nḏrt* (n. f.) **captivity; imprisonment**

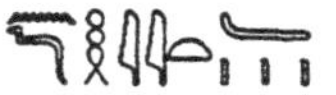 *nḏḥyt* var. of *nḥḏt* (n. f. pl.) **teeth; tusks**

 *nḏs* (adj.) **small, little; dim** (of eyes)

,  *nḏs* (n. m.) **poor man, commoner**

 *nḏsw* (n. m.) **poverty; low status**

 *r*

 *r* (prep.) 1) **to, towards** (a place, or thing); 2) **concerning, regarding, with relation to; according to**; 3) **at** (a location); 4) **from, apart** (with verbs of separation); 5) **into** (with verbs of motion/throwing); 6) **more than** ("*r* of comparison," used with adjectives and a few verbs); 7) (to act, do injury / injustice, etc.) **against** a person ("*r* of opposition"); 8) *r* + 1st prospective a) **until he hears;** b) **in order that / so that he hears** (§75, 2); 9) *r* + *sḏmt·f* **until he hears / has heard** (§156); 10) *r* + infinitive expresses futurity ("*r* of futurity," §§57, 2; 62) or purpose **in order to;** 11) *rdi* + *r* **to appoint... to be** (§77) 12) *r* + (period of time) **for** (a period of time); 12) **will be** ("*r* of futurity," the future counterpart of the "*m* of predication"). Cf. ? Hebrew אֶל (*ʾel*) and Arabic الى (*ilā*), both "to," "toward"

 *r* **mouth; statement, words; opening, entrance** For compounds, see below.

 *r-ʿ-ḫt* (n. m.) **war; combat**

 *r-w3t* (n. m.) **path,** perhaps **beginning of the path**

,  *r-pr* (n. m.) **temple**

 *r-ḏ3yw* (n. m.) **melee, time of battle**

*  See under *nr3w* **ibex.**

 See under *rdi* **to give, put, allow.**

, , ,  *rʿ* (n. m.) **sun; day** *only* in the idiom  (var. ) *rʿ nb* **every day**

, , , ,  *Rʿ* (divine name) **Rēʿ** (the solar god)

Rʿ-wsr(w) (man's name) **Rēʿ-woser**

rwi (vb. 3rd weak) **to depart, get away** (*r* **"from"** a place or thing); **to go away;** (transitive) **to leave (a place); to escape** (harm, trouble, etc.); **to drive out, eliminate**

rwty (n. m.) **outside;** *r rwty* **out, to the outside**

, *rwḏ*, var. *rwd*, *rd* (vb.) **to be strong, firm; to flourish, prosper; to succeed**

See under *iry-pʿt* **hereditary nobleman**

rf a (enclitic particle) **then, now,** cf. *irf*

, var. , *rmi, rmy* (vb. 3rd weak) **to cry; weep;** (participle) **weeper**

rmw (n. m.) **fish** (generic)

rmn (n. m.) **shoulder; side** *rmn n(y) ⸢iḥ⸣* **side of beef**

rmṯ n. m. (pl. *rmṯw*) **person, people**

rmṯt (n. fem. sing. collective) **people;** *n(y) rmṯt nbt* **public**

, *rn* (n. m.) **name**

rnpt (n. f.) **year**

rnpy (vb. 4th weak) **to be young, youthful**

Rnsy (man's name) **Rensi**

rhn (vb.) **to rely on, to trust in** (*ḥr*); **to lean on**

rḫ (vb. bi-cons.) **to learn, find out, to learn of** (something); in past tense / stative **to know** (i.e. having learned something is to know it); *rḫ m* **to know of** (something); *rḫ* + infin. **to know how to (do); to be able to (do)**

rḫ (m. s. participle) **learned man, scholar**

rḫ nsw (n. m.) **king's acquaintance** (a title)

, *rḫt* (n. f.) **knowledge; account; enumeration**

rsy (nisba) **southern**

rssy, var. , *rsy* (adverb) **quite, entirely;** (after negations) **at all**

rš (adj.) **joyful; happy**

ršwt (n. f.) **joy, a state of joy**

rqy (n. m.) **opponent**

rk (n. m.) **time; era; age**

rk enclitic particle similar to *rf*, but used especially when addressing a person (i.e. in the second person) and is fairly common after imperative forms **then, now**

See under *rmṯ*

, *rd* (vb. bi-cons.) **to grow**; for meaning **to flourish, prosper**, see *rwḏ*

rdi, (irregular verb) (hieratic variant *rdi* not *rᶜ*!) **to give; to put, place; to appoint** (a person) *m* **"as"** / *r* **"to be"** (§77); any form of *rdi* followed by the propspective (as its direct object) forms the causative (§75, 1): **to cause that someone (do something), to have someone (do something), to make someone (do something), to let someone (do something)**

rdi + prospective (causative)—some common idioms:

rdi rẖ·f **to inform him** ("to cause that he learn"); **let him know**

rdi sḏm·f **to tell him** ("to cause that he hear")

rdi šs3·f m **to acquaint him with**

Other idioms with *rdi*:

rdi ib r + infin. **to set one's heart on** (doing)

rdi ᶜ n **to give a hand to** (a person), **to help** (a person)

rdi m ḥr **to command** (a person); **to bring to the attention** (of someone)

rdi r t3 **to put on the ground; to abandon; to neglect; to leave alone; to land** (from a ship)

rdi ḥr gs **to lean / tilt to one side;** (of judges) **to be partial / biased**

rdi m3ᶜ r **to pay attention to**

rdi ḥr n (+ person) **to command** (a person)

rdi s3 (r) **to revoke, annul**

rdi tp nfr **to make a good start** (of journeys)

rdi ḏ3i·tw t3 r (+ thing / person) **to interfere with**

 *rd* (n. m.) **foot;** abbreviated:  *rdwy*, prob. cf. Sem. *rgl* foot, leg

 *rdm(w)t* (n. f. pl.) **rushes**

 *Rdḏdt* (woman's name) **Redjedet**

 *h*

 *h3i* (vb.) **to go down, descend** *ḥr* **"from"** (hill country);  (idiomatic expression §194) **a free for all.** The verb *h3i* must be clearly distinguished from *h3b* "to send."

 *h3w* (n. m.) of place **vicinity, neighbourhood;** (of time) **time,** (of king) **reign; affairs; belongings**

 *h3b* (vb.) **to send** (a person on an errand, etc.) *r* **"to** (a place)"; **to send (word)** *n* **"to** (a person)"; *h3b ḥr* **to send (word) about** (a matter)" *H3b* is not a "verb of motion." Cf. ?? Sem. *špr* "to send" cf. Ar. سفر (*safara*) 2nd stem (*faʿʿala*) "to send away"; Akkadian *šapāru* "to send" (*h* vs. *š*; *b* vs. *p* and metathesis)

 *hi* (n. m.) **husband**

 *hp* (n. m.) **law**

 *hnw* (n. m.) ***hin*** a liquid measure of ca. 0.5 litre

 *hrw* (n. m.) **day, daytime;** *m hrw pn* **today** N.B. *hrw* is the normal word corresponding to English "day." *Rʿ* occurs in this sense *only* in the expression *rʿ nb* "every day." The word *sw* means "date," although it is usually translated as "day" (of the month).

 *hrw* (adj.) **pleasing;** (vb. 3rd weak) **to be pleased, satisfied;**  *ir hrw* **Be so good as to... Take care that...**

 *hq* (vb. bi-cons.?) meaning unknown, perhaps **to break out**

 *ḥ*

 *ḥ3* (particle) introduces polite request **Would (you) please...** (§73); introduces contrary-to-fact wish **If only...!**

 *ḥ3* (prep.) **behind**

 *ḥ3t* (n. f.) **tomb**

 *ḥ3w* (n. m. pl.) **wealth; excess; exaggeration;** *rdi ḥ3w ḥr* **to do more than**

 See under  *ꜣḫt* **field**

 *ḥꜣt-sp* (reading and structure not entirely certain) **regnal year**

 *ḥꜣt* (n. f.) **forepart; forehead; vanguard** (of army); **beginning; foremost; the best of;**  *m-ḥꜣt* (compound prep.) **in front of; before; in the face of** (temporally and spatially);  *r-ḥꜣt* **in front of, before, to the front of;**  *ḫr-ḥꜣt* **in front of; before; previously**

 *ḥꜣt-ꜥ* (compound noun) **beginning;** *ḥꜣt-ꜥ m* **Here begins (the book of ...)** Used as the opening lines of a book or chapter in a compilation of texts. Do not confuse with  *ḥꜣty-ꜥ* "count," governor," etc.

 *ḥꜣty* (n. m. *nisba*) **heart, thought;** variant pl.  *ḥꜣtyw* (not **ḥꜣt ibw*!)

 *ḥꜣty-ꜥ* (n. m.) **count; regional governor; mayor**

 *ḥꜣtt* (n. f. *nisba*) **bow-warp** (of ship)

 *ḥꜣq* (vb.) **to plunder**

 *ḥꜣq* (n. m.) **plunder; booty** (can include severed hands, phalli, and live prisoners)

 *ḥꜥ* (n. m.) **flesh;** pl. *ḥꜥw* **body;** with suffixes: **~self;** (so-and-so), **in person**

 *ḥꜥi* (vb. 3rd weak) **to be joyous, rejoice** *m* **"over," "in"**

 *ḥꜥw(w)* (n. m. pl.) **ships; fleet**

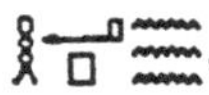,  *Ḥꜥp(y)* (proper noun) **Nile;** as god: **Ḥaꜥpy;**  *ḥꜥp ꜥꜣ* **high Nile;**

 *Ḥ(ꜥ)p-ḏf(ꜣ)* (man's name) **Ḥep-djefa**

 *ḥwt* (n. f.) **estate, large building;** ,  *ḥwt-nṯr* **temple**

 *ḥwi* (vb. 3rd weak, often without *t* in the infin.) **to beat, strike; tread** (on a road); **drive in** (a stake); verbal adjective (passive participle):  *ḥwy* **well-trodden, beaten** (path)

 *ḥwyt* (n. f.) **rain**

 *ḥwy* (particle) introducing polite request often followed by  *ꜣ* "please" (§73)

 *ḥwn* (n. m.) **youthful vigour**

 *ḥwrw* (n. m.) **poor man, humble man**

 *ḥb* (n. m.) **festival**

 *ḥbꜣbꜣ* (vb. 5-cons.) **to waddle**

 *ḥbs* (vb.) **to clothe; be clothed; put on** (garment); **cover,**  *ḥbs ḥr* **to be indifferent** *r* **"concerning";** *ḥbs ḥr* (infin.) **indifference** (to suffering or need), literally "covering the face" (in meaning similar to English: "looking the other way")

 *ḥbs* (n. m.) **garment;** pl. **clothing, clothes,** var. 

 *ḥpt* (vb.) **to embrace**

 See under *Ḥ(ᶜ)p-ḏf(3)* (man's name) **Ḥep-djefa**

 *ḥf3w* (n. m.) **serpent**

 *ḥm* (enclitic particle) **to be sure, surely, indeed** (§186, 3)

 *ḥm-ḫt* (compound verb) **to retreat**

,  *ḥmt* (n. f.) **wife, woman;** *iri ḥmt* **to marry a wife;**  *ḥmt-nsw* **Wife of the King;**  *ḥmt-nsw wrt* **Great Wife of the King** Cf. ? Semitic **ḥmt* "husband's mother"

 *ḥmw* (n. m.) **steering oar;** *iri ḥmw* **guide the helm** (Egyptian boats were steered with a steering oar, as rudders were unknown in antiquity.)

 *ḥm* (n. m.) **slave, servant;** (n. f.)  *ḥmt* **slave, servant woman**

 *ḥm-nṯr* (n. m.) ***ḥm-nṯr*-priest**

 *ḥm-k3* (n. m.) ***ḥm-k3*-priest, *k3* priest** (a category of priest who supervised the funerary cult of the deceased and supplied [under contract] offerings to the deceased person's *k3*)

 (n. m.) *Ḥm* **Majesty** (exact meaning unknown), esp. in the phrases: ,  *Ḥm·f* **His Majesty** (said of the king, *Ḥm·s* **Her Majesty** is used of female rulers); , ; *Ḥm·i* **My Majesty** (said by the king);  *Ḥm·k* **Your Majesty** (said to the king);  in the phrase *Ḥm n(y)* **the Majesty of** (+ name of a god or king)

 *ḥmt* (n. f.) **craft, art**

 *ḥmt* (n. f.) ⸢**glass flux**⸣ (an ingredient used in glass making)

 *ḥmww* (n. m.) **artisan, artist, craftsman**

 *ḥm3t* (n. f.) **salt** Cf. Semitic: Hebrew מֶלַח (*melaḥ*) "salt"; Arabic ملح (*milḥ*) "salt" (with metathesis)

 *ḥmsi* (vb. 4th weak) **to sit;** *ḥmsi m* **to live** (in/at a place), **dwell**

 *ḥn* (vb. bi-cons.) **to hurry, rush** (to a place)

 *ḥnᶜ* (prep.) **with** (a person), **together with** (things and people)

ḥnw **vessels;** generally **property, goods**

ḥnmnm (vb. 5-cons.) **to creep**

ḥnn, var. *ḥnnw* (n. m.) **phallus**

ḥnqt **beer** Cf. (?) the Semitic root **ḥmḏ* "to be sour, fermented."

ḥnkyt (n. f.) **bed**

Ḥr (divine name) **Horus** (The son of Osiris and Isis. Horus was identified with the reigning king.)

Ḥr-dd·f (man's name) **Ḥar-dedef** (a prince)

ḥr (n. m.) **face; surface**

ḥr (prep.) **on, upon; on account of, because; concerning, about; and, in addition to** (possibly cf. Semitic *ʿl* "upon"); *m-ḥr* (compound prep.) **before** (a person); **in (one's) sight**

ḥr-ỉb (compound prep.) **in the middle of;** *m ḥr-ỉb* **in the midst of, among**

ḥr-ʿwy (adv.) **immediately;** occasionally with the singular *ḥr-ʿ*

ḥr m (interrogative) **why?** (literally "on a account of what," §169)

ḥr-nt(y)t (conjunction) **because; on account of the fact that** (§114)

ḥr-ḫw (compound prep.) **except, apart from**

ḥr sy ỉšst (interrogative) **why?** (§169)

ḥr-tp (compound prep.) **on top of**

ḥry (*nisba*) **upper; (one) who/which is above/over**

ḥry-pr (n. m. *nisba*) **chief of household staff**

ḥry tꜣ (n. m. *nisba*) **survivor** (of a deceased person)

ḥry-tp (*nisba* of compound prep.) **who / which is upon; chief;** and as a noun, **headman, master**

ḥrty (vb. 4th weak, inf. without *t*) **to travel overland**

ḥḥ (cardinal number) **million**

ḥḥy (vb. 3rd weak, infin. without *t*) **to search (for), seek out**

See under *ḥry-ḥbt* **lector priest**

ḥs (n. m.) **excrement**

ḥsi (vb. 3rd weak) **to praise, honour, favour;** *ḥs·ti* (stative) **may it please you** (§99) Cf. ?? Semitic *šbḥ* "to praise," "laud"

ḥst (n. f.) **favour; praise;** *m ḥst* + divinity **through the favour of** (a god)

ḥsy (vb. 3rd weak, infin. without *t*) **to sing**

ḥsyw (n. m. [participle]) **singer**

, *ḥsb* (vb.) **to calculate; reckon**

ḥsb (n. m.) **fracture** (in bone)

ḥsbt (n. f.) **worm**

I , *ḥsmn* (n. m.) **natron** (a naturally occurring sodium carbonate [$Na_2CO_3 \cdot 10H_2O$] used in embalming and as a cleaning agent)

II , *ḥsmn* (n. m.) **bronze**

III , *ḥsmn* (n. m.) **amethyst**

ḥsq (vb.) **to sever, cut off**

, , *ḥq3* (n. m. [participle?]) **ruler;** *ḥq3-ḥwt* **local ruler, mayor, district governor**

, var. , , , , *ḥq3t* (n. f.) ***heqat*** a dry measure of ca. 4.54 litres

ḥqr (vb.) **to be hungry; to fast;** *ḥqr(w)* (participle) **hungry man**

ḥqr (n. m.) **hunger**

ḥkn (verbal adjective / participle) **(he who is) praised**

ḥknw (n. m.) **praise;** *rdi ḥknw* **to give praise** (i.e. to the gods)

ḥknw (n. m.) ***ḥknw*-oil** (a sacred oil)

ḥt3w (n. m.) **awning**

ḥtp (vb. intransitive) **to be satisfied** *m* **"with"; be at peace, go to rest, set** (of sun); (vb. transitive) **to satisfy, make content,** but cf. *sḥtp* "to satisfy"

ḥtp (n. m.) **peace, contentment;** *m ḥtp* **in safety, safely** (of travelling); **offering** *ḥtp di nsw* **an offering that the king makes** (offering formula §197) *ḥtp(w)t* (n. f. pl.) **offerings**

, *ḥḏ* (n. m.) **silver**

ḥḏ (adj. / vb. bi-cons.) **to be bright;** *ḥḏ t3* **the day dawns** (literally "the land becomes bright"); as noun **dawn, daybreak**

ḥḏ ḥr (adj.) **cheerful** (literally "bright of face")

ḥḏt (n. f.) **the White Crown** (of Upper Egypt)

ḥḏi (vb. 3rd weak) **to injure; destroy; annihilate; put an end to;** with *ib* **to disobey the heart**

ḥḏy (n. m.) **annihilation; destruction**

ḫ

, *ḫt* (n. f.—but sometimes masc.) **thing(s);** *r ḫt nbt* **more than anything; more, most** (§49)

ḫt (n. f.) **fire**

ḫ3 (n. m.) **office** (administrative bureau)

ḫ3i, abbreviated (vb. 3rd weak) **to examine** (a patient); **to measure** (grain, etc.)

ḫ3ʿ (vb.) **to throw down, cast aside; abandon** (property); *ḫ3ʿ r-s3* **to throw behind (someone)**

ḫ3wy (n. m.) **night**

ḫ3m (vb.) **to bend (the arm)** as a gesture of respect

ḫ3rt (n. f.) **widow**

ḫ3s (vb.) **to scramble**

, *ḫ3st* (n. f.) **country, foreign land; hill country**

(n. m. pl., *nisba*) *ḫ3styw* **foreigners**

ḫʿi (vb. 3rd. weak) **to rise** (sun); **to appear in glory** (king)

ḫʿw (n. m. pl.) 1) **weapons;** 2) **funerary furniture;** 3) **utensils; equipment; tackle** (of ship) *ḫʿw nw ʿḥ3* *ḫʿw ʿḥ3* **weapons of war**

ḫw in *ḥr-ḫw* (compound prep.) **except, apart from**

Ḫ(w)fw (man's name) **Ḫufu, Kheops** (a king of the Fourth Dynasty)

 *ḫbꜣ* (vb.) **to ravage, destroy**

 *ḫbi* (vb. 3rd weak) **to dance**

 *ḫbswt* (n. f.) **beard**

 *ḫpr* (vb. intransitive) **to become** (+ *m* of predication); **to change / turn** *m* **"into"; to come into existence; occur, happen,** *m-ꜥ* + person **"to a (person)"; to take place; to come, arrive** (time); **to go by, be past** (time); **to exist;** *ḫpr* + infinitive *n* + person **to be able** (for a person) **to do** (literally "[inifintive] happens for a person"); (of wealth) **to accrue** *n* **"to"** (a person); as an auxiliary verb **It happened that... / It will happen that...** (§172)

 *ḫprt* (participle, f. s. / pl.) **thing(s) that happened** *ḥr* + person **"to"** (a person); **event(s)**

 *ḫprw* (n. m.) **form, shape, manifestation, change** *iri ḫprw m* **to transform** (oneself) **into;** *iri ḫprw m* **to grow up in** (a place)

 See under *Ḫ(w)fw*

 *ḫft* **in accordance to; corresponding to; in front of; opposite; in proportion to;** *ḫft* + infinitive: **when.** Following verbs of speech and motion: **to** (a person of high rank or royalty), i.e. one does not speak *to* the king or approach him, but one speaks or stands merely *in his or her vicinity*. Note the writing! This is a case of graphic transposition (i.e. the *t* is normally placed in a convenient space for aesthetic reasons).

 *ḫft-nt(y)t* (conjunction) **in view of the fact that, since** (cf. *ḥr-nt(y)t* §114)

 *ḫft ḥr* (compound prep.) **before the face of, in front of**

 *ḫfty* (n. m. *nisba*) **enemy** ([one] who is opposed), pl. ,  *ḫftiw*

 *ḫm* **to not know** (something/somebody); **to be ignorant** (of something) The idiom **"to not know oneself"** means "to lose one's faculties" through fear, pain, etc. cf. "out of one's wits."

 *ḫmt* in the expression:  *m-ḫmt* + suffix / noun (compound prep.) **without; in (a person's) absence**

 *ḫn* (n. m.) **phrase, utterance, speech; matter, affair;**  *ḫn nfr* **a kind word;**
 *ḫn n(y) mdt* **proverb, saying**

 *ḫni* (vb. 3rd weak) **to land** (of flying, falling things); **to stop** (at a place); **to rest** (at a place—also of resting for refreshment) Cf. Semitic *nwḫ* e.g. Hebrew נוח (*nwḫ*) "to rest," "to settle," "to stop (at a place)"; Ar. نوخ (*nwḫ*) "to halt for a rest"

 *ḫny(w)t* (n. f. pl.) **dancing girls**

ḫnms (n. m.) **friend**

Ḫnsw (divine name) **Khonsu** (the moon god of Karnak)

ḫnt (n. m.) **front** *m ḫnt* **in the front,** *r ḫnt* **towards the front, forwards**

ḫnti (vb. 4th weak) **to sail upstream, travel south;** (travel, sail) **southward**

Ḫnty (divine name) **Ḫenty** (a crocodile god)

ḫntw (n. m.) **outside**

, *ḫntw, ḫnt(w)* (adv.) **before, beforehand; previously; earlier;** (adj.? *nisba?*) **previous; former**

ḫnd (vb.) **to trample, step on**

ḫr (prep.) **with, by, near,** (a god or king); **under** (a king's reign); (speak) **to** (a king); (come) **to, before** (a god or king)

ḫr (particle following a direct quotation) **so says** (a person) (§189)

, var. *ḫr* (sentence particle) **Now, ...; Then...; Thus, Further** (§185, 3); *ḫr m-ḫt* + prospective *sḏm·f* **Now after he heard / had heard** (§75, 2); with other sentence types **Now after; Now later** (§185, 4); *ḫr ir m-ḫt* **Now after; Now later; Now afterwards;** *ḫr ir m-ḫt ḥr-s3 nn* **Now later, after this; Now after this**

ḫrt (n. f.) **state; condition; affair; requirement**

, *ḫrw*, abbrev. (n. m. s./pl.) **enemy**

ḫrw **voice, sound;** , abbrev. , *m3ʿ ḫrw* / (fem.) *m3ʿt ḫrw* (epithet of deceased) **justified, vindicated** (I.e. in the trial court of the hereafter, the deceased has been declared innocent, and is admitted to the hereafter.)

ḫrw (n. m. pl.) **invocation offerings** (offerings that were believed to result from the recitation of the offering formula) used in conjunction with the verb *prỉ* "to go forth"

ḫr(y)·fy, var. (particle following direct quotation) **so says** (§189)

ḫrp (vb.) **to direct** (a project); **control** (affairs)

ḫrpw (n. m.) **mallet**

See under *ḫw* (This is a "sportive plural" writing.)

ḫsbd < *ḫsbḏ* (n. m.) **lapis lazuli**

ḫsf (vb.) transitive: **to drive away; ward off; oppose; thwart;** *ḫsf* … *ḥr* + infin. **prevent** (a person) **from** (doing); intransitive: *ḫsf ḥr* **fend for / defend** (a person); *ḫsf n* + person **to oppose** (a person); **to punish** (a person)

ḫt, (n. m.!) **tree, wood, lumber; stick; mast** (of ship); pl. *ḫtw*

ḫt (n. m.) ***khet*** a measure of 100 cubits

ḫt (prep.) **through; throughout; pervading** (often used as adverbial comment e.g. divine power pervaded his body); *m-ḫt* (compound prep.) **after, following, accompanying, behind; afterwards, later;** *m-ḫt* + prospective *sḏm·f* **when he heard / had heard** (§75, 2)

ḫt-ꜥȝ (n. m.) a type of bird

ḫtḫt (vb.) **to retreat, turn back**

ḫtḫt (n. m.) **reversal**

See under *ḫft*

ḫtm (vb.) **to seal; to put under contract** *m-ꜥ* **"with"** (+ person); **to lock** (doors, city gates) Cf. Semitic *ḫtm* "to seal"; "seal"

ḫtm (n. m.) **seal;** *ḥr ḫtm* **under** (a person's) **seal**

ḫdi (vb. 3rd weak) **to sail north; to travel / go north, to travel downstream**

ẖ

ẖt (n. f. occasionally m.) **belly; womb; abdomen; body; innermost being** (the belly was considered the seat of emotions)

ẖt (n. f.) **generation**

ẖȝyt (n. f.) **heap** (of corpses)

var. (n. m.) *ẖȝr* **sack** dry measure of 20 *ḥqȝt* (ca. 90.8 litres)

ẖnw (n. m.) **interior; home;** **royal Court;** *m-ẖnw (n[y])* (compound prep.) **within, on the inside of** (literally "in the interior of") Also written .

ẖni (vb. 3rd weak) **to row** (a boat)

ẖnw (n. m.) **brook**

Ḫnm(w) (divine name) **Khnum**

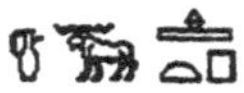

Ḫnm-ḥtp(w) (man's name) **Khnum-ḥotpe**

ẖr (prep.) **under,** and from the idea of "being under a burden": **bearing, carrying, holding, having; (being) in** (a state or condition)

ẖrt (n. f.) **belongings, property, possessions; obligation, requirement, demand, duty**

ẖrt hrw n(y)t rꜥ nb in the phrase  *m ẖrt hrw n(y)t rꜥ nb* **in the course of every day** The writing  *ẖrt hrw* is a visual pun, as the *ẖr*-sign is "*under* the sun"!

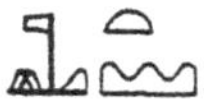

ẖrt-nṯr (n. f.) **necropolis**

ẖry (*nisba*) **who / which is under; (one) who is suffering from** (a medical condition), **(one) who has** (a medical condition); **having, possessing**

ẖry-ḥbt (n. m. *nisba*) **lector-priest** (lit. "the one holding the ritual book")

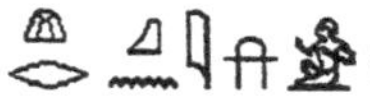

ẖr(y) qnỉ (n. m. *nisba*) **porter** (lit. "he who is under the baggage")

ẖrw (n. m.) **underside;** *r ẖrw* **downwards**

ẖrd (n. m.) **child**

ẖrdw (n. m.) **childhood**

(adj.) *ẖs* or *ẖs(y)* (adj. / verb) **cowardly; vile** (of enemy); **weak; of humble status, of modest means;** *ẖs ḥr ib* **to be incompetent**

ẖst (n. f.) **cowardice**

ẖsꜣyt (n. f.) a kind of spice

ẖkrw (n. m.) **panoply** (of war accoutrements)

S

s (n. m.) **man** Cf. ? Semitic, e.g. Hebrew אִישׁ (ʾīš) "man"

S-n(y)-Wsrt (man's name) **Senwosret**

(man's name) *S-n(y)-Wsrt-snb(w)* **Senwosret-sonbu,** sportive variant *st* (n. f.) **woman** Cf. ? Semitic, *ʾnṯ*: Arabic انثى (*ʾunṯā*) "female"; Hebrew אִשָּׁה (*ʾiššāh*) "woman"

st (n. f.) **place; seat, throne; space; proper place;** *m st iry* **in good order** (literally: "in their [proper] place[s]"). Cf. ? Arabic است (*ʾist*) "buttocks"; Hebrew שֵׁת (*šēt*) "buttocks," שָׁת (*šāt*) "foundation"

St occurs as the first element in compound abstract nouns (§193):

st-ib **affection**

st-ꜥ **blow, strike** (of gods against people)

st-nṯryt **divine state**

, *st-ḥr* (compound noun) **care, charge, supervision** in the expression *ḫr st-ḥr* **in the care of (a person), under (a person's) supervision**

st-swꜥb **purity, cleanliness**

st-skꜣ **ploughing**

st-štꜣw **mysteries**

sꜣ (n. m.) **back;** *m-sꜣ* **after; in the back of;** *r-sꜣ* + infinitive or + prospective *sḏm·f*: **after hearing** *or* **after he heard/has heard/had heard;** with nouns **behind, after;** *s r·s* **let it be revoked** (said of superseded legal documents—literally "away with it!")

, , *sꜣ* **son;** , *sꜣ nsw* **prince** (literally "son of the king") *sꜣ nsw n(y) ẖt·f* **king's true son** (literally "of his body"); as a priestly title: *sꜣ nsw tpy* **first king's son;** *sꜣ Rꜥ* **the Son of Rēꜥ** + king's Nomen in a cartouche (§69). The writing with the egg-sign is not particularly common.

Sꜣ-nht (man's name) **Sinuhe**

, *sꜣt* (n. f.) **daughter**

Sꜣt-Spdw (woman's name) **Sit-Sopdu**

, *sꜣ* (n. m.) **a phylē** (of priests); **regiment, company** (of troops) Phylē is a Greek word meaning "division" that was also used of the divisions within the Egyptian priesthood of a temple.

sꜣw (n. m.) **protection** (by means of magical amulets or spells)

sꜣi (vb. 3rd weak) **to guard, watch; ward off;** *sꜣꜣ·ti* (stative) + *ḥr* **beware! / take care not to (do) / be sure you don't (do)** (§99)

, *sꜣḥ* (vb. transitive) **arrive at, reach; to endow** *m* **"with"**; with , *tꜣ* as direct object: **to land** (from a ship), **to reach land**

Sꜣḫbw (place name) **Saḫbu**

sꜣq (vb.) **to pull (oneself) together, to be collected** (of mind)

sꜣtw (n. m.) **floor; ground**

sy, var. *s(y)* (3rd f. s. dep. pronoun) **her, it** (after particles taking the dependent pronoun, **she, it**)

sy (Late Egyptian pronoun, f. s.) **She; It** (§198) This pronoun is later replaced by the m. s. *sw*.

sy (interrogative pronoun) **what?** (precedes the noun); **who;** *sy išst* **what?;** *ḥr sy išst* **why? for what reason?;** *sy nw* **when? at what time?**

siꜣ (vb.) **to recognize; perceive; know**

siꜣ (n. m.) **perception; knowledge; prognostication** (a type of medical text that indicates how to predict the health of a patient); as a god **Sia**

sip (vb. *s*-causative of bicons.) **to inspect, examine; to take stock, to inventory**

sipty (n. m. *nisba*) **inventory**

sin (vb.) **to massage**

sini (vb. *s*-causative of 3rd weak) **to hesitate; to wait** *n* **"for"**

sꜥꜣi (vb. *s*-causative of 3rd weak) **to increase**

sꜥb (vb.) **to equip** (with weapons)

sꜥnḫ (vb. *s*-causative) **to feed, provide food for; to keep alive**

sꜥr (vb. *s*-causative of bi-cons.) **to cause to ascend** cf. Semitic *ꜥly* "to go up"

sꜥḥw (n. m. pl.) **nobles** (said of the blessed dead)

sꜥšꜣ (vb. *s*-causative) **to make numerous, many; to make (too) many**

sꜥq (vb. *s*-causative of bi-cons.) **to cause / make to enter, to send in; to bring in**

sw (3rd m. sing. dep. pronoun) **him, it** (after particles taking the dependent pronoun, **he, it**)

sw (Late Egyptian pronoun, m. s.) **He, It** (§198) (Later *sw* replaces the f. s. *sy* "She")

, common var. *swꜣ* (vb. intrans.) **to pass** *ḥr* **"by"** (a place); *ḥr* **"over"** (a legal case); *ḥr / m* **"along"** (the road); **to pass away** (die). Cf. Semitic *šwr*: Hebrew שׁור (*šwr*) "to journey"; Arabic سار (*sāra*) "to move on, go away, travel"

,  *sw3ḏ* (vb. *s*-causative of bi-cons.) **to make green; to make flourish**

 *swᶜb* (vb. *s*-causative) **to purify**

 *sww* (n. m. pl.) **dates;** (n. s.) abbreviated in dates ,  *sw* **day** (of the month) (§69)

,  *swr* (vb.) **to drink** (? an *s*-causative cognate to Semitic *rwy* "to drink one's fill")

 *swḥt* (n. f.) **egg;** *m swḥt* **in the egg,** meaning "unborn"

 *swsḫ* (vb. *s*-causative) **to widen, extend**

,  *swt* (enclitic particle) **however, but**

 *swtwt* (vb. 5-cons.) **to go for a walk**

 See under *nsw* **king**

 *sb* in the expression  *sb n(y) sḏt* (noun phrase) **burnt-offering**

 See under *sy* **what?**

 *sbi* (vb. 3rd weak) **to send** (a person) (but *not* letters); **to lead, accompany** (someone) *n* **"to** (a person)," *r* **"to** (a place)"; **to deliver** (materials, objects)

 *sbit* (n. f.) **load, cargo**

 *sb3* (vb.) **to teach** (can take two direct objects: "to teach a person a thing")

,  *sb3* (n. m.) **door; gate**

 *sb3* (n. m.) **star**

 *sbḥ* (n. m.) **cry**

 *sbḥwt* (n. f. pl.) **cries, wailing**

 *Sbk-m-ḥ3t* (man's name) **Sebek-em-ḥat**

 *sbt* < *sbṯ* (vb.) **to laugh** *m* **"at"**

 *sp* (n. m.) 1) **time, occasion;** 2) **deed, act;** 3) **misdeed, fault** 4) **matter, affair;** 5) **venture, undertaking;** 6) **success, accomplishment;** *iri sp ḥnᶜ* **deal with** (a person);  *sp sn* indicates to the reader that one or more sign, a word, or even a complete utterance is to be repeated (§70)

 var.  *sp3t* **district, nome** (the variant writing is found only in hieratic texts)

 See also under *ḏ3tt* **estate**

spỉ (vb. 3rd weak) **to remain over, survive;** *N sp* + Prospective *sḏm·f* **He never heard...** (§110)

spr (vb. transitive & intransitive) **to reach** (someone or a place) or with *r* + person; **to arrive** *r* **"at"**

spr (vb.) **to petition; to appeal** *ḥr* **"against** (a person)" *n* **"to"**; participle *sprw* (n. m., participle) **petitioner**

spd (adj.) **sharp; skilled;** *spd-ḥr* **alert (person); astute**

spdd (vb. 3rd gem.) **to supply**

sf (n. m.) **yesterday**

sfn (adj. / vb.) **(to be) kind, merciful; to show mercy; to be lenient**

sft < *sfṯ* (vb.) **to slaughter** (animal)

sft < *sfṯ* (n. m.) **oil**

sm (vb.) **to help, aid**

smꜣ (vb.) **to kill, slay**

smꜣ (n. m.) **associate; ally; accomplice**

smꜣ-tꜣ (compound vb.) **to unite the land; to be buried;** (n. m.) **interment; juncture, fork** (of a road—the meaning is not entirely certain)

, var. *smꜣr* (vb. *s*-causative) **to impoverish**

smwn (sentence particle) **probably, certainly** (§185, 6)

smn (vb. *s*-caus. of bi-cons.) **to establish; to make firm; to perpetuate; to set up** (an inscription)

smnḫ (vb. *s*-causative) **to enhance; improve; to advance; to embellish; to be servicable, of use**

smr (vb. *s*-causative of bi-cons.) **to inflict pain**

smr (n. m.) **Companion, Friend** of the king (a court title); *smr wꜥty* **Unique Friend; Sole Companion**

smsỉ, *smsy* (vb. *s*-causative of 3rd weak—infin. without *t*) **to deliver** (a woman in childbirth)

smsw (adj.) **eldest** (of persons) (Note the crook at the bottom of the staff.)

sn (3rd pl. dep. pron.) **them** (after particles requiring the dependent pronoun, **they**)

sn (n. m.) **brother**

snt (n. f.) **sister**

, *sn* (vb. bi-cons.) **to kiss; to smell; to breathe**

snỉ (vb. 3rd weak) **to pass by**

snwy (n. dual) **two**

, *sn-nw* (ordinal number) **second;** **mate, fellow, companion, partner**

snwḫ (vb. *s*-causative) **boil, cook** *ḥr* **"in"**

snb (adj.) **healthy; safe;** (vb.) **to be healthy;** *snb·t(ỉ)* (stative) **may you be healthy; Safe journey!** (cf. Semitic *šlm* "to be whole, in good condition, safe"—here Egy. *n* corresponds to *l* and with interchange of *m* and *b*).

snb (n. m. or infin. of preceding) **recovery** (from illness)

snf (n. m.) **blood**

snḫt (vb. *s*-causative) **to strengthen**

, *sntr* < *snṯr* (n. m.) **incense**

snḏ (vb.) **to fear; to respect** (n. m.) **fear** (Suggestion: when *snḏ* is followed by a reference to a god or king, translate "the fear of him" rather than "his fear.")

snḏt (n. f.) **fear**

snḏm (vb. *s*-causative) **to make happy; to sit, be seated;** **dwelling-place; home** Cf. Semitic *nʿm* "pleasant, comfort," etc.

, *sr* (n. m.) **official**

sr (vb. bi-cons.) **to predict; foretell**

srwỉ (vb. *s*-causative of 3rd weak) **to remove**

srwḫ (vb. 4-cons.) **to treat** (medically); **to tend**

srwd < *srwḏ*; (vb. *s*-causative) **to strengthen; to perpetuate** (offerings to the gods or ancestors); **to make flourish**

srmỉ (vb. *s*-causative of 3rd weak) **to make cry; to cause weeping**

sḥ3ỉ (vb. *s*-causative of 3rd weak) **to let down, lower**

sḥq3 (vb. *s*-causative) **to install as ruler, to make (someone) a ruler**

 *sḥqr* (vb. *s*-causative) **to cause hunger; to let starve**

 *sḥtp* (vb. *s*-causative) **to satisfy; to please**

, var.  *sḥtm* (vb. *s*-causative) **to destroy**

 *sḥḏ* (vb. *s*-causative of bi-cons.) **to illuminate; to brighten**

 *sḫt* (n. f.) **fields, meadow, country** (in contrast to the town)

 *sḫty* (*nisba* from *sḫt*) **peasant**

 *sḫ3* **to remember**

 See under *wsḫ* **width**

 *sḫpr* (vb. *s*-causative) **to create, bring into existence, cause to be, bring about**

 *sḫm* (adj. and vb.) **powerful;** as verb: **to have power** *m* **"over"; to prevail** *m* **"over,"** *r* **"over"; to have control** *m* **"over"**

 *sḫm* (n. m.) **power**

 *sḫr* See under *sẖr* **to sweep**

 *sẖr* (n. m.) **plan, idea, (piece of) advice**

 *sẖry* (n. m. *nisba*) **captain** (of a ship or boat)

 *sẖr*, var.  *sẖr* (vb.) **to sweep; to overlay** (to apply gold leaf, etc.)

 *ss* (n. m.) **ashes**

 *ss3i* (vb. *s*-causative of 3rd weak) **to satisfy, to make wise**

*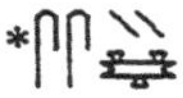 See under *rssy*.

 *sspd* (vb. *s*-causative) **to prepare, to make ready, to supply** *m* **"with"**

 *ssm(w)t* (n. f. pl.) **horses** (Eighteenth Dynasty accounts indicate that chariot teams were almost exclusively mares.)

 See under *sww* **dates** (This is a "sportive plural.")

 *sš? sn?* (vb. bi-cons.) **to spread out; to pass** *ḥr* **"by"**

 *sš* (n. m.) **threshold**

 *sš* (vb. bi-cons.) **to write**

sš (n. m.) **document; writing;** *ỉrỉ m sš* **to put in writing**

sš (n. m.—participle) **scribe;** *sš nsw* **royal scribe**

sš3 See under *šs3* **to be wise**

sš3 (n. m.) **prayer**

sšm (vb.) **to lead, guide; rule govern; direct; show the way; conduct** (work)

sšmw (m. s. participle) **director; leader; guide; ruler**

sšmw (n. m.) **conduct; behaviour**

sšn (n. m.) **lotus** also with the determinative Cf. Semitic *ššn* "lily."

sq3 (vb. *s*-causative of bi-cons.) **to exalt; extol**

sqbb (vb. 3rd gem.) **to make cool**

sqbbwy (n. m.) **cool hall** or perhaps **bathroom** (shower-room?)

sqr-ᶜnḫ (n. m.) **captive** (prisoner of war)

, *sqdỉ* (vb. *s*-causative of 3rd weak, infin. apparently without *t*) **to sail, to sail on** (can be transitive); (more generally) **to travel** (even on land)

sqdw (m. participle) **sailor**

See under *isṯ*

sk (vb. bi-cons.) **to wipe out** (pots, etc.); *sk ẖt* **pour out one's heart** (literally "wipe out one's belly")

ski (vb. 3rd weak) **to destroy; annihilate**

, , *sgr* (vb. *s*-causative of bi-cons.) **to silence;** *rdỉ sgr m* + person **to silence** (a person)

st (3rd pl. dep. pron.) **them, it** (after particles taking the dependent pronoun, **they, it**)

st (Late Egyptian pronoun, com. pl.) **They** (§198)

See under *sṯ(y)*

sti (vb. 3rd weak) **to shoot**

st(w)t (n. f. pl.) **shooting pains**

stwt (n. f. pl.) **rays** (of sun)

stp (n. m.) **strip** (of cloth)

stpw (n. m. pl.) **the choicest, the pick** (said of troops, crews, etc.)

Stẖ the god **Sutekh** (Seth)

See under *isṯ* **Now** or *st* **them**

sṯꜣ, *stꜣ* (vb.) **to drag, drag off** (persons); **to pull, draw** (wagon)

sṯꜣt (n. f.) ***aroura*** land measure of 100 cubits squared (2735 sq. metres or a little more than ⅔ acre) (§68, 4)

stꜣw (n. m. pl.) **secretions**

sṯ(y), *st(y)* (n. m.) **fragrance, aroma, smell**

sṯsi (vb. *s*-causative of 3rd weak, infin. with *t*) **to raise**

sṯsi (vb. 4th weak, infin. without *t*) **to be prostrate, sprawled out**

sd (vb. bi-cons.) **to clothe**

sd (n. m.) **tail**

sd < *sḏ* (vb. bi-cons.) **to break, to crush, to smash**

sdb (n. m.) **fringe** (of cloth)

sdm (vb.) **to apply** (cosmetics, medicines) **to the eyelids**

sḏt (n. f.) **fire, flame**

sḏwy (vb. *s*-causative of 3rd weak) **to slander, vilify**

sḏm (vb.) **to hear; to listen;** *sḏm n* **to listen to** (a person); **obey** (a person) Only rarely written with a determinative: Cf. Semitic *šmꜥ* "to hear"

See under *sdm* **to apply to the eyelids**

sḏmw (participle, m.) **judge**

sḏr (vb. *s*-causative of bi-cons.) **to lie down; go to bed; sleep; spend the night** (doing)

sḏd (vb. *s*-causative of bi-cons.) **to recount; relate; converse; talk** *m* **"about"; recite**

sḏdwt (n. f. pl.) **quotations; literary works**

Š

š (n. m.) **pool, pond, lake; garden**

š3 (vb. bi-cons.) **to ordain; to order**

š3w (n. m.) **fate**

š3(w) in *n š3w n(y)* (compound prep.) **to the extent of; in the capacity of**

š3ꜥ (vb.) **to begin** *m* + infin. **to (do something)**

š3ꜥ (n. m.) **beginning** *š3ꜥ m* **beginning from;** *m š3ꜥ m* **beginning from;** *š3ꜥ r* **as far as;** *r š3ꜥ r* **down to**

š3ꜥs (n. m.) (an unknown luxury product)

š3s (vb.) **to travel, go, make a trip**

š3d (vb.) **to excavate, dig out, dredge**

šꜥt variant of *šꜥyt* (n. f.) a type of cake

šꜥd(w) (n. m. pl.) **incisions**

Šw (divine name) **Shu** (the god of the air)

šw (adj. / vb. bi-cons.) **to be empty; free** *m* **"of, from"; devoid** *m* **"of"; to be lacking**

šwyt (n. f.) **shadow, shade**

šw3w (n. m. pl.) **commoners**

šp (vb. bi-cons.) **to flow out; to pass out of** (said of evil spirits departing the body)

špsy (adj.) **noble, splendid, costly, elegant, luxurious;** (of gods) **august**

špssw (n. m. pl.) **precious things, luxuries, riches, wealth; delicacies**

Šft (woman's name) **Šaftu**

, *šm* (vb. bi-cons., anomalous infin. with *t* *šmt*) **to go; to walk**

šmꜥ (n. m.) **Upper Egyptian barley**

šmꜥ (vb.) **to make music**

šmꜥw (n. m.) **musician**

šmw (n. m.) **summer** (a season §69)

šmw (n. m.) **harvest**

šms (vb.) **to follow, accompany;** *šms wḏ3* **a funeral procession**

šmsw (m. participle) **retainer, attendant**

šni (vb. 3rd weak) 1) **to enquire into a matter, to investigate, to question** (someone); 2) **to conjure / exorcise** (an illness); **to curse**

šnyt (n. f. collective) **courtiers**

šn(w) (n. m.) **net**

See under *šnṯ* **to revile**

šnṯ, var. *šnt* **to revile; denounce**

šndyt (n. f.) **kilt;** figuratively **apron** i.e. protector of the motherless

šri (n. m.) **lad; youth** (young man)

šrr, *šri* (adj. & vb. 2nd gem.) **to be little, small, diminished, lessened**

šs3 var. *sš3* (vb.) **to be wise;** *rdi šs3 m* **to inform** (someone) **of, acquaint** (someone) **with**

šs3w (n. m.) **treatment** (medical)

šsp (vb.) **to take, accept, receive; take up** (an object)

šsp (n. m.) **light**

šspt (n. f. collective) **cucumbers**

šspt (n. f.) **summer house**

št3 (adj.) **mysterious; secret; difficult;** (n. m. pl.) *št3w* **secrets, mysteries**

šdi (vb. 3rd weak) **to dig out, cut out, carve (out); remove**

šdyt (n. f.) **pool** (i.e. "that which is dug out")

q

q3 (adj.) **tall, high; exalted; loud** (cf. English "at the top of one's voice"); *q3 s3* **arrogant,**

presumptuous (and as a noun denoting such a person);  *q3 ḫrw* **noisy** ("loud-mouthed")

 *q3b* (n. m.) **intestine; interior;**  *m-q3b* (compound prep.) **in the midst of** (people, places, things)

, var.  *q3q3* (n. m.) **travelling barge**

 *Qi-na* (place name) **Qina** (written in New Kingdom style group writing)

 *qʿḥ* (n. m.) **bend** or **fold** (of a fishing net)

 *qbb* (adj. and vb. 2nd gem.) **(to be) cool, calm;** with *ib* **refreshed**

, var.  *qm3* (vb.) **to produce, create; to engender**

 *qni* (adj. and vb. 3rd weak) **to be brave; strong; sturdy; to conquer** Cf. ? Semitic *dnn*: Ugaritic *dnn* "to be strong, powerful"; Akkadian *danānu* "to be strong, powerful"

 *qnt* (n. f.) **valour**

 *qni* (vb. 3rd weak) **to embrace** *m* + person; *qni šwyt* **to fall unconscious, black out**

 *qni* (n. m.) **embrace;** *mḥ qni m* + person **to fill (one's) embrace with** (a person)

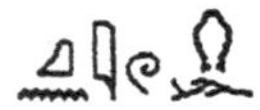 *qniw* (n. m.) **palanquin** (an open seat carried on poles by porters)

,  *qnbt* (n. f.) **court** (of magistrates); as collective **magistrates**

 *qnbty* (n. m. *nisba*) **magistrate;**  *qnbty n(y) w* **district magistrate** ("magistrate of the district")

 *qri* (n. m.) **thunder, thunderstorm**

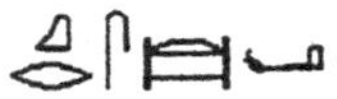 *qrs* (vb.) **to bury**

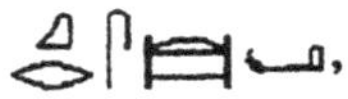,  *qrs* (n. m.) **burial**

 *qsn* (adj.) **painful, troublesome, difficult, nasty;** of injuries *qsn r·f* **too painful for him** (*r* of comparison, §49, literally "[It] is painful beyond him," i.e. beyond his tolerance); (n. m.) **pain** Cf. Hebrew קָשָׁה (*qāšā*) "difficult, hard, severe"; Arabic قسا (*qasā*) "to be hard, harsh, cruel"

, var.  *qd* (vb. bi-cons.) **to build; fashion** (humans)

 *qd* (n. m.) **reputation, character, nature; extent;**  *mi qd·f* **in its entirety** (§80)

 *qdt* (n. f.) ***qidet*** a weight of 9.1 grams, one tenth of a *deben* (§68,3)

 *Qdš* (place name) **Kadesh** a city on the Orontes River

k

, *k3* (sentence particle) **Then... Next...** (§185, 2)

k3 (particle following a direct quote) **so** (a speaker) **will say** (§189)

k3 (n. m.) ***ka (ku)*; spirit; soul** The *ka* was a part of the person's makeup that among other things received nourishment—real or spiritual—and to which offerings were made after the person's death.

, var. , , *k3* **bull** (can refer to the king)

k3t (n. f.) **construction project; work;** *imy-r k3(w)t* **overseer of works**

k3w (n. m. pl.) **sycamore figs**

k3p (n. m.) **hut, lean-to**

k3hs (vb. 4-cons.) **to be harsh**

K3š (place name, feminine in gender) **Kush** (in Nubia)

ky (n. m.) (precedes the noun) **another; another man** (sometimes with a seated man determinative), **another thing, another one**

ky (n. m.) **baboon**

kt (n. fem.) (precedes the noun) **another;** used as *ky*

Kbi (man's nickname) **Kebi**

Kpny (also spelled *Kbn*) (place name) **Byblos** (an Egyptian "colony town" in Lebanon)

kf (vb.) **to uncover**

kf3 (vb.) **to be discreet;** *kf3 ib* **trustworthy;** **trusted man**

, *km* **to complete; to come to a total of, to total up to;** *m km* (infinitive) *n(y) 3t* **in the blink of an eye** ("in the completing of an instant"

, *Kmt* (place name, f.) **Egypt** (literally, "the Black Land")

ksw (n. m. pl.) **bowings,** esp. in the phrase *m ksw* (foreigners come) **bowing** (to the king)

kkt (n. f.) an unknown animal that eats grain

 *kkw* (n. m.) **darkness**

 *kt* (adj.) **little**

 *g*

 *gwf* (n. m.) **long-tailed monkeys** The word was loaned into Hebrew: קוֹף (*qōf*) "monkey."

 *Gb* (divine name) **Geb** (the earth god)

 *gbgbyt*: *m gbgbyt* **headlong**

 *gfn* (vb.) **to dismiss** (a person)

 *gmi* (vb. 3rd weak) **to find** Cf. (?) the Semitic root(s) **mḏʾ / mṯʾ / mǵy* "to find; come; come upon," e.g. Hebrew מָצָא (*māṣāʾ*) "to find," Ugaritic *mǵy* "to come upon"

 *gmḥ* (vb.) **to catch sight of** (someone), **to spot** (someone)

 *gmgm* (vb. 4-cons., intransitive) **to break; to crash; smash**

 *grt* (enclitic particle) **however; moreover; now** (can occur after the particle *iw* and can have suffix pronouns attached)

 *gr* (vb. bi-cons.) **to be silent; to be motionless**

 *gr(w)* (adv.) **also, too; still**

 *grḥ* (n. m.) **night** *m grḥ* **at night, in the night,** *grḥ mi hrw* **both night and day**

,  *grg* (vb.) **to establish, re-establish, found; to prepare (for);** *grg pr* **set up a household** (start a family)

,  *grg* (n. m.) **falsehood, lie**

 *gḥs* (n. m.) **gazelle**

, , 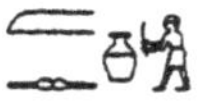 *gs* (vb. bi-cons.) **to anoint**

 *gs* (n. m.) 1) **side;** 2) **half;** 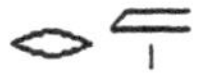 *r-gs* (compound prep.) **beside; at the side of; next to**

 *gs-pr* (compound noun, m.) **temple**

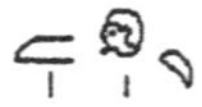 *gs-tp* (compound noun, m.) **migraine headache** (literally "half the head") The Greek and Latin names from which "migraine" derives (*hēmikrania, hemicrania*) are very likely loan-translations from Egyptian.

t

t (n. m.) **bread**

tꜣ (f. s. demonstrative / definite article) **this; the** (§78)

, var. , *tꜣ* (n. m.) **land; earth; ground** Dual: , , *Tꜣwy* **The Two Lands** (Egypt, i.e. Upper and Lower Egypt); *Nb Tꜣwy* **The Lord of the Two Lands** (an epithet of the king)

Tꜣ-mri (place name) **Egypt**

Tꜣ-nṯr (place name) **God's Land** (often refers to Punt, but also to other distant lands)

tꜣš (n. m.) **boundary**

See under *tmt* **sprinkle**

tiḥwy (n. m. pl.) **peas**

tišps (n. m.) a spice

I , , *tw* (indefinite pron.) **one** (can occur as subject or as topic in non-verbal sentences, e.g. §62); in 18th Dynasty texts, "One" may refer to the king. The passive marker is derived from this word. Note that true passive forms occur far more frequently than does the indefinite pronoun.

II *tw* See

III *tw* (f. s. demonstrative) **this** (§78) archaic

, *twꜣ* (n. m.) **inferior; a person of low status**

twi (Late Egyptian pronoun, com. s.) **I** (§198)

twn (Late Egyptian pronoun, com. pl.) **We** (§198)

twk (Late Egyptian pronoun, m. s.) **You** (§198)

twt (Late Egyptian pronoun, f. s.) **You** (§198)

tw·tw (Late Egyptian pronoun) **One** (§198)

twtn (Late Egyptian pronoun, com. pl.) **You** (§198)

twy (f. s. demonstrative) **this** (§78) archaic

twt (vb.) **to be in accord with; to resemble, be like;** *twt ib ḥnꜥ* **to agree with**

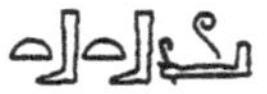 *tbtb*, var. 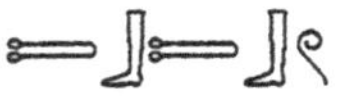 *ṯbṯb* (vb. 4-cons.) **to haul up**

 *tp* (n. m.) **head; °principal°** (of a loan);  *m tp ḥr m3st* (to sit) **with head on knee** (a gesture of mourning)

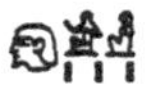 *tp* (n. m.) **person**

 *tp* (prep.) **on**

 *tp-ᶜ* (compound prep.) **before** with the infinitive ("before going to bed"), and with the prospective *sḏm·f* ("before one could / might go," etc.)

 *tp-m* (coumpound prep.) **before**

 *tp-ḥr(y)* (compound noun m.) **master**

 *tp-dw3yt* (n. phrase) **dawn**

 *tpt* (n. f.) **fine oil** (i.e. "first class")

, var.  *tpy* (*nisba*) **which is on; principal, chief; the best (of);** ,  **first;** 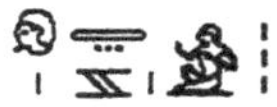 *tpyw-t3* **those who are on earth**

 *tf*, var.  *tf3* (f. s. demonstrative adj.) **that** (§78)

 *tm*, var. , ,  negative auxiliary verb—negates purpose clauses (§175); prospective forms as direct object and object of preposition (§176); conditional sentences (§177); infinitives (§178); participles and *sḏm·ty·fy* (§179); relative verb (§179)

,  *tm3* (n. m.) **mat**

 *tmm* (vb. intrans.) **to close up (abnormally)** (said of wounds)

 *tmt*, var.  *tmtm* (vb.) **to sprinkle, to dust** (with a powder)

I  *tn* (f. s. demonstrative adj.) **this** (follows the noun and agrees in gender with it). Sometimes it is better translated **that.**

II  *tn* See  *ṯn* (also for words beginning with *tn*)

 *tn* See 

 *tnỉ* (vb. 3rd weak) **to grow old**

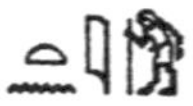 *tnỉ* (n. m.) **old age**

 See *ṯnỉ* **to distinguish**

tr (n. m.) **time, season**

tr (enclitic particle) **indeed, certainly, then** (§186, 4)

thỉ (vb. 3rd weak) **to go astray; lead astray, mislead**

tḫỉ (vb. 3rd weak) **to get / be drunk**

tḫt (n. f.) **the land of drunkenness**

tḫb (vb.) **to irrigate** (a wound)

See under *twt*

Tti (woman's name) **Teti**

ṯ

ṯ3y (n. m.) **male**

ṯ3w (n. m.) **wind; breath;** *ṯ3w ꜥnḫ* **the breath of life / life-giving breath**

ṯ3ty **the vizier** (The highest official in Egypt)

ṯw (2nd m. sing. dep. pron.) **you**

ṯwy var. of *twy* **this**

See under *tbtb* **to haul up**

ṯm3-ꜥ (adj. phrase) **strong of arm, strong-armed**

ṯn, var. *tn* (2nd f. sing. dep. pron.) **you**

ṯn, var. *tn* (2nd pl. dep. pron.) **you**

ṯn (interrogative) **where?**

ṯnỉ, *tnỉ* (vb.) **to distinguish** (one thing *r* **"from"** another); **to be distinguished, elevated** (of actions, speech, character, etc.)

ṯnw, *tnw* (n. m.) **distinction, eminence**

ṯnw, *tnw* (n. m.) **number**

, *ṯs* (n. m.) **vertebra**

ṯs (vb. bi-cons.) **to attach; join; knit together** (broken bones); **to tie**

ṯst (n. f. collective) **troops; gang**

ṯsw (n. m.) **commander; leader**

ṯsi (vb. 3rd weak) **to raise up, lift up, get up**

ṯsm (n. m.) **hound, dog**

d

dꜣbw (n. m. pl.) **figs**

dꜣr (vb.) **to control** (one's temper, etc.); *dꜣr ib* **to get control of oneself**

di ʿnḫ, ḏd, wꜣs (perf. passive particilple) **given life, stability, and dominion** (an exclamation used after the mention of the king's nomen, see §§69; 121, 2b)

dwꜣw (n. m.) **tomorrow; morning**

dwꜣ-nṯr (compound verb—suffixes follow the entire unit) *dwꜣ-nṯr ... n* + person **to thank** (someone) (literally "praise god for [person]")

dwn (vb.) **to stretch** (limbs of body)

db (n. m.) **horn** (of an animal); **wing** (of an army)

For words written , see under *ḏbꜣ*

dbyt (n. f.) a type of plant

dbn (vb.) **to go around, circulate, travel around**

dbn (n. m.) ***deben*** a weight of ca. 91 grams

dbdb (vb. 4-cons.) *iri dbdb* **to pound** (heart)

dp (vb. bi-cons.) **to taste; to experience**

dpt (n. f.) **taste; experience**

dpt (n. f.) **boat**

dm (vb. bi-cons.) **to pronounce, to mention**

dmꜣ (vb.) **to stretch out**

dmỉ (n. m.) **town; harbour**

dmỉ (vb. 3rd weak) **to touch** generally, but also in the sense of harming; **to reach** (a place)

dns (adj.) **heavy; serious**

dr (vb. bi-cons.) **to drive out; expell**

drp (vb.) **to offer; make offerings**

drf, var. *ḏrf* (n. m.) **title deed**

dhn (vb.) **to appoint** (a person to an office); *dhn-tꜣ* var. *ḏh<n>-tꜣ* **to touch one's head to the ground** (as a gesture of respect)

ds (n. m.) **jug** (also as a beer measure)

ds (n. m.) **flint**

dgꜣỉ (also *dgỉ*) (vb. 4th weak) **to see, look at;** also with prep. *n* **look "at"** Cf. Semitic: Hebrew דָּגוּל (*dāgûl*) "visible; distinguished"; Akkadian *dagālu* "to see"

dgỉ (vb. transitive) **to hide** (something); (intransitive) **to be in hiding, to be hidden**

dgm (n. m.) **castor oil plant**

ḏ

ḏt (n. f.) **eternity, for ever**

ḏꜣ (n. m.) **fire-drill** (an implement to start fires)

ḏꜣỉ (vb. 3rd weak) **to ferry (someone) across; to cross** (sky, river, etc.); *ḏꜣỉ tꜣ r* **to interfere with** (land claims, property, etc.) *Ḏꜣỉ* is not a "verb of motion."

ḏꜣyt (n. f.) **wrongdoing**

ḏꜣỉsw (n. m.) **disputant, adversary, opponent**

ḏꜣmw (n. m. pl.) **young men;** frequently in a military context **the boys, the lads**

ḏꜣtt (n. f.) **estate**

See also under *spꜣt* **district, nome**

ḏᶜ (n. m.) **wind storm, tempest** Cf. ? Hebrew סַעַר (*saᶜar*, probably */tsaᶜar/*) "heavy windstorm" and the unique word סְעָה (*sōꜥā*) "rushing wind," "tempest"

, *ḏꜥmw* (n. m.) **electrum** (or some type of fine gold)

ḏꜥr (vb.) **to search; seek out; probe, palpate** (wound); **investigate**

ḏw (n. m.) **mountain**

ḏw (n. and adj.) **misfortune, evil;** and as adjective **bad, wicked; sad**

ḏbꜣ (vb.) **to block, stop up** *m* **"with"**

ḏbꜣ, *ḏbꜣ* (vb.) **to restore, repay, replace**

ḏbꜣw, var. *ḏbꜣw* (n. m. pl.) **payments; compensation; bribe;** *r ḏbꜣ* **in place of, instead of**

ḏbꜥ **finger**(cf. Semitic *ꜣṣbꜥ "finger")

ḏbꜥ **10,000**

, , , , , *ḏfꜣw* (n. m. pl.) **provisions, sustenance, abundance**

ḏnnt (n. f.) **skull**

ḏrt (n. f.) **hand**

, *ḏr* (prep.) **since**

ḏr (vb. bi-cons.) auxiliary verb **to end up** (§174)

ḏr in *r ḏr·f*, see under *ḏrw* **limit**

ḏrw (n. m.) **limit, boundary** (concrete and abstract); **border;** *r ḏr·f* **in its entirety** (§80); *nn ḏrw* **without limit**

See under *drf* (n. m.) **title-deed**

ḏrḏry (adj.) **strange; foreign**

See under *dhn*

Ḏḥwty (divine name) **Thoth** (the god of learning and the "weigher of the soul" in the court of the hereafter)

ḏs· (reflexive pronoun) **~self** (requires suffixes): *ḏs·f* **himself,** *ḏs·s* **herself,** *ḏs·k* **yourself,** etc. (The words formed with *ḏs·* are emphatic and are not used for the simple reflexive. I.e. the sense is like French *moi-même* "me–myself" and not "myself" as in "I saw myself in the mirror.")

ḏd (vb. bi-cons.) **to say, speak, talk, tell;** *m ḏd* **saying** (*ḏd* is an infinitive) introduces direct discourse (a word for word quotation); it can be left out of translations if colon and quotation marks are used. Also occurring with the same function is the phrase *r ḏd* **saying**

, abbreviated *ḏd mdw* **words to be recited** (*ḏd* is the infinitive [§57, 7] literally "the saying of words"): a phrase to introduce the text of rituals, incantations, and lines of dialogue of divinities in dramatic performances or on temple walls accompanying illustrations (the speaker is identified by the agent particle *in* "by")

Ḏdi (a man's name) **Djedi**

Ḏd-Snfrw (*mꜣꜥ ḫrw*) (place name) **Djed-Snofru, justified**

Ḏdw (place name) **Busiris** (modern Abu Ṣir Banā); *Nb Ḏdw* **Lord of Busiris** (an epithet of Osiris)

Reading uncertain or unknown

⌜*qꜣw*⌝ (n. m.) **powder**

GRAMMATICAL & GENERAL INDEX

Note that in this index, the Egyptian words are listed by *English* alphabetic order, and *not* by Egyptian alphabetic order. Letters requiring diacritical marks in Egyptian are, however, listed in the Egyptian order (e.g. *ḥ* before *ḫ*). This index was compiled for quick reference, and items may be found in more than one location, which it is hoped will save the user time and trouble.

ᶜḥᶜ·n sḏm·n·f and related constructions §90–96

AB nominal sentence §56, 1; §128

  Explicatory sentence §148

Abbreviations §52

Adjective verb §76; §82

Adjectives

  Bound to following noun §48

  Comparison §49

  Declension §19; §20

  Demonstrative §78

  Exclamatory *wy* §45

  Fem. sing. as "thing" §21, 2; §47

  Modifiers §20

  Nisba forms §54

  Nominal use §21, 1

  Overview of uses §43

  Predicate adjective §44

    Impersonal with dative §46

  Superlative notion §50

Adverbs and adverb equivalents §9; §97

  Adverbial comments

   in explicatory sentences §148

  Adverbial comments

    in non-verbal statements of fact §10; §16

   Stative as, §85 (See also Pseudo-verbal constructions)

  Adverbial modifiers §9; §10

   Stative as, §86

   Following the relative adjective *nty* §112

Afroasiatic languages §1

  Affinity of Egyptian suffix pronouns §23, 7

Apposition §22, 2

Articles

  Lack of §8

  Possessive §132

Bi-partite nominal sentences with *pw* §129

  With other demonstrative pronouns §130

Bound constructions (direct genitive) §22, 1a

Calendar §69
Captions (narrative infinitive) §57, 7
Circumstantial clauses §16; §32
  Modifying nouns §38
  Progressive action §61
  Relative clause with indefinite antecedent §38
Circumstantial family of forms §35
Circumstantial *sḏm·f*
  Active forms §29
  Passive forms §34
  Relative clause with indefinite antecedent §38
Circumstantial *sḏm·n·f*
  Active forms §30
  After *ꜥḥꜥ·n* and related constructions §§90–96
  Modifying nouns (relative clauses) §38
  Passive counterpart—*sḏm(w)·f* passive §35
Combination signs §42
Commands (imperative) §145
  With reflexive dative §195
Comment, Adverbial §10
Compound prepositions §54; §81
  Nisba derivatives of compound prepositions §81
Conditional sentences §§137–139
  Negation of §177
  Without *ỉr* §139
Coordinating words §63
Coptic §3

Dates §69
Dative
  Following impersonal predicate adjective §46
  Position in sentence (word order) §51
  Reflexive use in commands and exhortations §195
Declension of nouns and adjectives §19
Defective writings §52
Demonstratives §78
Demotic §3
Dependent pronouns §39
Determinatives §12

Direct genitive, see Bound constructions
Direct object
  Position in sentence (word order) §51
Disjunctive words, lack of §63
Dual §19

Egyptian language
  Connection to African and West Asian languages §1
  Historical phases §2
  Scripts §3
Emphatic sentence, see "Explicatory sentence"
Exclamatory *wy* (in predicate adjective) §45
Exhortations §72
  Negation of §164
  With reflexive dative §195
Existential sentences §100
  Negation of §103 (*nn wn*; *nn*; *n wnt*)
Explanations
  ỉnk pw §144
  sḏm·f pw §143
Explicatory sentences §148
  Common in questions for specification §169
  Negations of §184

Fronting of nouns
  ỉw·f sḏm·f §37
  Noun *sḏm·f* §36
  With *ỉr* §133
Funerary offering formula §197
Future tense §62
  Negated by *nn sḏm·f* (first prospective) §109

Genitival relations §22, 1
Genitival adjective (indirect genitive) *n(y)*, etc. §22, 1b
  Before prepositional phrases §191
  Verbs following §190
Graphic transposition §41, 2
Group writing §53

Hieratic script §3
Hieroglyphic script §3
  Principles of §4; §6; §11
Honorific transposition §41, 1
ḥr + infinitive §58; §59; §61
ḥtp di nsw (offering formula) §197

Idiomatic phrases used as nouns §194
Imperative §145
  Negation of §166
  With reflexive dative §195
Independent pronouns §56
Indirect genitive, see Genitival adjective
Infinitives §57
  As direct object of verbs §57, 6
  Forms §57, 1
  ḥr + infinitive §58; §59; §61
  Logical direct object following §57, 3
  Logical indirect object following §57, 5
(infinitives)
  Logical subject following §57, 4
  m + infinitive §60
  nn + infinitive "without (doing)" §105
  Narrative infinitive §57, 7
  Negative infinitive §178
  Object of preposition §57, 2
  r + infinitive (purpose) §57, 2
  r + infinitive (future tense) §62
  Subject of verbs / predicate adjectives §57, 8
  See also Pseudo-verbal constructions
Interrogative pronouns §128
Interrogative words and phrases in questions for specification §169
iw (sentence particle) §9; §23, 6; §31; §32
iw·f ḥr sḏm §59
iw·f m iit §60
iw·f r sḏm §62
iw·f sḏm·f §37
iw sḏm·f §9

Journal entry style (narrative infinitive) §57, 7

"Know": *rḫ* in stative §89

Late Egyptianisms
  Personal pronouns *tw·i*, etc. §198
  Writing conventions §199
Logical direct object (after infinitive) §57, 3
Logical indirect object (after infinitive) §57, 5
Logical subject (after infinitive) §57, 4

m + infinitive §60
m of predication §24
M-preformative nouns §192
Measurements §68
mk (sentence particle) §17; §31; §40
n (negative particle)
  n negating bi-partitite nominal sentences with *pw* §130
  n ... is negating bi-partite nominal sentences with *pw* §130
  n sp sḏm·f (first prospective) §110
  n sḏm·f (past) §107, 1
  n sḏm·n·f (present) §108, 1
  n sḏm·n·tw·f (present passive) §108, 2
  n sḏm·tw·f (past passive) §107, 2
  n sḏmt·f ("before he has heard") §155
Narrative infinitive §57, 7
Narrative past tense
  ʿḥʿ·n sḏm·n·f and related constructions §90–96; 153
  šmt pw ir(w)·n·f with verbs of motion §136
Negation
  Conditional sentences §177
  Existential sentences §103
  Explicatory sentences §184
  Imperative §166
  Infinitives §178
  Non-verbal statements of fact with adverbial predicate §102
  Noun clauses §176

Negation, cont.
Participles §179
Predicate adjectives §106 ff.
Purpose clauses §175
Rare or archaic negations
nfr n §181
nfr pw §181
w §182
Relative verb forms §179
Statements of fact, non-verbal with adverbial predicate §102
Statements of fact, verbal §§106–109
Wishes and exhortations §164
See also under *n* and *nn* for specific constructions.
Negatival complement §165
Negative relative adjective *iwty* §183
n·f imy "of his own" and as partative "of them" §127
n·f imy X (possession) §126, 3
Nisba adjectives §54
From compound prepositions §81
nn (negative particle)
Negating non-verbal sentences with adverbial comment §102
Negating existential sentences §103; *nn wn* §103
Negating infinitives ("without doing") §105
Negating future statements of fact: *nn sḏm·f* (first prospective) §109
Negating nouns ("without") §104
Non-enclitic sentence particles §185
Non-verbal sentences
AB nominal sentences §56, 1; §128
Bi-partite nominal sentences with *pw* §129
Explicatory sentences §148
Non-verbal sentences with adverbial comment §10; §16
Negation of §102
Reciprocal sentence §152
Tripartite nominal sentences with *pw* §135
See also Pseudo-verbal constructions
Noun phrases
As adverbial modifiers §79
Negation of §176
Prospective *sḏm·f* in §75
Nouns
Abstract nouns formed with *bw* and *st* §193
Apposition §22, 2
Declension §19
Fronting
in participial statments §134
in verbal statement of fact §37
with *ir* §133
Gender §19
Genitival relations §22
Introduction to nouns §14
M-preformative nouns §192
Number §19
Vocative §64
ntf X (possession) §126, 2
nty (etc.) §111
Numbers
Cardinal §65
Ordinal §67
Use of §66
n(y) sw X (possession) §126, 1

Object
Infinitive as object of preposition §57, 2
Omission of §141
Prospective *sḏm·f* as object of preposition §75, 2
For objects of verbs, see Direct object
Offering formula §197
Old perfective, See Stative
Omission
of the direct object §141
of the object of a preposition §141
of the subject §140

Parsing, See Exercise IIC
Participial statment §134

Participles §§117–25
  Adjectival functions §119
    As predicate adjective §119
  Basic uses §118
  Forms
    Future active *sḏm·ty·fy* (etc.) §125
    Imperfect active §121, 1a
    Imperfect passive §121, 1b
    Perfect active §121, 2a
    Perfect passive §121, 2b
    Prospective active §121, 3a
    Prospective passive §121, 3b
  Introduction to participles §117
  Negation of §179
  Passive particples
    Extended use (with indirect reference to the antecedent) §123
    Followed by a noun in a bound construction §124
  Verbal aspects §120
Particles
  Enclitic §186
  Sentence particles (non-enclitic particles)
    ḫr §185, 3
    ḫr m-ḫt / ḫr ir m-ḫt §185, 4
    ir m-ḫt §185, 4
    isṯ, isk §185, 1
    iw §9; §23, 6; §31; §32
    k3 §185, 2
    mk, mṯ, mṯn §17; §31; §40
    nḥmn §185, 7
    smwn §185, 6
Partitive §66; §127
Passive voice §33
  See also under specific verb form.
Past tense narrative constructions
  ʿḥʿ·n sḏm·n·f and related constructions §§90–96; §153
  narrative infinitive §57, 7
  šmt pw ir(w)·n·f with verbs of motion §136
Plural forms of nouns §19
Polite requests §73; §146
Possession §126–127
  n·f imy X §126, 3
  ntf X §126, 2
  n(y) sw X §126, 1
Possessive Articles §132
Predicate adjective §44 (and see "Adjective")
Prepositions
  Compound §54; §81
Present tense (generally expressed by *sḏm·f*—see under specific form)
Progressive constructions §58; §59; §60; §61
Pronouns, interrogative §128
Pronouns, personal
  See under Suffix pronouns, Dependent pronouns, and Independent pronouns
  Movement ahead in verbal sentences §51
Prospective *sḏm·f* (first prospective)
  Forms and overview §71
  Noun clauses formed with §75
    As direct object of verbs §75, 1
    As object of prepositions §75, 2
    As subject of verbs §75, 3
    Negation of noun clauses §176
  Purpose clauses §74
    Negation of §175
  Wishes, exhortations §72
Prospective *sḏm(w)·f* (sencond tense) §138; §188
Pseudo-participle, See Stative
Pseudo-verbal constructions
  ḥr + infinitive §58; §59; §61
  m + infinitive §60
  r + infinitive §62
  Introduced by *wn·in·f* §131
  Stative as adverbial comment §85
Purpose, expressed by *r* + infinitive §57, 2
Purpose clauses §74
  Negation of §175

Questions §§167–169
  Explicatory sentences as questions for specification §169
  Participial statements with *in-m* or *nm* §134
Quotations
  Introduced by *m dd* §57, 2
  Parenthetic quotations: *ḫr*, *ḫr(y)·fy*; *in*; *k3* "so says" §189

r of futurity §62
  after *rdi* "appoint to be" §77
Reciprocal sentences §152
Relative adjective *nty* (etc.) §111
  Feminine singualar *nt(y)t* "what exists" §113
    "That" (after verbs of knowing & seeing) §116
    ḥr nt(y)t §114; §115
    r nt(y)t §115
  Followed by adverbs / adverbials §112
  Negative relative adjective *iwty* §183
Relative clauses
  with indefinite antecedent §38
  with relative adjectives §112; §183
  with relative verb forms §§157–163
  with the genitival adjective *n(y)* + second tense verb form §190
Relative verb forms §§157–163
  Imperfect §159
  Negation of §179
  Passive forms §162
  Perfect §158
  Prospective §160
  sdm(w)·n·f past tense §161
Requests §73; §146
Result clauses §74
Royal titulary §69

s-causative verb stem §27
  Infinitives with *t* §57, 1
sdm·f Forms, See under Circumstantial, Prospective, Relative, and Second tense
sdm·f pw §143
sdm·ḫr·f §131
  Negation of §180
sdm·in·f §131
sdm·k3·f §131
sdm·n·f Forms, See under Circumstantial, Prospective, Relative, and Second tense
sdmt·f §154
  As objects of prepositions §156
  n sdmt·f ("before he has heard") §155
  Negation of §180
sdm·ty·fy (etc.) future active participle §125
  Negation of §179
sdm(w)·f passive §35
Seasons §69
Second tense *(sdm·f & sdm·n·f)* §147
  Direct objects of verbs §151
  Following genitival adjective *n(y)* §190
  Independent use of §149
  Objects of prepositions §150
  Reciprocal sentences §152
Second tense prospective *(sdm(w)·f)* §138; §188
Sentance particles, see "Particles"
Statements of fact
  Non-verbal (with adverbial comment) §10
    Negation of §102
  Noun *sdm·f* §36
  Pseudo-verbal constructions
    ḥr + infinitive §58; §59; §61
    m + infinitive §60
    r + infinitive §62
    Stative as adverbial comment §85
      Impersonal use §196
  Verbal §9; §31
    Negation of §§106–109
    Word order in §51
Stative
  Adverbial comment in non-verbal statement of fact §85
  Adverbial modifier (circumstantial clause) §86

Stative, cont.
Exclamatory use §99
Forms §83; §84
Impersonal use with topic omitted §196
Independent use of first person singular §98
Modifying nouns §87
Overview §82
rḫ in stative "to know" §89
Verbs of motion §88
See also Pseudo-verbal constructions
Stroke (determinative of logograms) §13
Subject
omission of §140
position in sentence (word order) §51
noun as §9; §15; §51
suffix pronoun as §23, 5
Subordinate clauses §16
(See also Circumstantial clauses)
Suffix conjugation
Introduction §25
Suffix pronouns §23
Affinity of Egyptian suffix pronouns to those of Afro-Asiatic §23, 7
Affixed to:
Nouns §23, 2
Prepositions §23, 4
Verbs §23, 5
As subject in verbal sentences §23, 5
As topic in non-verbal sentences §23, 6
Defective writing of the third plural (*·s* for *·sn*) §187
Dual forms §23, 3

šmt pw ir(w)·n·f with verbs of motion §136; §163

Tense §26
Titulary, royal §69
Topic §10
Second tense phrase as topic in explicatory sentence §148

Transposition
Graphic §41, 2
Honorific §41, 1
Tri-partite nominal sentences with *pw* §135

Verbal sentences
Word order in §51
(See also Statements of fact and the specific construction.)
Verbs (For detailed references to verb forms, consult the main entries—under the name of the particular verb form)
After genitival adjective *n(y)* §190
Auxiliary verbs
ꜥḥꜥ·n §§90–96
ḏr §174
ḫpr §172
ii §174
iri §171
pꜣ(w) §173
pri §174
rdi + (first) prospective as causative §75, 1
Circumstantial family of forms §35
sḏm·f §29
sḏm·n·f §30
sḏm·tw·f §34
sḏm(w)·f passive §35
Classes of verbs §28; §170
Derived stems §27
Imperative §145
Infinitives §57
Participles §§117–25
Prospective (first) *sḏm·f* §§71–75
Prospective (second) *sḏm(w)·f* §138; §188
s-causative stem §27
sḏmt·f §§154–156
Second tense §147
Stative §§82–88
Verbs of motion §31
m + infinitive §60

Verbs of motion, cont.
Past tense requires stative §88
šmt pw ỉr(w)·n·f §136
Vocalic writing §53
Vocative use of nouns §64
Vocative particle *ỉ* §142
Vocative *pw* §142
Wechselsatz §152
Wishes §72
Negation of §164
Word order in verbal sentences §51

Appendix 1: Forms of the Mutable and Irregular Verbs

	3rd Weak	2nd Gem.	"Give"	"Bring"	"See"	"Be"	"Come"
SUFFIX CONJUGATION:							
Circumst.	*mrỉ·*	*qbb·*	*dỉ·*, *rdỉ·*	*ỉnỉ·*	*mꜣꜣ·*	*wn·*	*ỉw·*, *ỉy·*
Prospect.	*mr·*, *mry·*	*qb·*	*dỉ·*	*ỉnt·*	*mꜣ·*, *mꜣn·*	*wn·*	*ỉwt·*
2nd Tense	*mrr·*	*qbb·*	*dd·*	*ỉnn·*	*mꜣꜣ·*	*wnn·*	*ỉw(w)·*
Old Indic.	*mr·*, *mry·*	*qb·*	*dỉ·*, *rdỉ·*	*ỉn·*	*mꜣ·*, *mꜣn·*	*wn·*	*ỉw·*, *ỉy·*
***Sḏm·n·f*[1]**	*mrỉ·n·*	*qb·n·*	*rdỉ·n·*	*ỉn·n·*	*mꜣ·n·*	*wn·*	*ỉy·n·*
STATIVE:							
	mr-	*qb-*	*rdỉ-*, *dỉ-*	*ỉn-*	*mꜣ-*	*wn-*	*ỉw-*, *ỉy-*
INFINITIVE:							
	mrt	*qbb*	*rdỉt*	*ỉnt*	*mꜣꜣ*, *mꜣ*, *mꜣn*	*wnn*	*ỉyt*, *ỉwt*
IMPERATIVE:							
	mr	*qb*	*ỉmỉ*	*ỉn*	*mꜣ*, *mꜣꜣ*	??	*mỉ*

[1]All of the *sḏm·n·f* forms (circumstantial, "old indicative," and 2nd tense) are identical in their written forms.

Appendix 2: Basic Verbal Constructions

I ACTIVE VOICE

	affirmative	pseudo-verbal	negative
STATEMENTS OF FACT: (§9, 16, 18)			
Present	*ỉw mr·f* (§31)	*ỉw·f ḥr mrt* (§59) / *ỉw·f m ỉỉt* (60)	*n mr·n·f* (§108, 1)
	ỉw·f mr·f / (*ỉw*) Noun *mr·f* (§36, 37)		*n mr·n·f*
Future		*ỉw·f r mrt* (§62)	*nn mr(y)·f* (§109)
Past	*ỉw mr·n·f* (§31)	*ỉw·ỉ ỉỉ·kwỉ* (§85)	*n mr·f* (§107, 1)
CIRCUMSTANTIAL CLAUSES:			
Present	..., *mr·f* (*qbb·f*) (§32)	*ḥr mrt* (§61) / *~·ỉ ỉỉ·kwỉ* (§86)	*nn mrt* (§105) *n mr·n·f* (§108, 1)
Past	..., *mr·n·f* (§32)	*ḥr mrt* / *~·ỉ ỉỉ·kwỉ*	*nn mrt* / *n mr·f* (§107, 1)
EXPLICATORY SENTENCES			
Present/Future	*mrr·f* (+ ADVERB) (§148)		*tm·f mr(w)* (+ ADVERB) (§)
Past	*mr·n·f* / *ỉy·n·f* (§148)		*???*[1]
PROSPECTIVE OR SUBJUNCTIVE:			
Wishes	*mr(y)·f* (§72)		*ỉmỉ·f mr(w)*[2] (§164)
"In order that..."	*mr(y)·f* (§74)		*tm·f mr(w)* (§)
IMPERATIVE (COMMANDS):			
	mr (§145)		*m mr(w)* (§166)

[1]One would expect *tm·n·f mr(w)*, but it is not yet attested.
[2]The prospective of the negative verb *ỉmỉ* + negatival complement.

Appendix 2: Basic Verbal Constructions

II PASSIVE VOICE

	affirmative	pseudo-verbal	negative
STATEMENTS OF FACT: (§9, 16, 18)			
Present	*ỉw mr·tw·f* (§34)		*n mr·n·tw·f* (§108, 2)
Future		*ỉw·tw r mrt* (§33, 62)	*nn mr·tw·f* (§109)
Past	*ỉw mr(w)·f* (§35)	*ỉw·ỉ ỉn·kwỉ* (§82, 85)	*n mr(w)·f / n mr·tw·f* (§107, 2)
CIRCUMSTANTIAL CLAUSES:			
Present	…, *mr·tw·f* (§32, 34)		*n mr·n·tw·f* (§108, 2)
Past	…, *mr(w)·f* (§32, 35)		*n mr(w)·f / n mr·tw·f* (§107, 2)
EXPLICATORY SENTENCES:[1]			
Present/Future	*mrr·tw·f* (+ ADVERB) (§148)		*tm·tw mr(w)* + Noun Subj.[2] (§)
Past	*mr·n·tw·f* (§148)		*???*[3]
PROSPECTIVE OR SUBJUNCTIVE:			
Wishes	*mr·tw·f / mr(w)·f* (§72)		
"In order that…"	*mr·tw·f* (§74)		*???*
IMPERATIVE (COMMANDS):[4]			
	ỉmỉ mr·tw·k (§)		*m rdỉ(w) mr·tw·k*

[1]All verb forms used are second tense forms. There are four negations of the expository. The construction shown here negates the verbal idea.
[2](+ ADVERB). One would expect the negative form with pronoun to be **tm·tw·f mr(w)*.
[3]One would expect **tm·n·tw·f mr(w)*, but it is not yet attested.
[4]These constructions involve the causative use of *rdỉ* and the 2nd pers. suffixes: "cause yourself to be loved"; "do not let yourself be loved."